BY HARUKA FUKUSHIMA
VOL. 3

HAMBURG // LONDON // LOS ANGELES // TOKYO

The making of CHERRY JUICE

チェリージュースのつくりかた

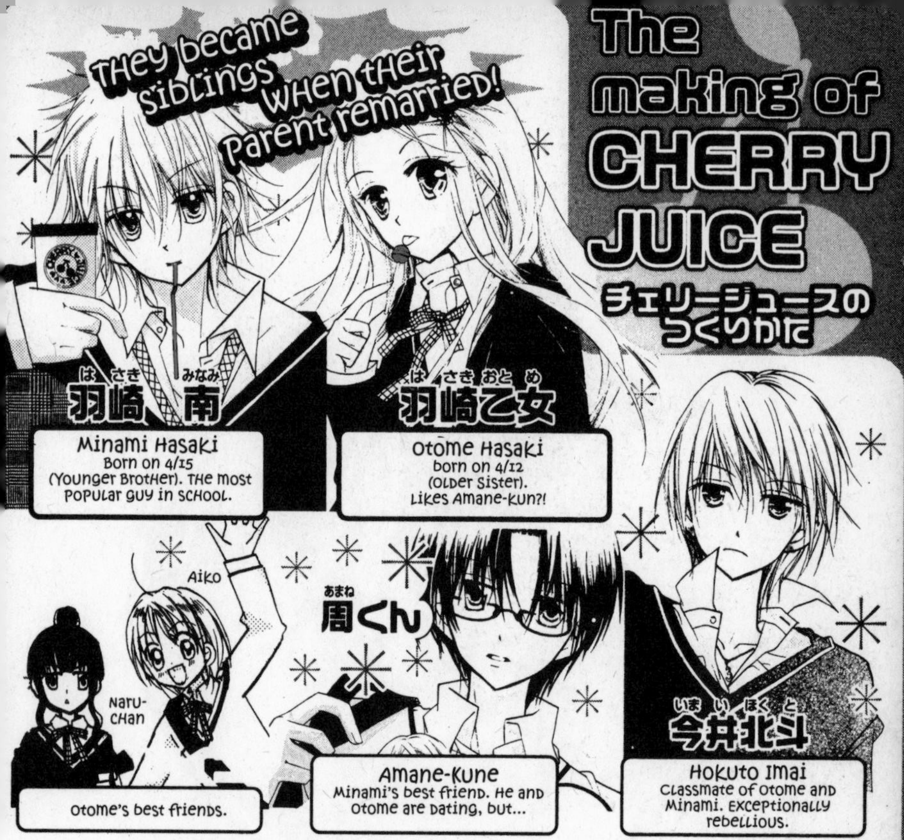
They became siblings when their parent remarried!
羽崎南
はさき みなみ
Minami Hasaki
Born on 4/15 (Younger Brother). The most popular guy in school.
羽崎乙女
はさき おとめ
Otome Hasaki
born on 4/12 (Older Sister). Likes Amane-kun?!
今井北斗
いまい ほくと
Hokuto Imai
Classmate of Otome and Minami. Exceptionally rebellious.
周くん
あまね
Amane-kune
Minami's best friend. He and Otome are dating, but...
Aiko
Naru-chan
Otome's best friends.

Although they are not blood related, Otome and Minami became siblings six years ago when their parents remarried. The pair gets along as well as true siblings should, but truthfully, Minami has recently developed deeper feelings for Otome. And though Otome has begun dating her beloved Amane-kun, Minami's existence has become unexpectedly important to her... What will come of this complicated love triangle?

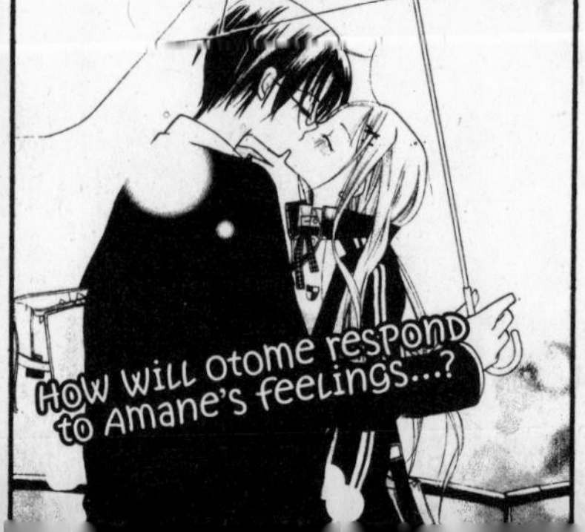
How will Otome respond to Amane's feelings...?

Now high school students, Otome and Minami are being harassed by jerky Hokuto Imai. In the midst of this, after witnessing a tender kiss between Otome and Amane, Minami finds himself pinning Otome down...?!

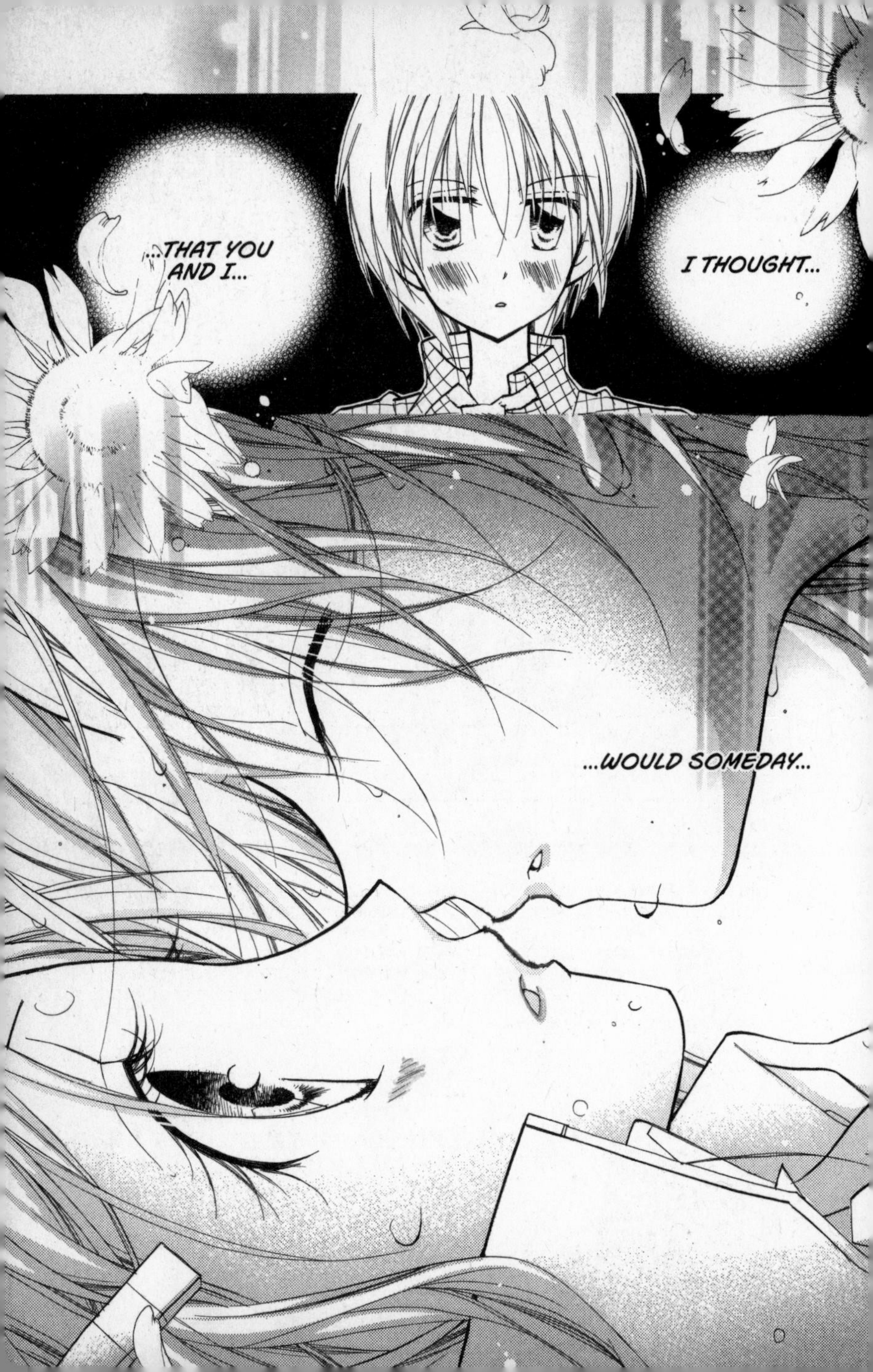
I THOUGHT...
...THAT YOU AND I...
...WOULD SOMEDAY...

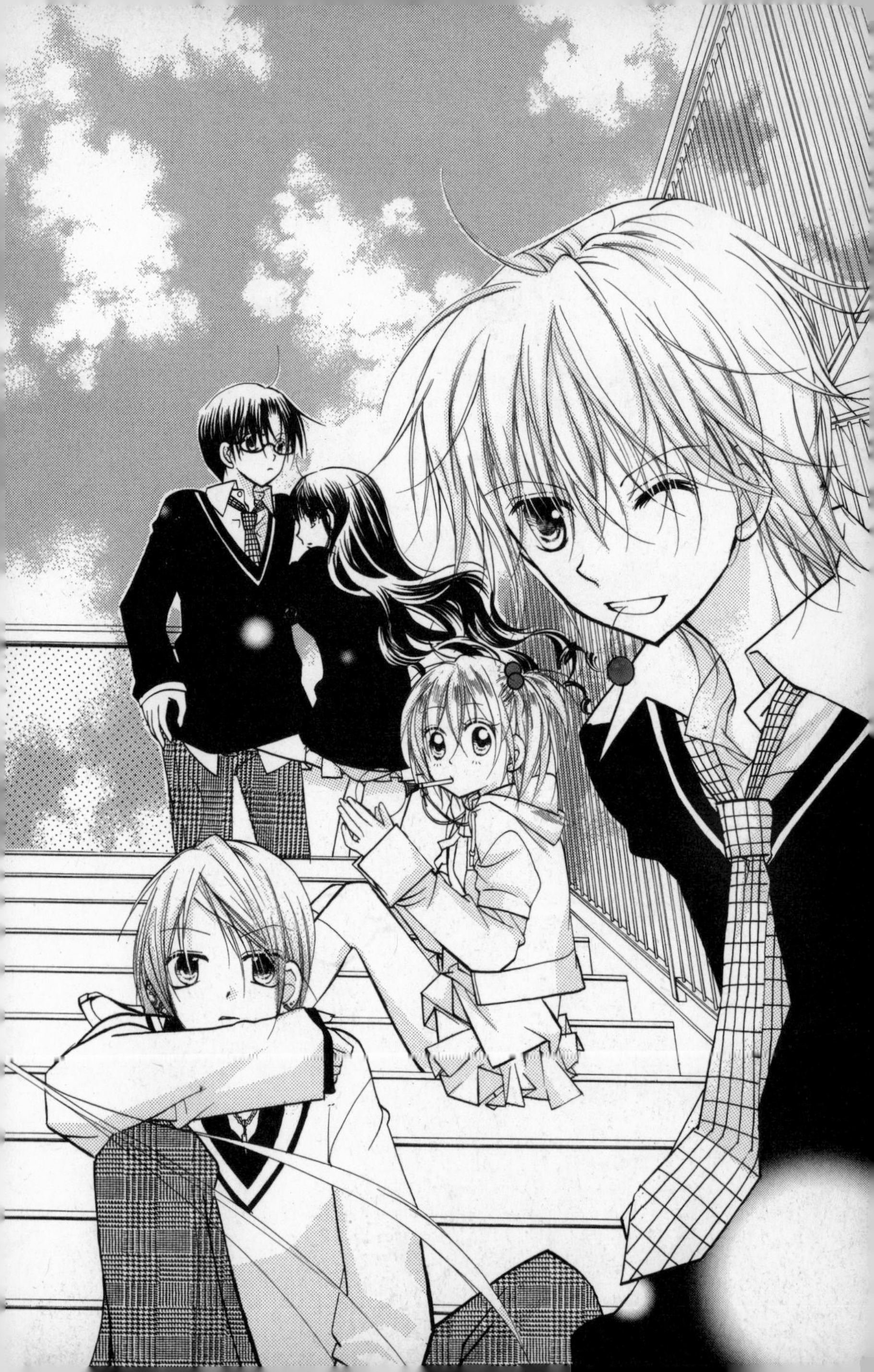

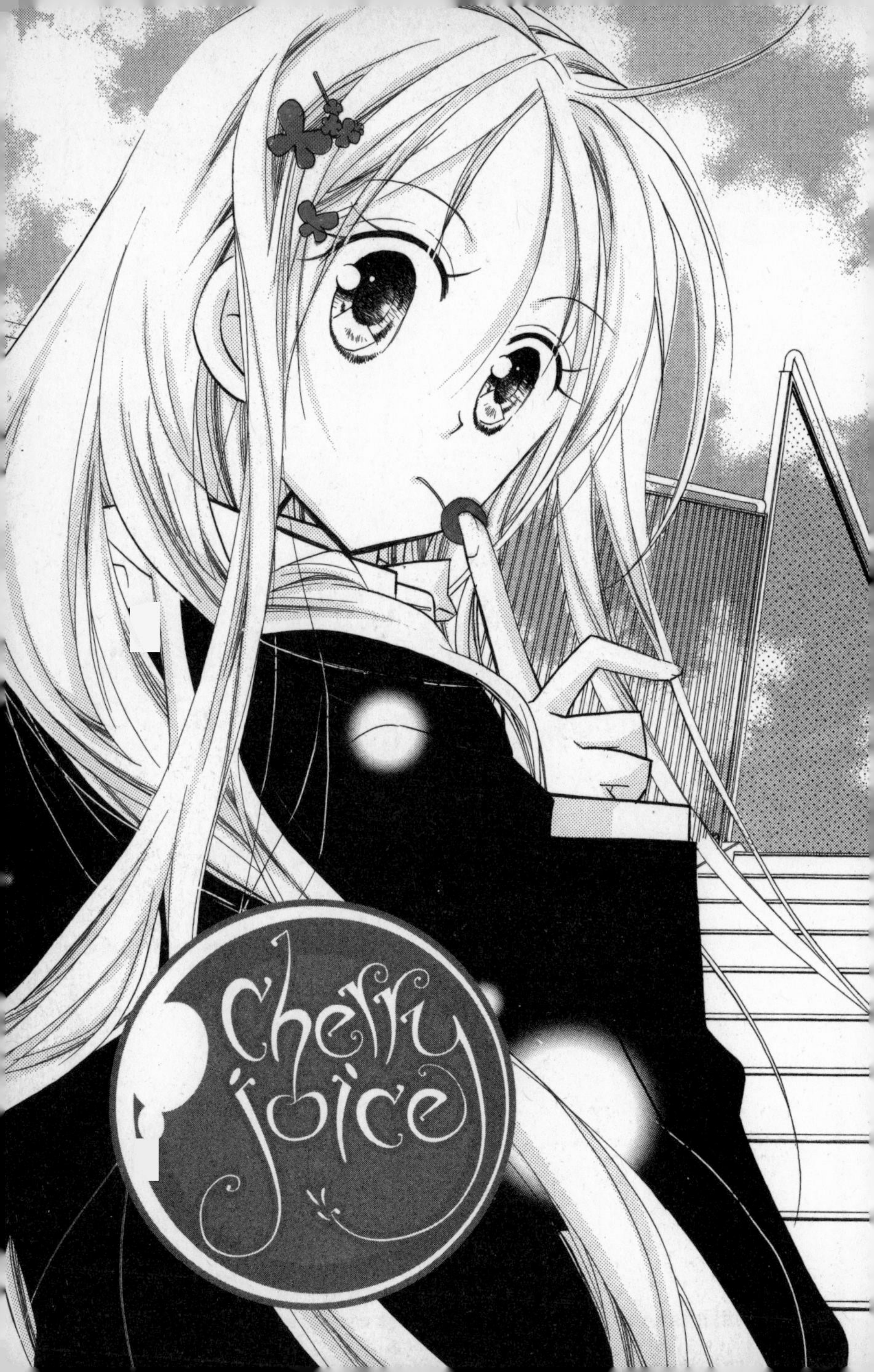
Cherry Juice

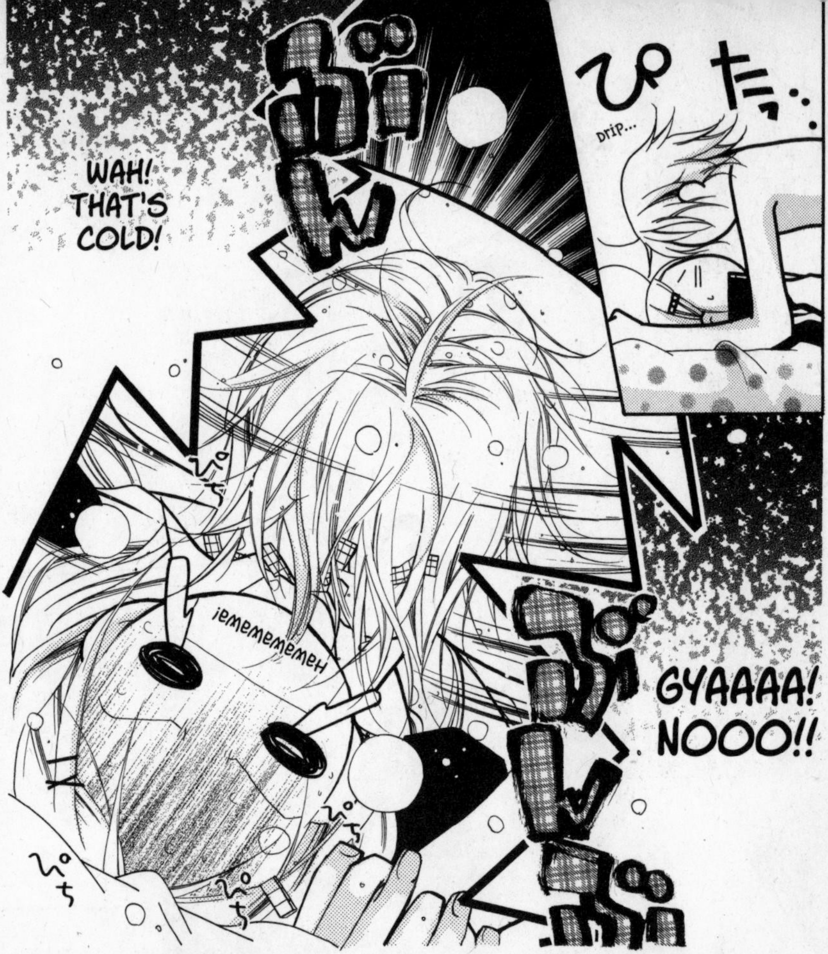
ぴ た…
Drip...
GYAAAA! NOOO!!
Hememememe!
WAH! THAT'S COLD!

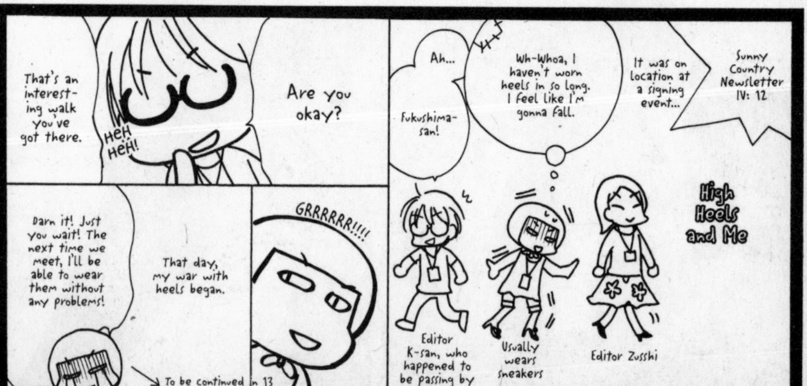
Sunny Country Newsletter IV: 12
High Heels and Me
It was on location at a signing event...
Wh-Whoa, I haven't worn heels in so long. I feel like I'm gonna fall.
Ah...
Fukushima-san!
Editor Zusshi
Usually wears sneakers
Editor K-san, who happened to be passing by
Are you okay?
That's an interesting walk you've got there.
HEH HEH!
GRRRRRR!!!!
That day, my war with heels began.
Darn it! Just you wait! The next time we meet, I'll be able to wear them without any problems!
To be continued in 13

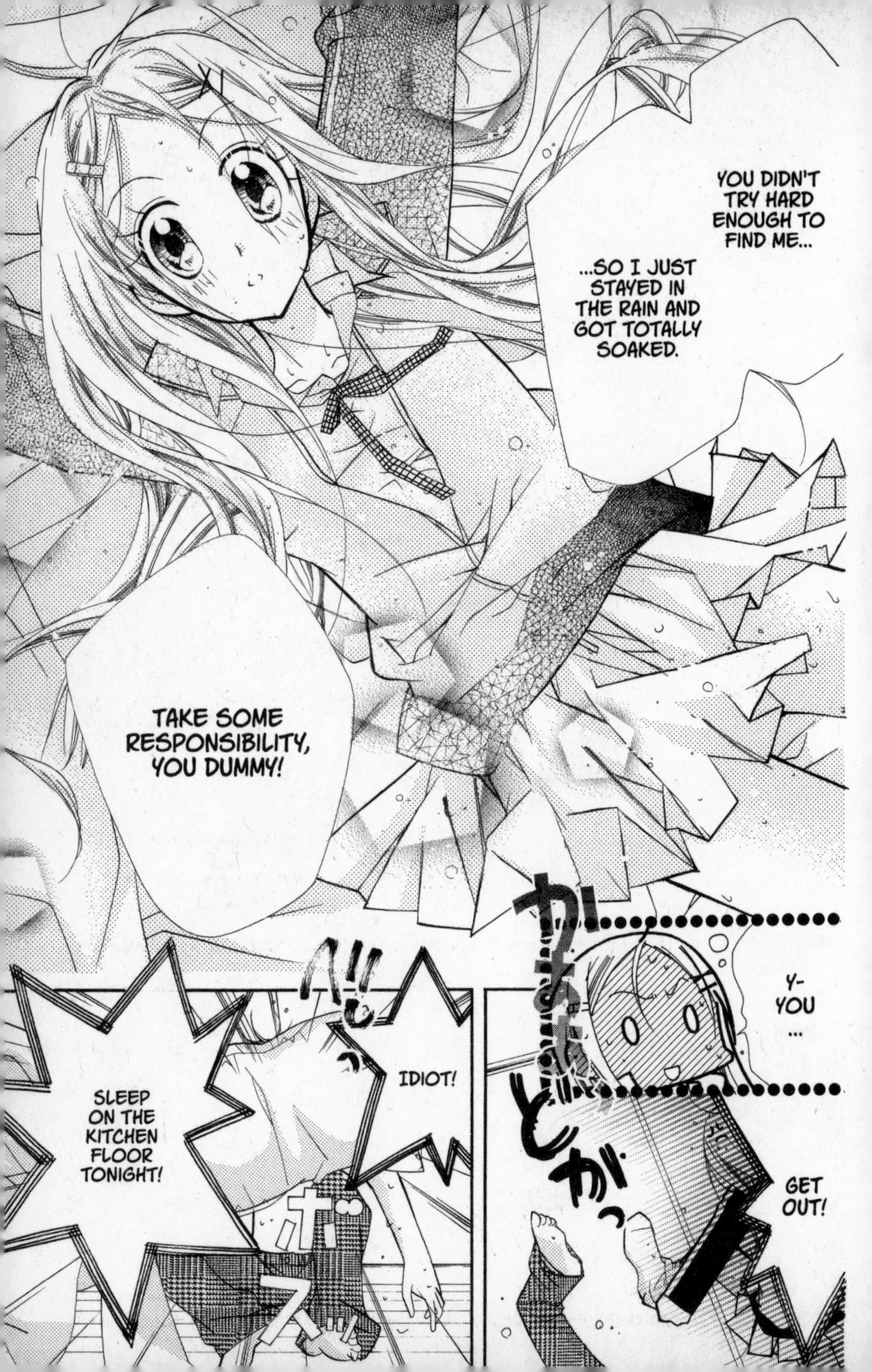
YOU DIDN'T TRY HARD ENOUGH TO FIND ME...
...SO I JUST STAYED IN THE RAIN AND GOT TOTALLY SOAKED.
TAKE SOME RESPONSIBILITY, YOU DUMMY!
Y- YOU ...
GET OUT!
IDIOT!
SLEEP ON THE KITCHEN FLOOR TONIGHT!

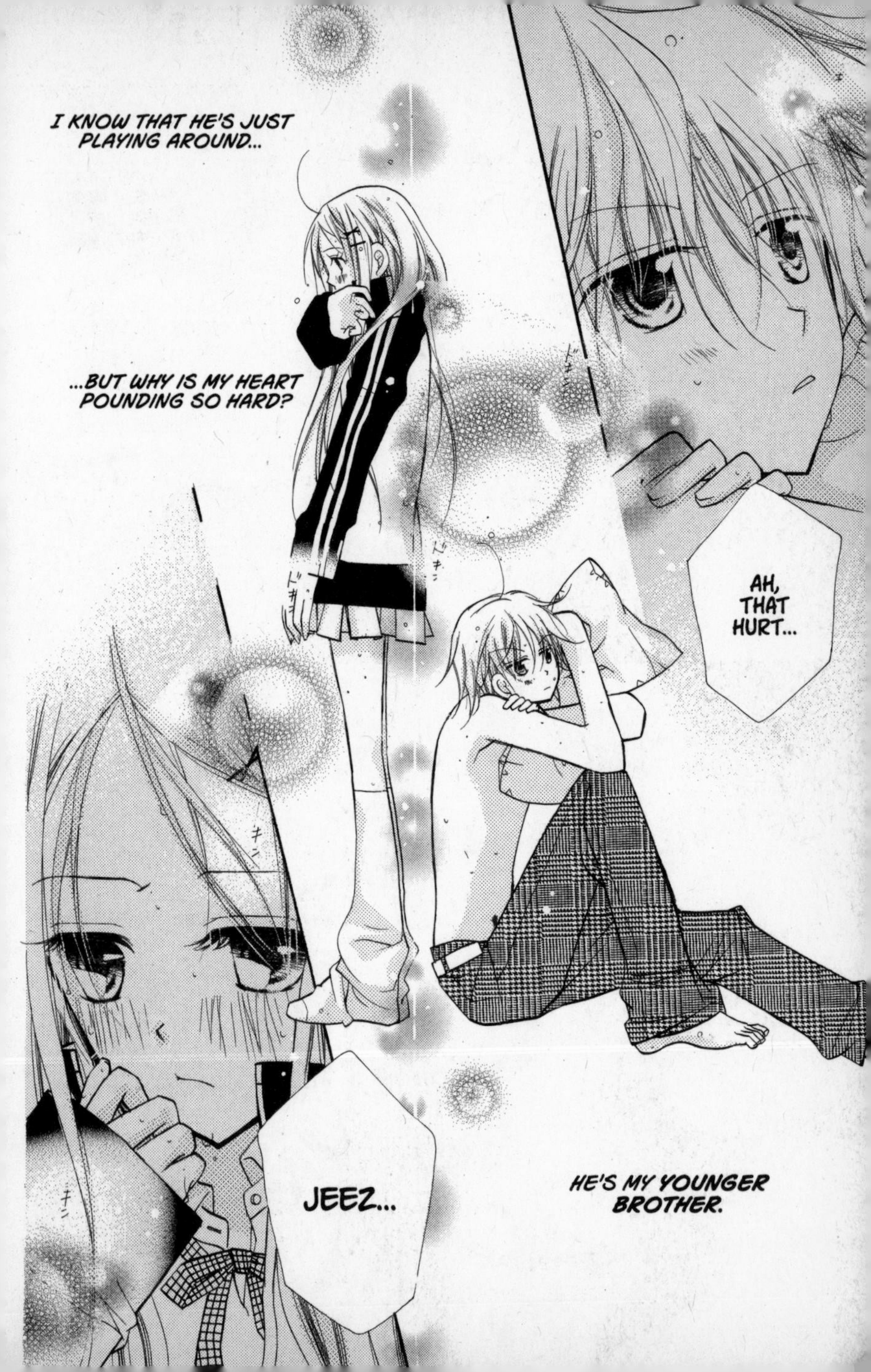
AH, THAT HURT...
I KNOW THAT HE'S JUST PLAYING AROUND...
...BUT WHY IS MY HEART POUNDING SO HARD?
HE'S MY YOUNGER BROTHER.
JEEZ...

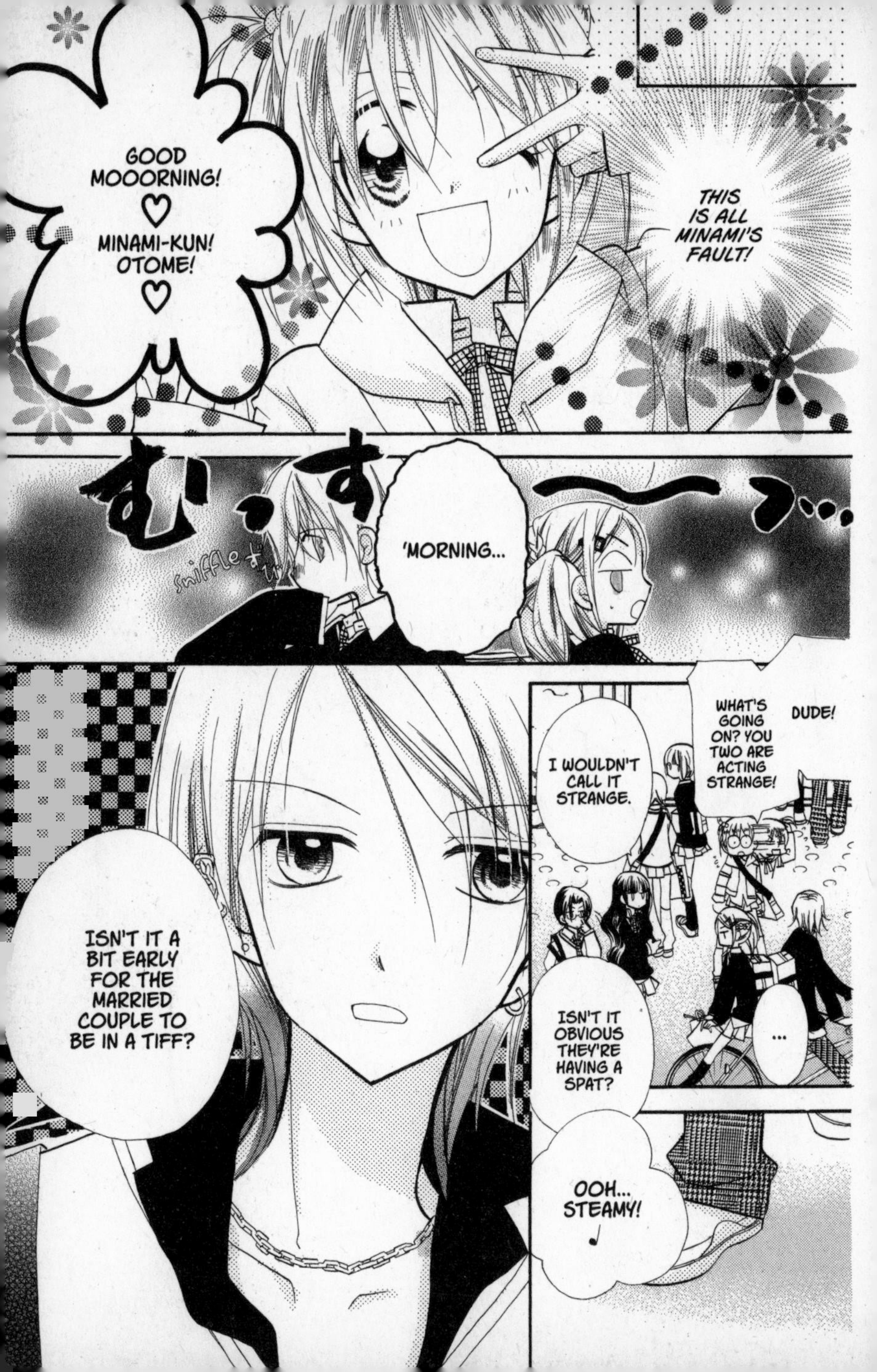
THIS IS ALL MINAMI'S FAULT!
GOOD MOOORNING! ♡ MINAMI-KUN! OTOME! ♡
むっすーーっ...
'MORNING...
sniffle ずび
DUDE!
WHAT'S GOING ON? YOU TWO ARE ACTING STRANGE!
I WOULDN'T CALL IT STRANGE.
...
ISN'T IT OBVIOUS THEY'RE HAVING A SPAT?
OOH... STEAMY! ♪
ISN'T IT A BIT EARLY FOR THE MARRIED COUPLE TO BE IN A TIFF?

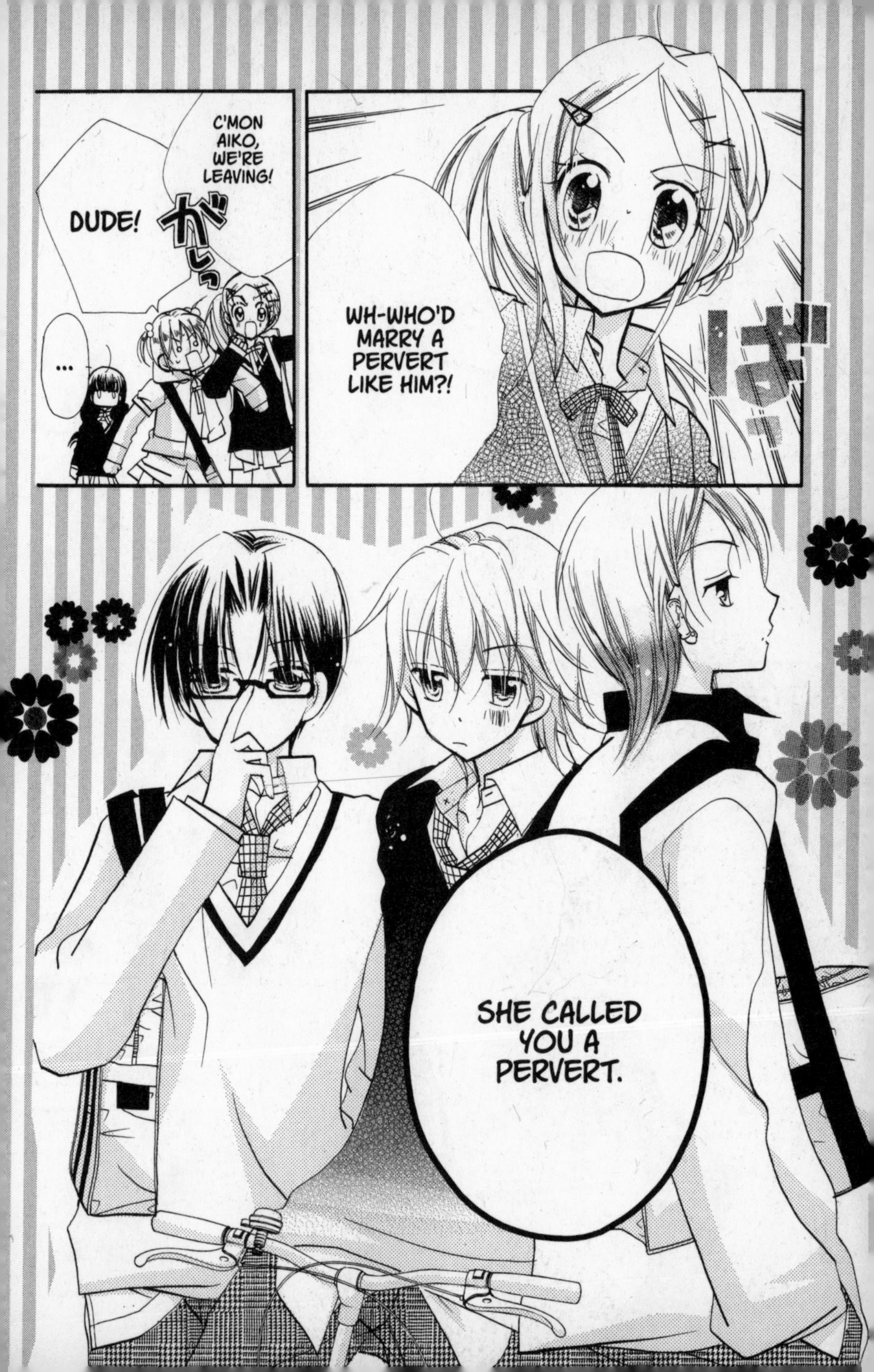
WH-WHO'D MARRY A PERVERT LIKE HIM?!
ばっ
C'MON AIKO, WE'RE LEAVING!
がしっ
DUDE!
...
SHE CALLED YOU A PERVERT.

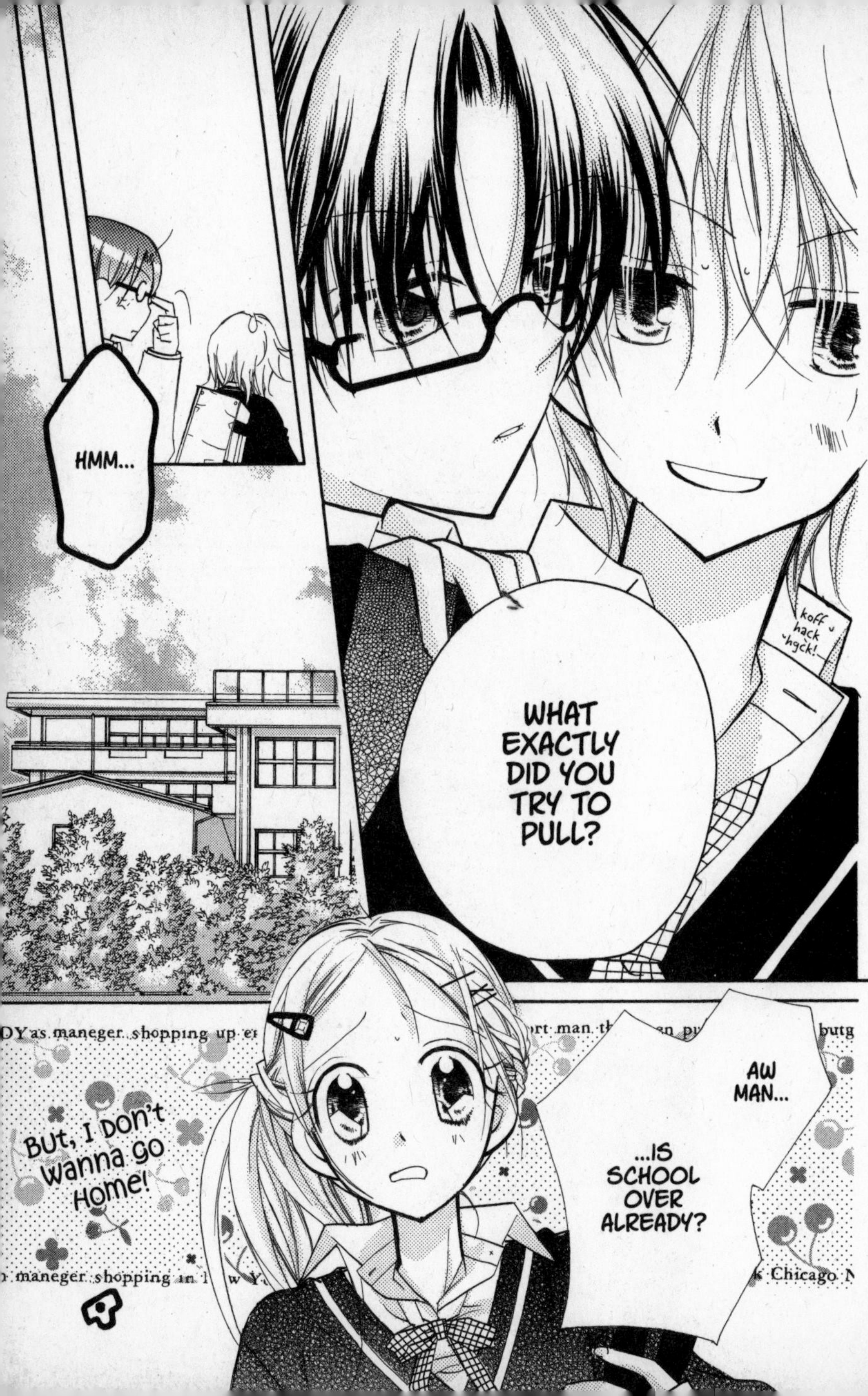
koff hack hgck!
WHAT EXACTLY DID YOU TRY TO PULL?
HMM...
AW MAN...
...IS SCHOOL OVER ALREADY?
But, I Don't wanna go Home!

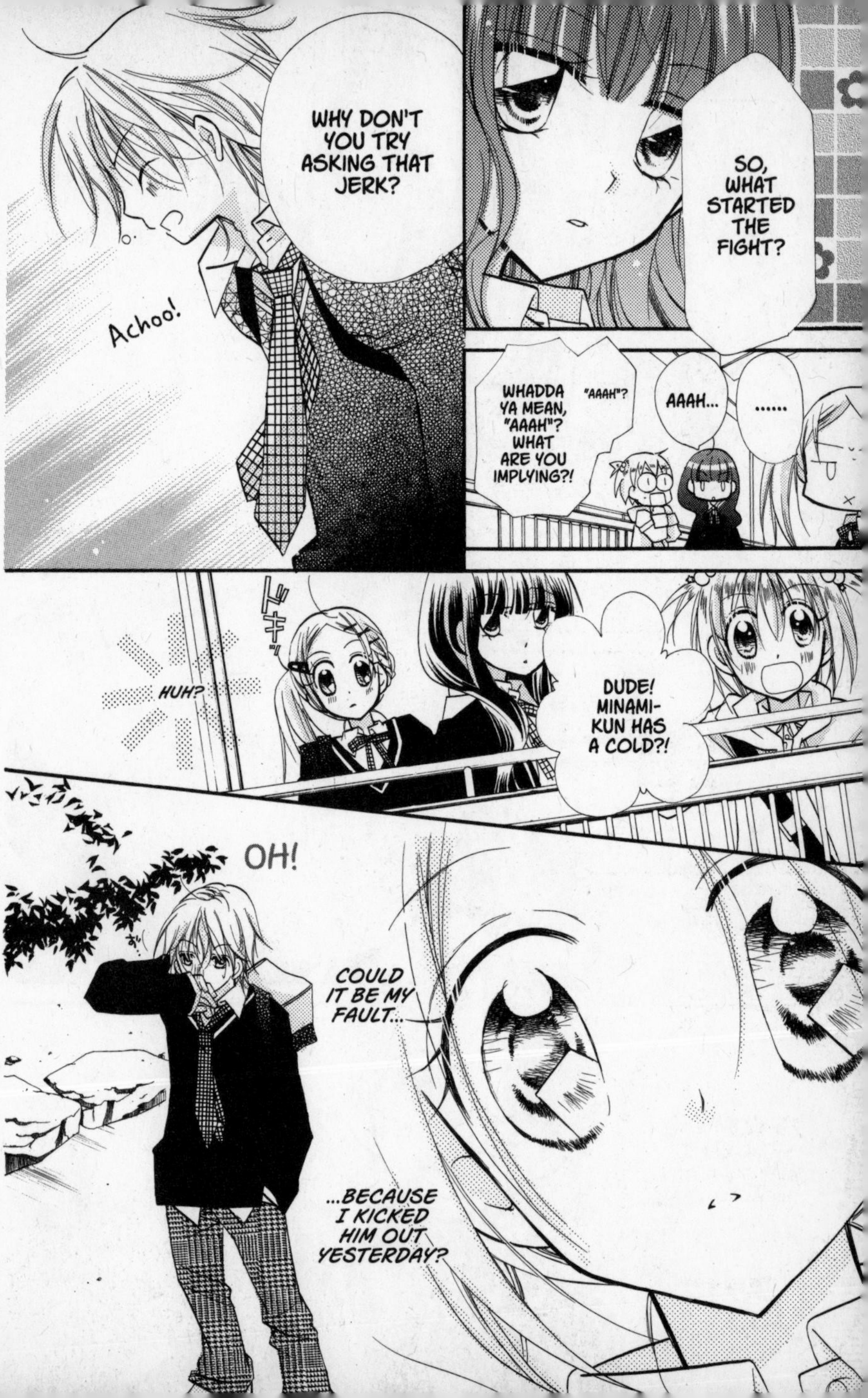
SO, WHAT STARTED THE FIGHT?
......
AAAH...
"AAAH"?
WHADDA YA MEAN, "AAAH"? WHAT ARE YOU IMPLYING?!
WHY DON'T YOU TRY ASKING THAT JERK?
Achoo!
DUDE! MINAMI-KUN HAS A COLD?!
HUH?
OH!
COULD IT BE MY FAULT...
...BECAUSE I KICKED HIM OUT YESTERDAY?

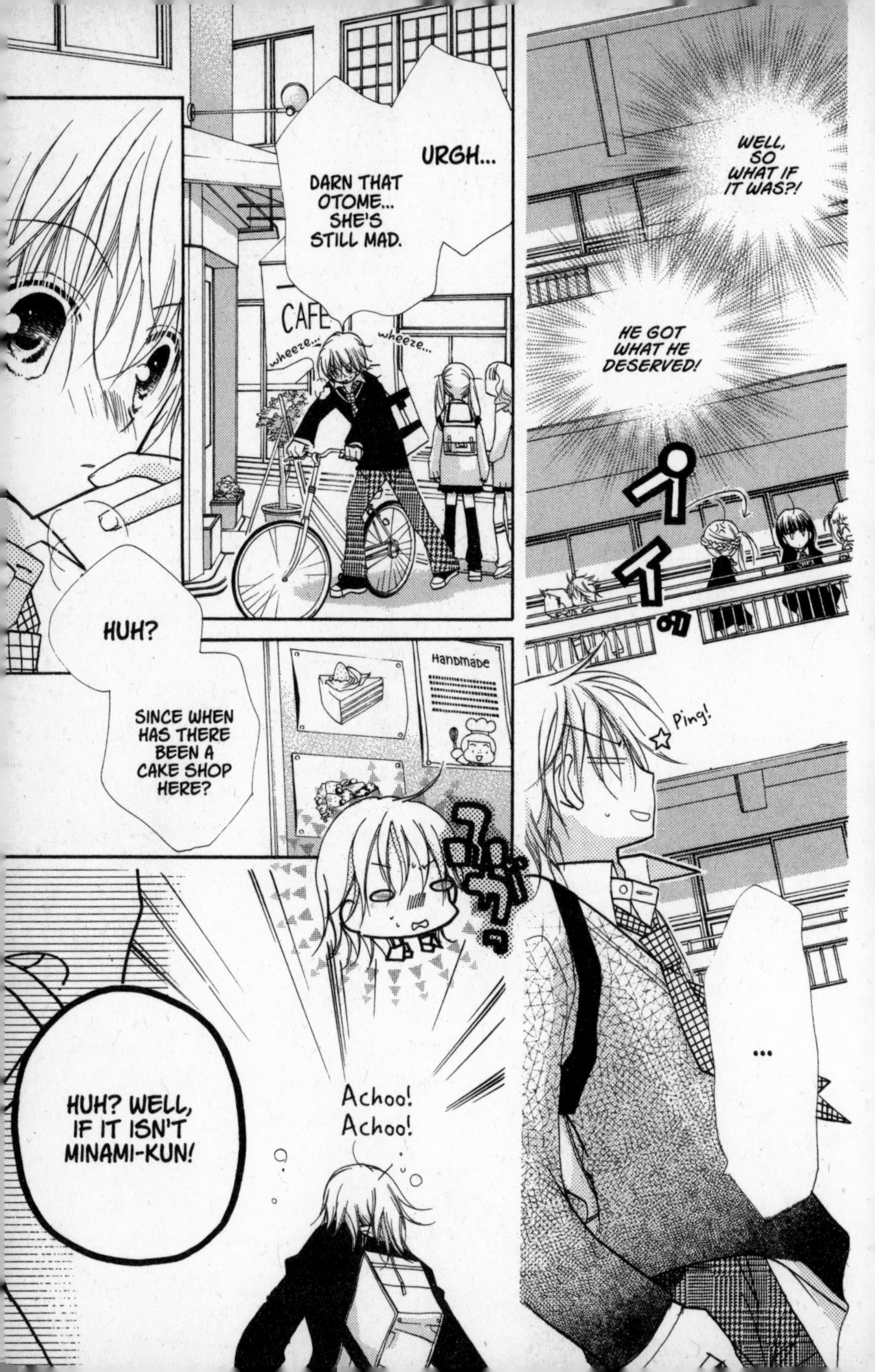
WELL, SO WHAT IF IT WAS?!
HE GOT WHAT HE DESERVED!
URGH...
DARN THAT OTOME... SHE'S STILL MAD.
CAFE
wheeze...
wheeze...
HUH?
Handmade
SINCE WHEN HAS THERE BEEN A CAKE SHOP HERE?
Ping!
...
Achoo! Achoo!
HUH? WELL, IF IT ISN'T MINAMI-KUN!

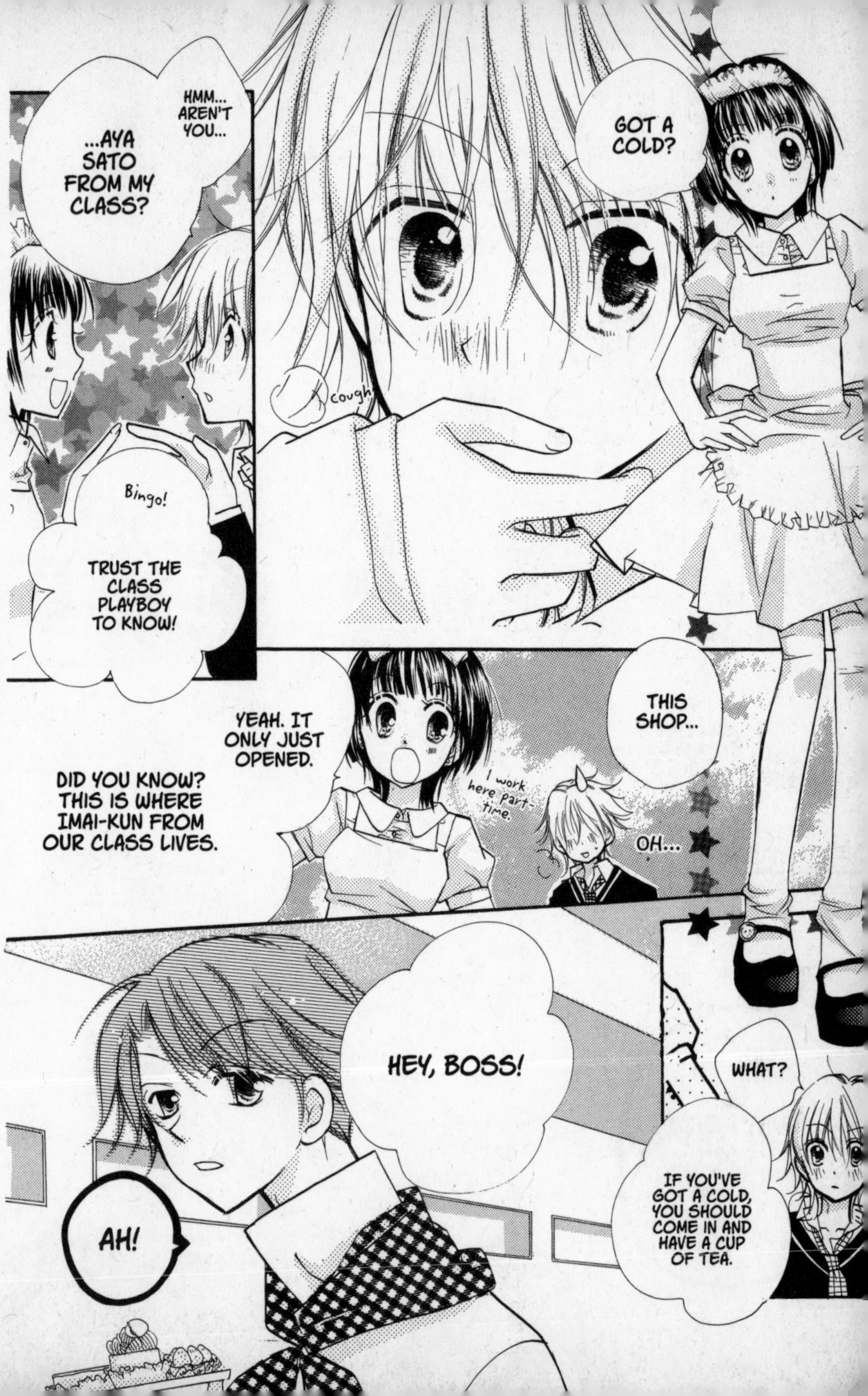
GOT A COLD?
cough
HMM... AREN'T YOU...
...AYA SATO FROM MY CLASS?
Bingo!
TRUST THE CLASS PLAYBOY TO KNOW!
THIS SHOP...
OH...
I work here part-time.
YEAH. IT ONLY JUST OPENED.
DID YOU KNOW? THIS IS WHERE IMAI-KUN FROM OUR CLASS LIVES.
WHAT?
IF YOU'VE GOT A COLD, YOU SHOULD COME IN AND HAVE A CUP OF TEA.
HEY, BOSS!
AH!

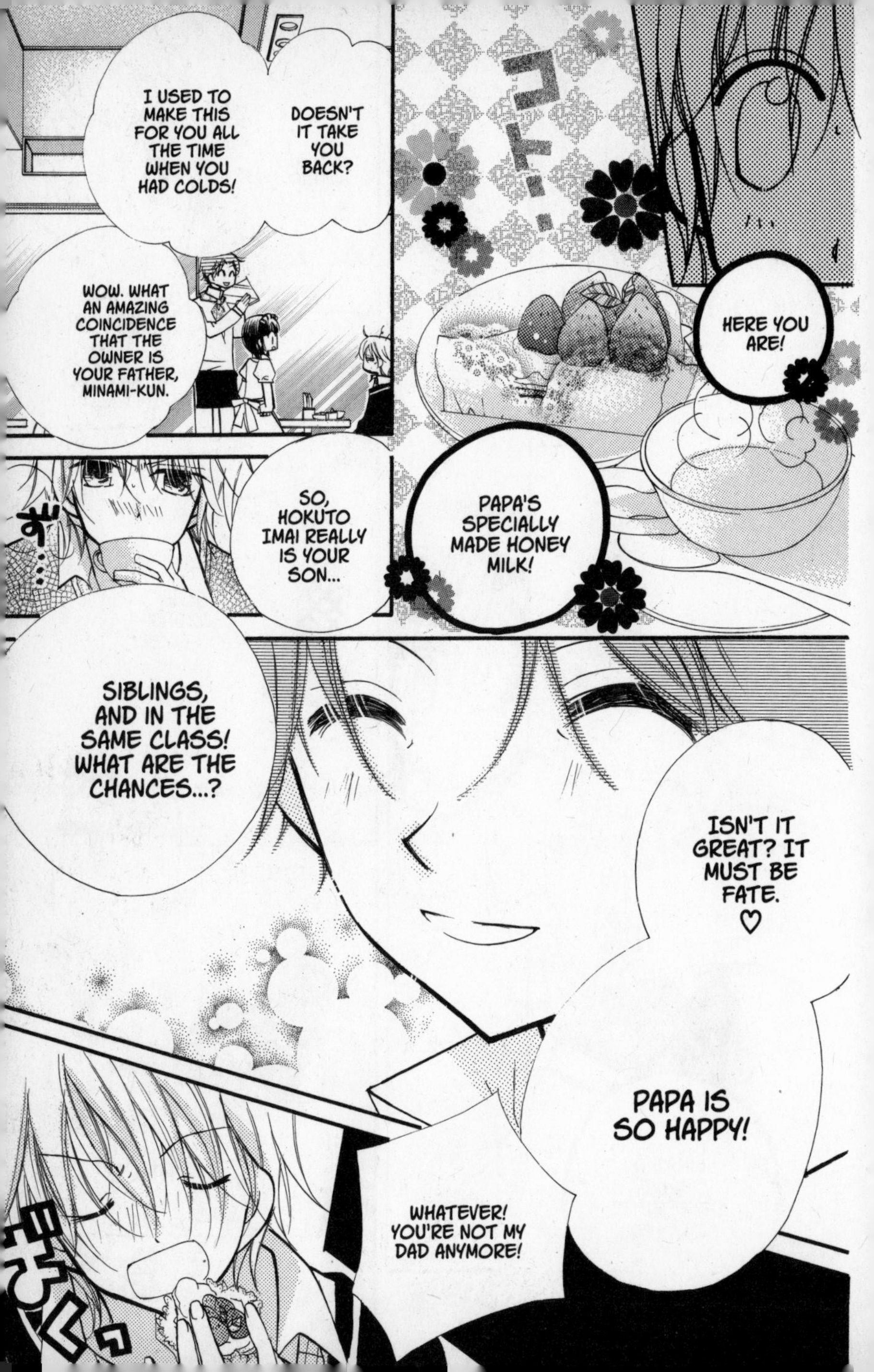
HERE YOU ARE!
PAPA'S SPECIALLY MADE HONEY MILK!
I USED TO MAKE THIS FOR YOU ALL THE TIME WHEN YOU HAD COLDS!
DOESN'T IT TAKE YOU BACK?
WOW. WHAT AN AMAZING COINCIDENCE THAT THE OWNER IS YOUR FATHER, MINAMI-KUN.
SO, HOKUTO IMAI REALLY IS YOUR SON...
SIBLINGS, AND IN THE SAME CLASS! WHAT ARE THE CHANCES...?
ISN'T IT GREAT? IT MUST BE FATE. ♡
PAPA IS SO HAPPY!
WHATEVER! YOU'RE NOT MY DAD ANYMORE!

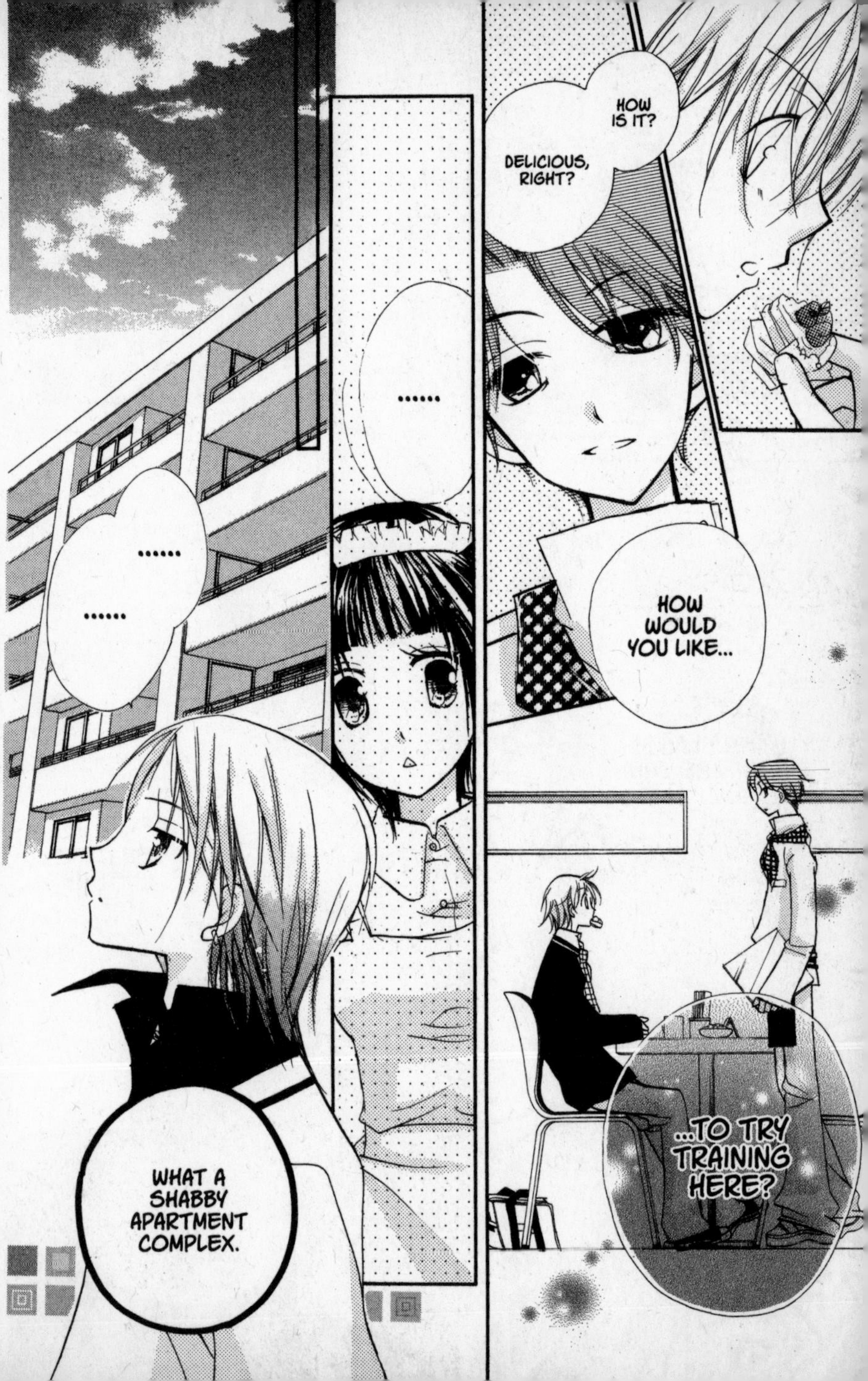
HOW IS IT?
DELICIOUS, RIGHT?
HOW WOULD YOU LIKE...
...TO TRY TRAINING HERE?
......
....
WHAT A SHABBY APARTMENT COMPLEX.

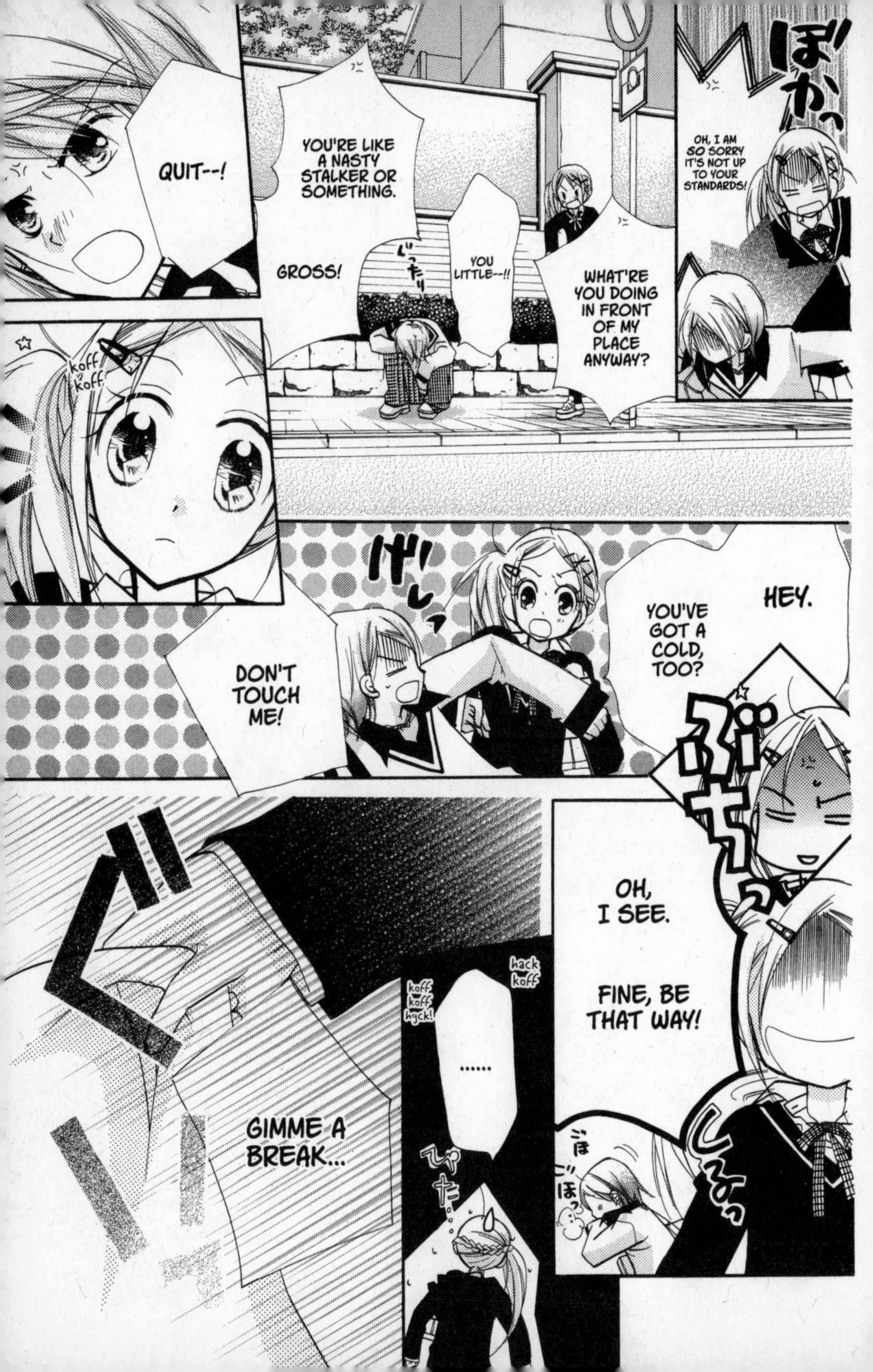
ぽかっ
OH, I AM SO SORRY IT'S NOT UP TO YOUR STANDARDS!
WHAT'RE YOU DOING IN FRONT OF MY PLACE ANYWAY?
YOU'RE LIKE A NASTY STALKER OR SOMETHING.
YOU LITTLE--!!
ぐったり
GROSS!
QUIT--!
koff koff
HEY.
YOU'VE GOT A COLD, TOO?
げしっ
DON'T TOUCH ME!
ぷちっ
OH, I SEE.
FINE, BE THAT WAY!
hack koff
koff koff hgck!
......
GIMME A BREAK...

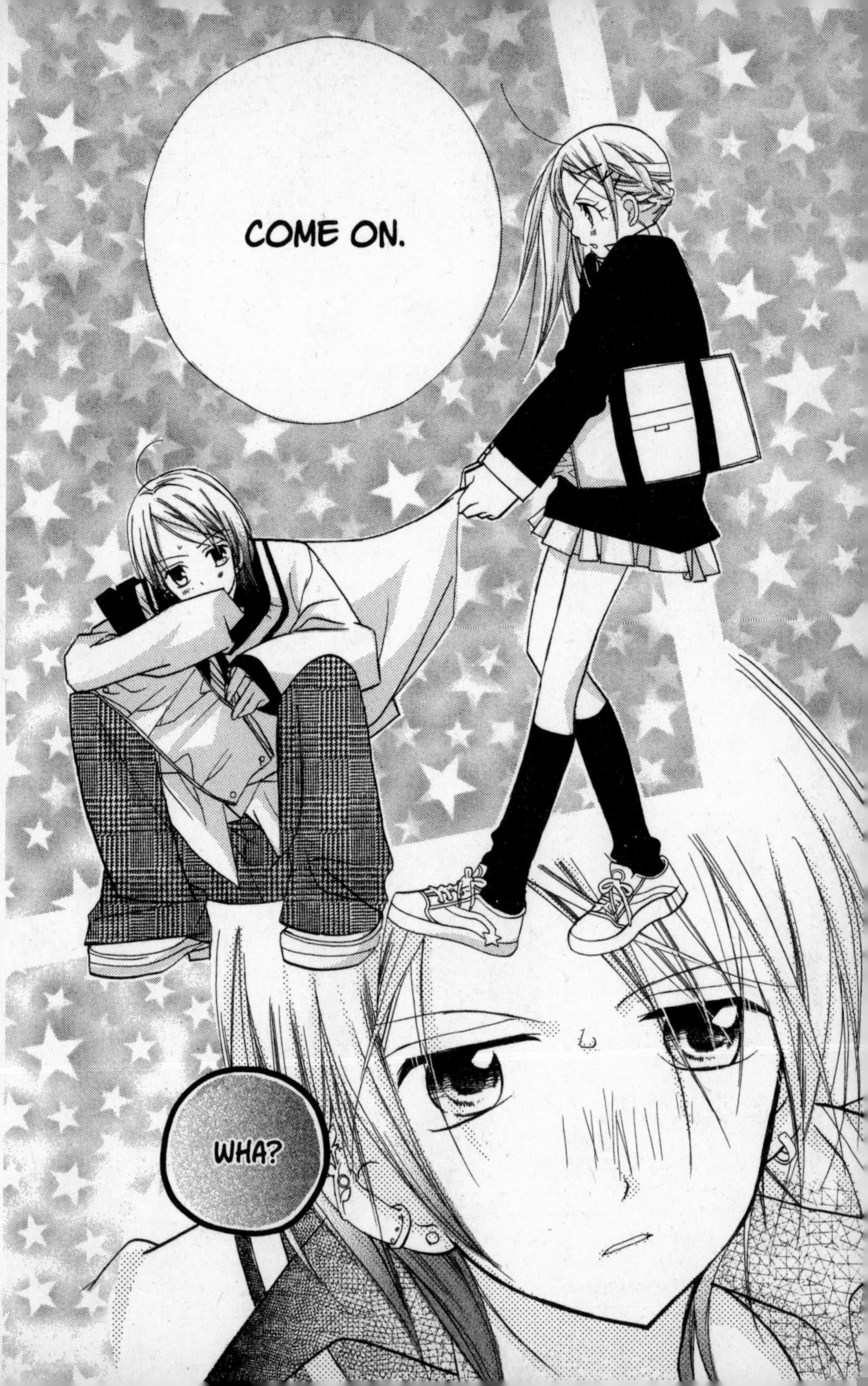
COME ON.
WHA?

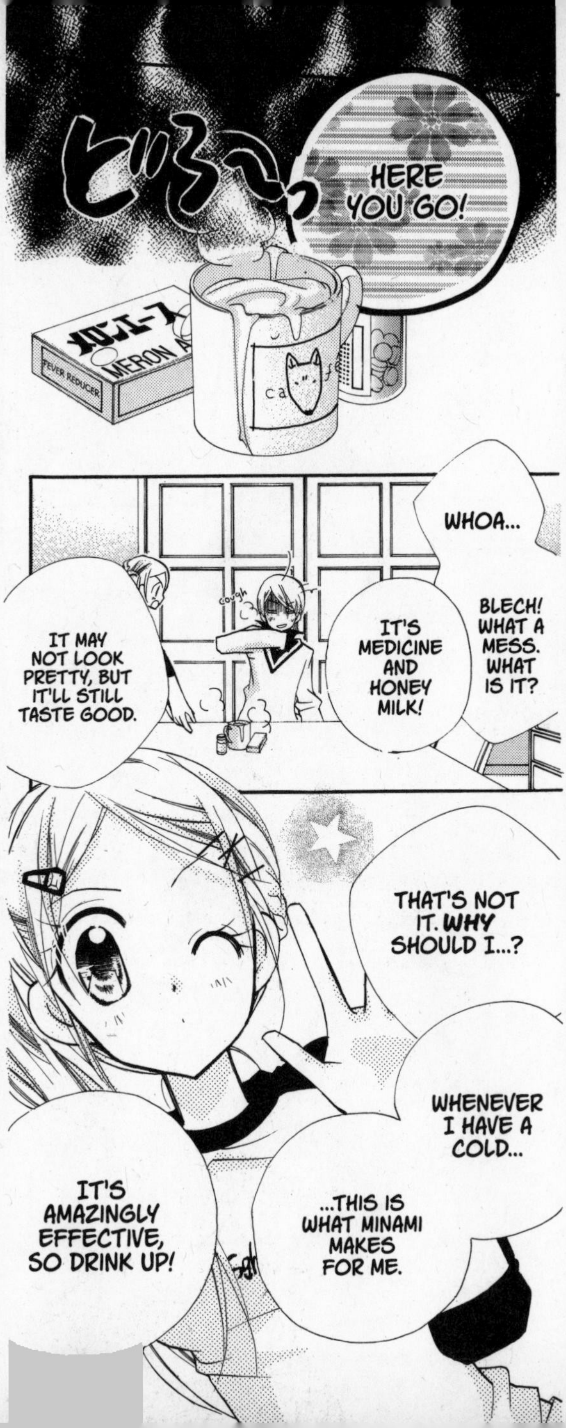
HERE YOU GO!
FEVER REDUCER
MERON A
WHOA...
BLECH! WHAT A MESS. WHAT IS IT?
cough
IT'S MEDICINE AND HONEY MILK!
IT MAY NOT LOOK PRETTY, BUT IT'LL STILL TASTE GOOD.
THAT'S NOT IT. WHY SHOULD I...?
WHENEVER I HAVE A COLD...
...THIS IS WHAT MINAMI MAKES FOR ME.
IT'S AMAZINGLY EFFECTIVE, SO DRINK UP!

ONE

Hello!

Are you all okay? Right now, I'm...

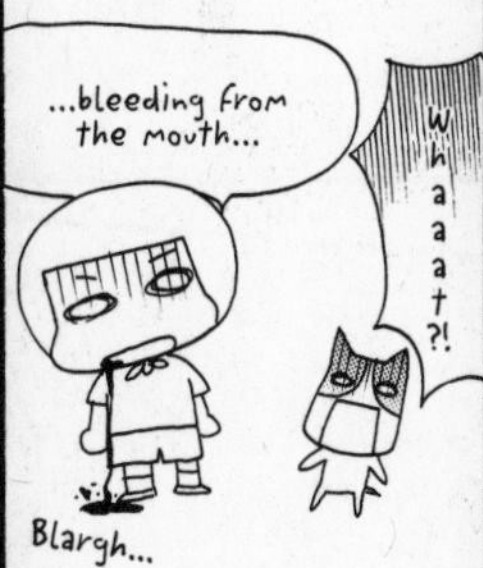
...bleeding from the mouth...
Whaaaat?!
Blargh...

...because my gums were recently mutilated by the dentist. (Heh.)

You know, it seems I'm always telling you about my teeth and my dentist. Sorry about that... Other than my teeth, I'm doing fine. These days, I keenly feel that dental care is oh-so-important!

So let's be diligent about teeth brushing!

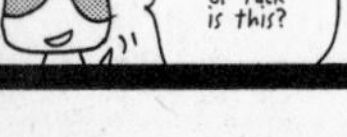
What kind of talk is this?

To TWO

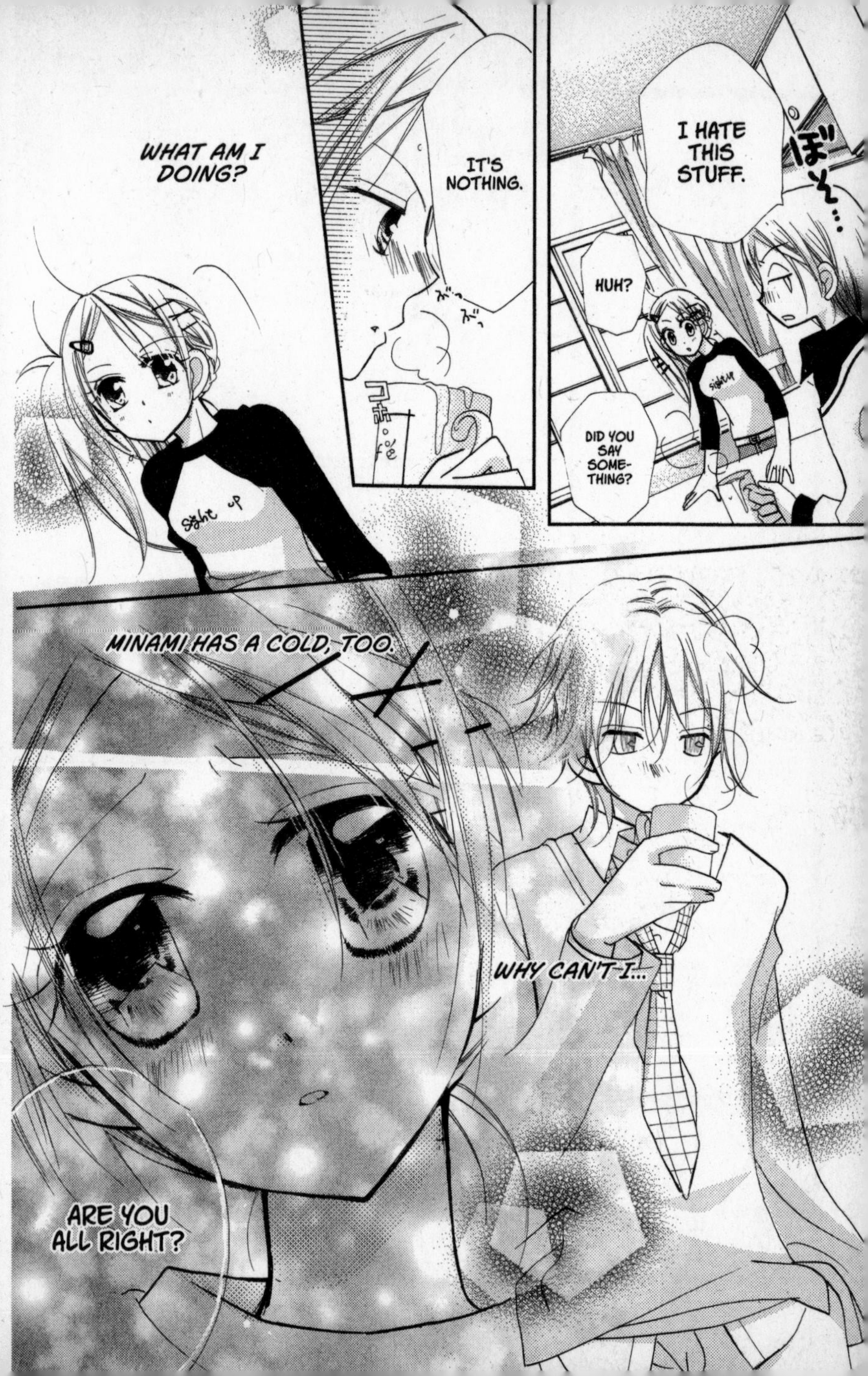
I HATE THIS STUFF.
ぼそ…
HUH?
DID YOU SAY SOME-THING?
IT'S NOTHING.
WHAT AM I DOING?
MINAMI HAS A COLD, TOO.
WHY CAN'T I...
ARE YOU ALL RIGHT?

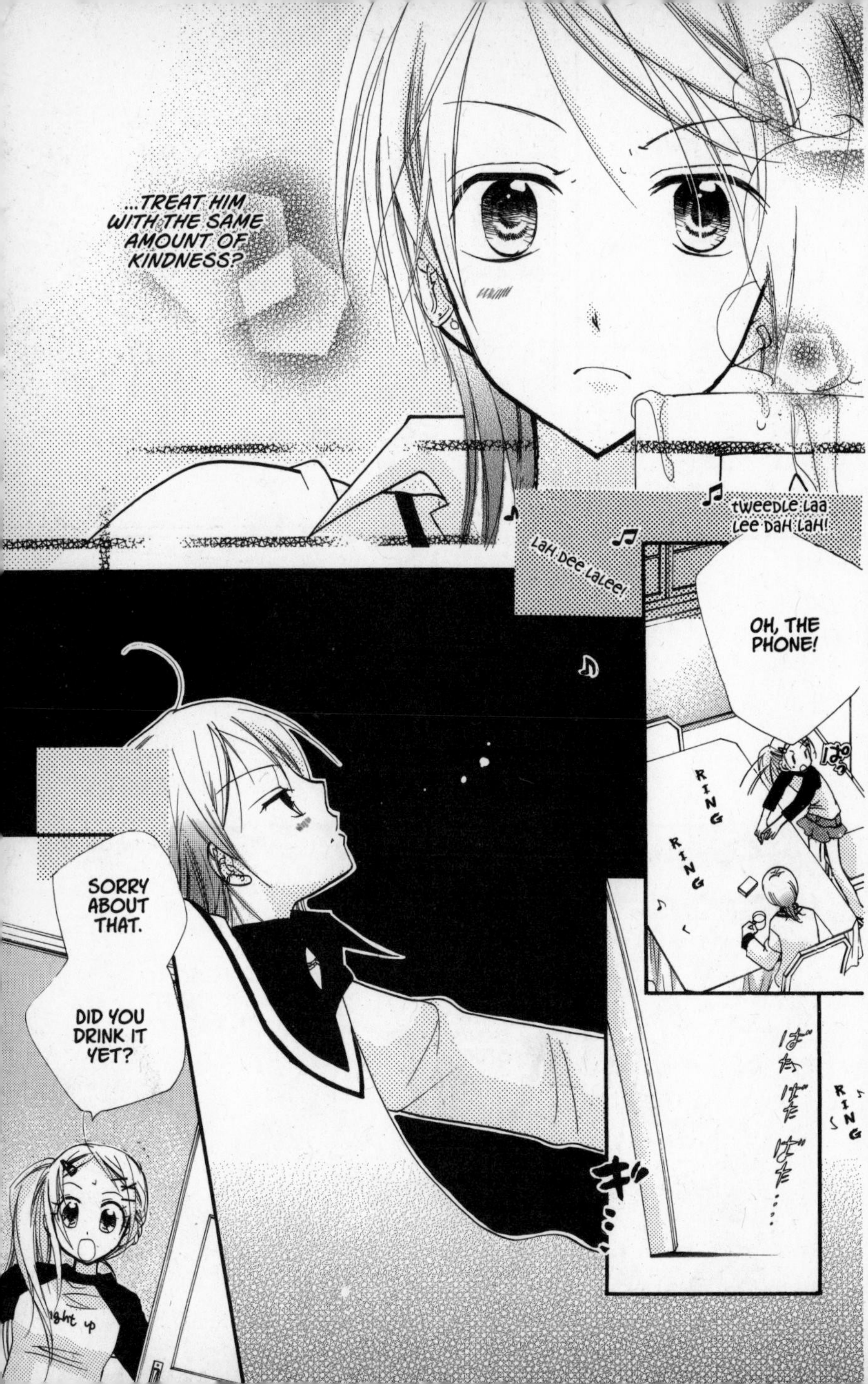
...TREAT HIM WITH THE SAME AMOUNT OF KINDNESS?
TWEEDLE LAA LEE DAH LAH!
LAH DEE LALEE!
OH, THE PHONE!
RING RING
ぱっ
ばたばた…
RING RING
ギ…
SORRY ABOUT THAT.
DID YOU DRINK IT YET?

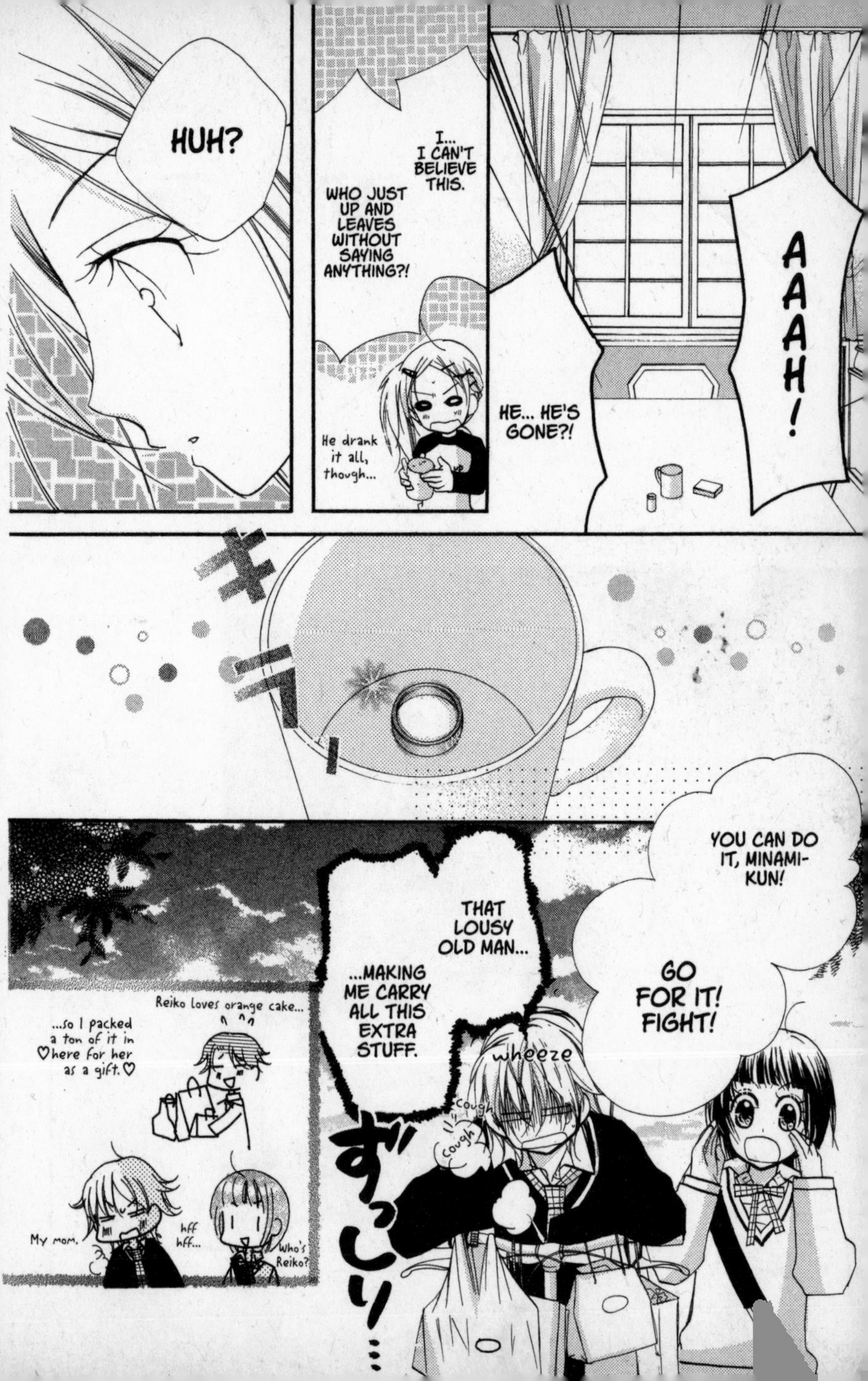
AAAAH!
HE... HE'S GONE?!
I... I CAN'T BELIEVE THIS.
WHO JUST UP AND LEAVES WITHOUT SAYING ANYTHING?!
He drank it all, though...
HUH?
YOU CAN DO IT, MINAMI-KUN!
GO FOR IT! FIGHT!
THAT LOUSY OLD MAN...
...MAKING ME CARRY ALL THIS EXTRA STUFF.
wheeze
cough
cough
ずっしり
Reiko loves orange cake...
...so I packed a ton of it in ♡here for her as a gift.♡
hff hff...
Who's Reiko?
My mom.

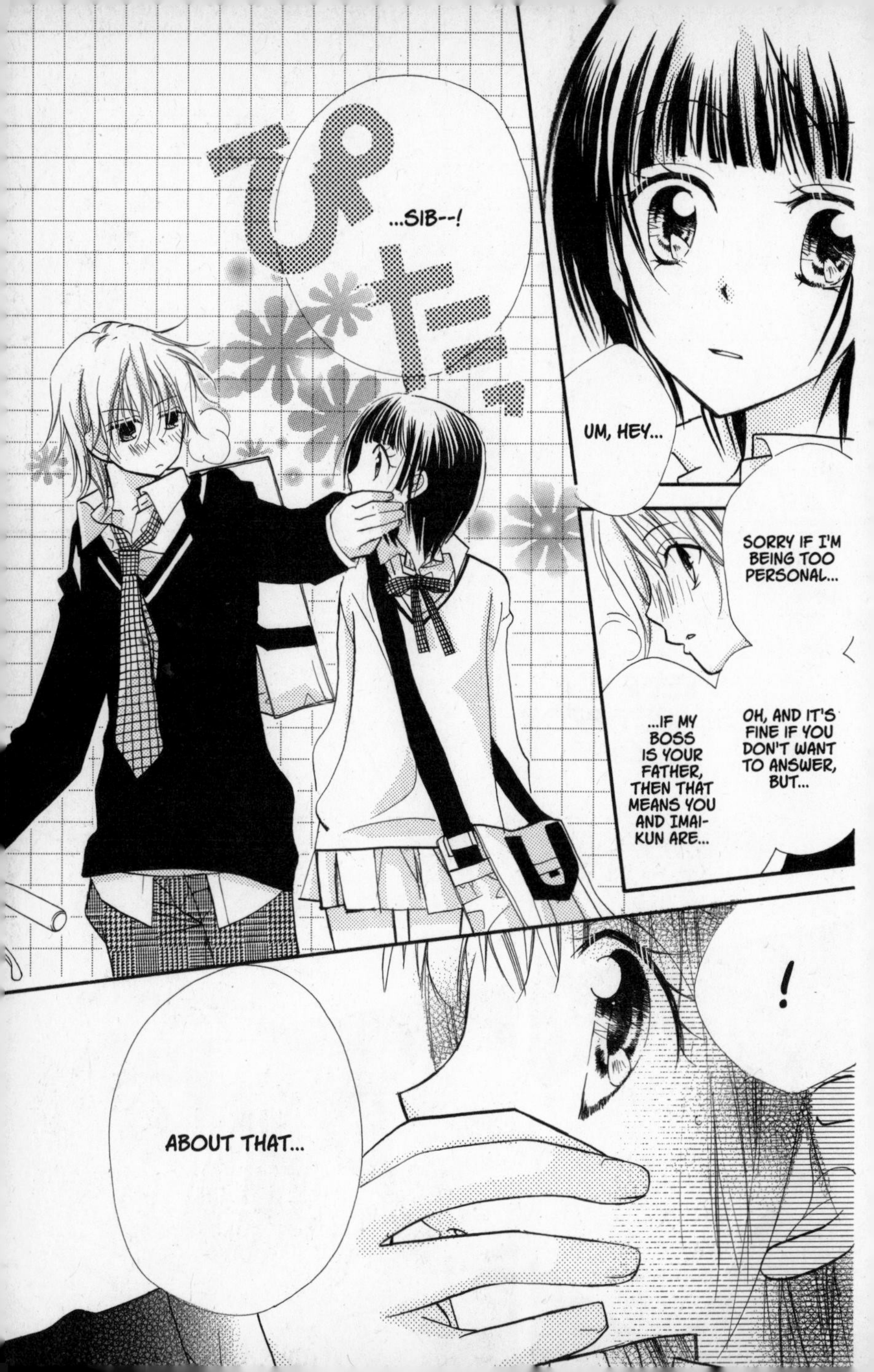
UM, HEY...
SORRY IF I'M BEING TOO PERSONAL...
OH, AND IT'S FINE IF YOU DON'T WANT TO ANSWER, BUT...
...IF MY BOSS IS YOUR FATHER, THEN THAT MEANS YOU AND IMAI-KUN ARE...
...SIB--!
!
ABOUT THAT...

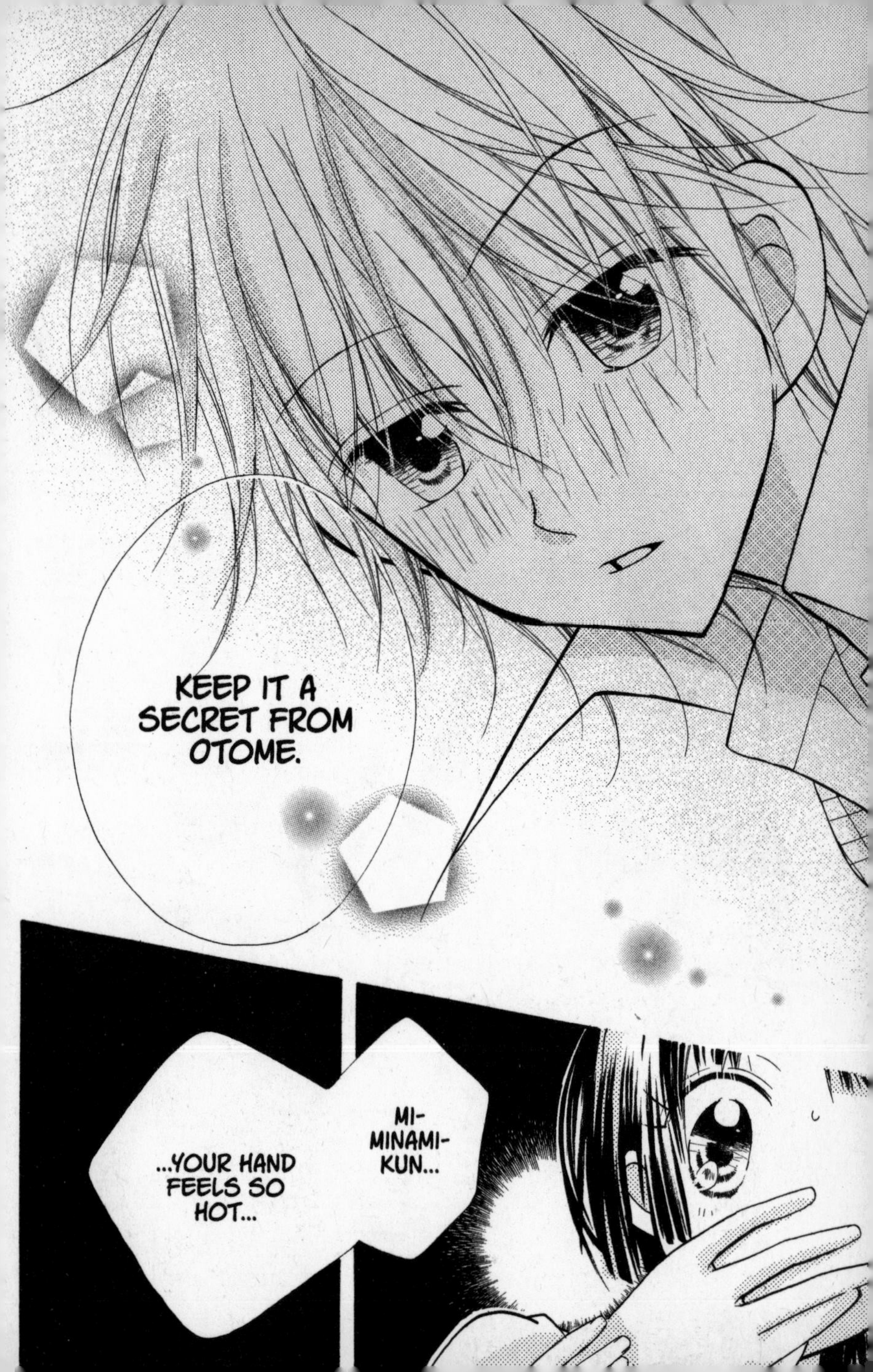
KEEP IT A SECRET FROM OTOME.
MI-MINAMI-KUN...
...YOUR HAND FEELS SO HOT...

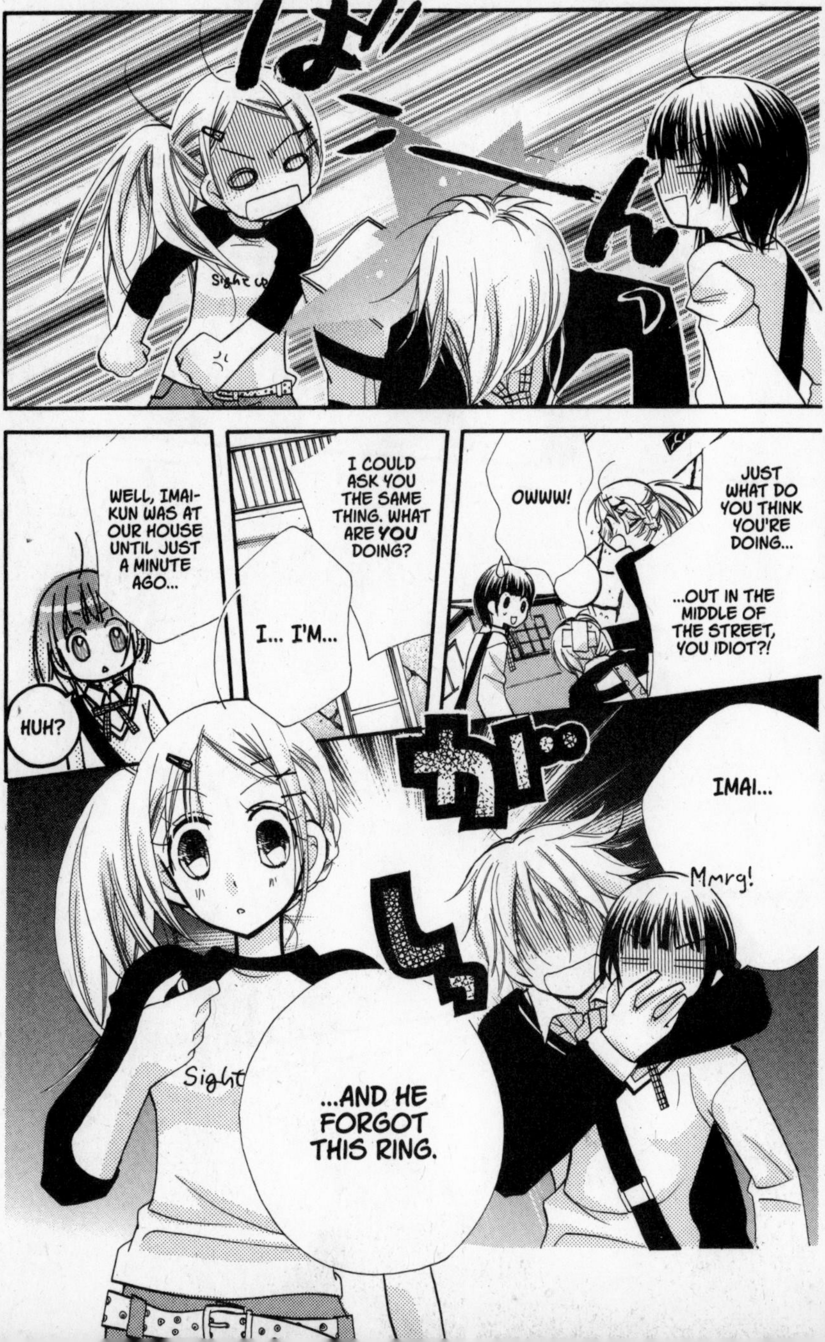
ばこーん
JUST WHAT DO YOU THINK YOU'RE DOING...
...OUT IN THE MIDDLE OF THE STREET, YOU IDIOT?!
OWWW!
I COULD ASK YOU THE SAME THING. WHAT ARE YOU DOING?
I... I'M...
WELL, IMAI-KUN WAS AT OUR HOUSE UNTIL JUST A MINUTE AGO...
HUH?
IMAI...
Mmrg!
がしっ
...AND HE FORGOT THIS RING.

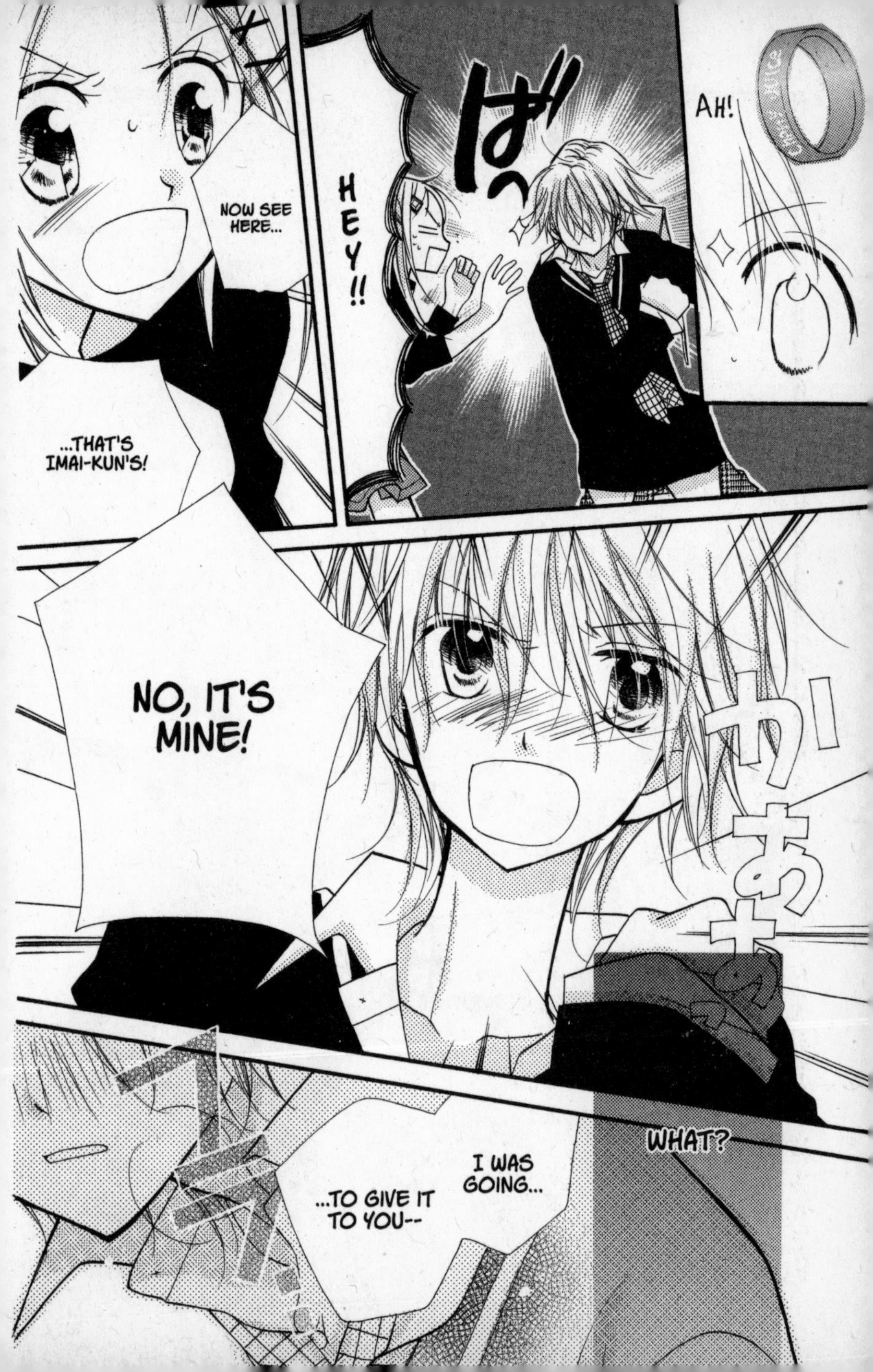
AH!
HEY!!
NOW SEE HERE...
...THAT'S IMAI-KUN'S!
NO, IT'S MINE!
WHAT?
I WAS GOING...
...TO GIVE IT TO YOU--

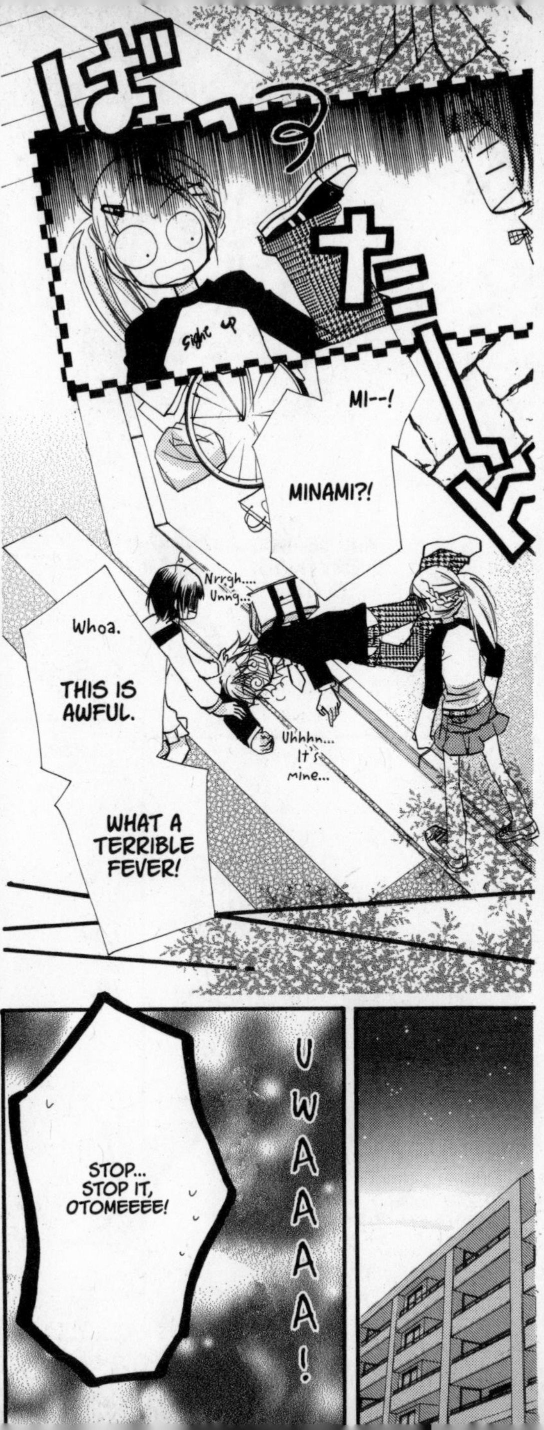
MI--!
MINAMI?!
Nrrgh.... Unng...
Whoa.
THIS IS AWFUL.
Uhhhn... It's mine...
WHAT A TERRIBLE FEVER!
UWAAAAA!
STOP... STOP IT, OTOMEEEE!

TWO

I wrote in this very spot in volume 2 that I would talk about Otome and the other's high school uniforms in volume 3...so, I will do that right here!

↓

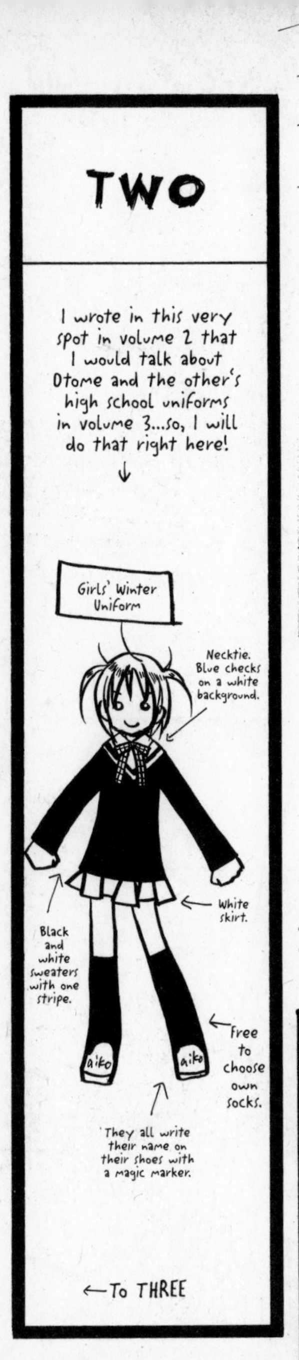
Girls' Winter Uniform
Necktie. Blue checks on a white background.
White skirt.
Black and white sweaters with one stripe.
Free to choose own socks.
aiko
aiko
They all write their name on their shoes with a magic marker.

←To THREE

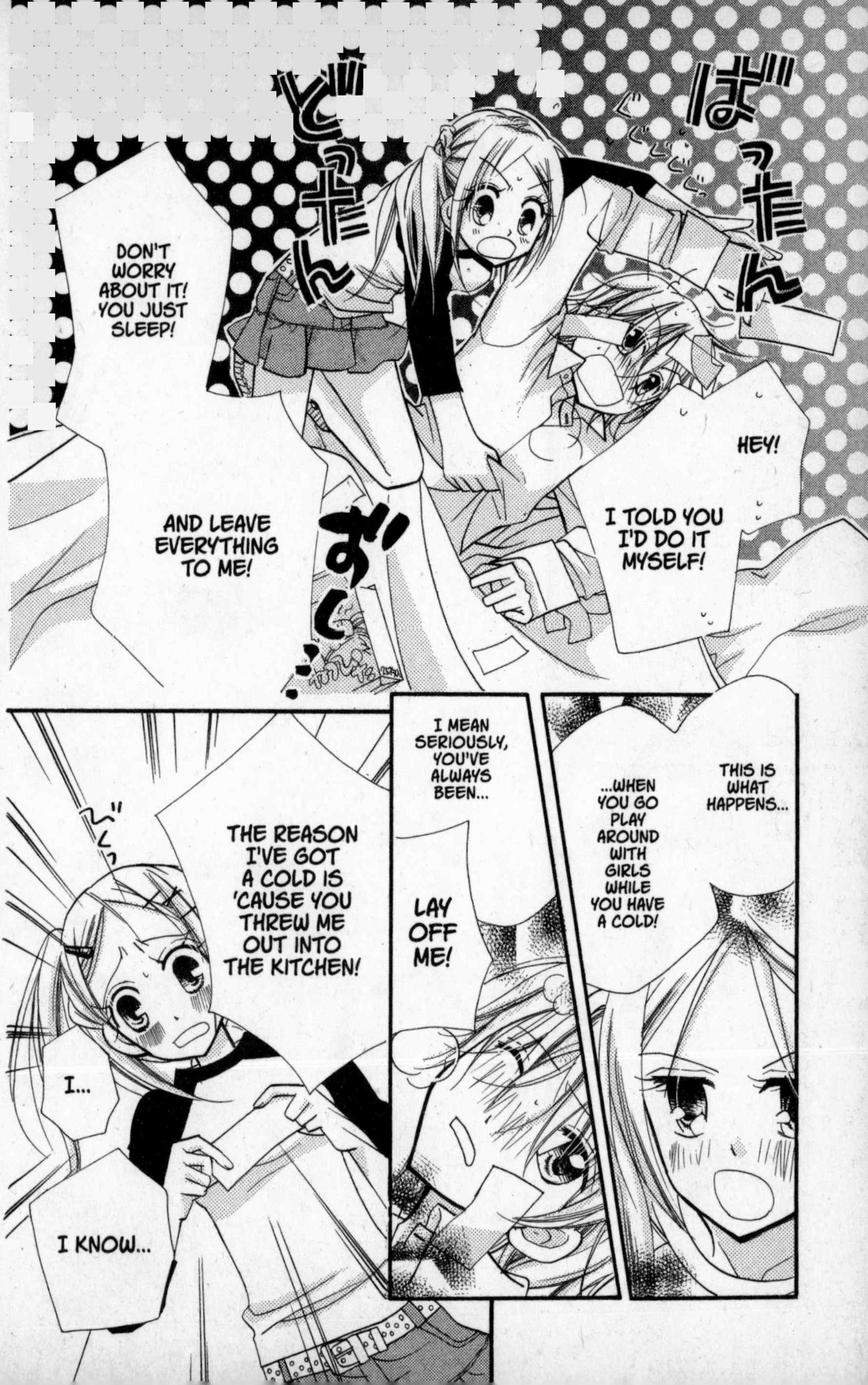
ばったん
どったん
HEY!
I TOLD YOU I'D DO IT MYSELF!
DON'T WORRY ABOUT IT! YOU JUST SLEEP!
AND LEAVE EVERYTHING TO ME!
THIS IS WHAT HAPPENS...
...WHEN YOU GO PLAY AROUND WITH GIRLS WHILE YOU HAVE A COLD!
I MEAN SERIOUSLY, YOU'VE ALWAYS BEEN...
LAY OFF ME!
THE REASON I'VE GOT A COLD IS 'CAUSE YOU THREW ME OUT INTO THE KITCHEN!
I...
I KNOW...

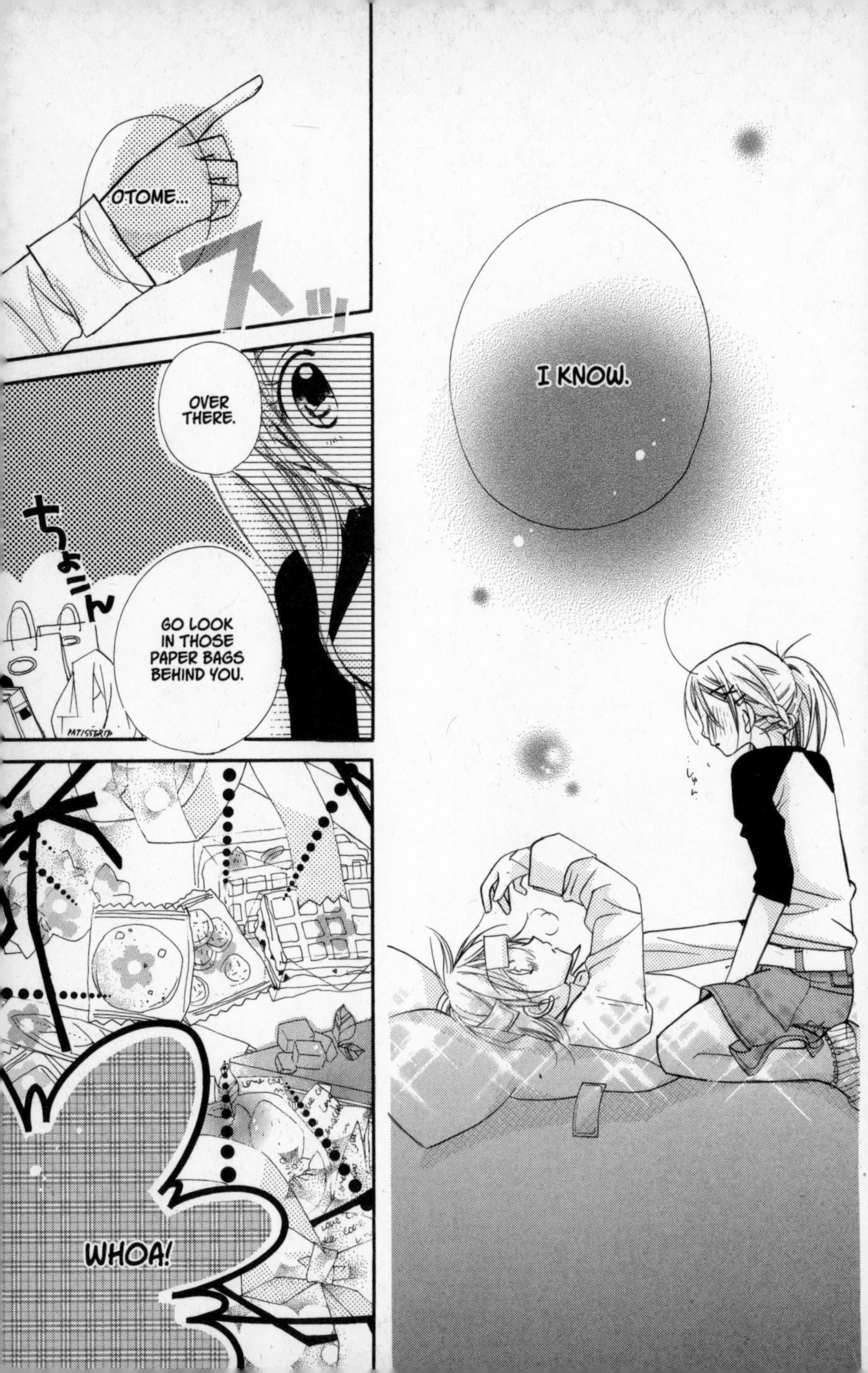
I KNOW.
OTOME...
OVER THERE.
GO LOOK IN THOSE PAPER BAGS BEHIND YOU.
WHOA!

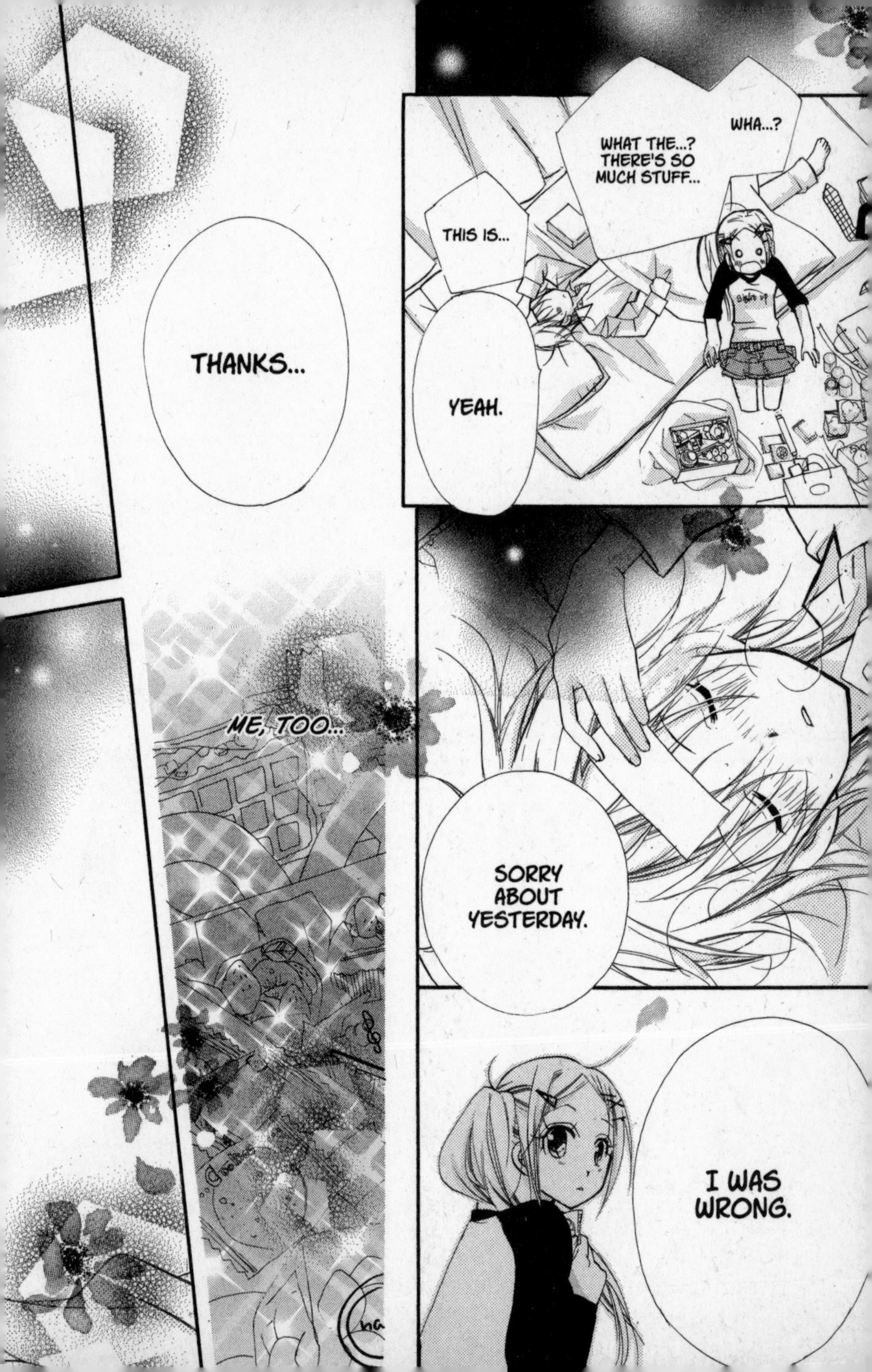
WHA...?
WHAT THE...? THERE'S SO MUCH STUFF...
THIS IS...
YEAH.
SORRY ABOUT YESTERDAY.
I WAS WRONG.
THANKS...
ME, TOO...

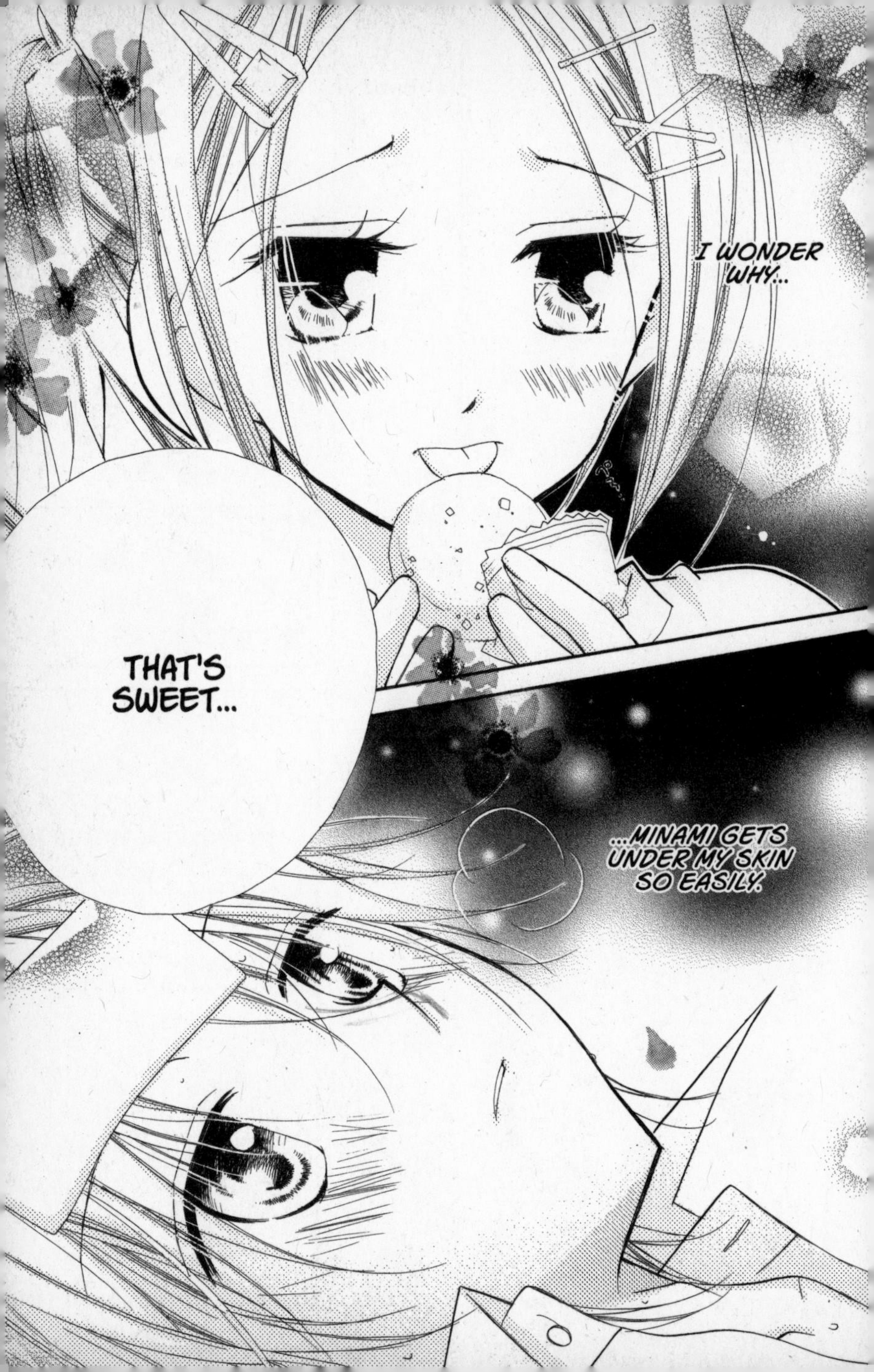
I WONDER WHY...
THAT'S SWEET...
...MINAMI GETS UNDER MY SKIN SO EASILY.

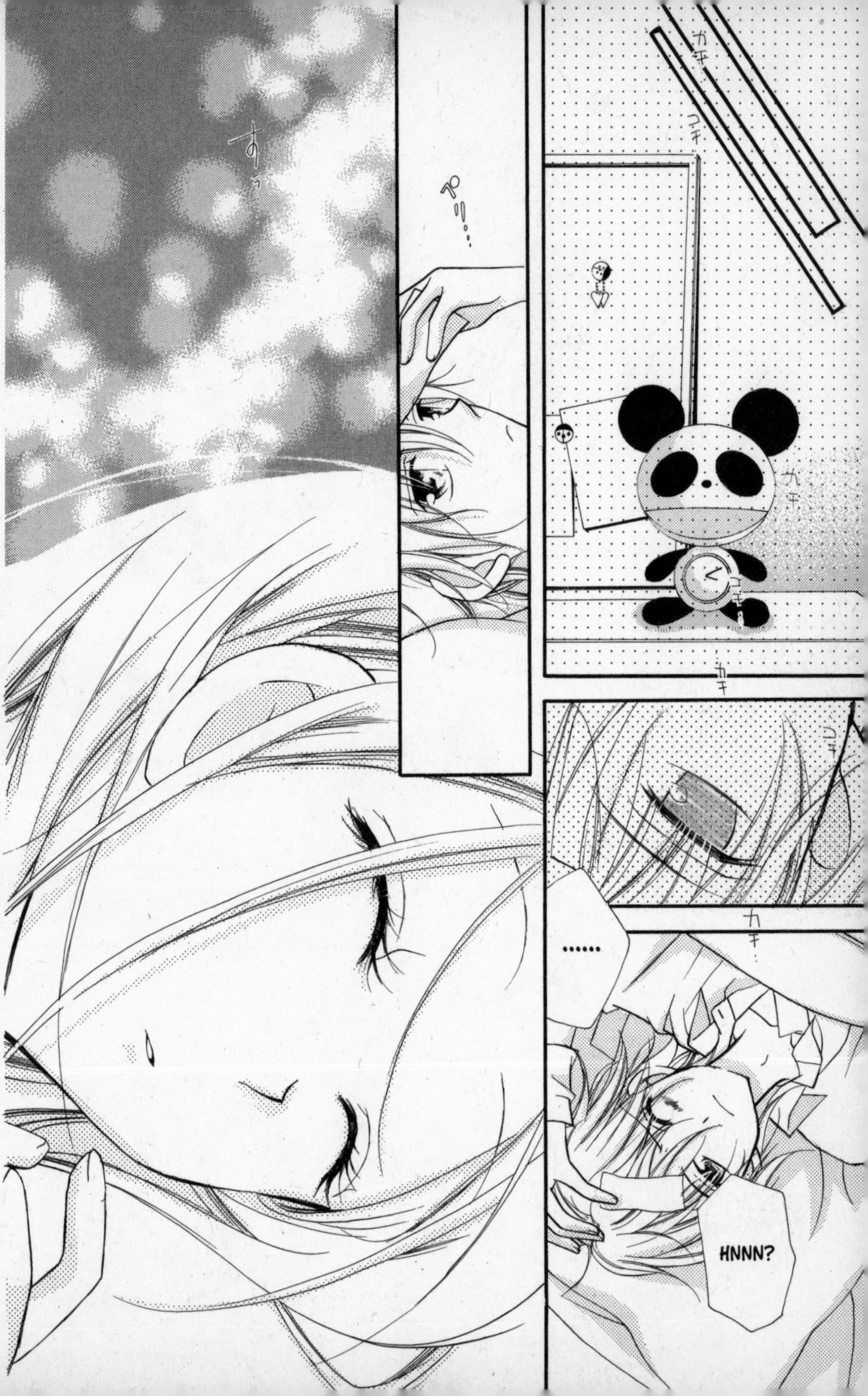

......
HNNN?

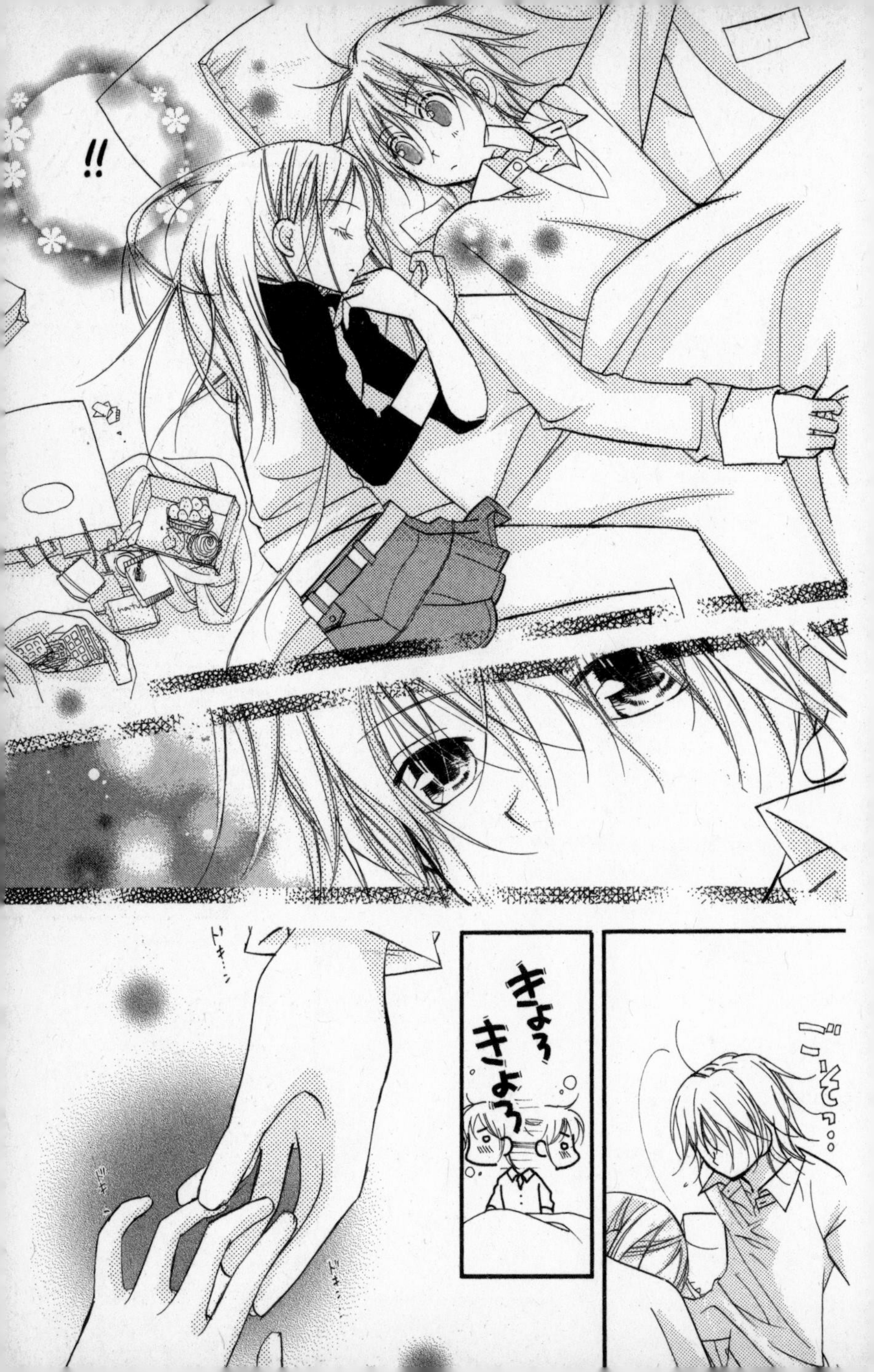
!!
ごそっ…
きょろ
きょろ
ドキ…ン
ドキ…

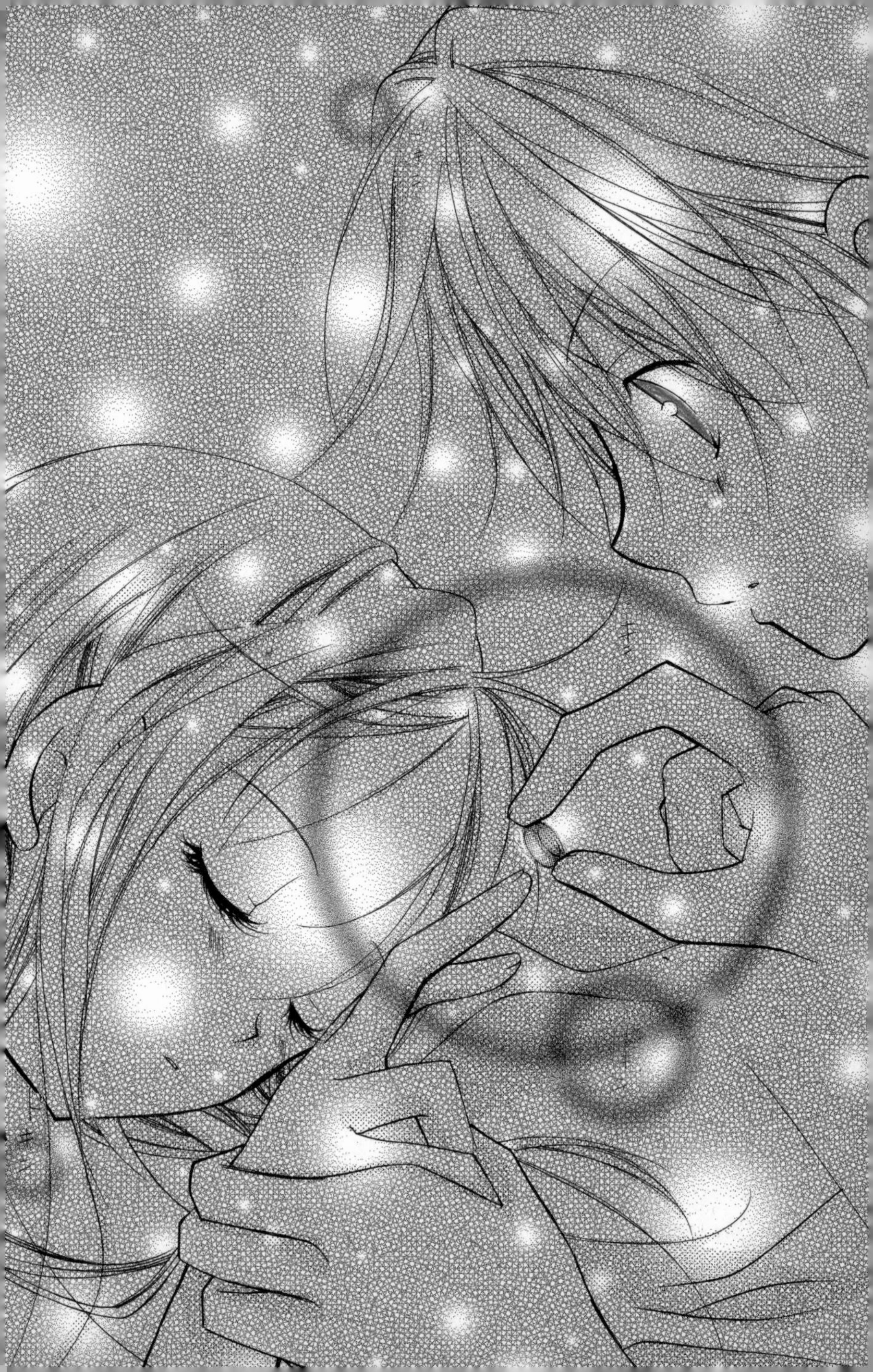

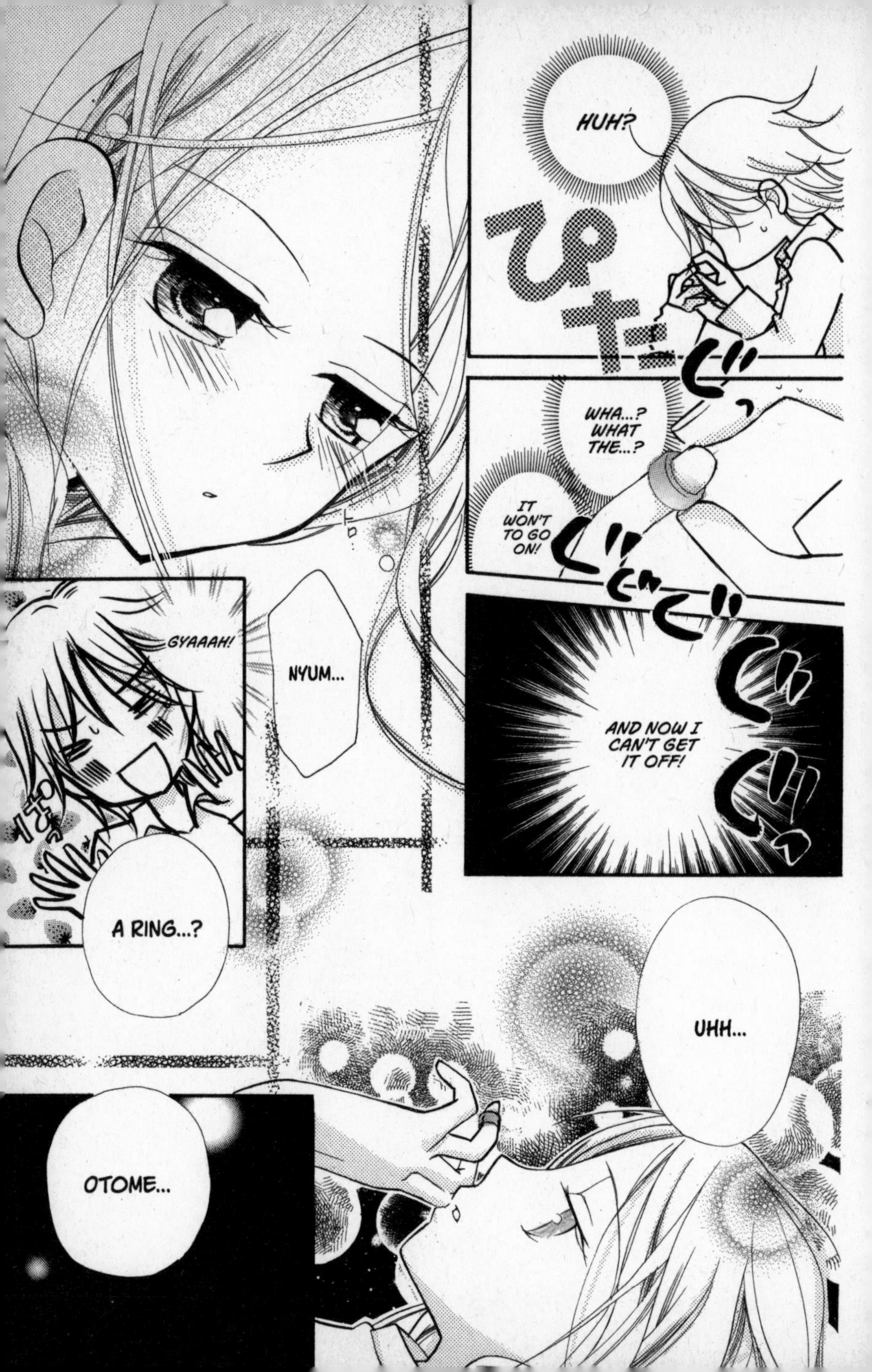
HUH?
WHA...? WHAT THE...?
IT WON'T TO GO ON!
AND NOW I CAN'T GET IT OFF!
NYUM...
GYAAAH!
A RING...?
UHH...
OTOME...

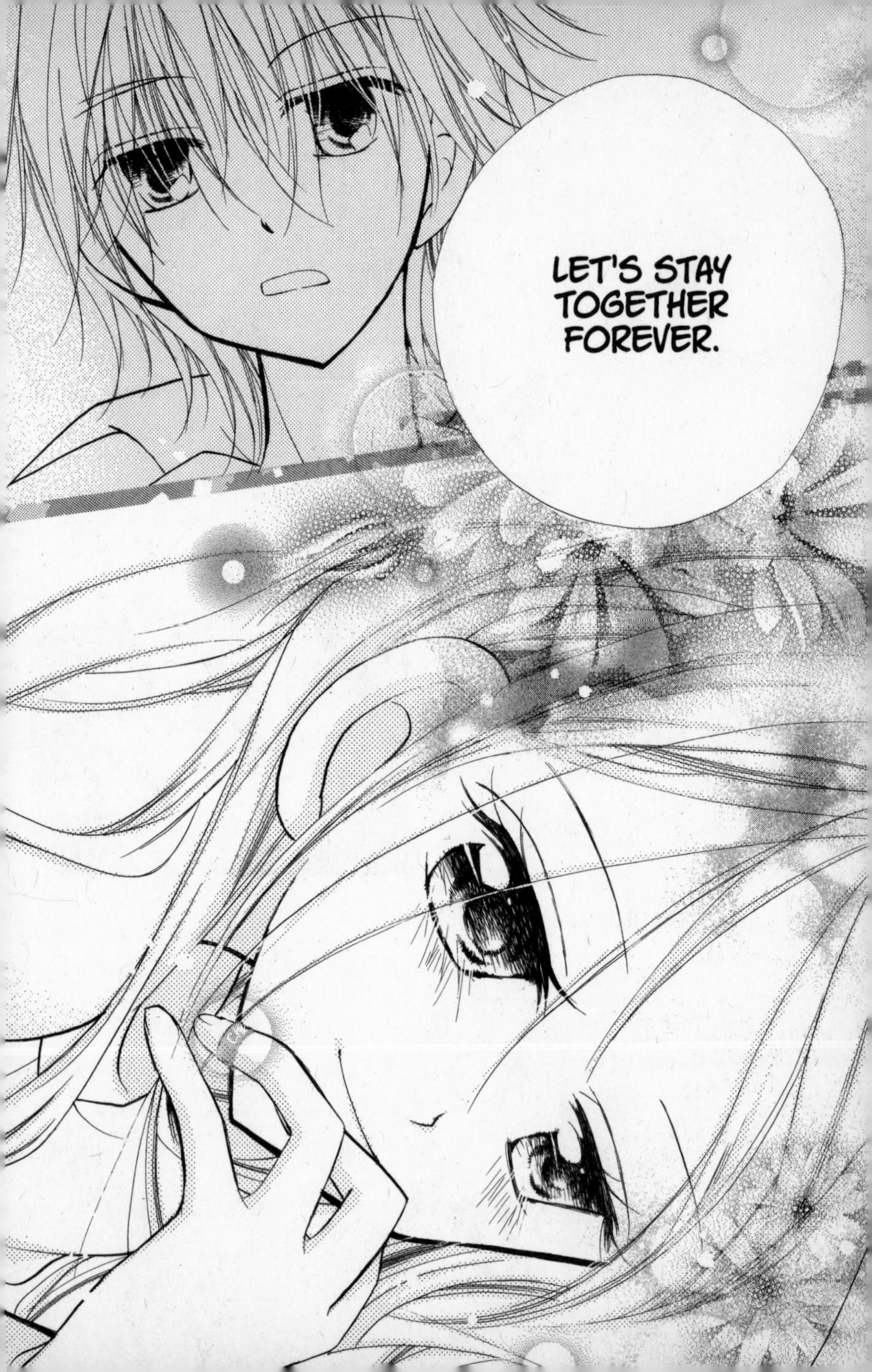
LET'S STAY TOGETHER FOREVER.

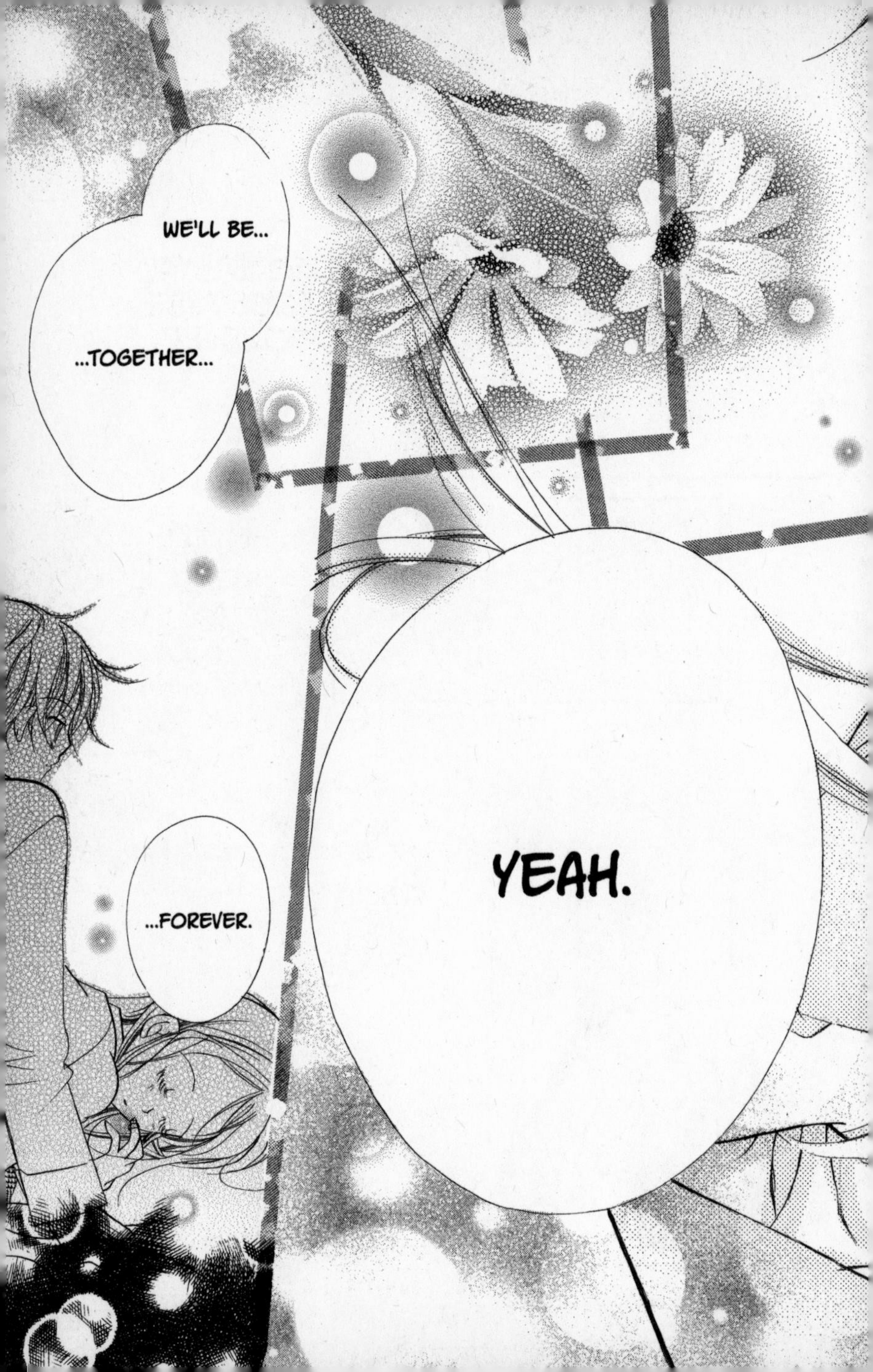
WE'LL BE...
...TOGETHER...
...FOREVER.
YEAH.

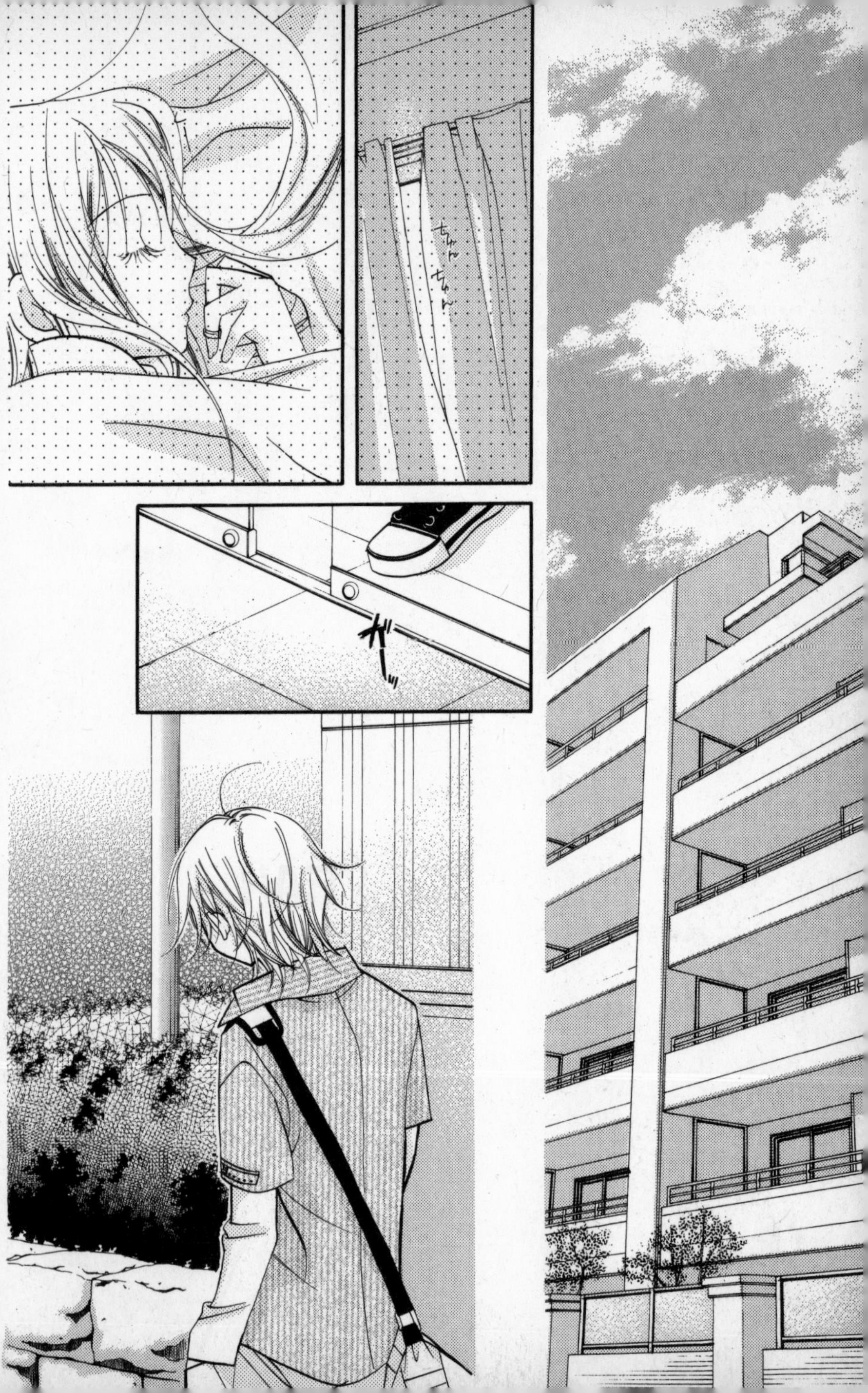
ちゅん ちゅん
ガーッ

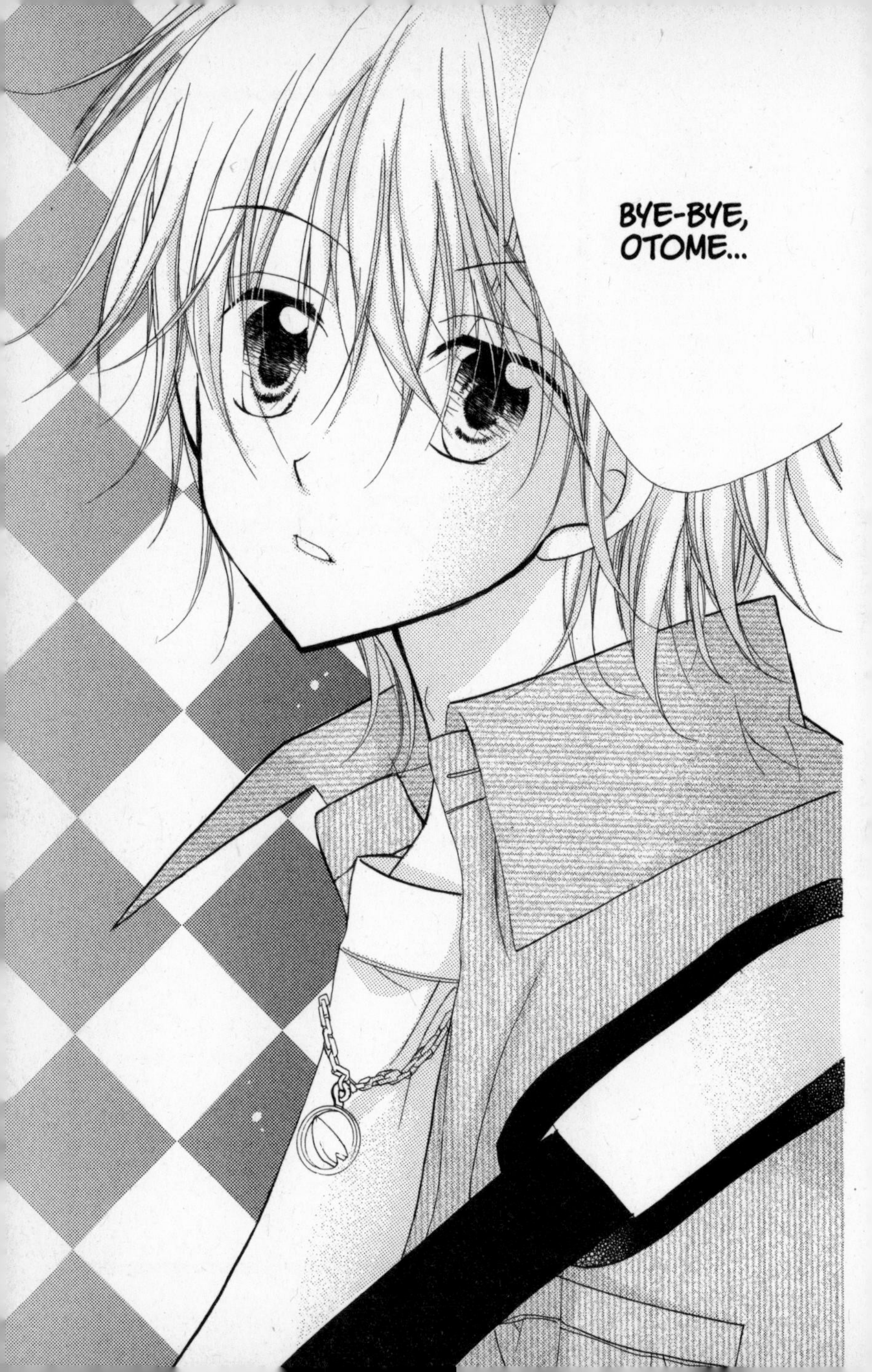
BYE-BYE, OTOME...

FOR starters!

Yo!

Japanese pears are delicious. ♡

This is Cherry Juice volume 3!

Japanese Pears

Hello! Haruka Fukushima here.
Thanks for buying this.

Before I knew it, we had come to volume
3 of this story. The farther along I
am in the story, the more it hits me
how difficult school romances are.

It's constantly spinning through my head
day after day that, if I can get your hearts
pounding even a little bit, I'll be happy...

And with that, back to
the story we GO!

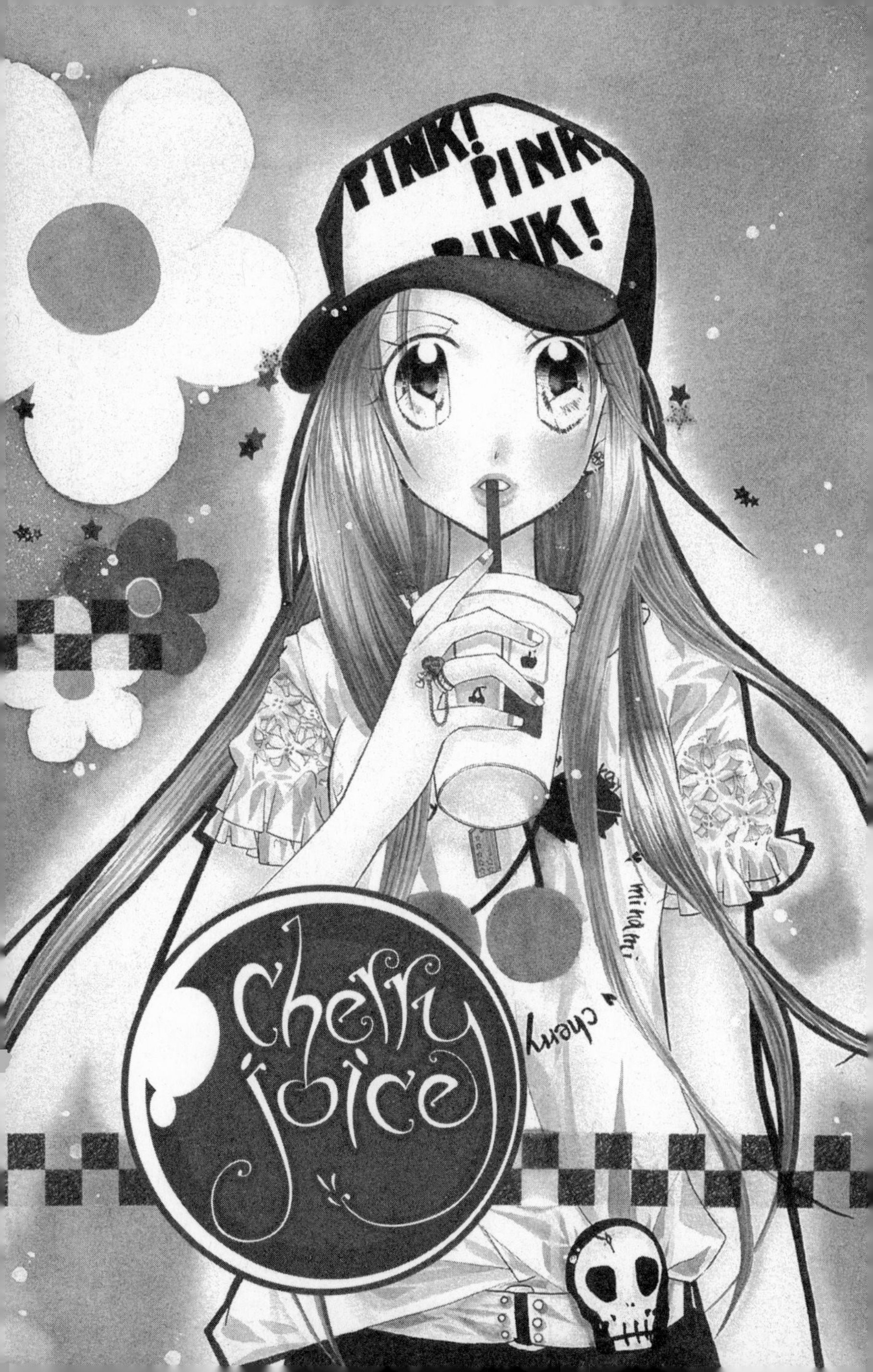
PINK!
Cherry Juice

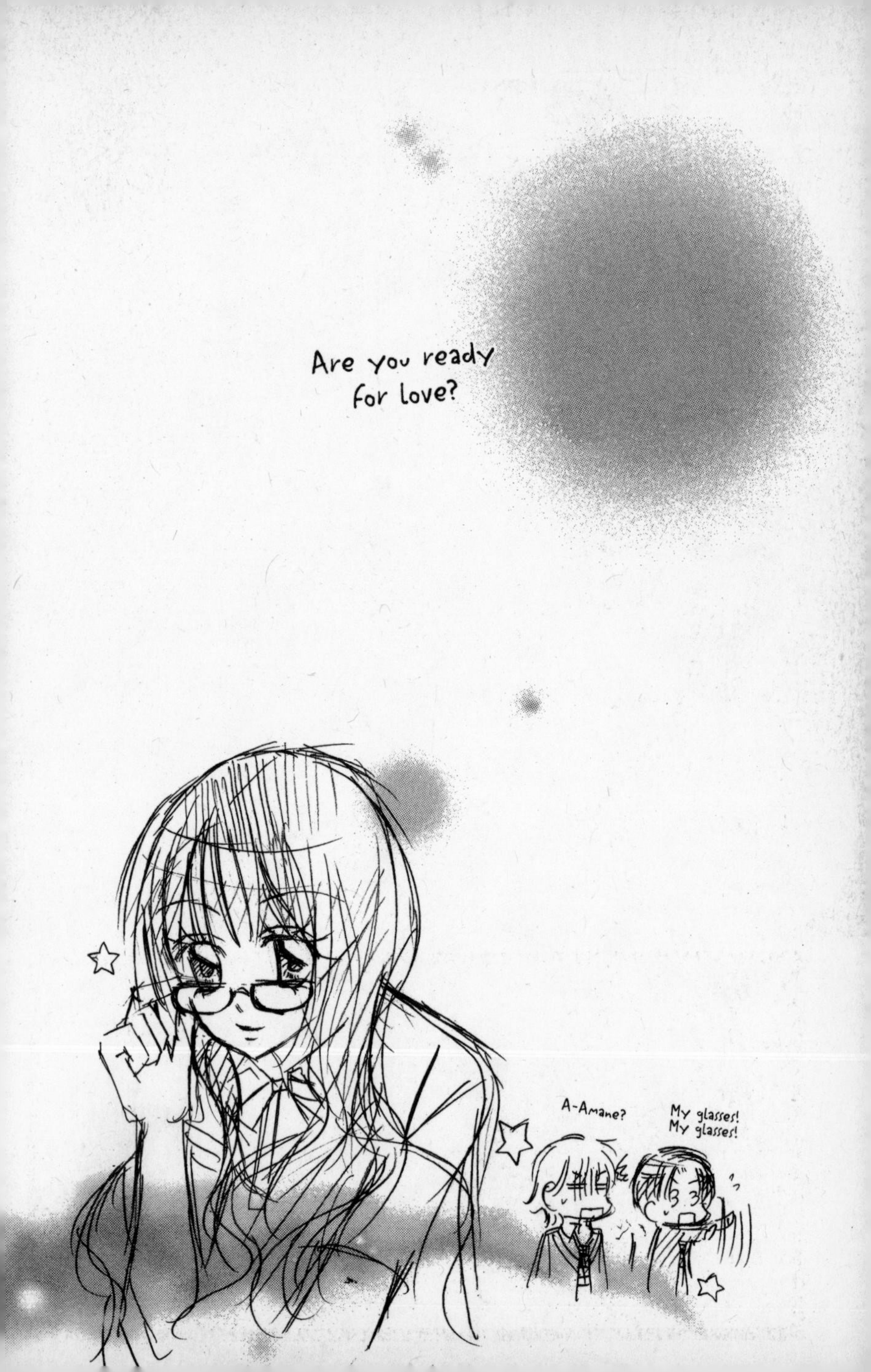
Are you ready for love?
My glasses! My glasses!
A-Amane?

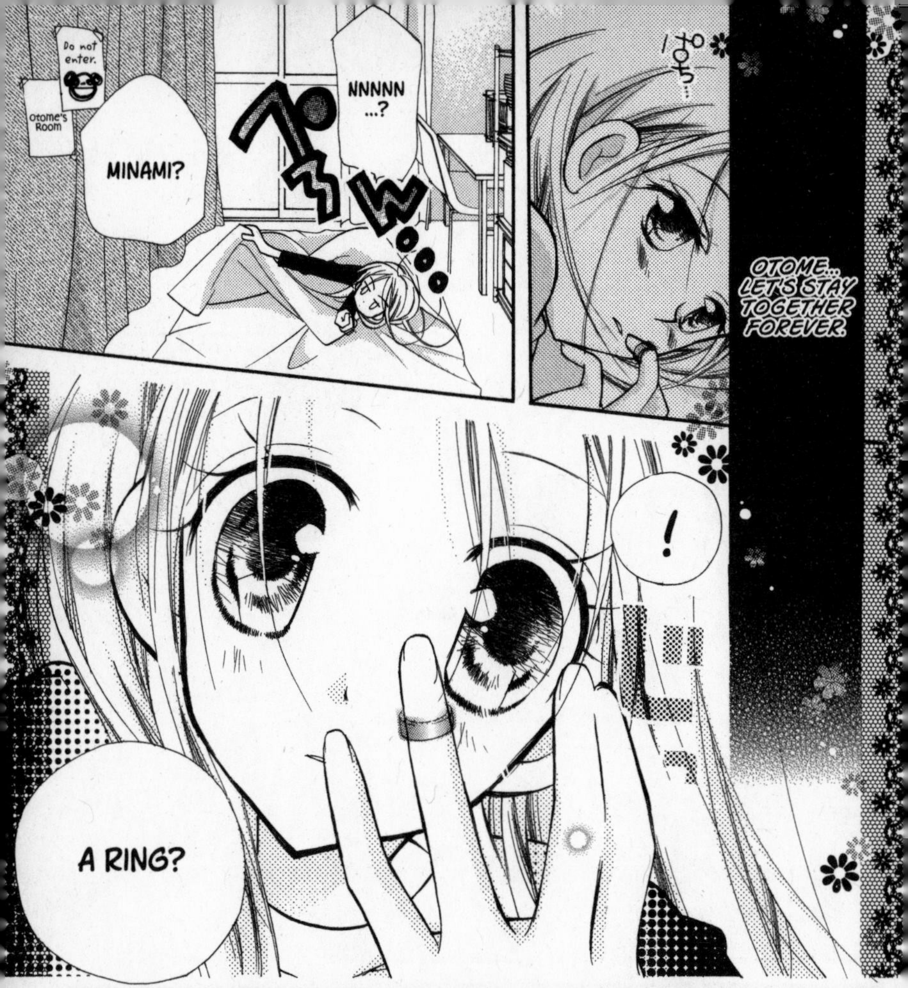
ぱち…
OTOME... LET'S STAY TOGETHER FOREVER.
Do not enter.
Otome's Room
NNNNN ...?
MINAMI?
!
A RING?

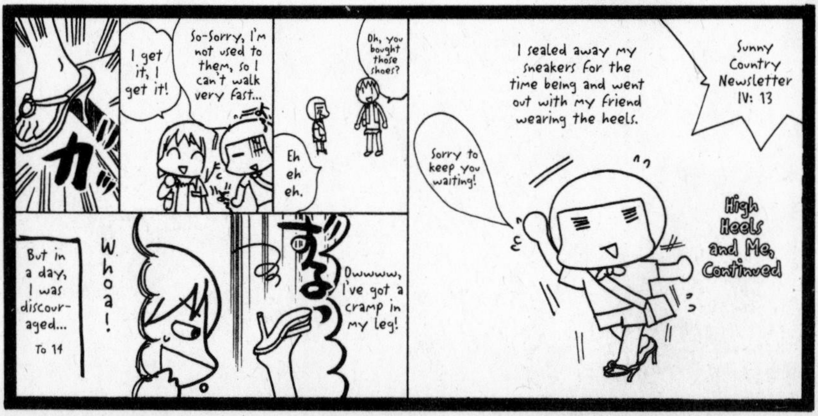
Sunny Country Newsletter IV: 13
High Heels and Me, Continued
I sealed away my sneakers for the time being and went out with my friend wearing the heels.
Sorry to keep you waiting!
Oh, you bought those shoes?
Eh eh eh.
So-Sorry, I'm not used to them, so I can't walk very fast...
I get it, I get it!
Owwww, I've got a cramp in my leg!
Whoa!
But in a day, I was discouraged...
To 14

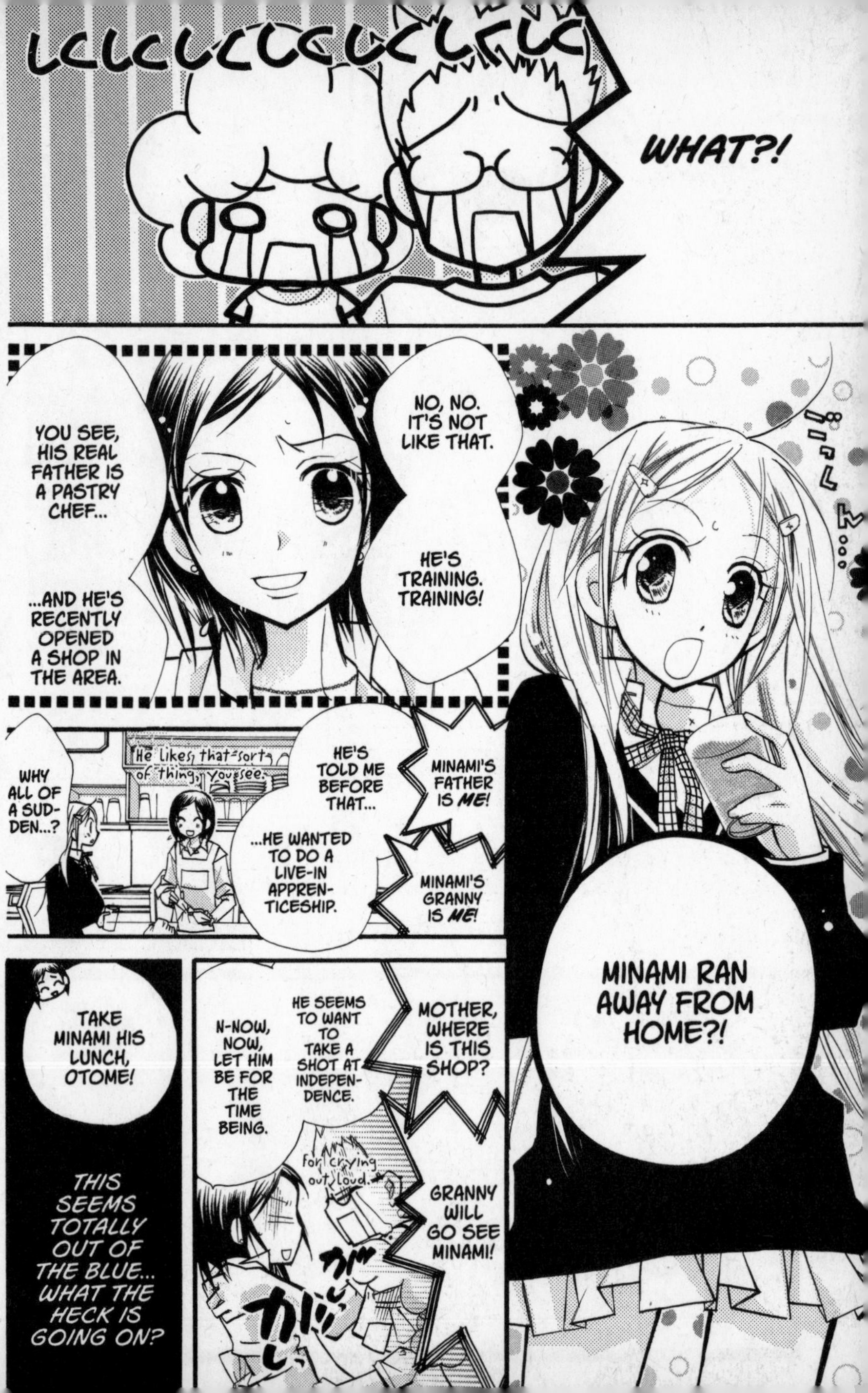
WHAT?!
MINAMI RAN AWAY FROM HOME?!
NO, NO. IT'S NOT LIKE THAT.
HE'S TRAINING. TRAINING!
YOU SEE, HIS REAL FATHER IS A PASTRY CHEF...
...AND HE'S RECENTLY OPENED A SHOP IN THE AREA.
MINAMI'S FATHER IS ME!
MINAMI'S GRANNY IS ME!
HE'S TOLD ME BEFORE THAT...
...HE WANTED TO DO A LIVE-IN APPRENTICESHIP.
He likes that sort of thing, you see.
WHY ALL OF A SUDDEN...?
MOTHER, WHERE IS THIS SHOP?
GRANNY WILL GO SEE MINAMI!
HE SEEMS TO WANT TO TAKE A SHOT AT INDEPENDENCE.
N-NOW, NOW, LET HIM BE FOR THE TIME BEING.
for crying out loud.
TAKE MINAMI HIS LUNCH, OTOME!
THIS SEEMS TOTALLY OUT OF THE BLUE... WHAT THE HECK IS GOING ON?

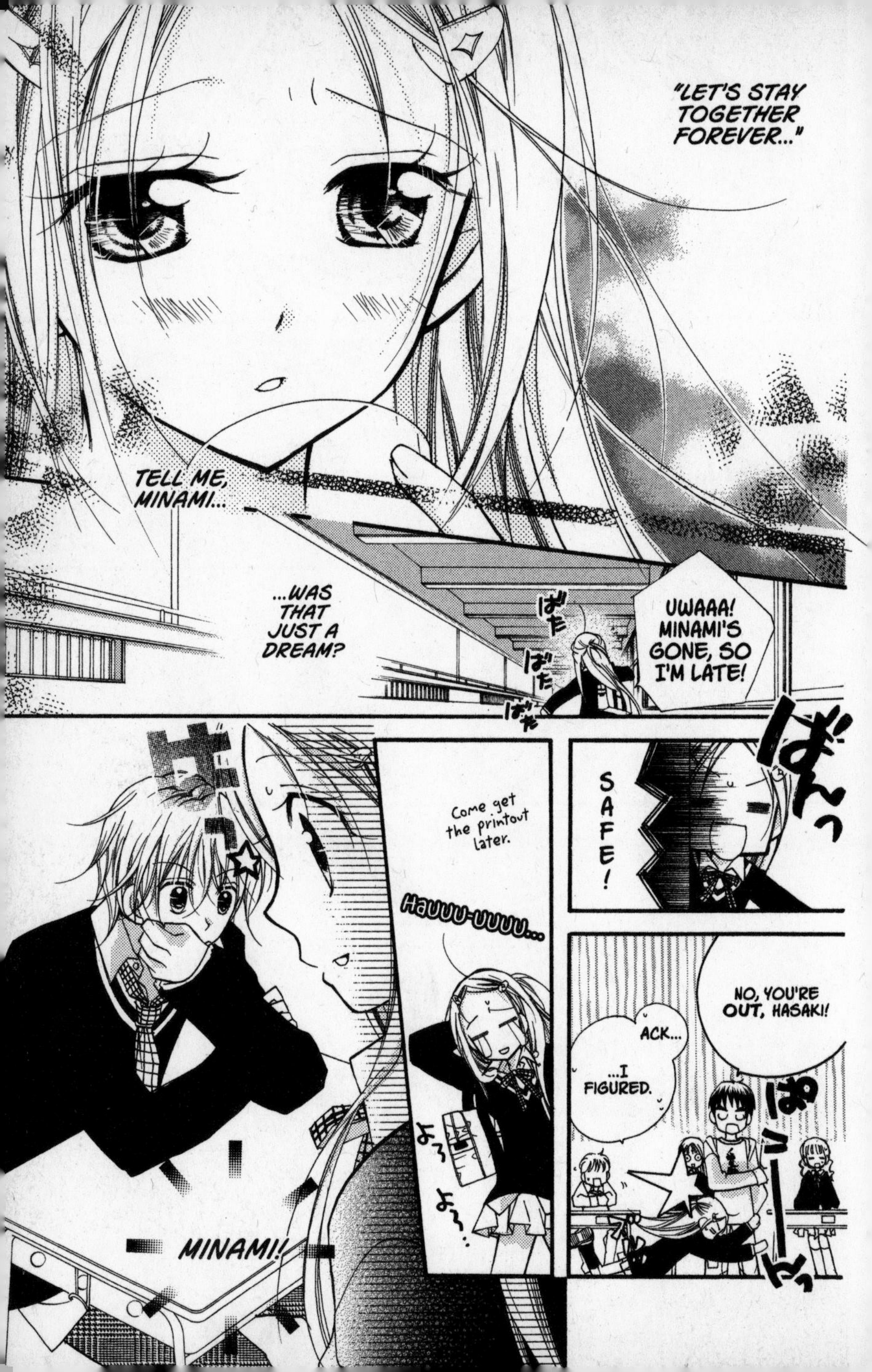
"LET'S STAY TOGETHER FOREVER..."
TELL ME, MINAMI...
...WAS THAT JUST A DREAM?
UWAAA! MINAMI'S GONE, SO I'M LATE!
ばた
ばた
ばた
ばんっ
SAFE!
NO, YOU'RE OUT, HASAKI!
ACK...
...I FIGURED.
ぱこーんっ
Come get the printout later.
HAUUU-UUUU...
よろ
よろ~...
MINAMI!

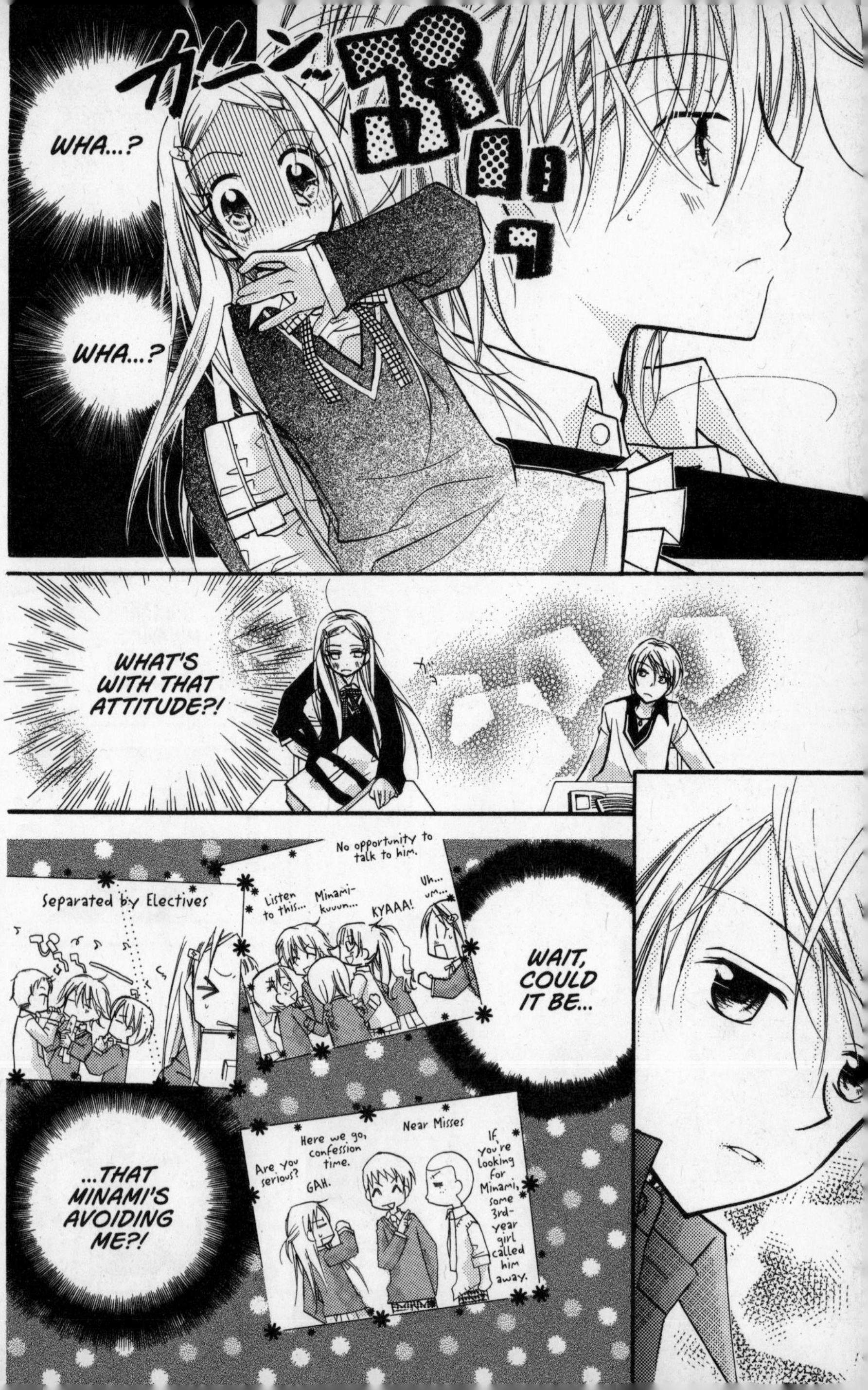
WHA...?
WHA...?
WHAT'S WITH THAT ATTITUDE?!
No opportunity to talk to him.
Uh... um...
KYAAA!
Minami-kuuun...
Listen to this...
WAIT, COULD IT BE...
Separated by Electives
Near Misses
If you're looking for Minami, some 3rd-year girl called him away.
Here we go, confession time.
GAH.
Are you serious?
...THAT MINAMI'S AVOIDING ME?!

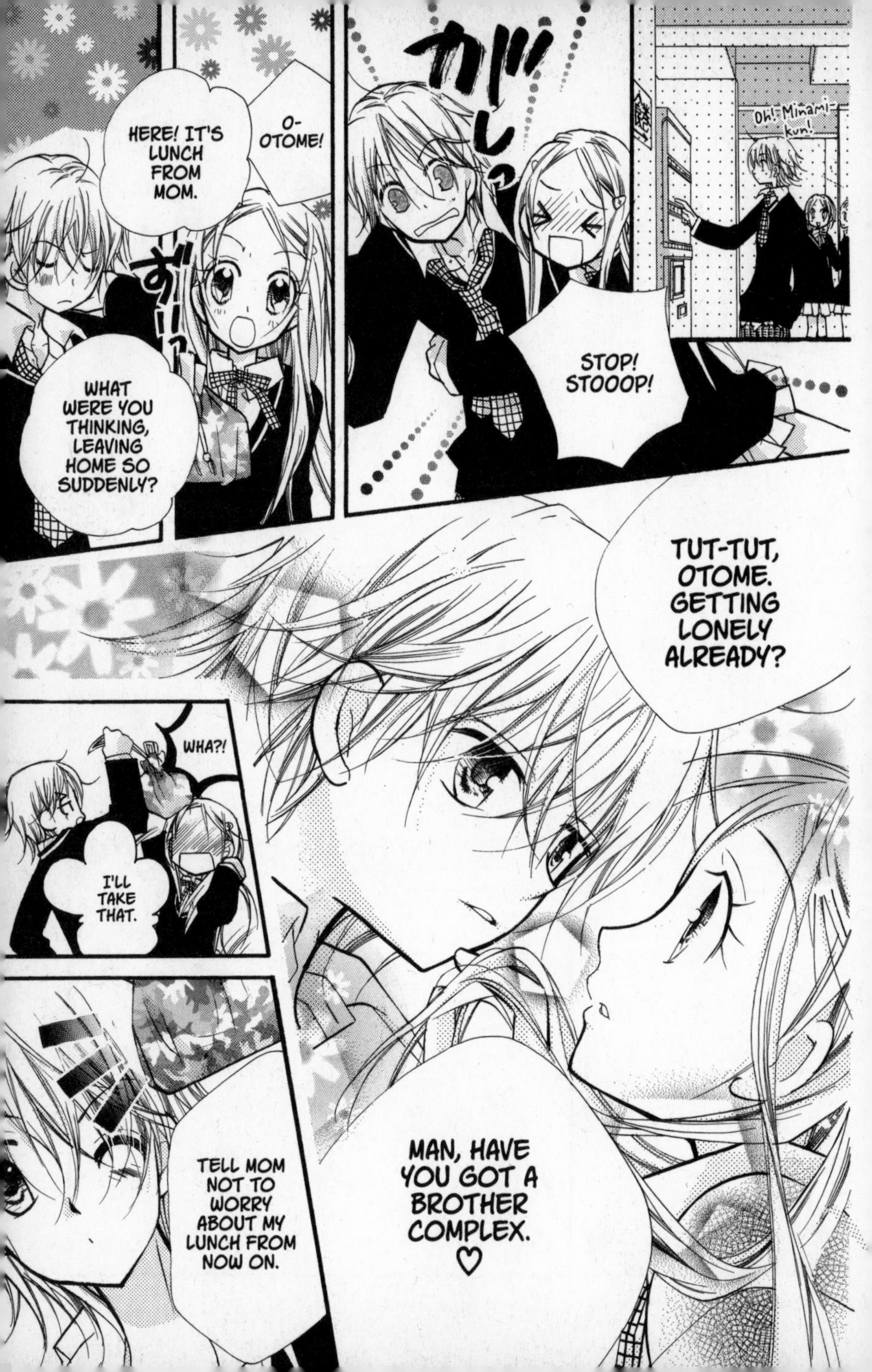
Oh! Minami-kun!
STOP! STOOOP!
O-OTOME!
HERE! IT'S LUNCH FROM MOM.
WHAT WERE YOU THINKING, LEAVING HOME SO SUDDENLY?
TUT-TUT, OTOME. GETTING LONELY ALREADY?
MAN, HAVE YOU GOT A BROTHER COMPLEX. ♡
WHA?!
I'LL TAKE THAT.
TELL MOM NOT TO WORRY ABOUT MY LUNCH FROM NOW ON.

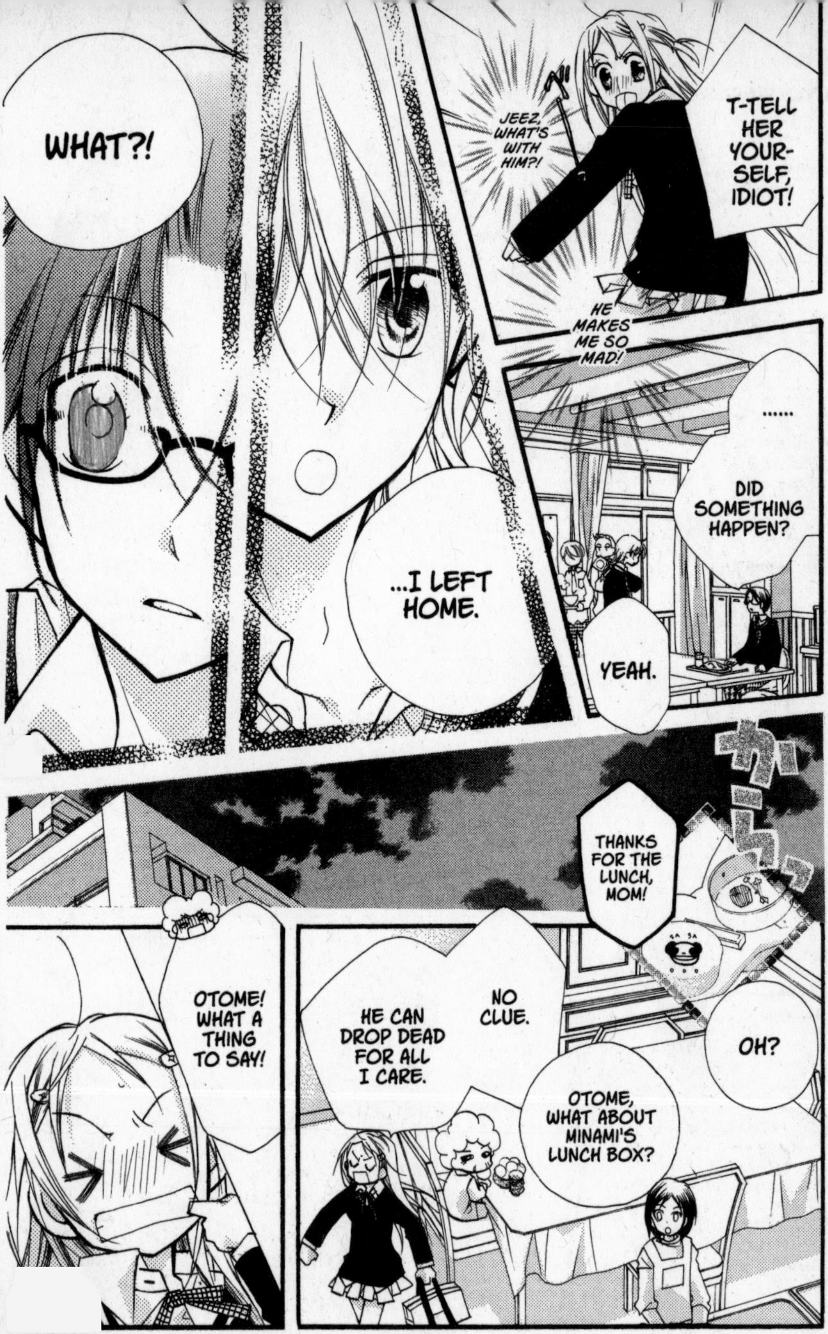
T-TELL HER YOURSELF, IDIOT!
JEEZ, WHAT'S WITH HIM?!
HE MAKES ME SO MAD!
......
DID SOMETHING HAPPEN?
YEAH.
...I LEFT HOME.
WHAT?!
THANKS FOR THE LUNCH, MOM!
OH?
OTOME, WHAT ABOUT MINAMI'S LUNCH BOX?
NO CLUE.
HE CAN DROP DEAD FOR ALL I CARE.
OTOME! WHAT A THING TO SAY!

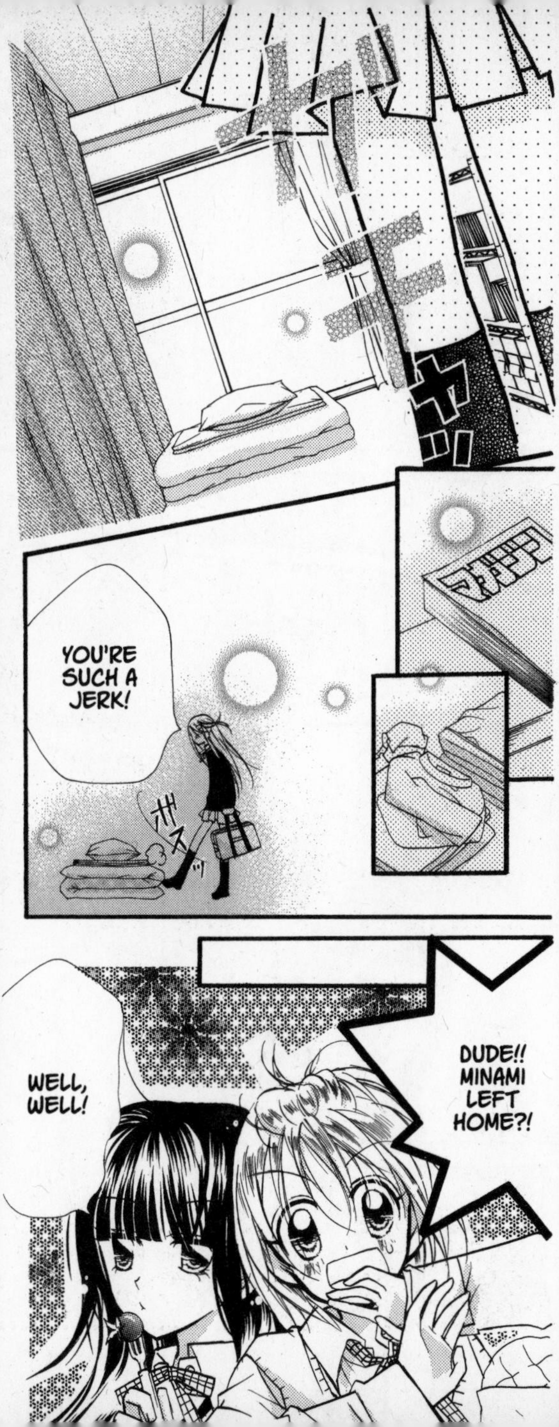
YOU'RE SUCH A JERK!
DUDE!! MINAMI LEFT HOME?!
WELL, WELL!

THREE

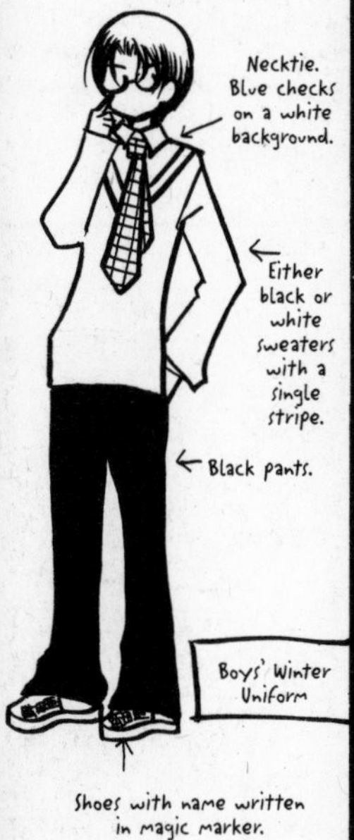
Necktie. Blue checks on a white background.
Either black or white sweaters with a single stripe.
Black pants.
Boys' Winter Uniform
Shoes with name written in magic marker.

Truthfully, I had planned to put checks on both the boys' and girls' shirts, but when I think about the amount of work... Yeah, well, I don't want to think about it. And so, for such a pathetic reason as that, I decided to make only the ribbons and ties checkered.

← To FOUR

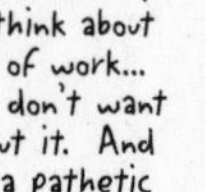

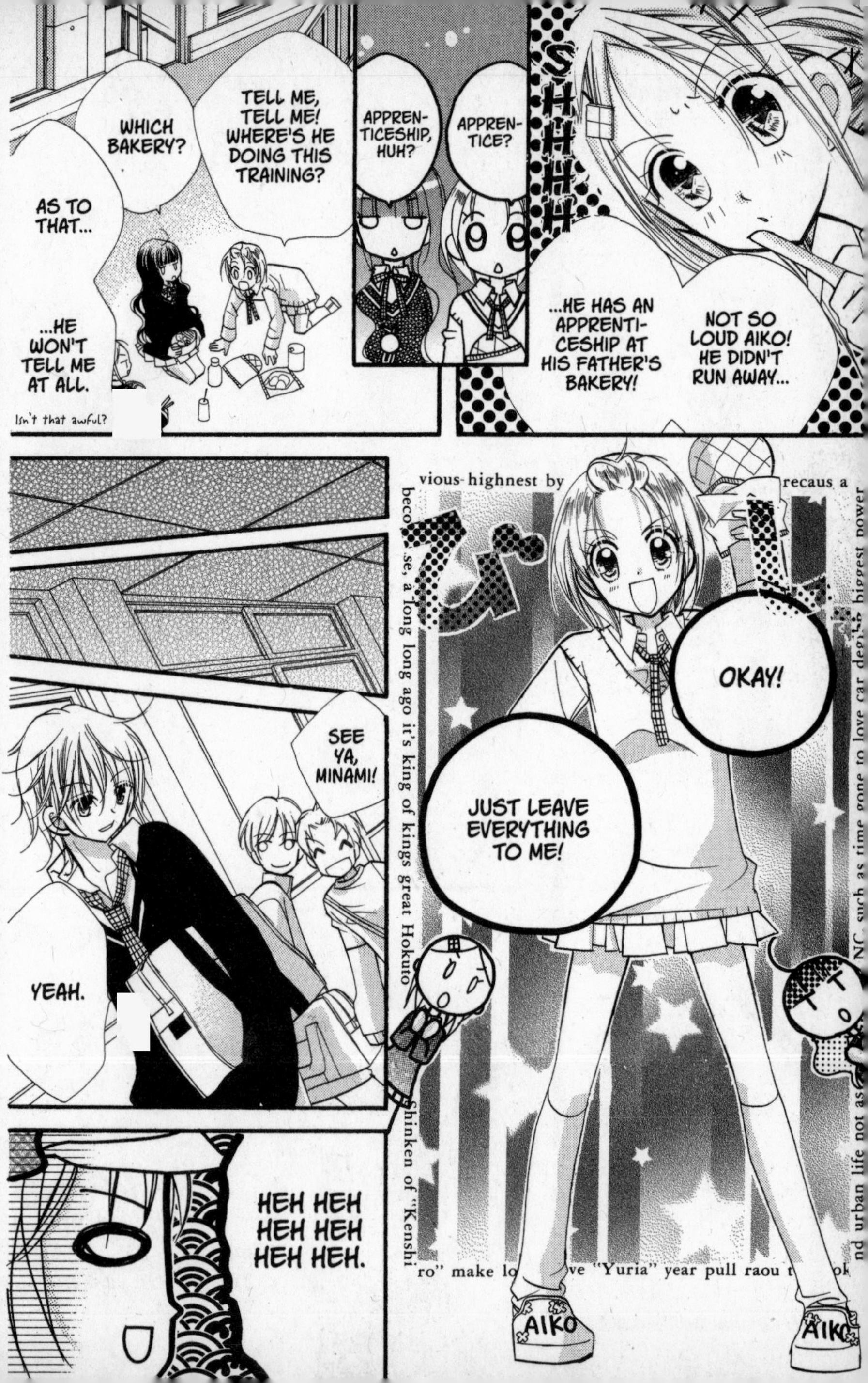
SHHHH
NOT SO LOUD AIKO! HE DIDN'T RUN AWAY...
...HE HAS AN APPRENTICESHIP AT HIS FATHER'S BAKERY!
APPRENTICE?
APPRENTICESHIP, HUH?
TELL ME, TELL ME! WHERE'S HE DOING THIS TRAINING?
WHICH BAKERY?
AS TO THAT...
...HE WON'T TELL ME AT ALL.
Isn't that awful?
vious-highnest by
recaus a
se, a long long ago it's king of kings great Hokuto Shinken of "Kenshi
"ro" make lo
ve "Yuria" year pull raou t
OKAY!
JUST LEAVE EVERYTHING TO ME!
AIKO
AIKO
SEE YA, MINAMI!
YEAH.
HEH HEH HEH HEH HEH HEH.

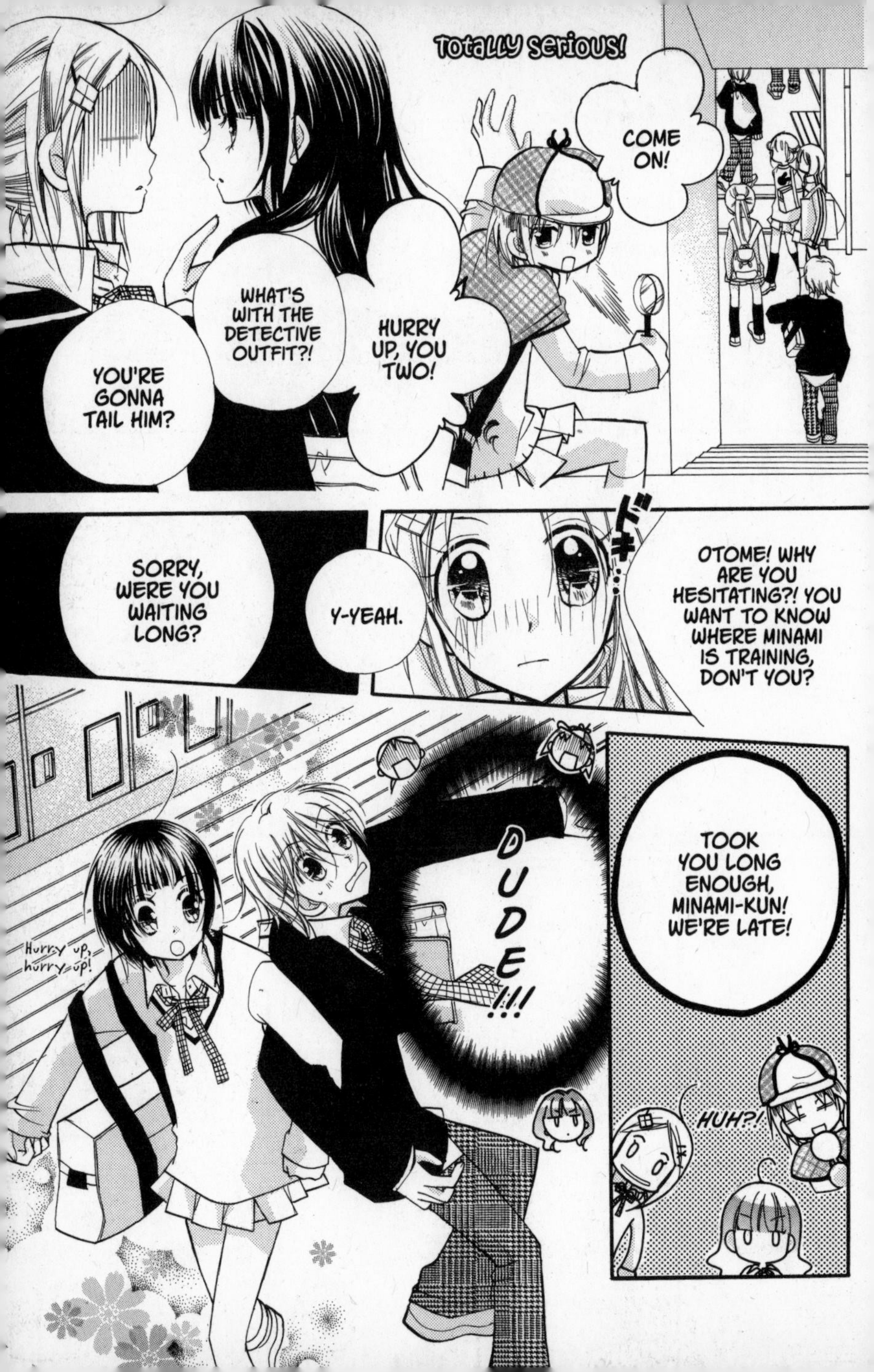
TOTALLY SERIOUS!
COME ON!
HURRY UP, YOU TWO!
WHAT'S WITH THE DETECTIVE OUTFIT?!
YOU'RE GONNA TAIL HIM?
OTOME! WHY ARE YOU HESITATING?! YOU WANT TO KNOW WHERE MINAMI IS TRAINING, DON'T YOU?
ドキ
Y-YEAH.
SORRY, WERE YOU WAITING LONG?
TOOK YOU LONG ENOUGH, MINAMI-KUN! WE'RE LATE!
HUH?!
DUDE!!!
Hurry up, hurry up!

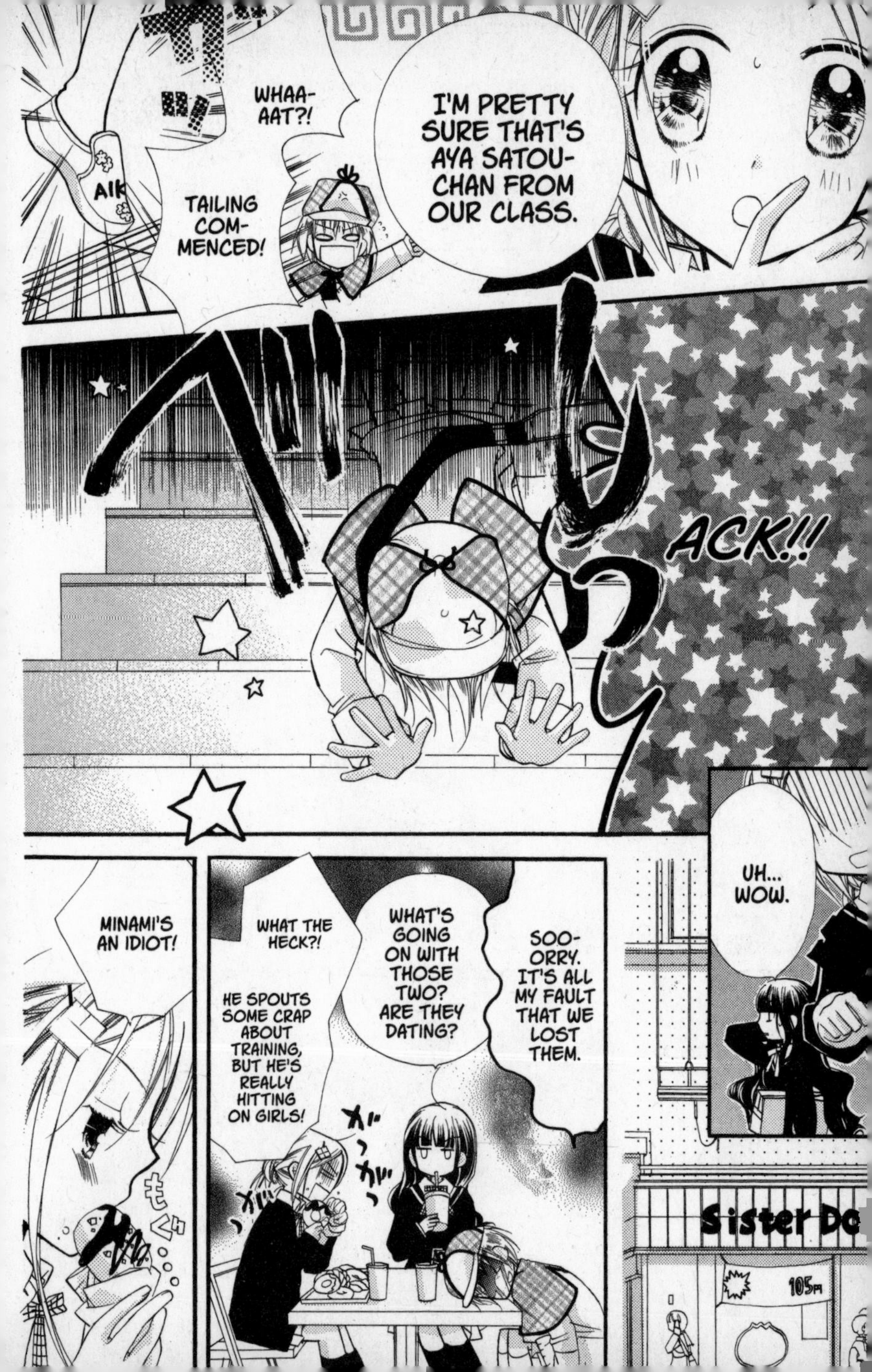
I'M PRETTY SURE THAT'S AYA SATOU-CHAN FROM OUR CLASS.
WHAA-AAT?!
TAILING COM-MENCED!
AIK
ACK!!
UH... WOW.
Sister Do
105
SOO-ORRY. IT'S ALL MY FAULT THAT WE LOST THEM.
WHAT'S GOING ON WITH THOSE TWO? ARE THEY DATING?
WHAT THE HECK?!
HE SPOUTS SOME CRAP ABOUT TRAINING, BUT HE'S REALLY HITTING ON GIRLS!
MINAMI'S AN IDIOT!

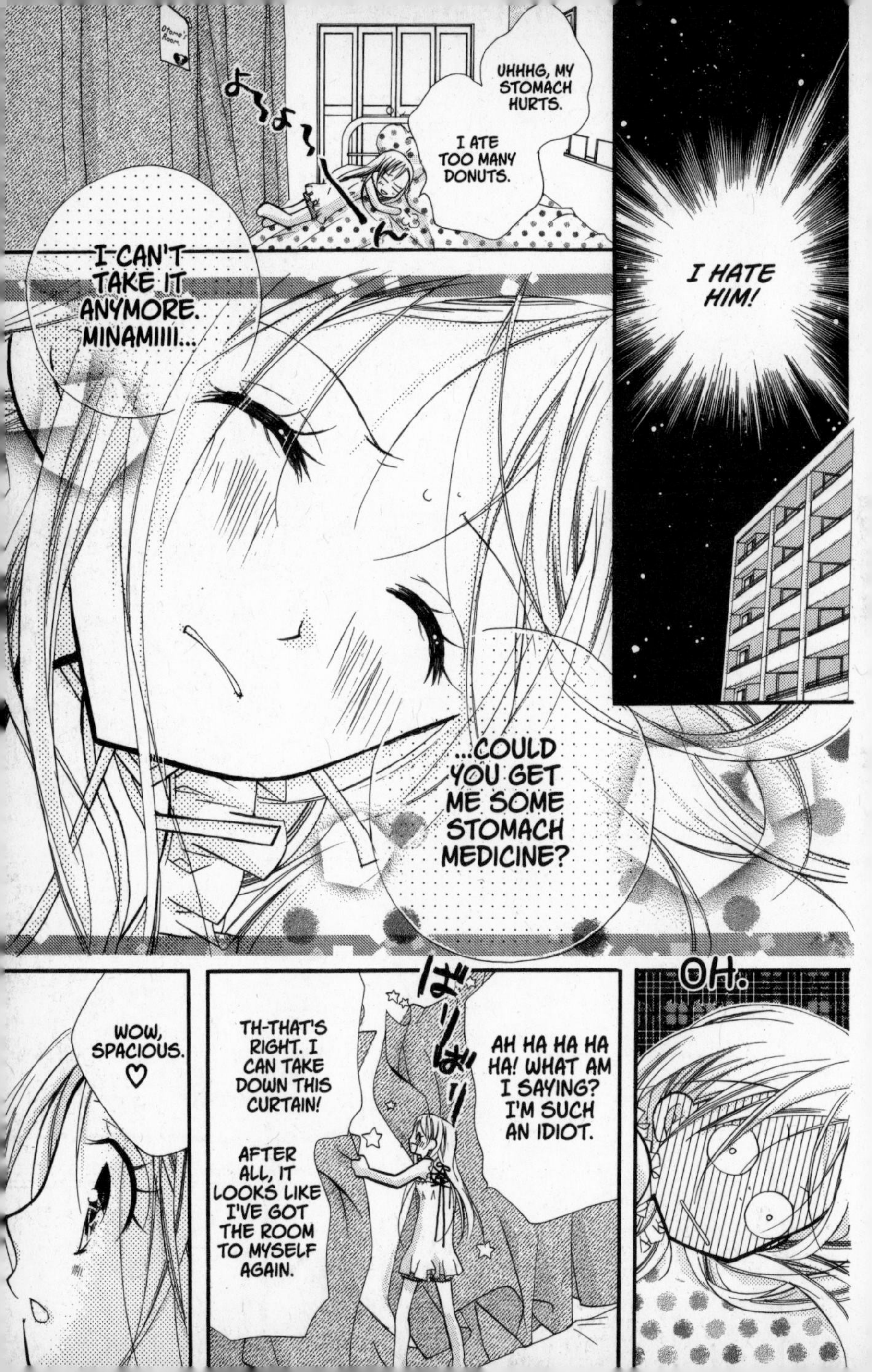
I HATE HIM!
UHHHG, MY STOMACH HURTS.
I ATE TOO MANY DONUTS.
よろよろ
I CAN'T TAKE IT ANYMORE. MINAMIIII...
...COULD YOU GET ME SOME STOMACH MEDICINE?
OH.
ばっばっ
TH-THAT'S RIGHT. I CAN TAKE DOWN THIS CURTAIN!
AFTER ALL, IT LOOKS LIKE I'VE GOT THE ROOM TO MYSELF AGAIN.
AH HA HA HA HA! WHAT AM I SAYING? I'M SUCH AN IDIOT.
WOW, SPACIOUS. ♡

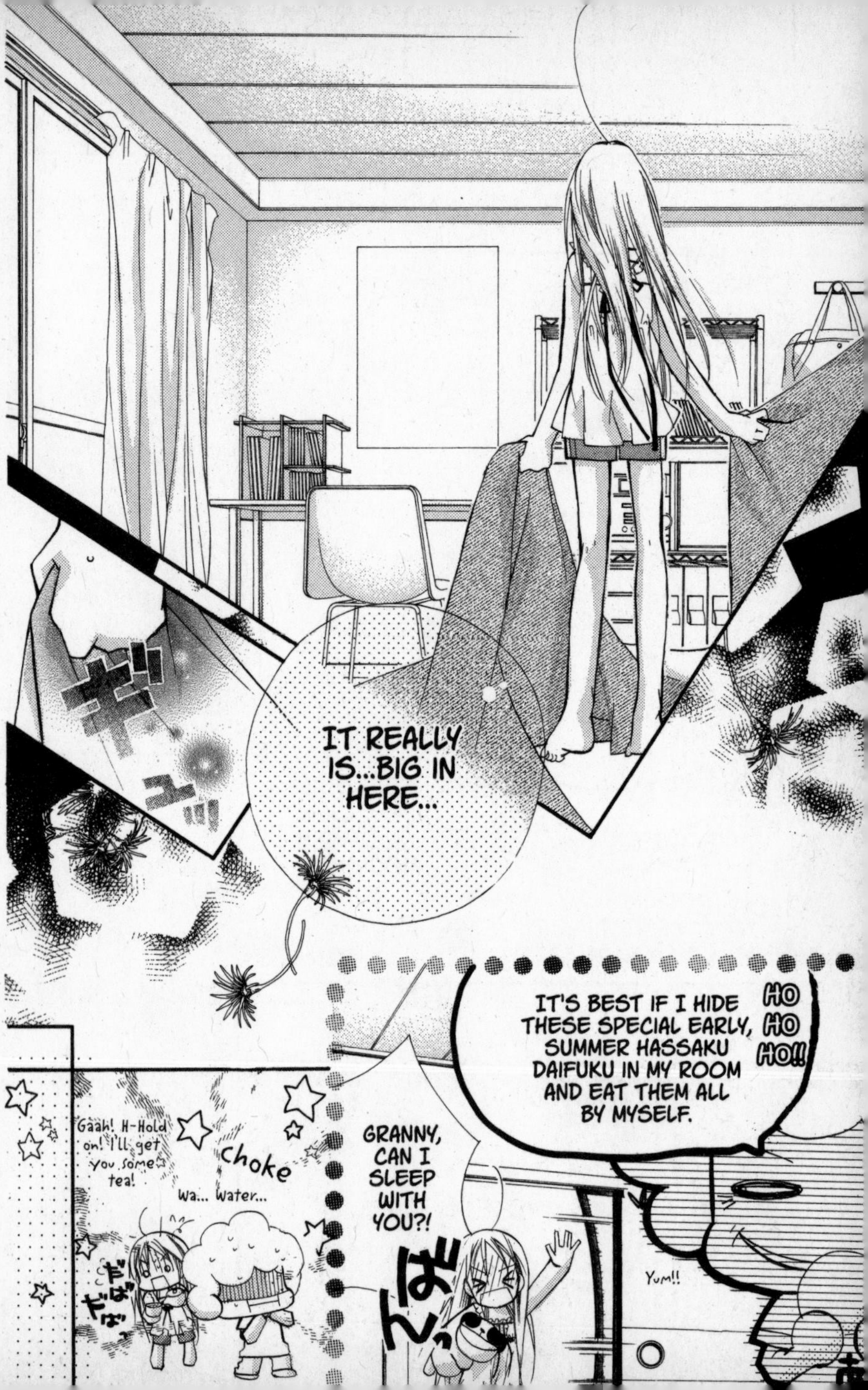
ギュッ!!
IT REALLY IS...BIG IN HERE...
HO HO HO!!
IT'S BEST IF I HIDE THESE SPECIAL EARLY, SUMMER HASSAKU DAIFUKU IN MY ROOM AND EAT THEM ALL BY MYSELF.
Yum!!
GRANNY, CAN I SLEEP WITH YOU?!
ばんっ
Choke
wa... water...
Gaah! H-Hold on! I'll get you some tea!
だばだばっ

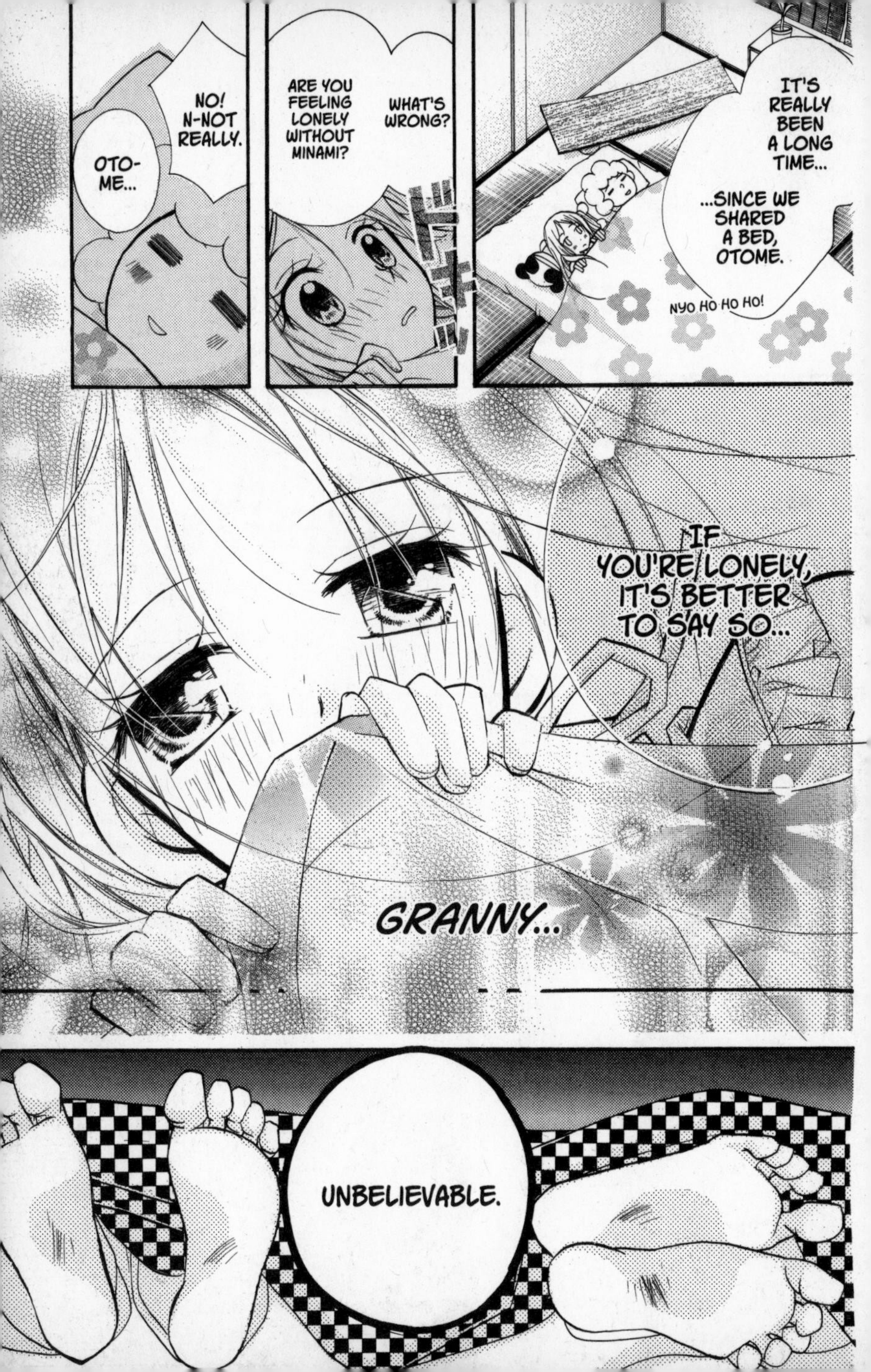
IT'S REALLY BEEN A LONG TIME...
...SINCE WE SHARED A BED, OTOME.
NYO HO HO HO!
WHAT'S WRONG?
ARE YOU FEELING LONELY WITHOUT MINAMI?
NO! N-NOT REALLY.
OTO-ME...
IF YOU'RE LONELY, IT'S BETTER TO SAY SO...
GRANNY...
UNBELIEVABLE.

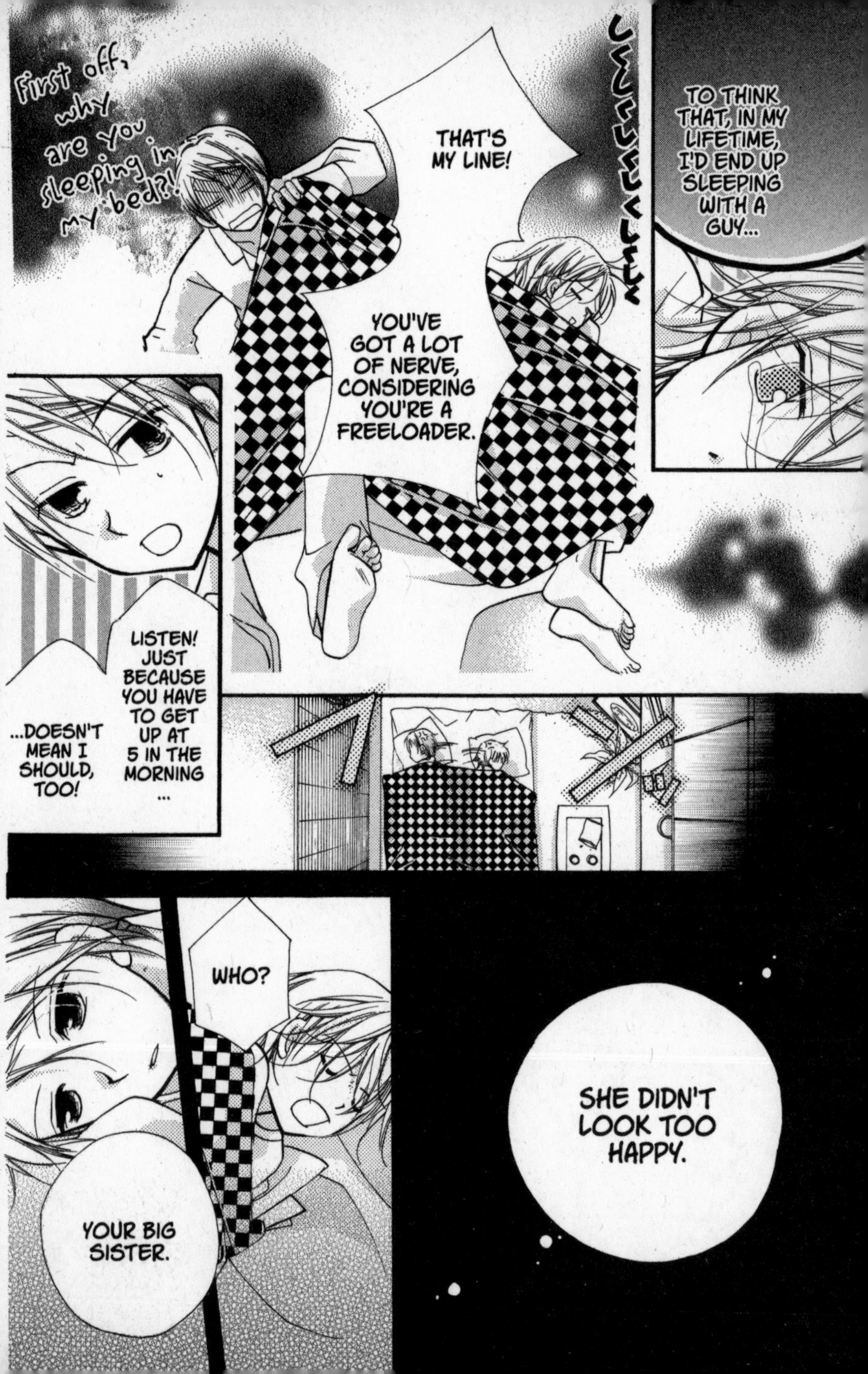
TO THINK THAT, IN MY LIFETIME, I'D END UP SLEEPING WITH A GUY...
THAT'S MY LINE!
First off, why are you sleeping in my bed?!
YOU'VE GOT A LOT OF NERVE, CONSIDERING YOU'RE A FREELOADER.
LISTEN! JUST BECAUSE YOU HAVE TO GET UP AT 5 IN THE MORNING...
...DOESN'T MEAN I SHOULD, TOO!
SHE DIDN'T LOOK TOO HAPPY.
WHO?
YOUR BIG SISTER.

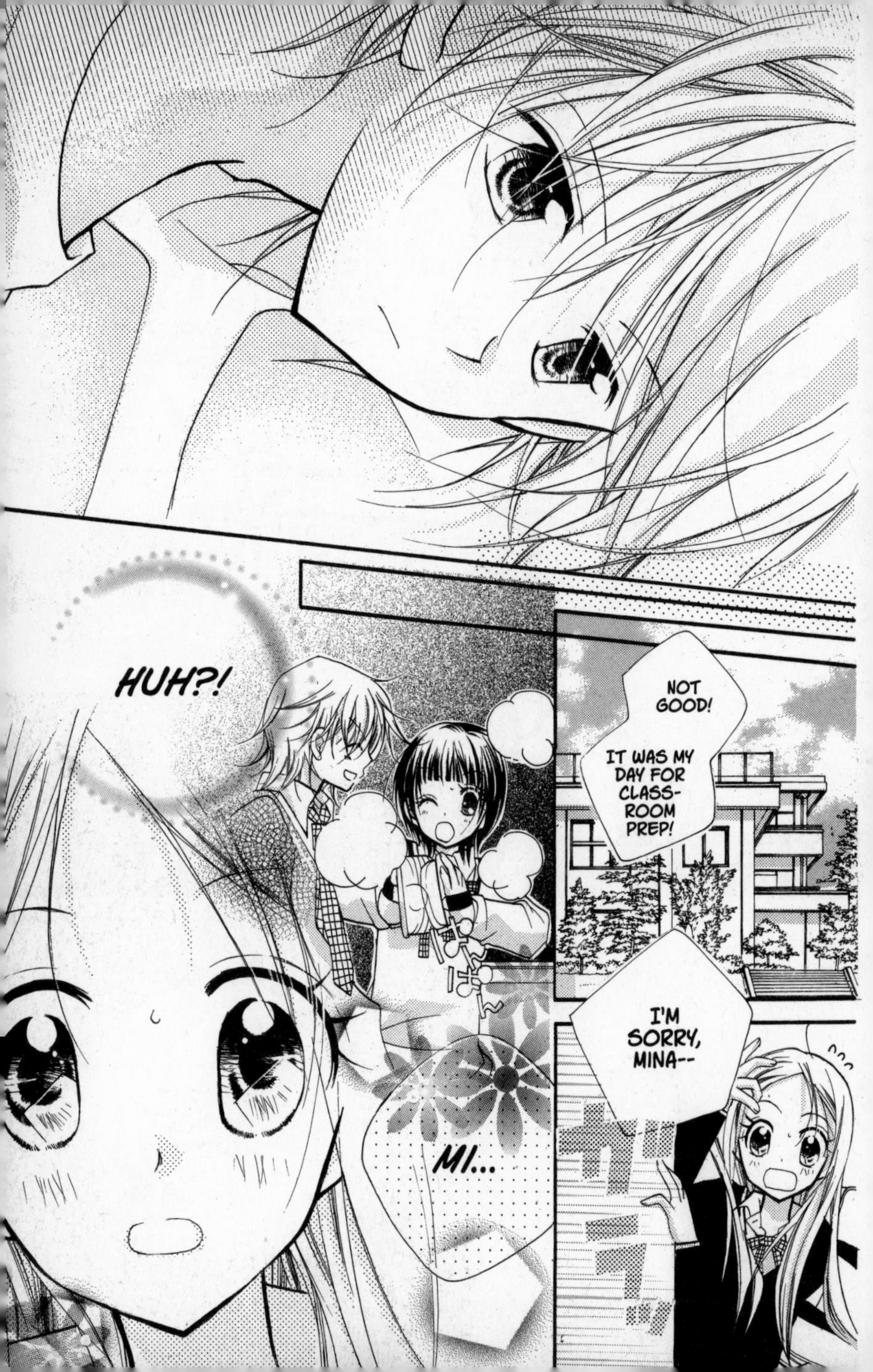
NOT GOOD!
IT WAS MY DAY FOR CLASS-ROOM PREP!
I'M SORRY, MINA--
HUH?!
MI...

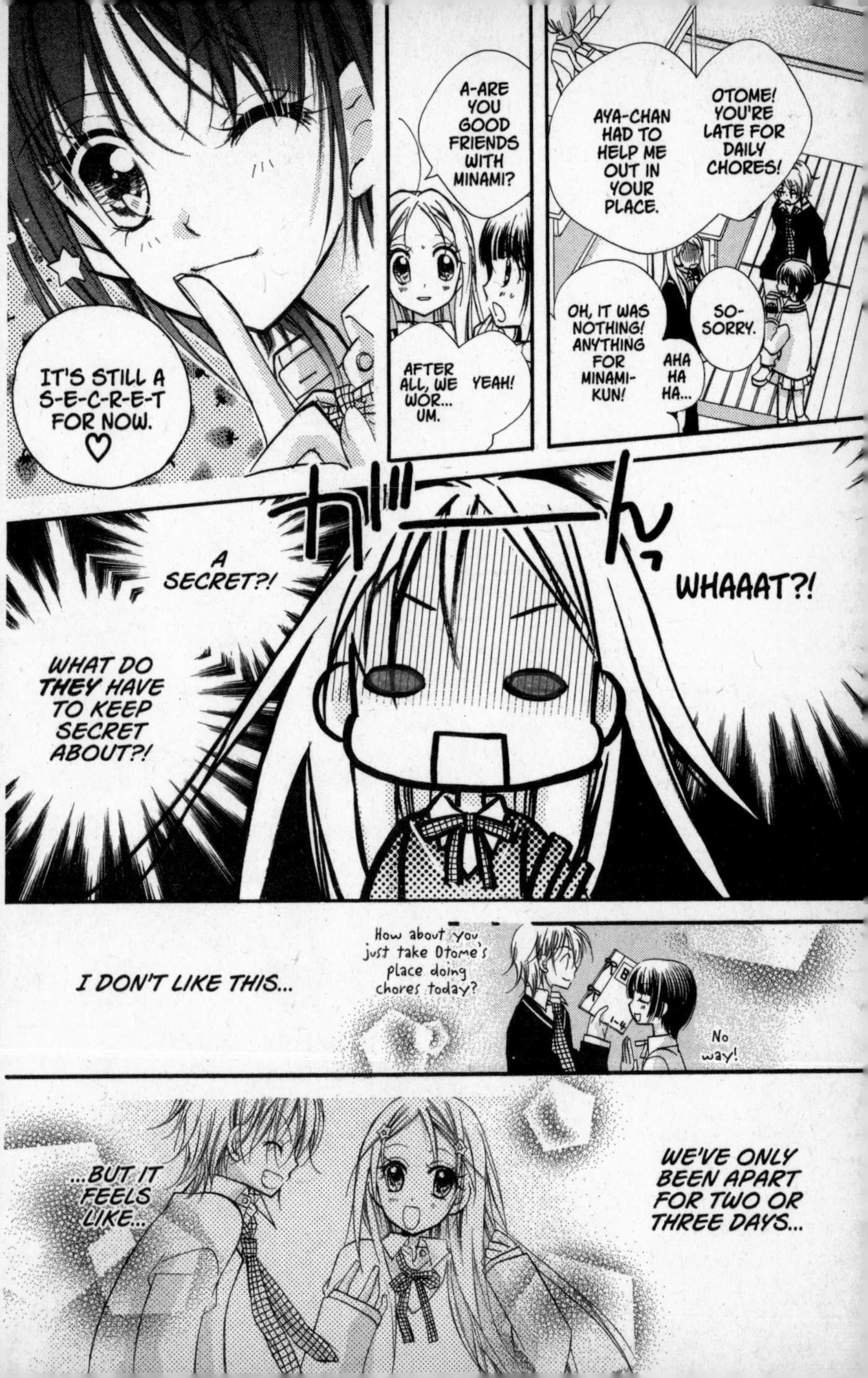
OTOME! YOU'RE LATE FOR DAILY CHORES!
AYA-CHAN HAD TO HELP ME OUT IN YOUR PLACE.
SO-SORRY.
AHA HA HA...
OH, IT WAS NOTHING! ANYTHING FOR MINAMI-KUN!
A-ARE YOU GOOD FRIENDS WITH MINAMI?
YEAH!
AFTER ALL, WE WOR... UM.
IT'S STILL A S-E-C-R-E-T FOR NOW. ♡
がーん
WHAAAT?!
A SECRET?!
WHAT DO THEY HAVE TO KEEP SECRET ABOUT?!
No way!
How about you just take Otome's place doing chores today?
I DON'T LIKE THIS...
WE'VE ONLY BEEN APART FOR TWO OR THREE DAYS...
...BUT IT FEELS LIKE...

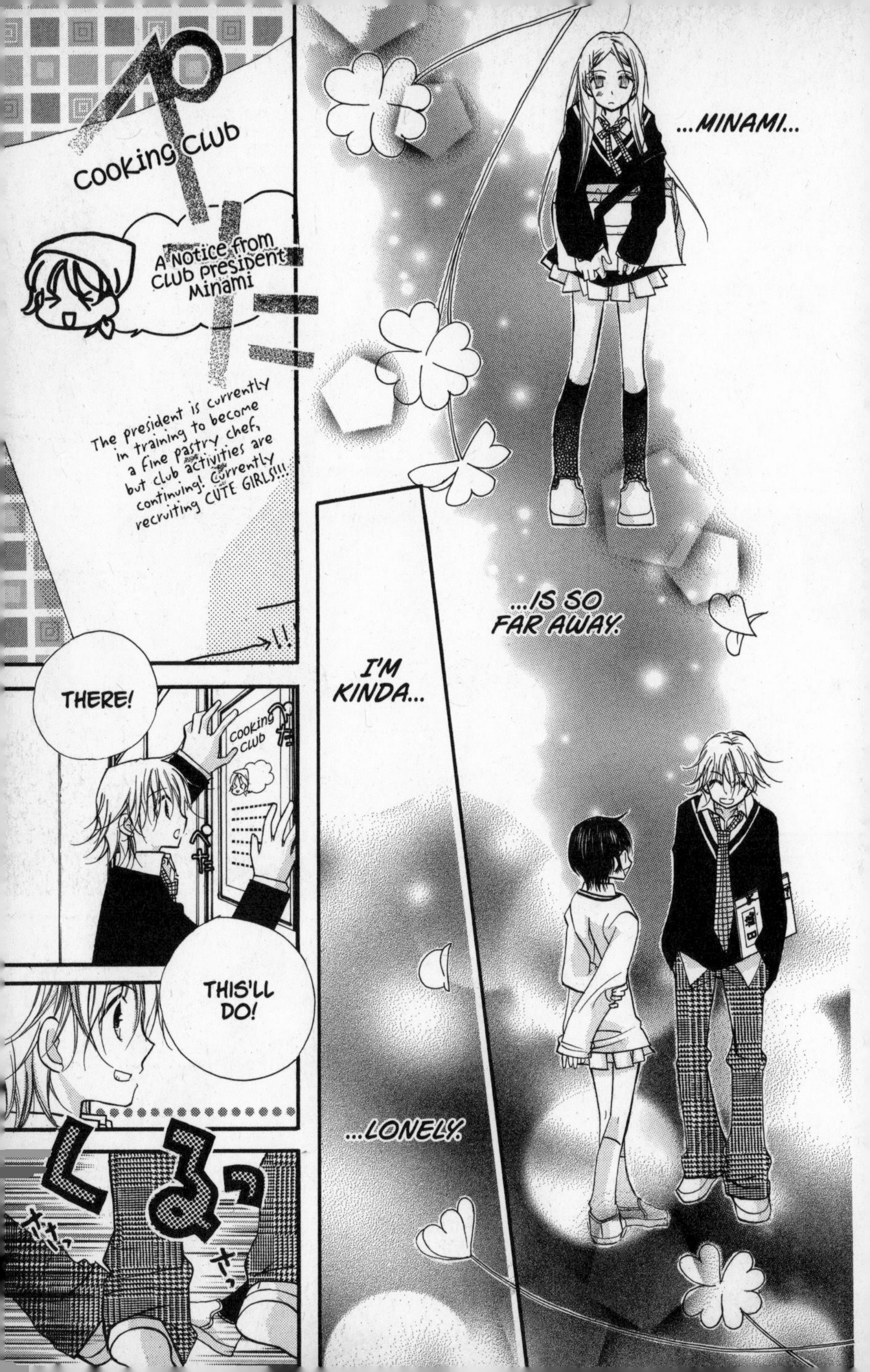
...MINAMI...
...IS SO FAR AWAY.
I'M KINDA...
...LONELY.
COOKING CLUB
A Notice from CLUB PRESIDENT Minami
The president is currently in training to become a fine pastry chef, but club activities are continuing! Currently recruiting CUTE GIRLS!!!
!!
THERE!
COOKING CLUB
THIS'LL DO!

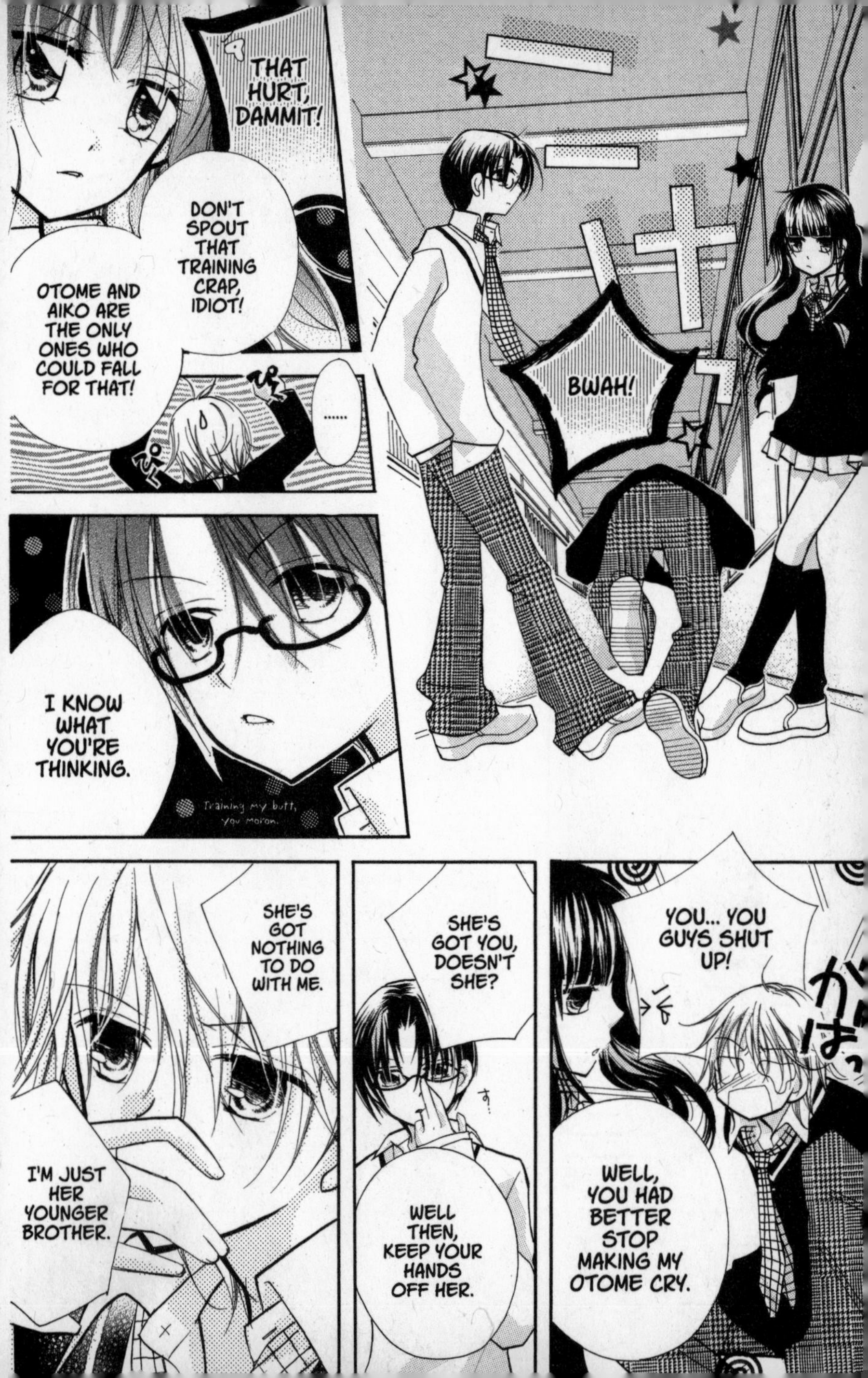
BWAH!
THAT HURT, DAMMIT!
DON'T SPOUT THAT TRAINING CRAP, IDIOT!
OTOME AND AIKO ARE THE ONLY ONES WHO COULD FALL FOR THAT!
......
I KNOW WHAT YOU'RE THINKING.
Training my butt, you moron.
YOU... YOU GUYS SHUT UP!
WELL, YOU HAD BETTER STOP MAKING MY OTOME CRY.
SHE'S GOT YOU, DOESN'T SHE?
WELL THEN, KEEP YOUR HANDS OFF HER.
SHE'S GOT NOTHING TO DO WITH ME.
I'M JUST HER YOUNGER BROTHER.

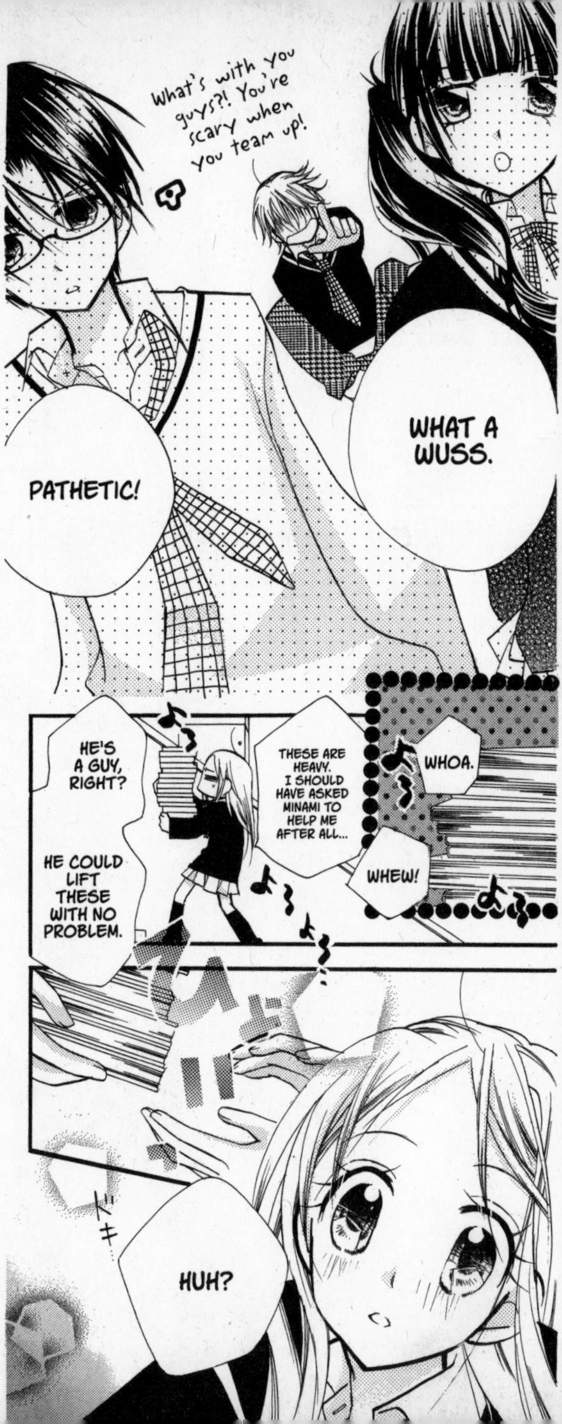
WHAT A WUSS.
PATHETIC!
What's with you guys?! You're scary when you team up!
WHOA.
WHEW!
THESE ARE HEAVY. I SHOULD HAVE ASKED MINAMI TO HELP ME AFTER ALL...
HE'S A GUY, RIGHT?
HE COULD LIFT THESE WITH NO PROBLEM.
HUH?

FOUR

Lately, many schools have adopted things like vests and sweaters as their school uniform's winter outerwear.

Once, when I saw my friend's little sister wearing a red sweater, I decided, "Otome and the other's high school sweaters MUST be red!" But when I was drawing it in the original black and white, I began to think that the sweater looked kind of black, and before I knew it, I made it black... Hmm...

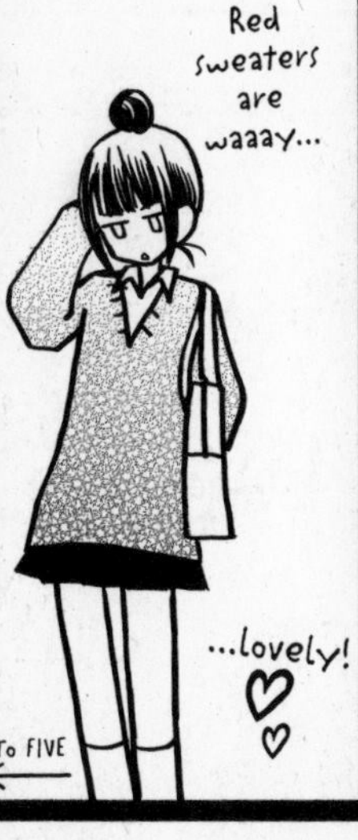
Red sweaters are waaay...
...lovely!

To FIVE

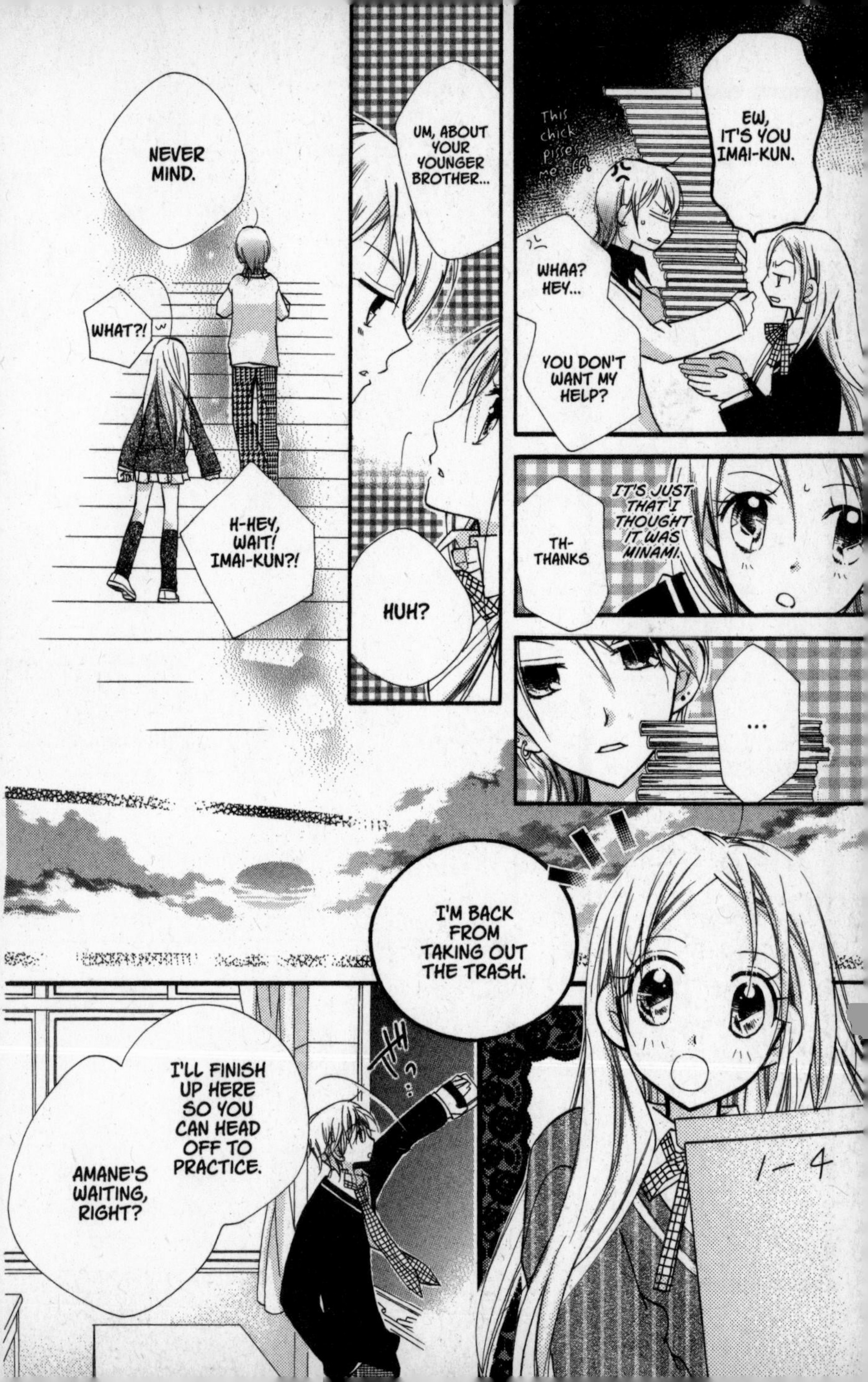
EW, IT'S YOU IMAI-KUN.
This chick pisses me off!
WHAA? HEY...
YOU DON'T WANT MY HELP?
IT'S JUST THAT I THOUGHT IT WAS MINAMI.
TH-THANKS
...
UM, ABOUT YOUR YOUNGER BROTHER...
HUH?
NEVER MIND.
WHAT?!
H-HEY, WAIT! IMAI-KUN?!
I'M BACK FROM TAKING OUT THE TRASH.
1-4
I'LL FINISH UP HERE SO YOU CAN HEAD OFF TO PRACTICE.
AMANE'S WAITING, RIGHT?

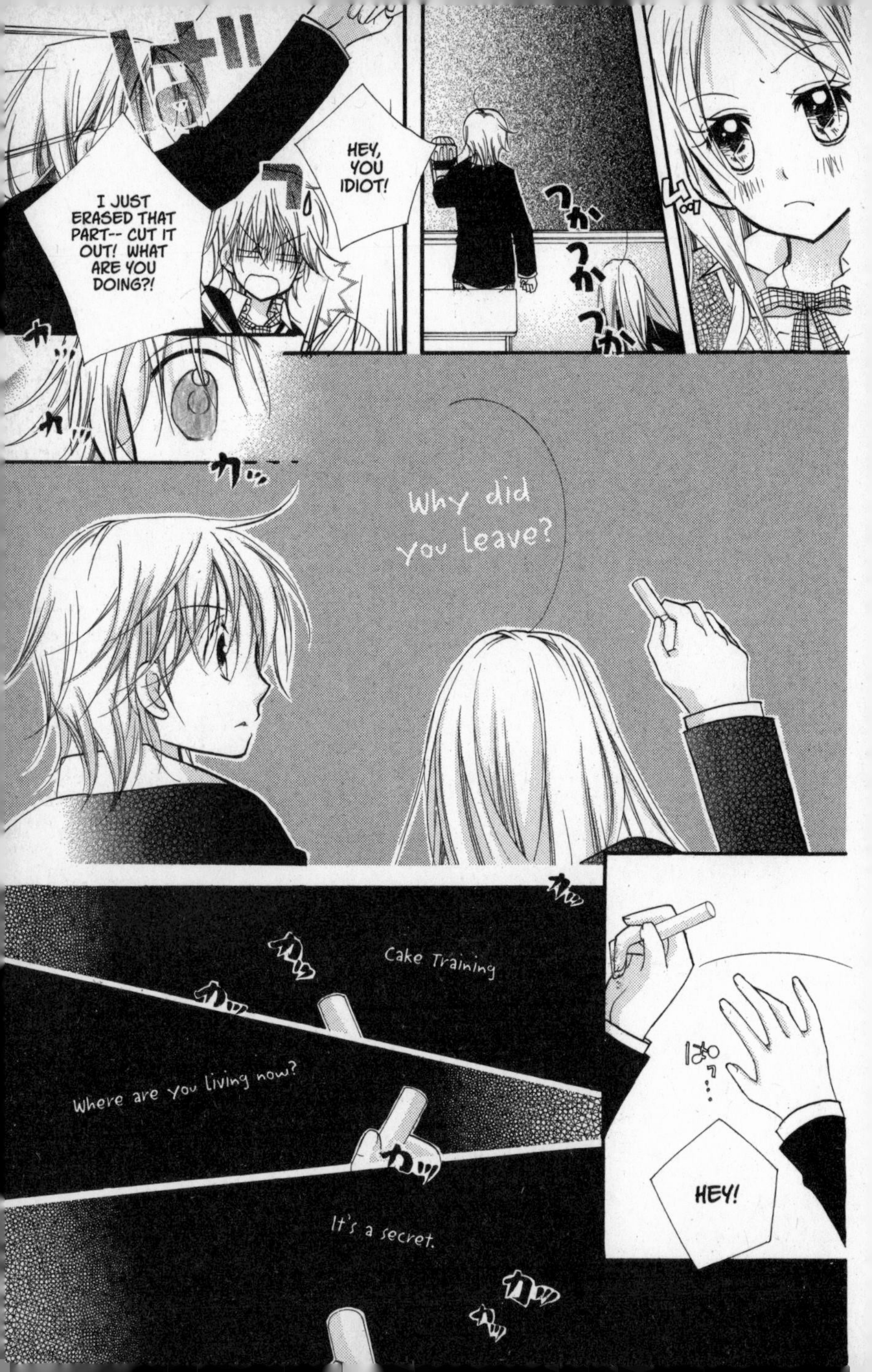

HEY, YOU IDIOT!
I JUST ERASED THAT PART-- CUT IT OUT! WHAT ARE YOU DOING?!
Why did you leave?
HEY!
Cake Training
Where are you living now?
It's a secret.

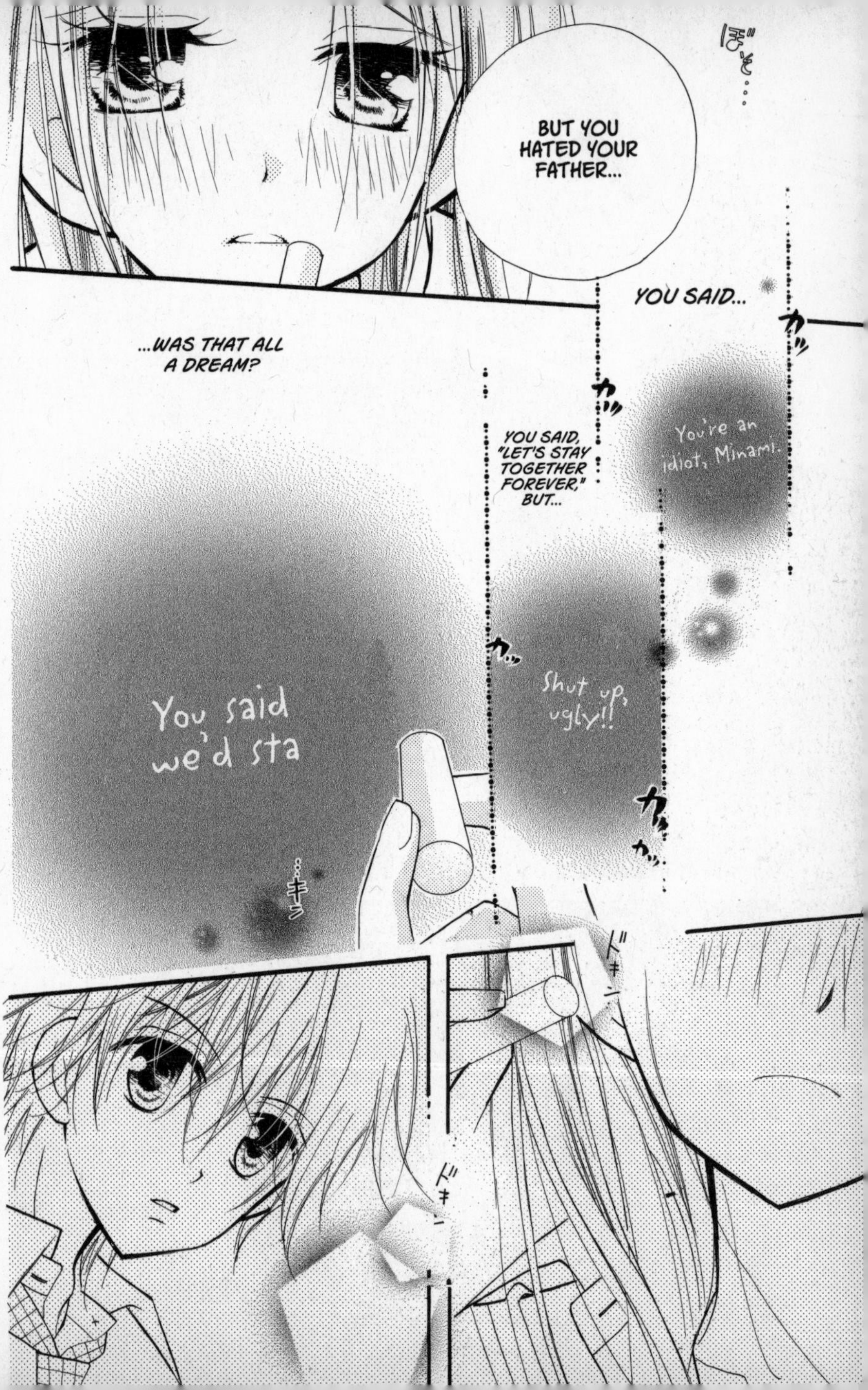
BUT YOU HATED YOUR FATHER...
YOU SAID...
You're an idiot, Minami.
YOU SAID, "LET'S STAY TOGETHER FOREVER," BUT...
Shut up, ugly!!
...WAS THAT ALL A DREAM?
You said we'd sta

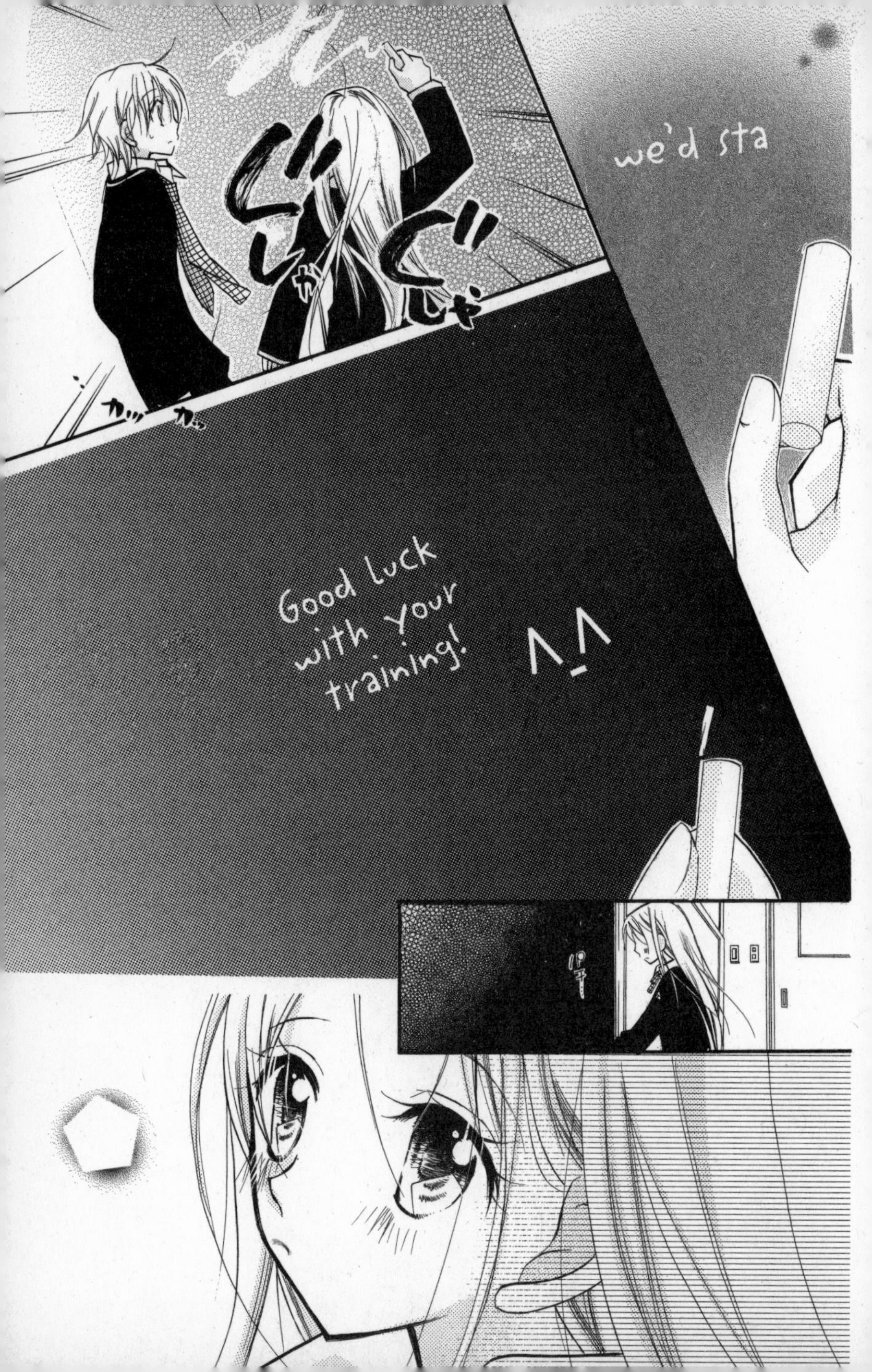
we'd sta
Good luck with your training!
^_^

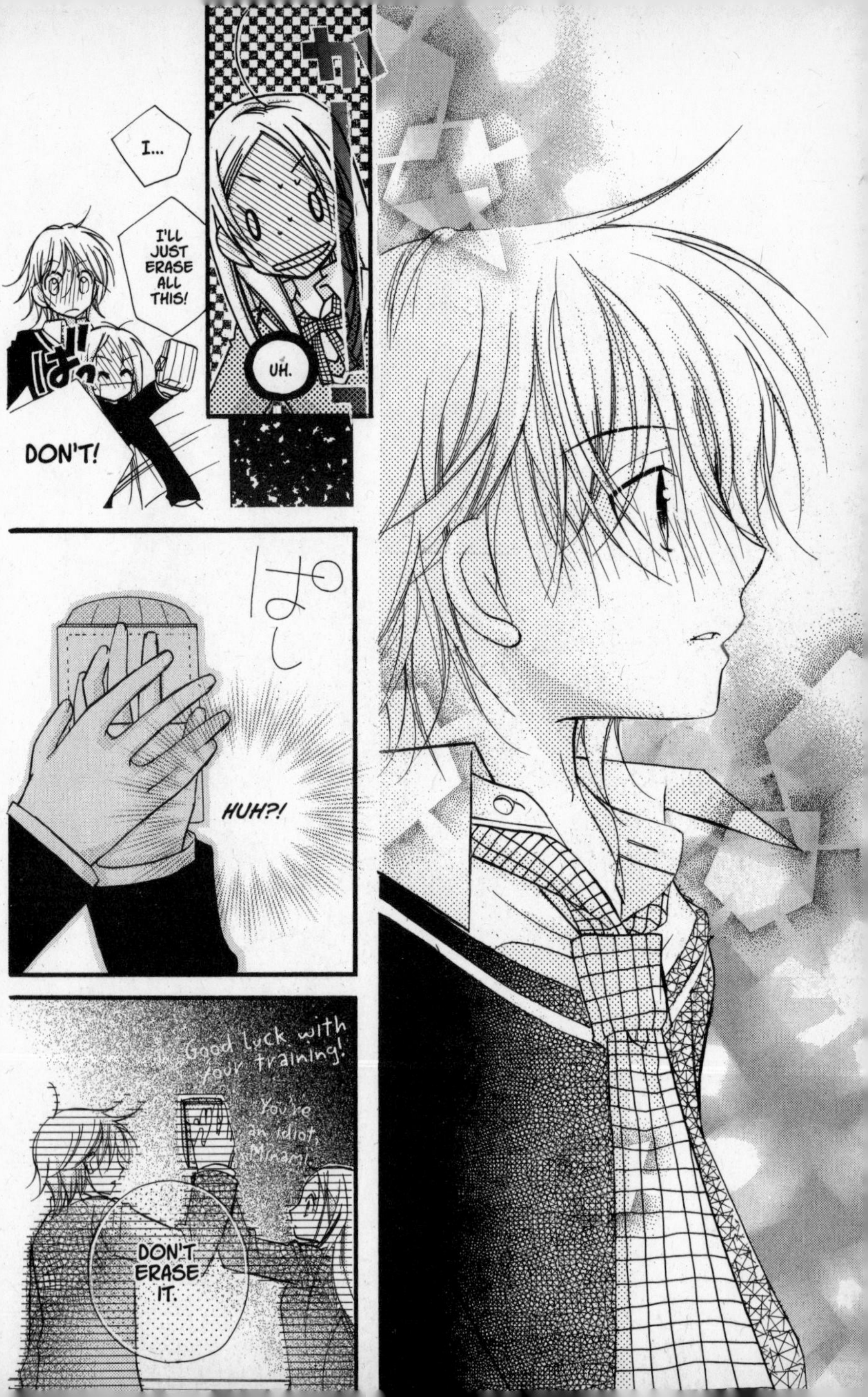
UH.
I...
I'LL JUST ERASE ALL THIS!
DON'T!
ぱし
HUH?!
Good luck with your training!
You're an idiot, Minami!
DON'T ERASE IT.

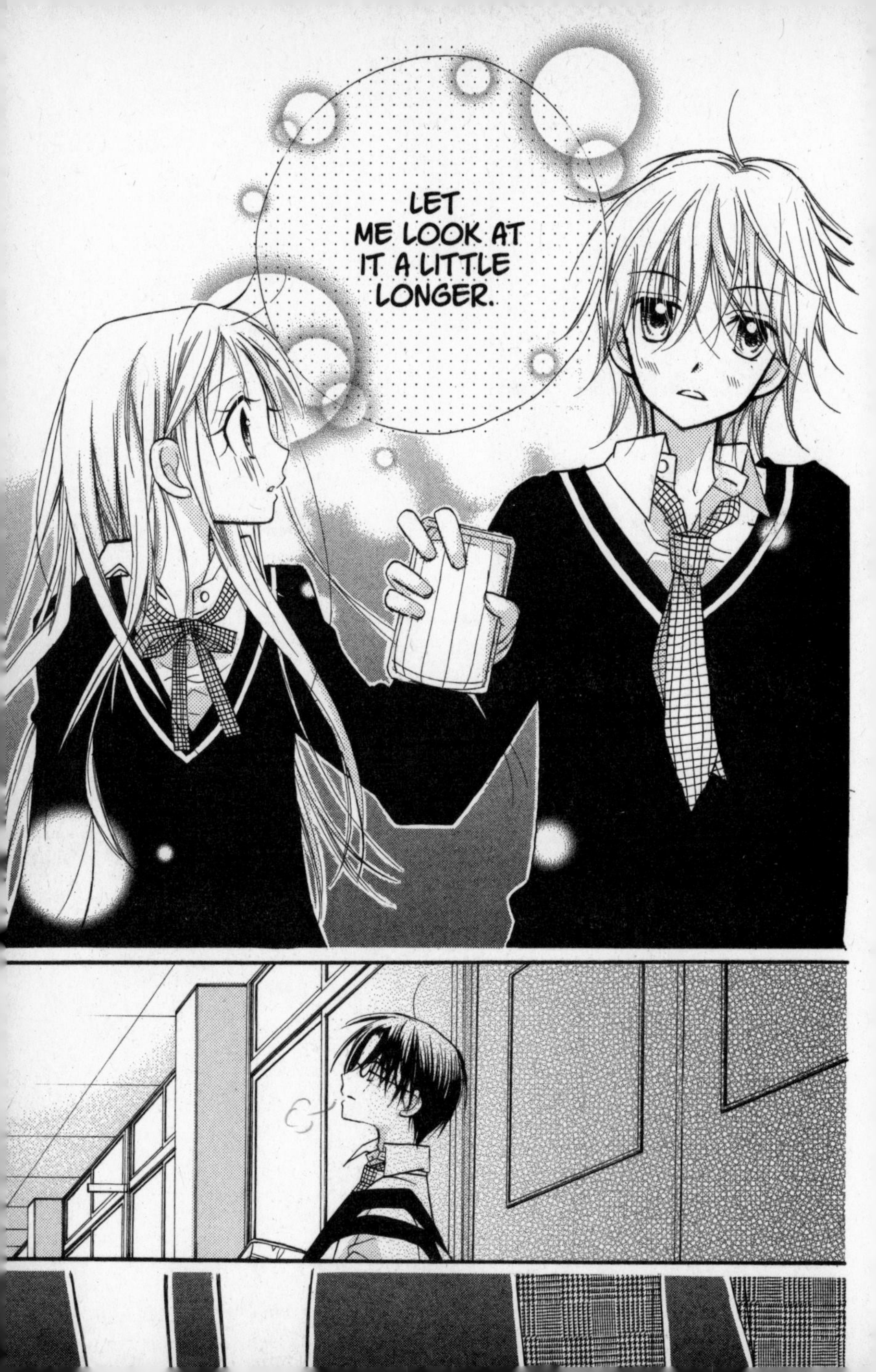
LET ME LOOK AT IT A LITTLE LONGER.

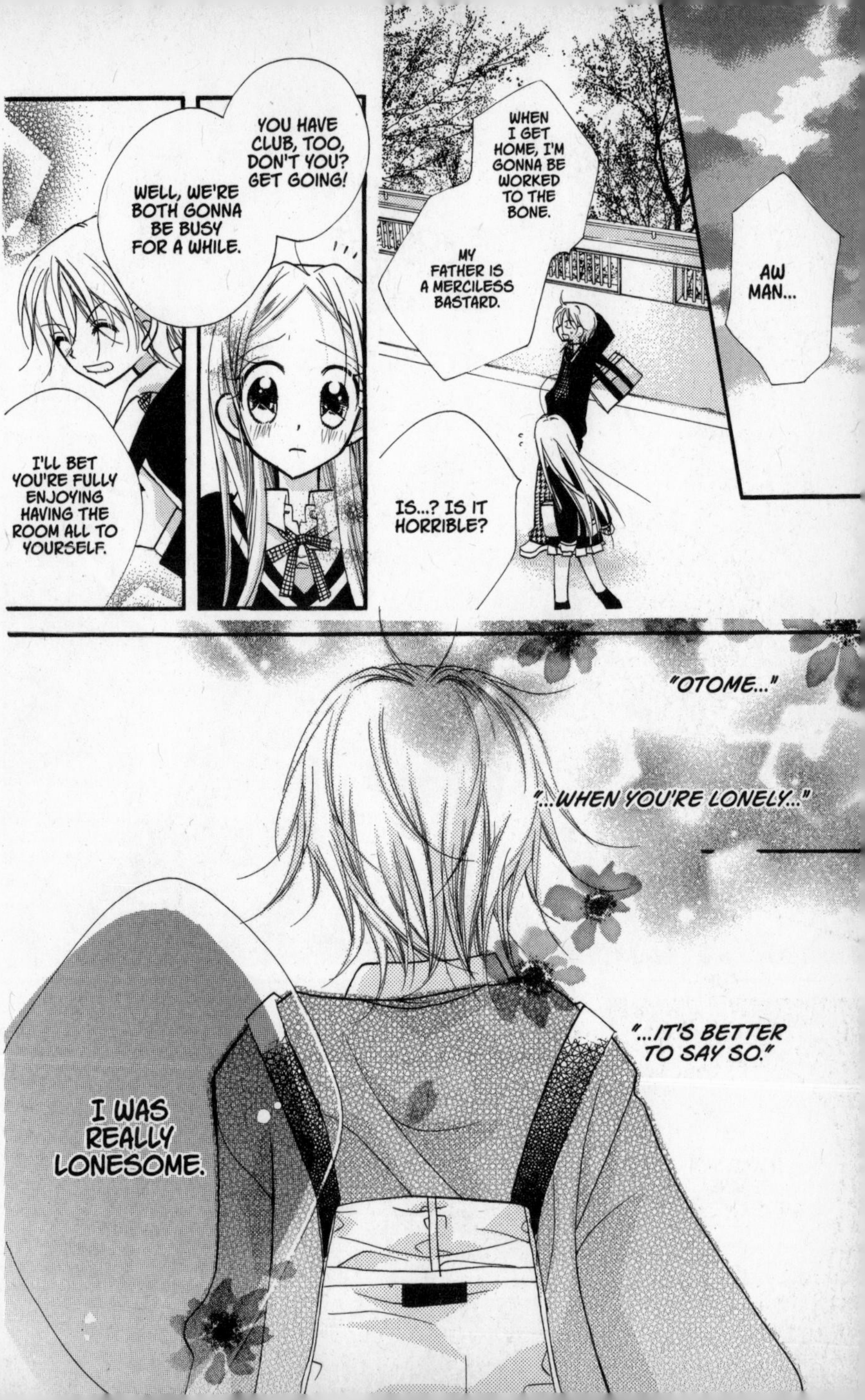
AW MAN...
WHEN I GET HOME, I'M GONNA BE WORKED TO THE BONE.
MY FATHER IS A MERCILESS BASTARD.
IS...? IS IT HORRIBLE?
YOU HAVE CLUB, TOO, DON'T YOU? GET GOING!
WELL, WE'RE BOTH GONNA BE BUSY FOR A WHILE.
I'LL BET YOU'RE FULLY ENJOYING HAVING THE ROOM ALL TO YOURSELF.
"OTOME..."
"...WHEN YOU'RE LONELY..."
"...IT'S BETTER TO SAY SO."
I WAS REALLY LONESOME.

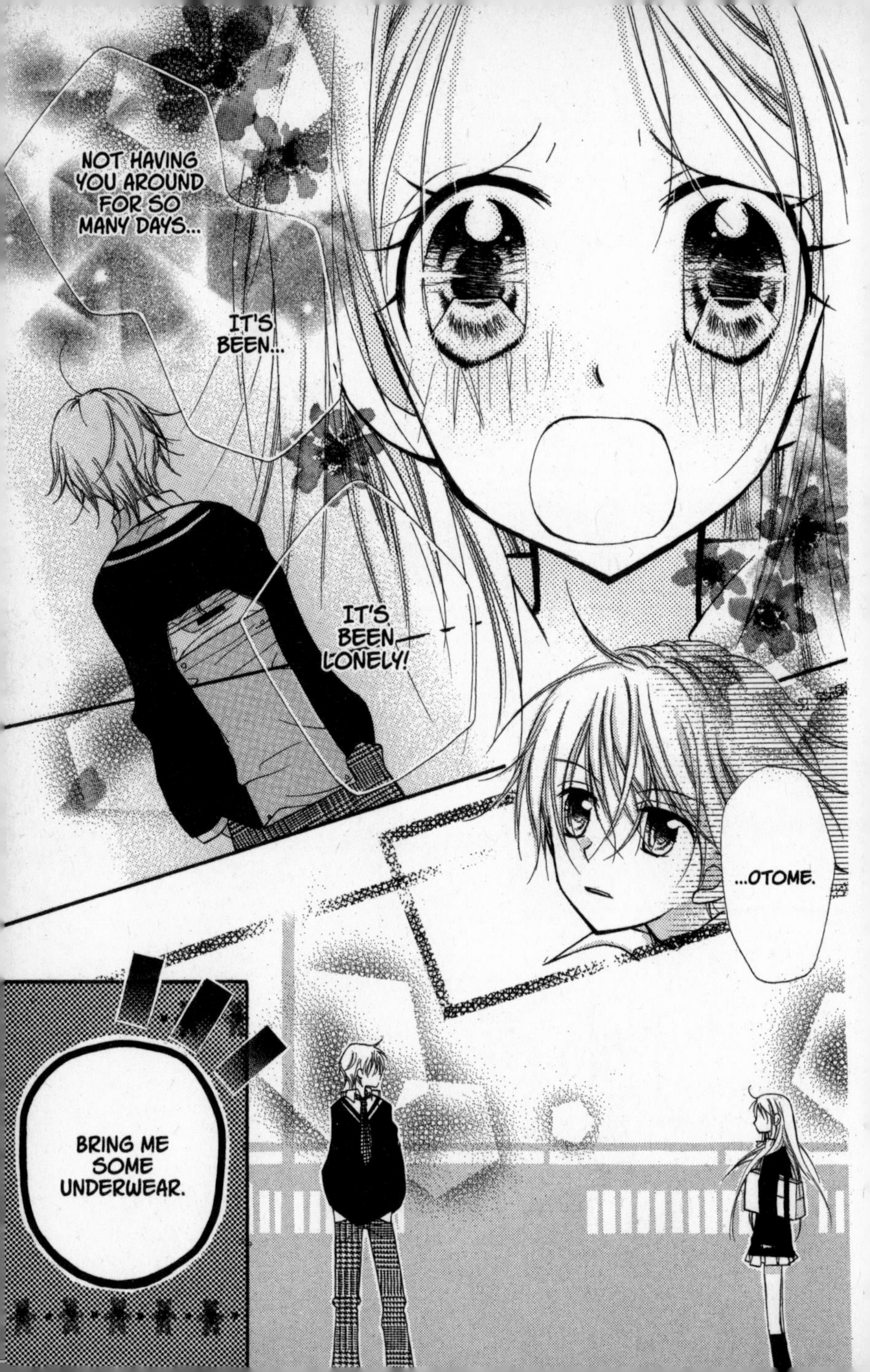
NOT HAVING YOU AROUND FOR SO MANY DAYS...
IT'S BEEN...
IT'S BEEN LONELY!
...OTOME.
BRING ME SOME UNDERWEAR.

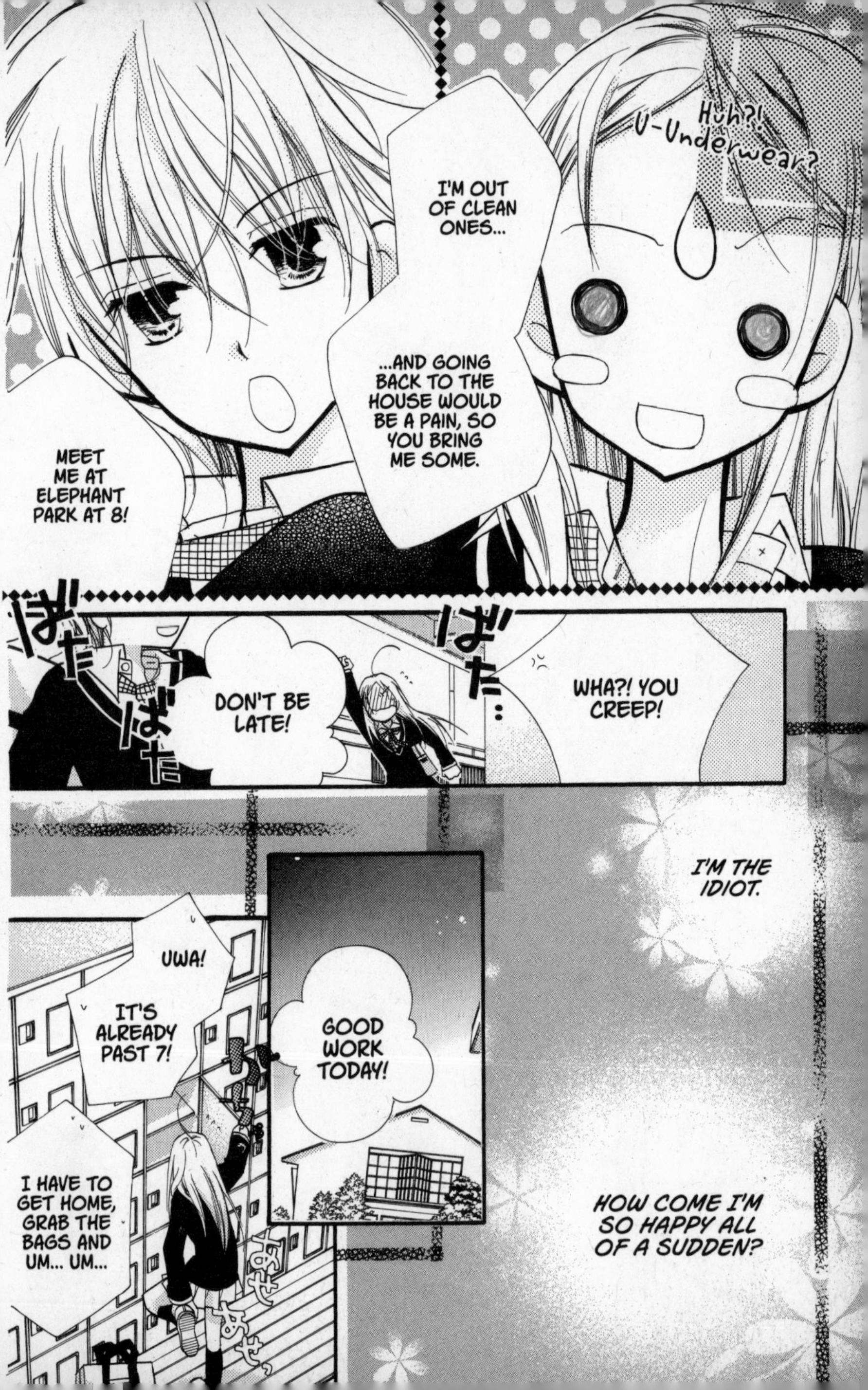
Huh?! U-Underwear?
I'M OUT OF CLEAN ONES...
...AND GOING BACK TO THE HOUSE WOULD BE A PAIN, SO YOU BRING ME SOME.
MEET ME AT ELEPHANT PARK AT 8!
WHA?! YOU CREEP!
ばた
DON'T BE LATE!
ばた
ばた
I'M THE IDIOT.
HOW COME I'M SO HAPPY ALL OF A SUDDEN?
GOOD WORK TODAY!
UWA!
IT'S ALREADY PAST 7!
I HAVE TO GET HOME, GRAB THE BAGS AND UM... UM...
あせ
あせ

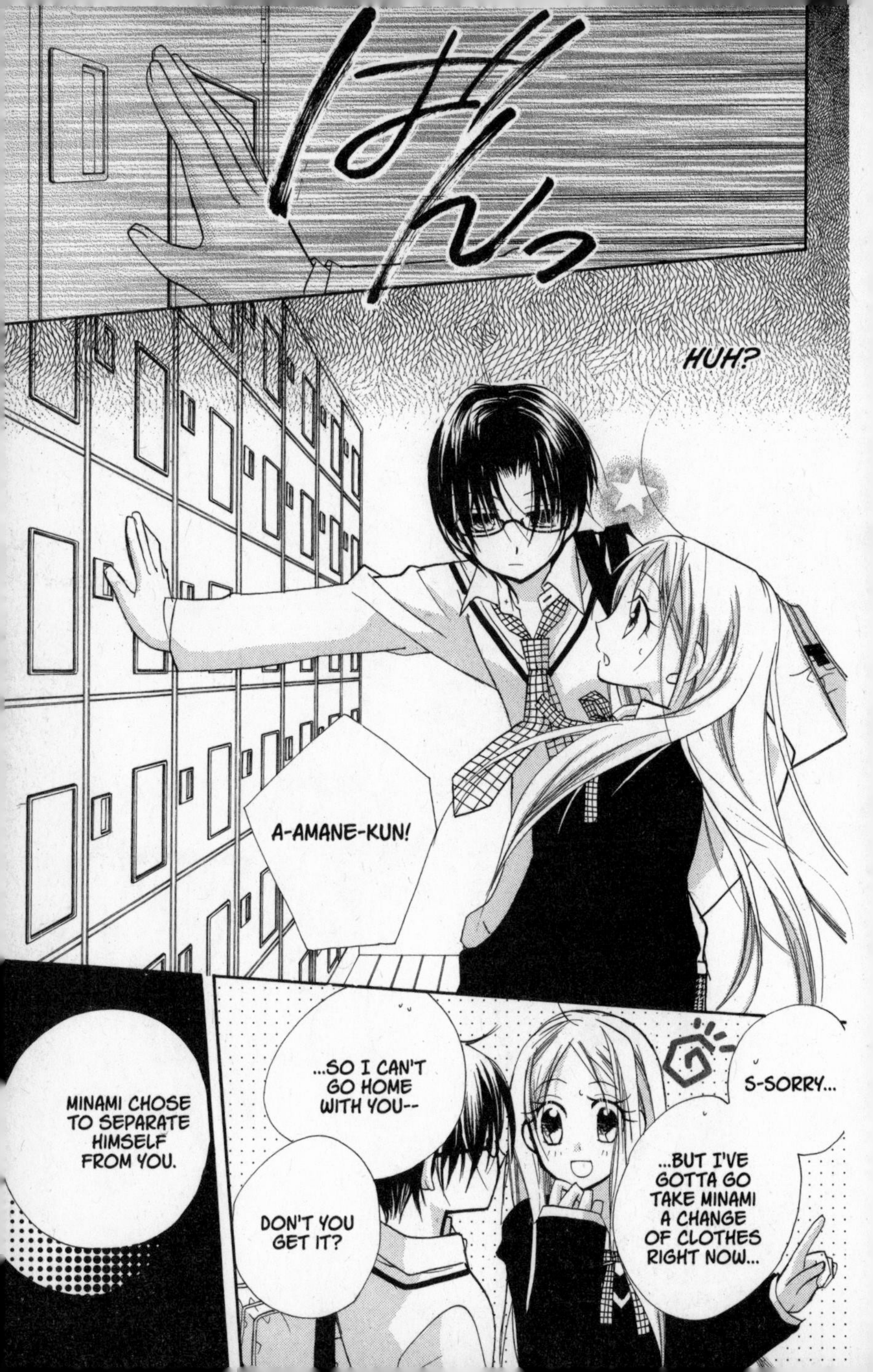
はんっ
HUH?
A-AMANE-KUN!
S-SORRY...
...BUT I'VE GOTTA GO TAKE MINAMI A CHANGE OF CLOTHES RIGHT NOW...
...SO I CAN'T GO HOME WITH YOU--
DON'T YOU GET IT?
MINAMI CHOSE TO SEPARATE HIMSELF FROM YOU.

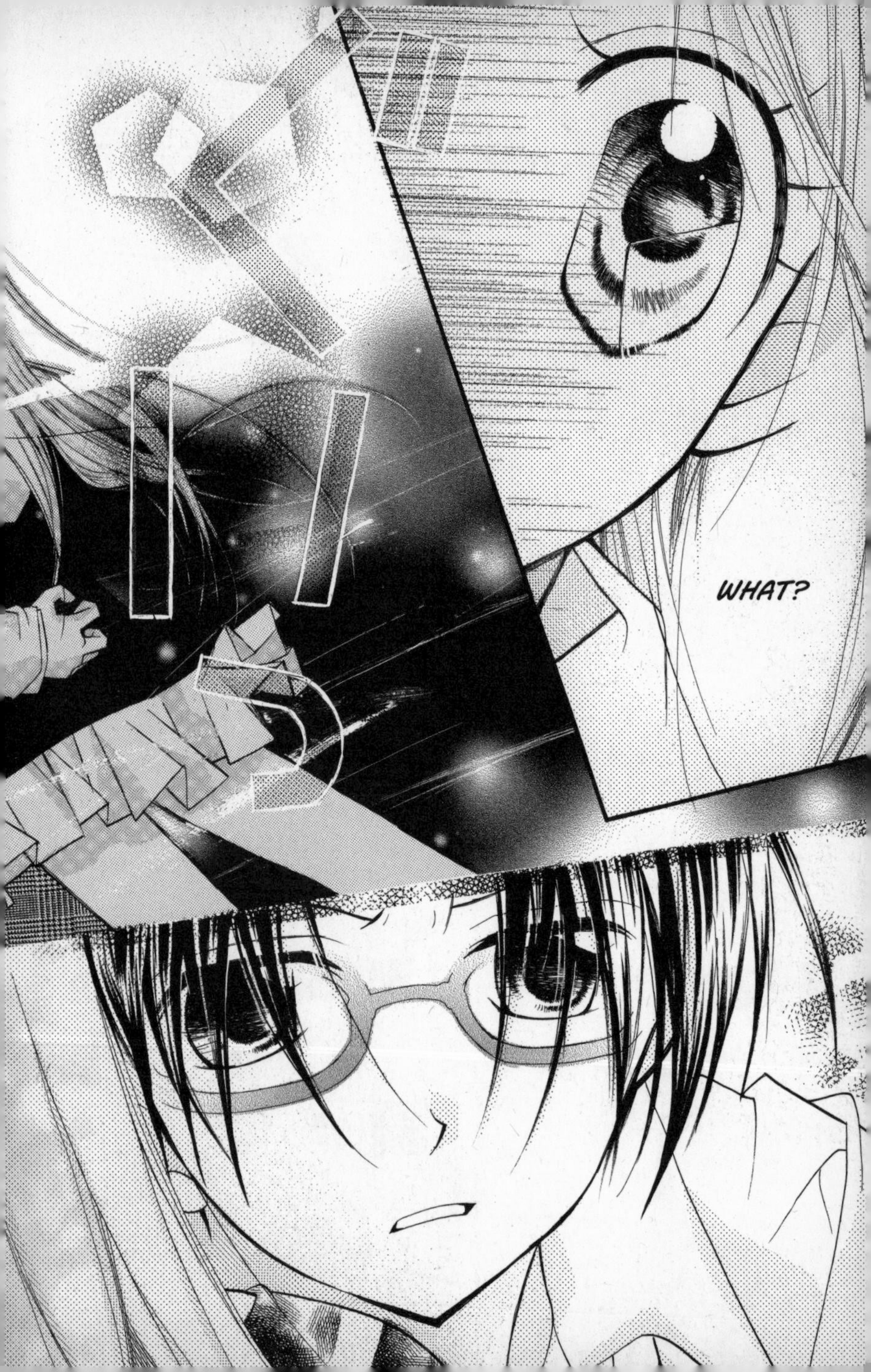
WHAT?

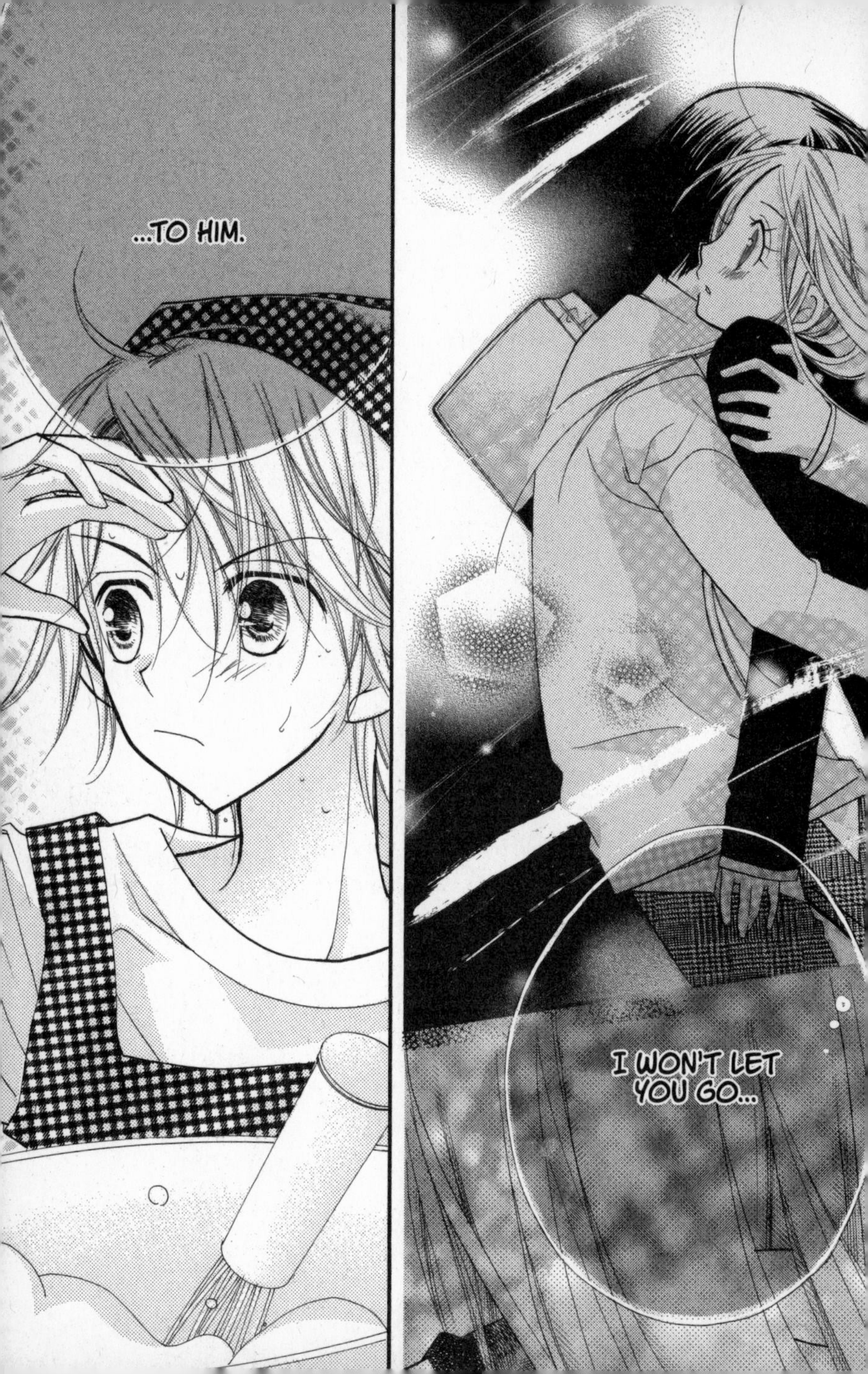
I WON'T LET YOU GO...
...TO HIM.

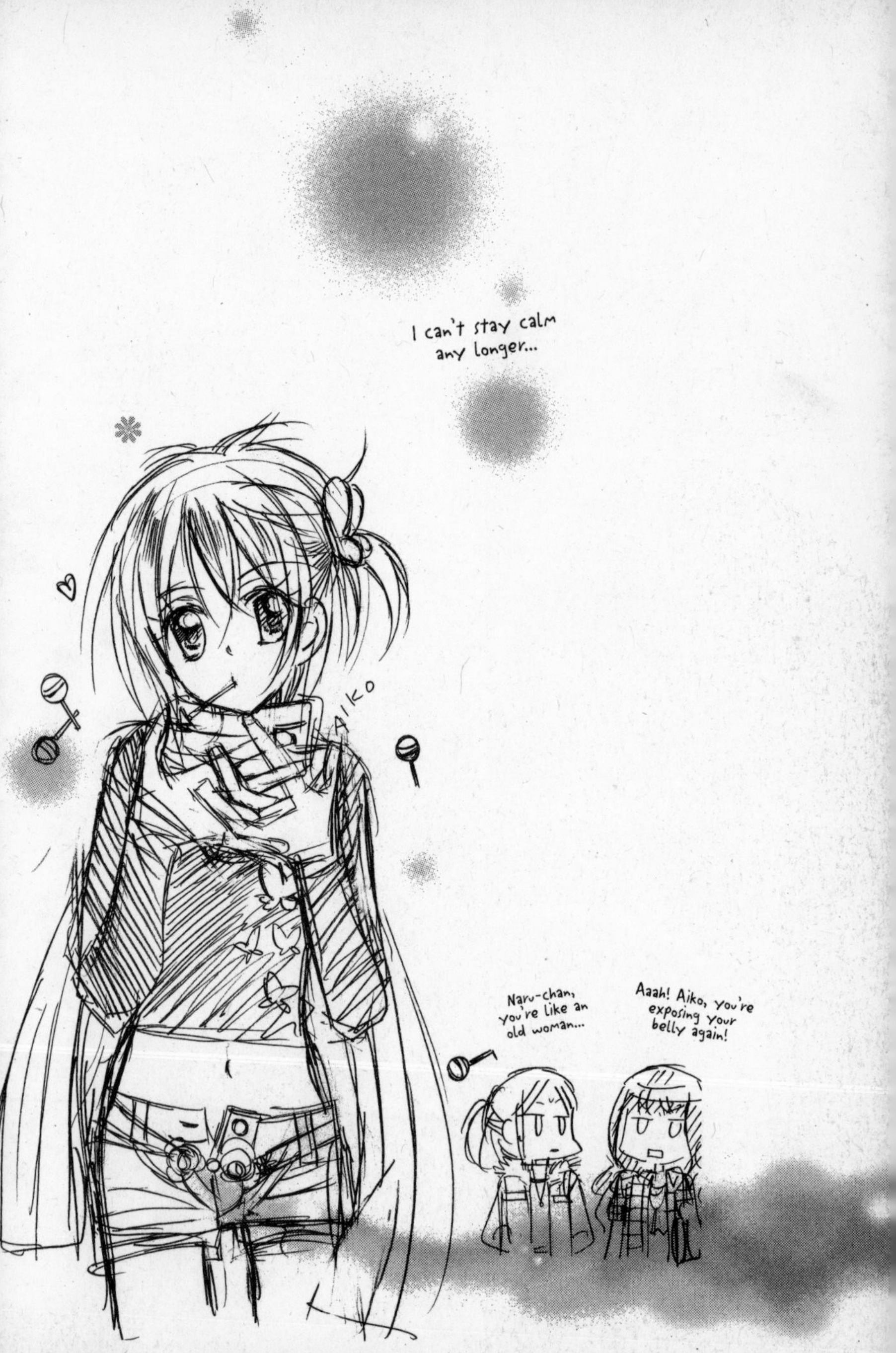
I can't stay calm any longer...
AIKO
Aaah! Aiko, you're exposing your belly again!
Naru-chan, you're like an old woman...

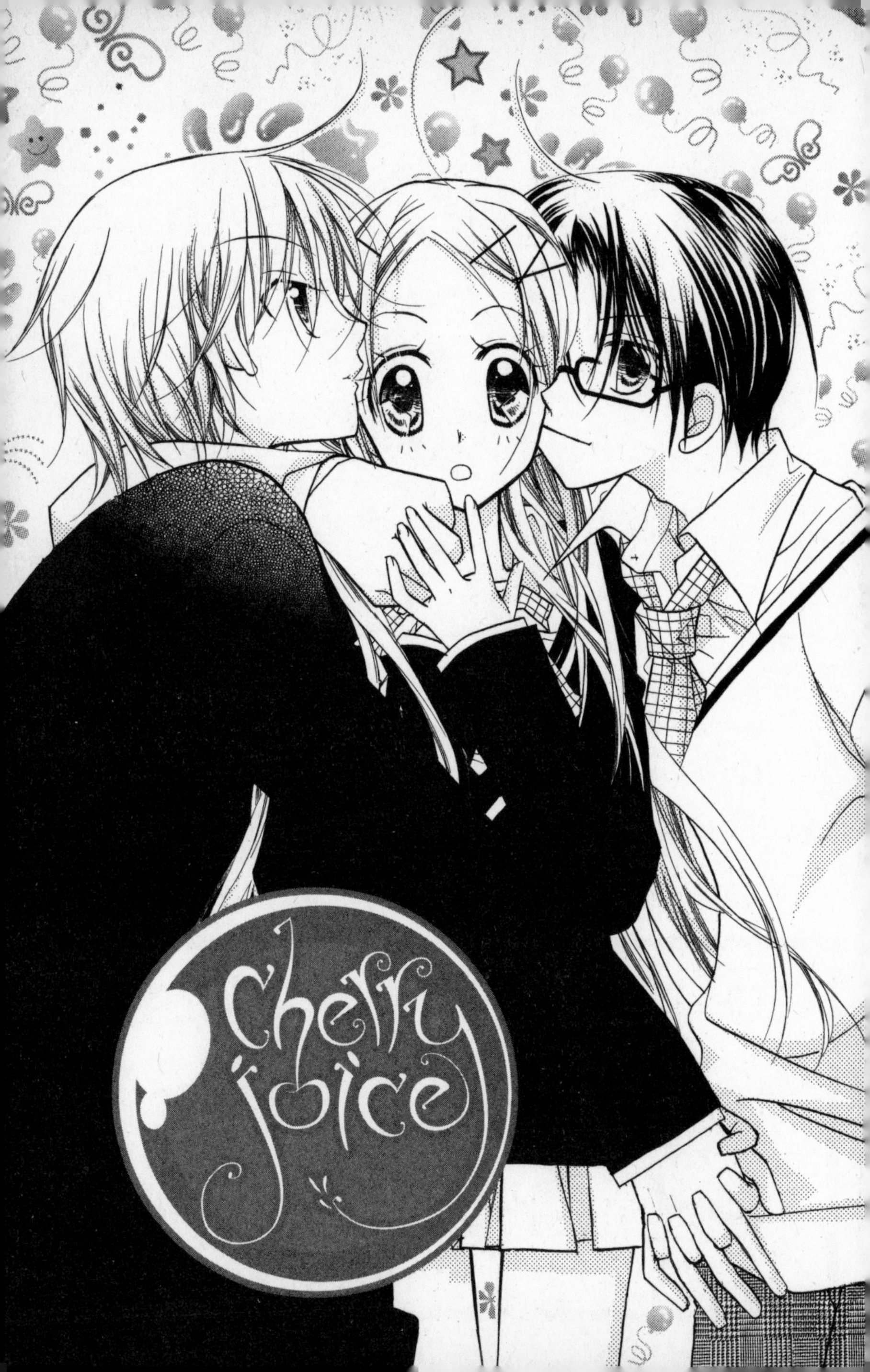
Cherry Juice

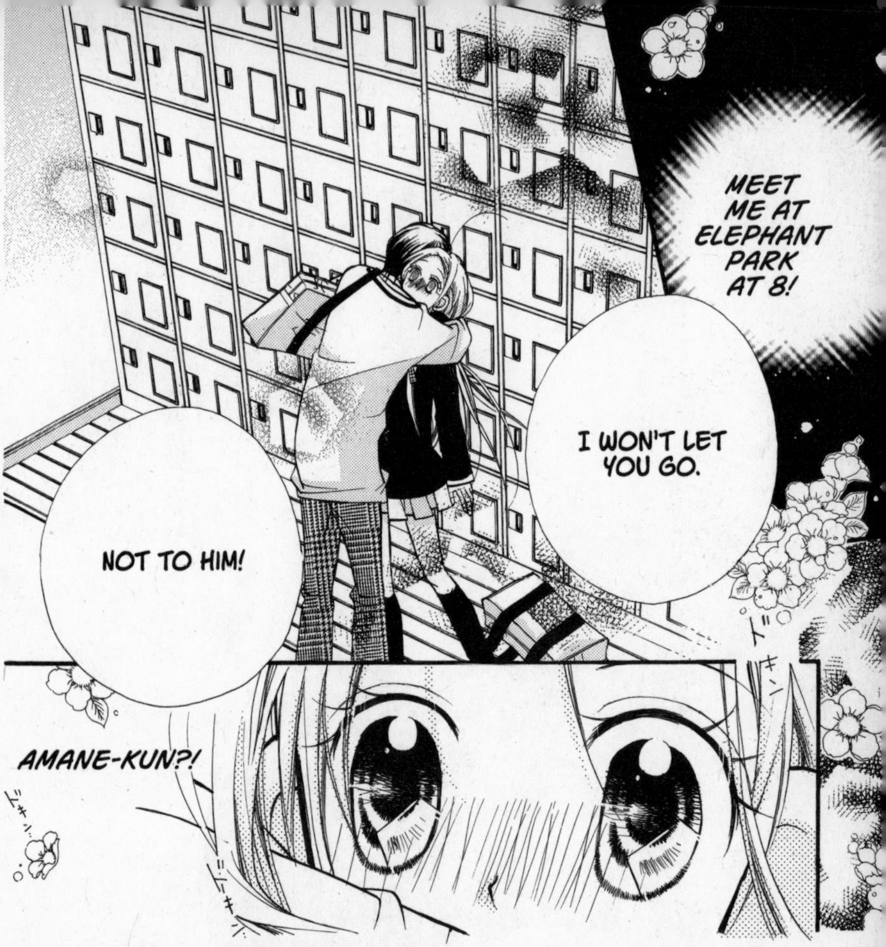
MEET ME AT ELEPHANT PARK AT 8!
I WON'T LET YOU GO.
NOT TO HIM!
AMANE-KUN?!

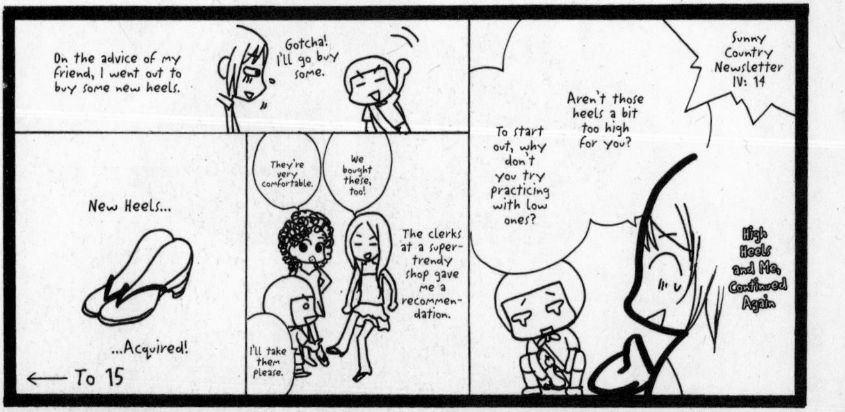
Sunny Country Newsletter IV: 14
High Heels and Me, Continued Again
Aren't those heels a bit too high for you?
To start out, why don't you try practicing with low ones?
On the advice of my friend, I went out to buy some new heels.
Gotcha! I'll go buy some.
We bought these, too!
They're very comfortable.
The clerks at a super-trendy shop gave me a recommendation.
I'll take them please.
New Heels...
...Acquired!
← To 15

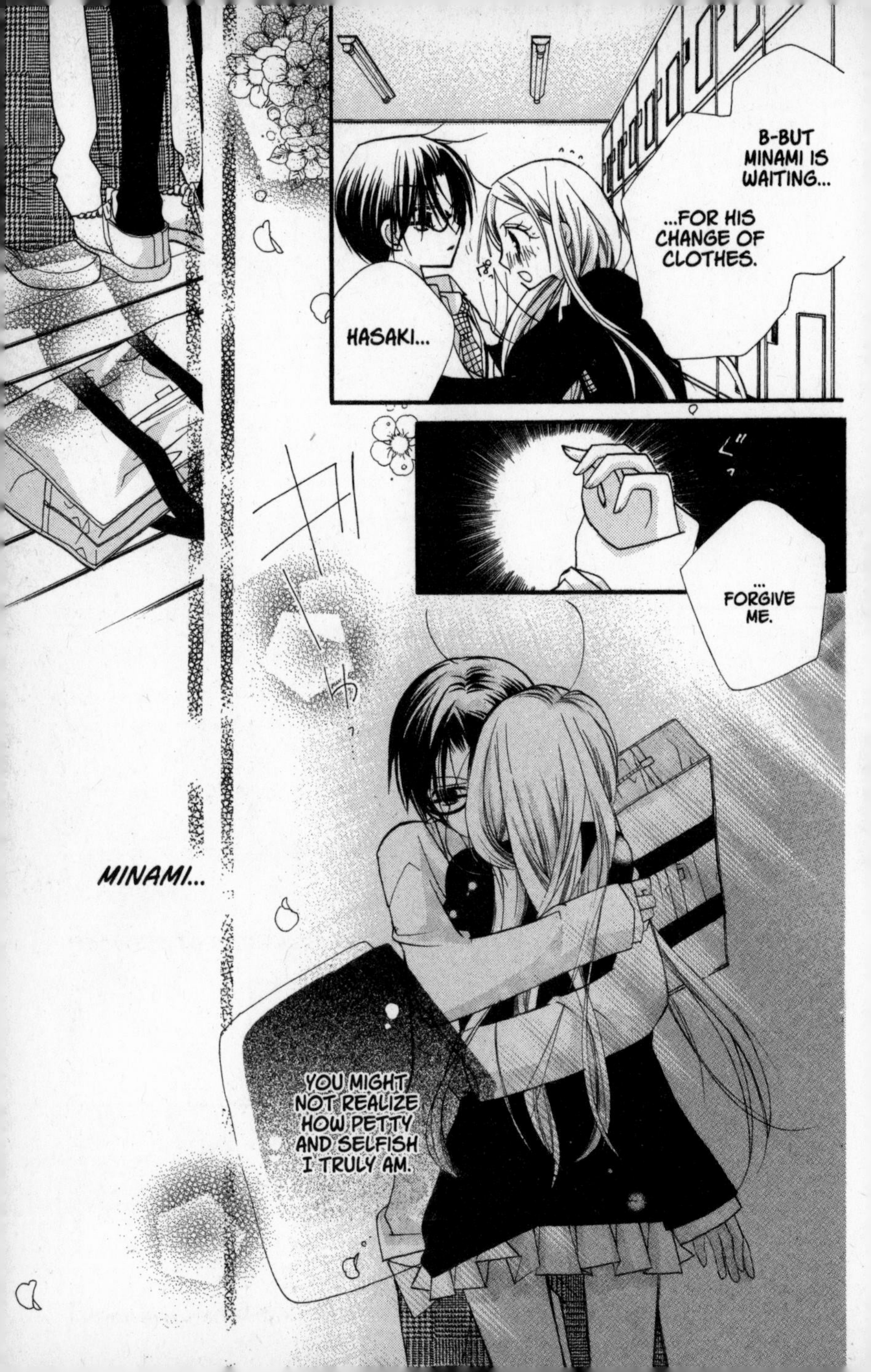
B-BUT MINAMI IS WAITING...
...FOR HIS CHANGE OF CLOTHES.
HASAKI...
... FORGIVE ME.
YOU MIGHT NOT REALIZE HOW PETTY AND SELFISH I TRULY AM.
MINAMI...

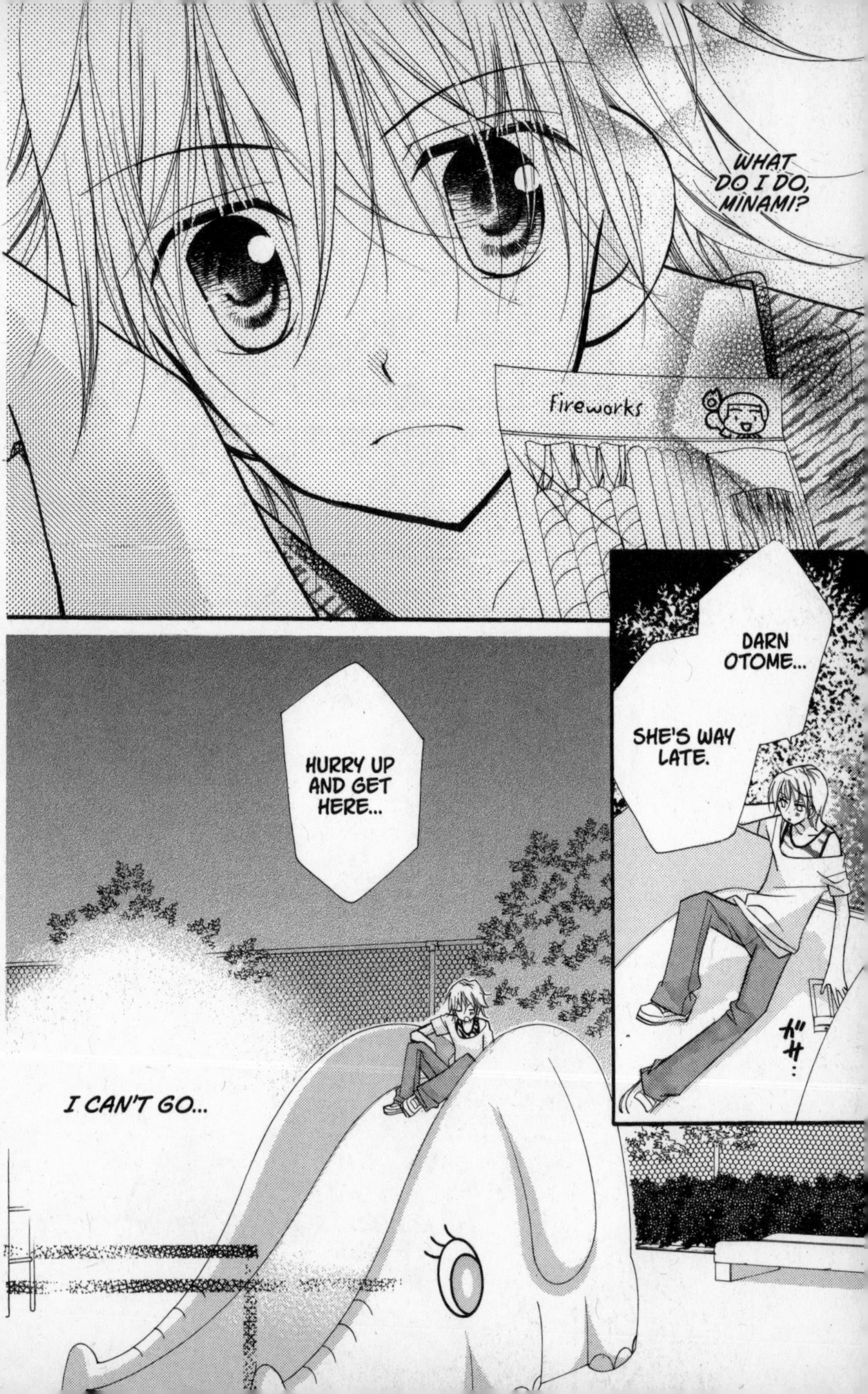
WHAT DO I DO, MINAMI?
fireworks
DARN OTOME...
SHE'S WAY LATE.
ガサ…
HURRY UP AND GET HERE...
I CAN'T GO...

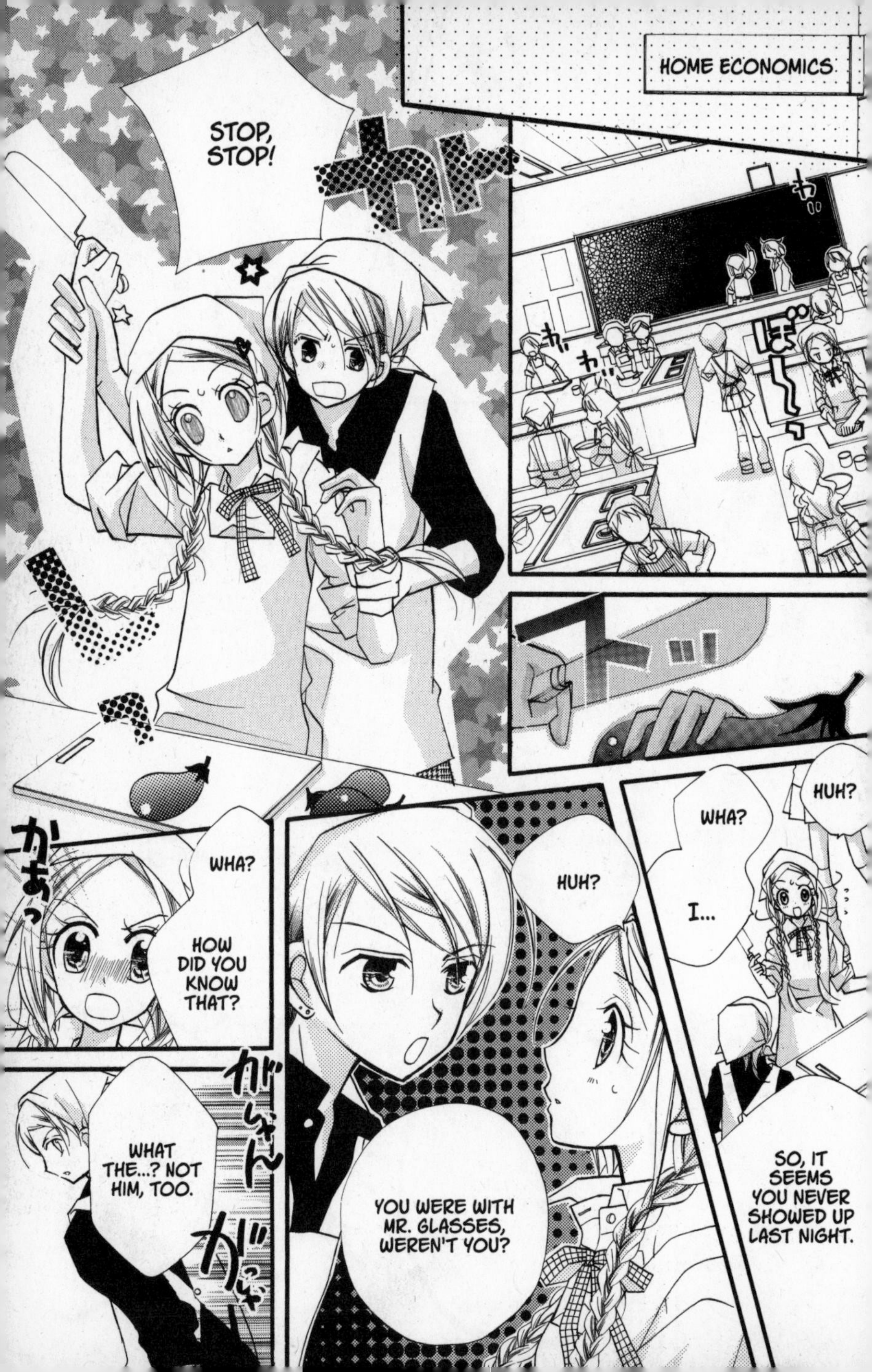
HOME ECONOMICS
STOP, STOP!
HUH?
WHA?
I...
SO, IT SEEMS YOU NEVER SHOWED UP LAST NIGHT.
HUH?
YOU WERE WITH MR. GLASSES, WEREN'T YOU?
WHA?
HOW DID YOU KNOW THAT?
WHAT THE...? NOT HIM, TOO.

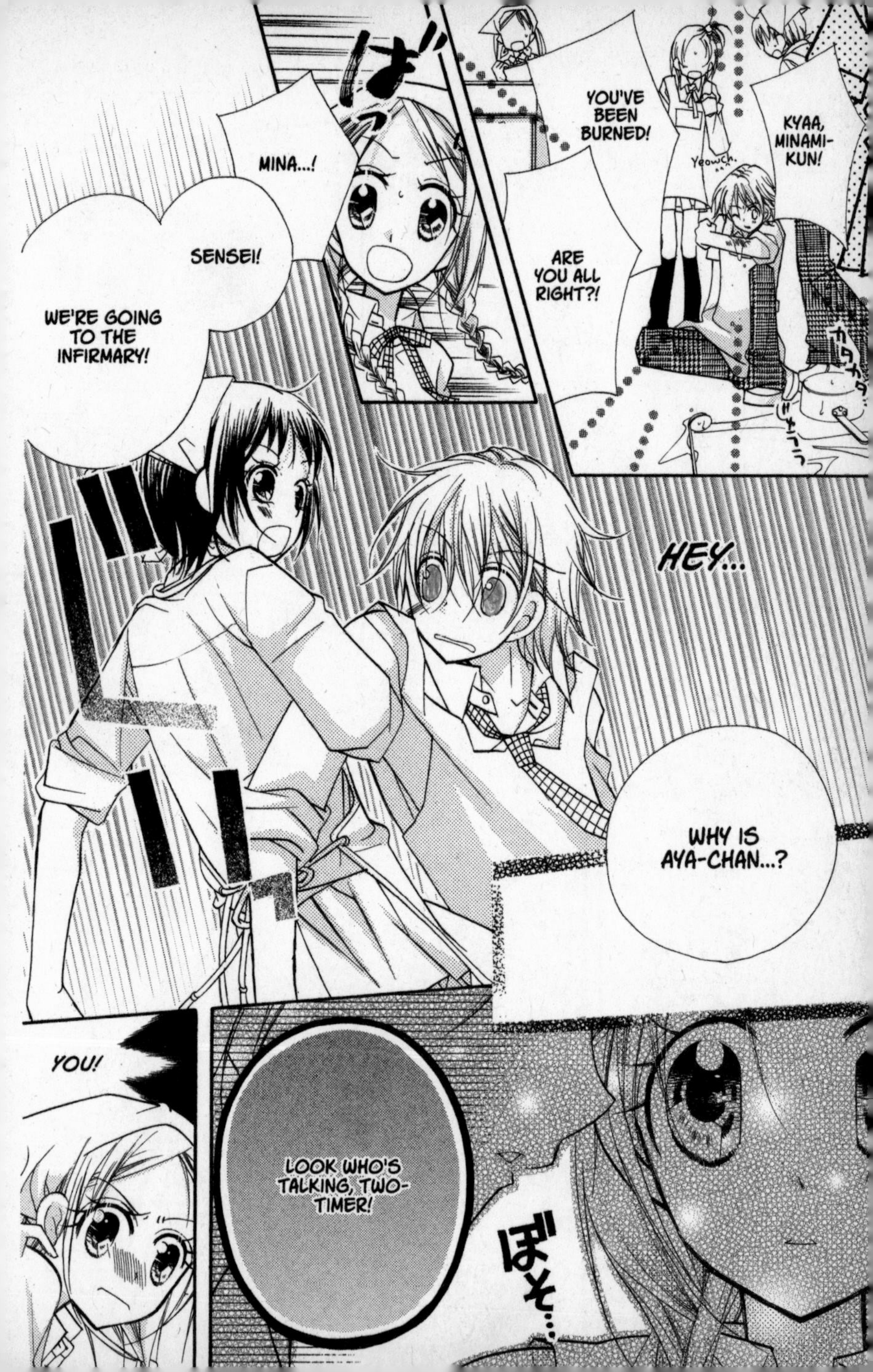
KYAA, MINAMI-KUN!
Yeowch.
YOU'VE BEEN BURNED!
ARE YOU ALL RIGHT?!
ばっ
MINA...!
SENSEI!
WE'RE GOING TO THE INFIRMARY!
HEY...
WHY IS AYA-CHAN...?
ぼそ...
LOOK WHO'S TALKING, TWO-TIMER!
YOU!

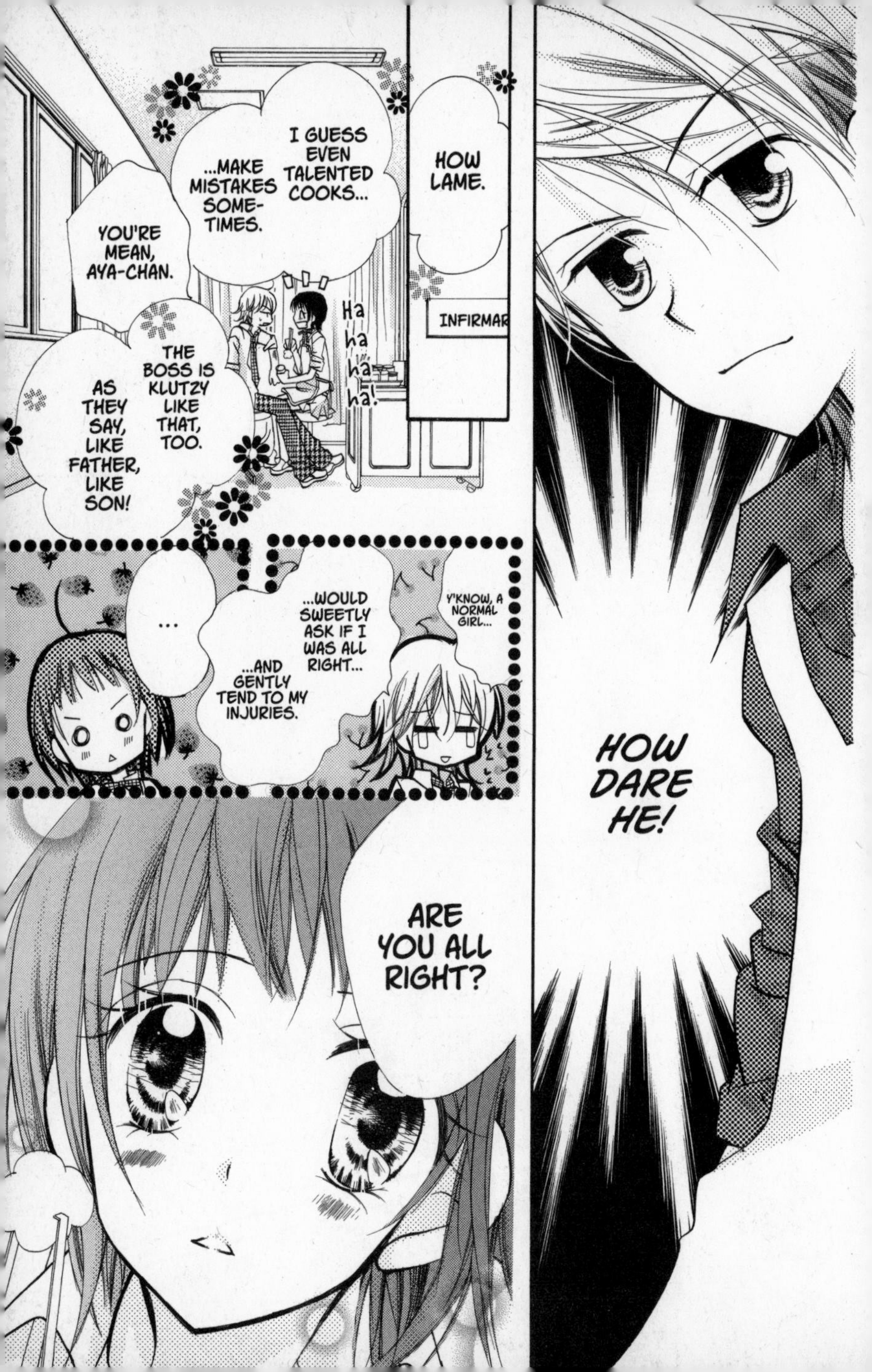
HOW LAME.
Ha ha ha ha ha!
I GUESS EVEN TALENTED COOKS...
...MAKE MISTAKES SOME-TIMES.
YOU'RE MEAN, AYA-CHAN.
INFIRMAR
THE BOSS IS KLUTZY LIKE THAT, TOO.
AS THEY SAY, LIKE FATHER, LIKE SON!
Y'KNOW, A NORMAL GIRL...
...WOULD SWEETLY ASK IF I WAS ALL RIGHT...
...AND GENTLY TEND TO MY INJURIES.
...
ARE YOU ALL RIGHT?
HOW DARE HE!

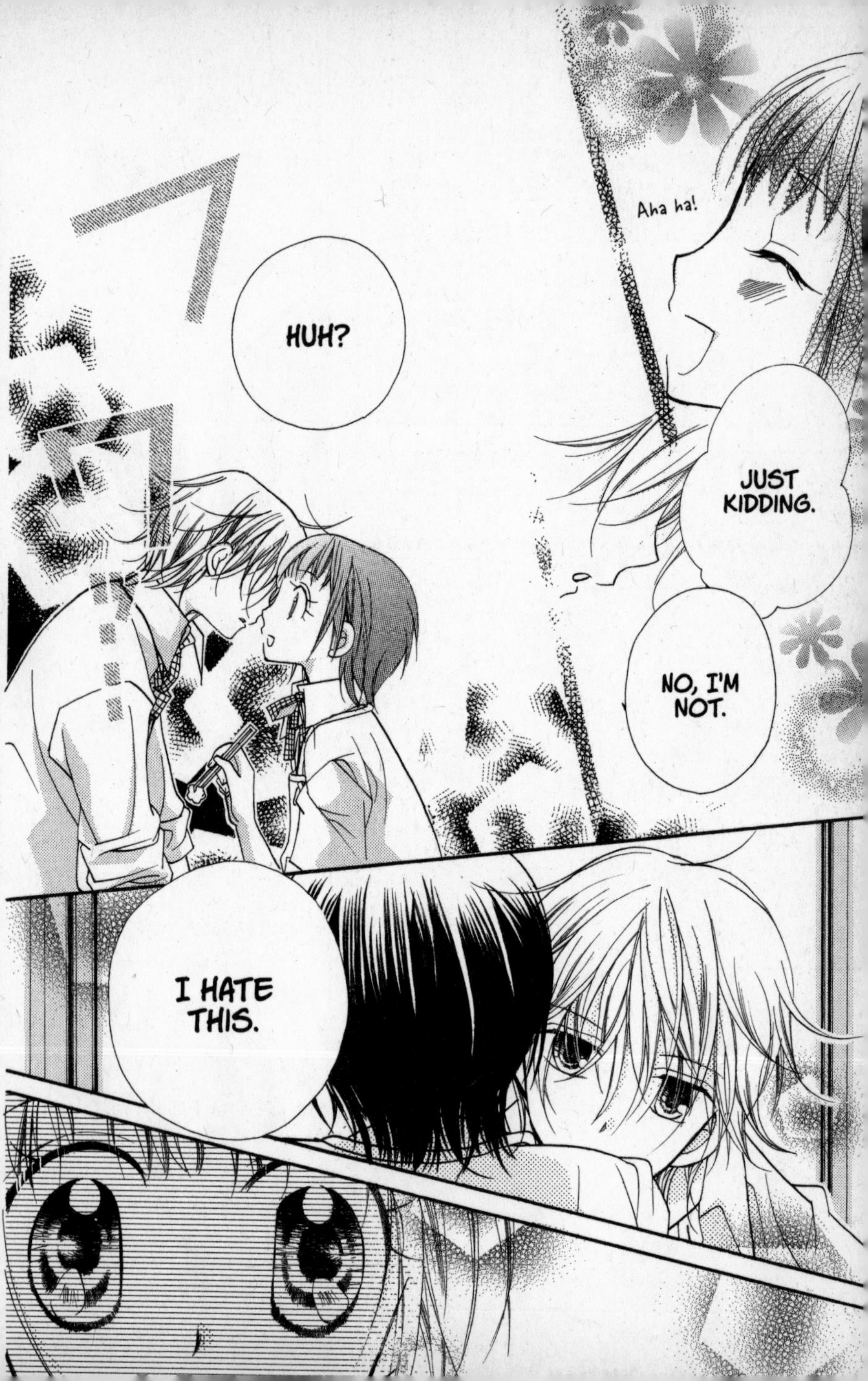
Aha ha!
JUST KIDDING.
NO, I'M NOT.
HUH?
I HATE THIS.

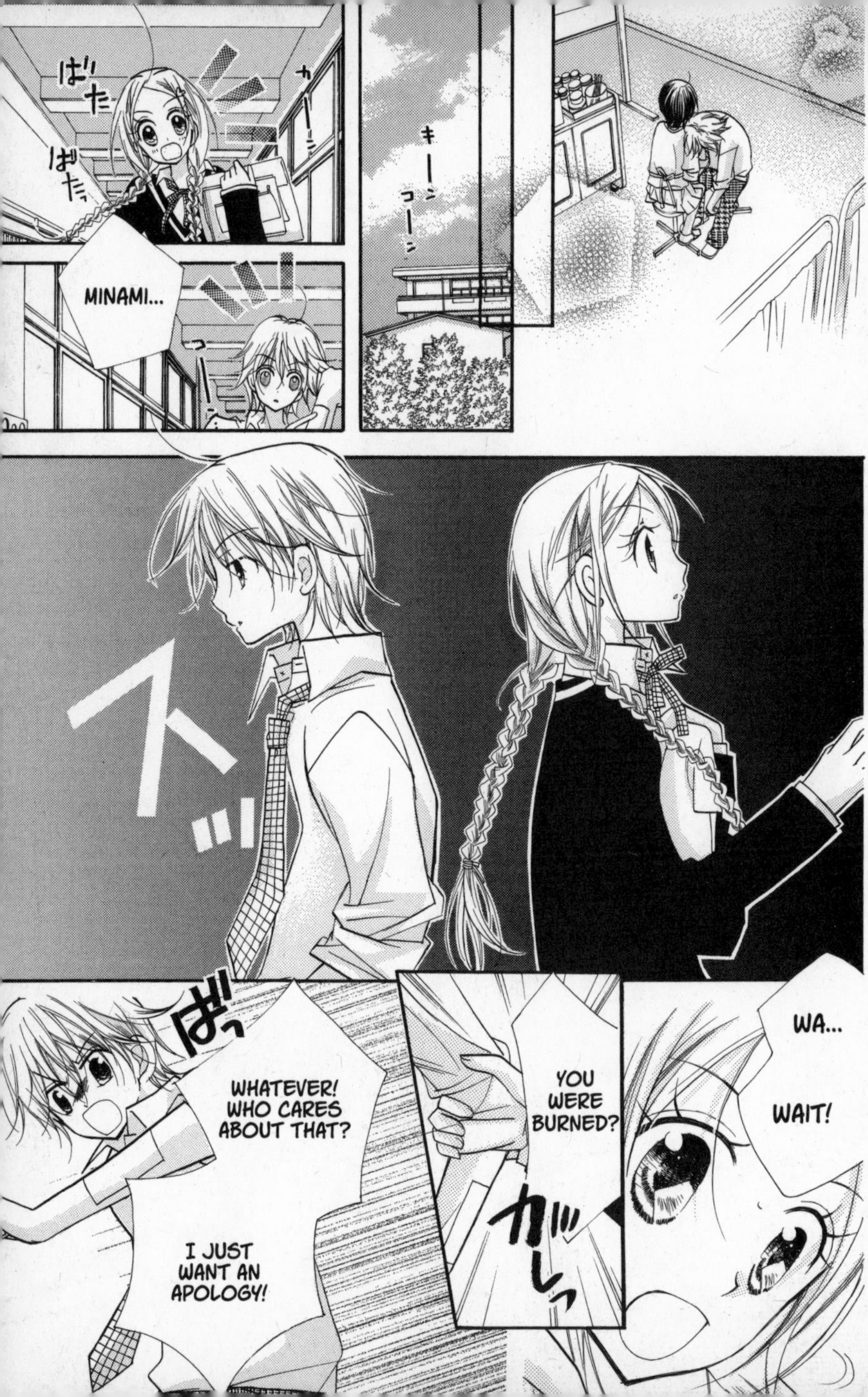
MINAMI...
WA...
WAIT!
YOU WERE BURNED?
WHATEVER! WHO CARES ABOUT THAT?
I JUST WANT AN APOLOGY!

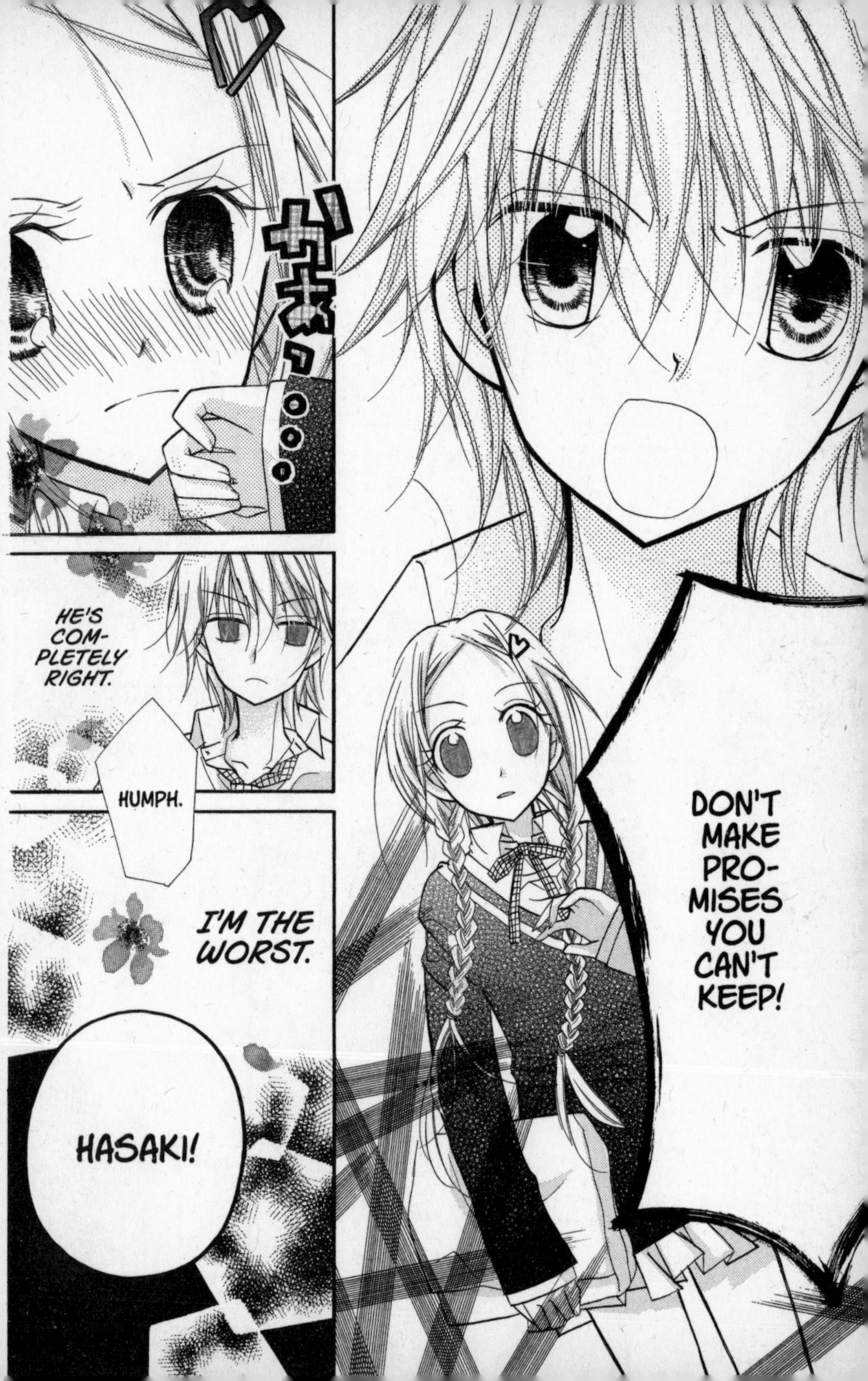
DON'T MAKE PRO-MISES YOU CAN'T KEEP!
HE'S COM-PLETELY RIGHT.
HUMPH.
I'M THE WORST.
HASAKI!

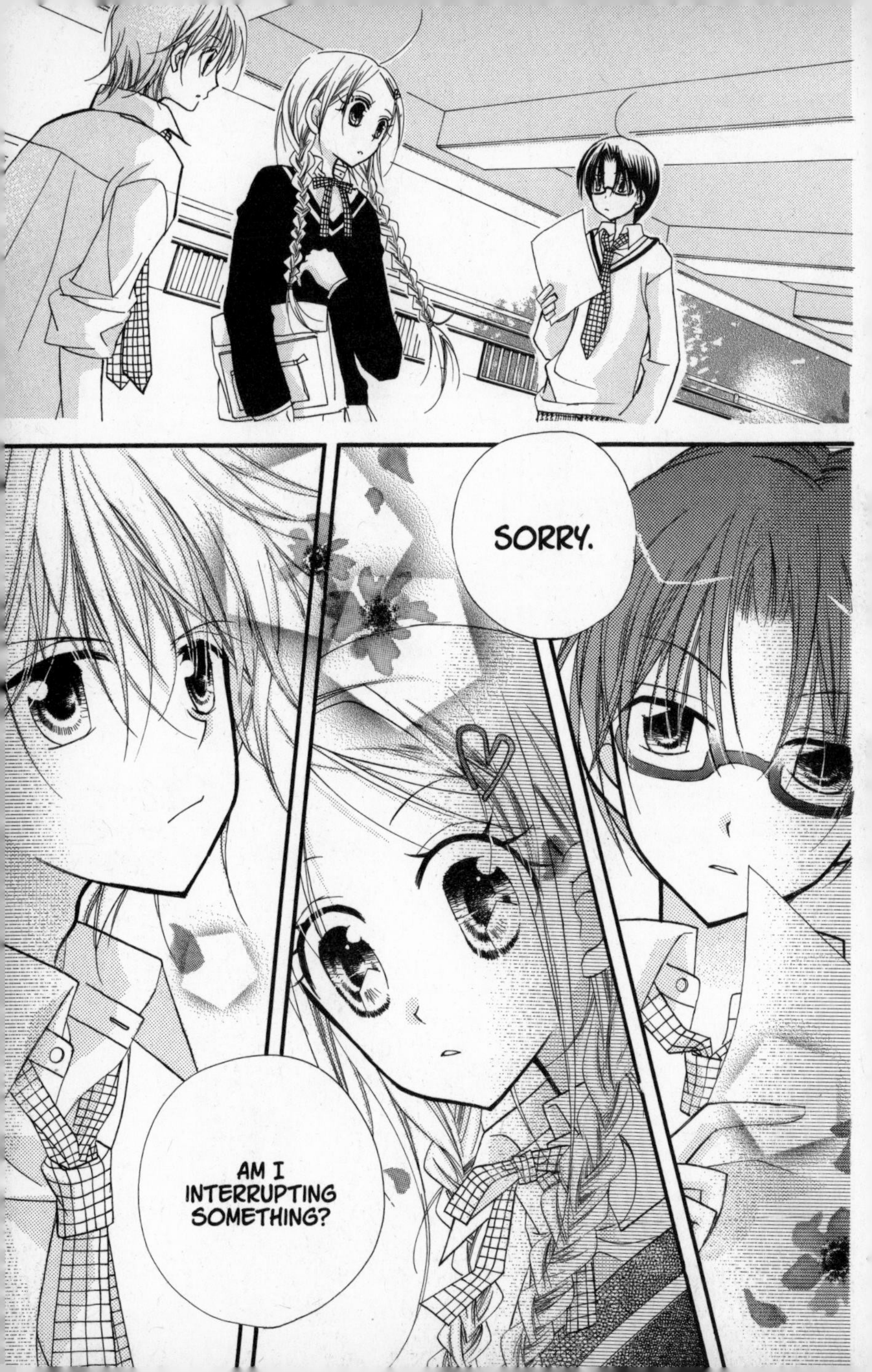
SORRY.
AM I INTERRUPTING SOMETHING?

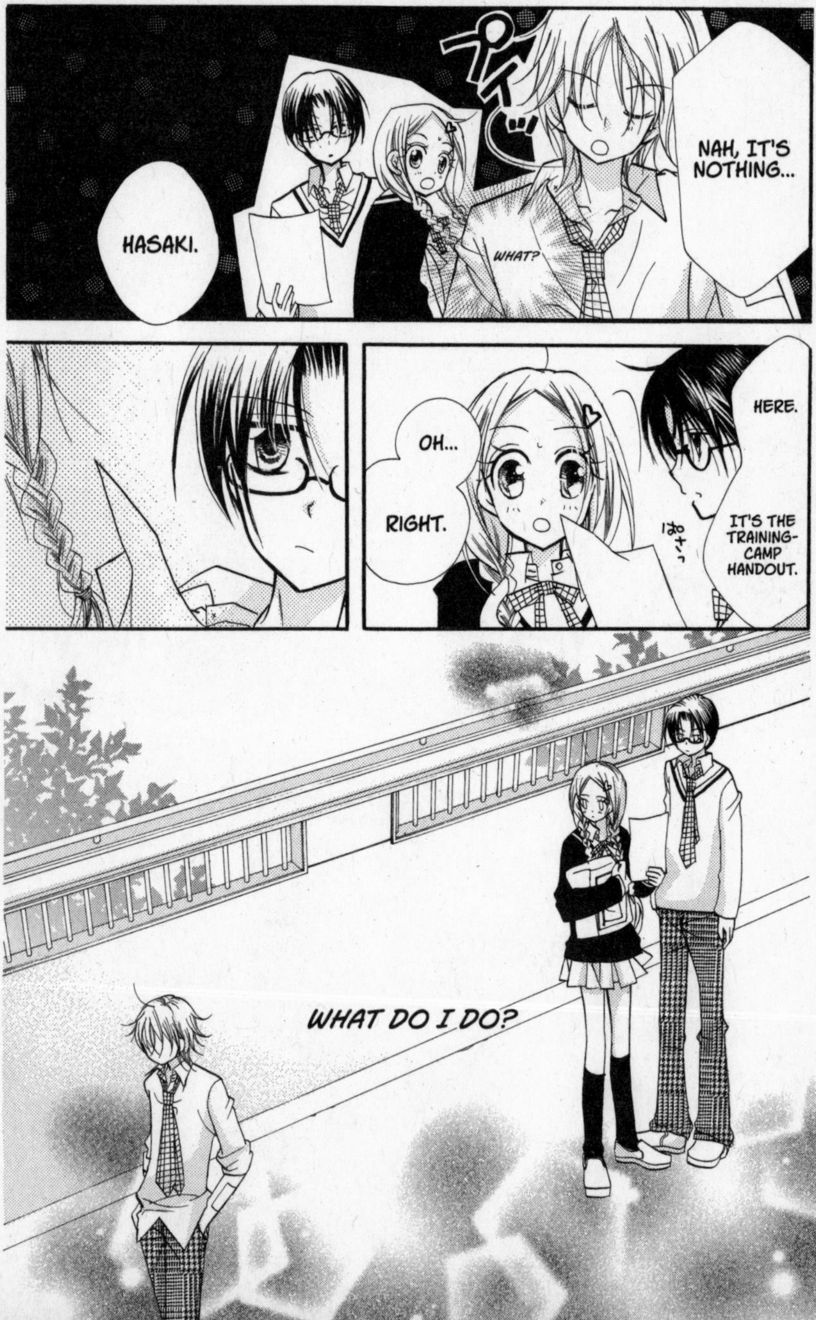
NAH, IT'S NOTHING...
WHAT?
HASAKI.
HERE.
IT'S THE TRAINING-CAMP HANDOUT.
OH... RIGHT.
WHAT DO I DO?

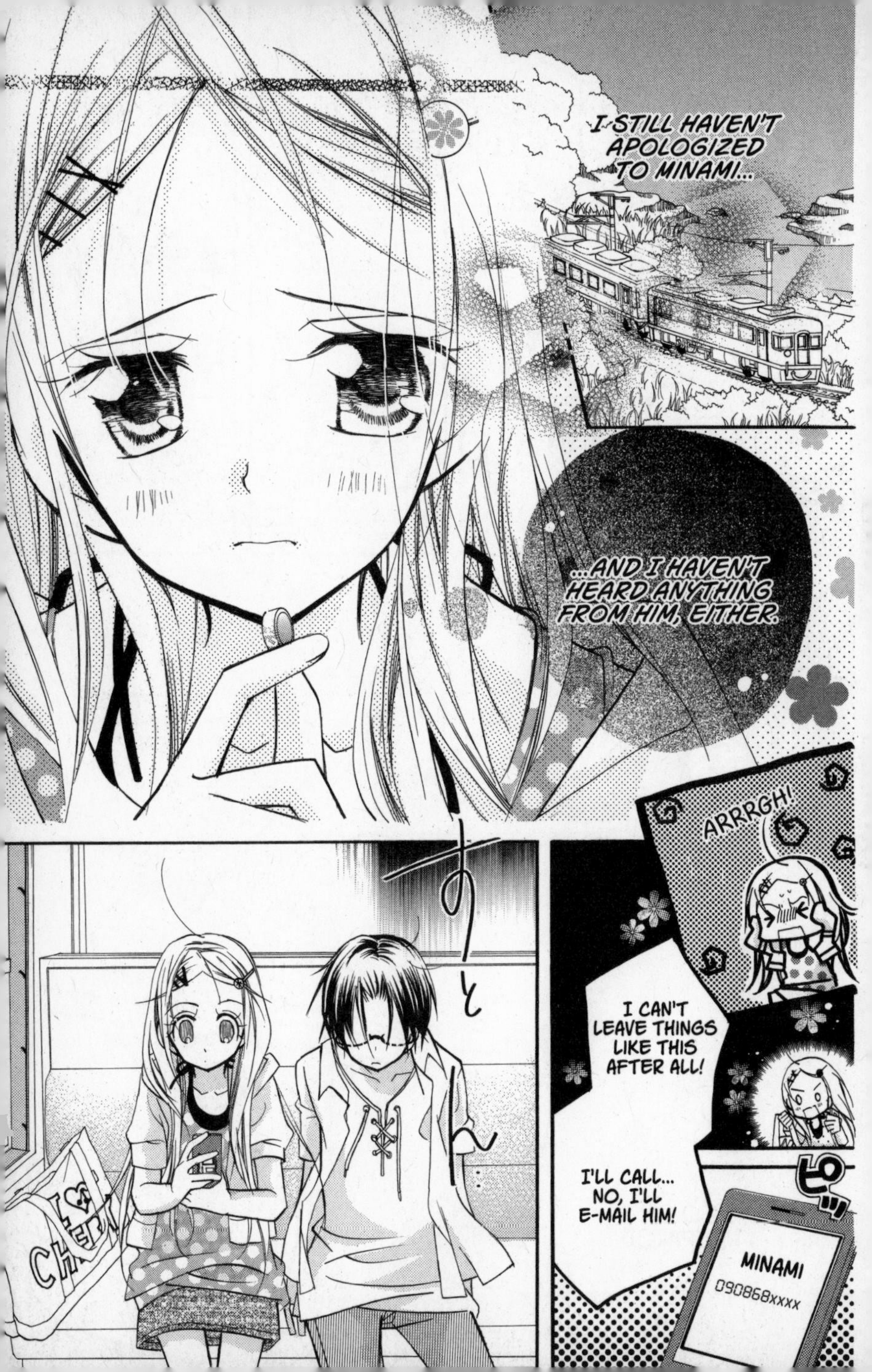
I STILL HAVEN'T APOLOGIZED TO MINAMI...
...AND I HAVEN'T HEARD ANYTHING FROM HIM, EITHER.
ARRRGH!
I CAN'T LEAVE THINGS LIKE THIS AFTER ALL!
I'LL CALL... NO, I'LL E-MAIL HIM!
ピッ
MINAMI
090868xxxx

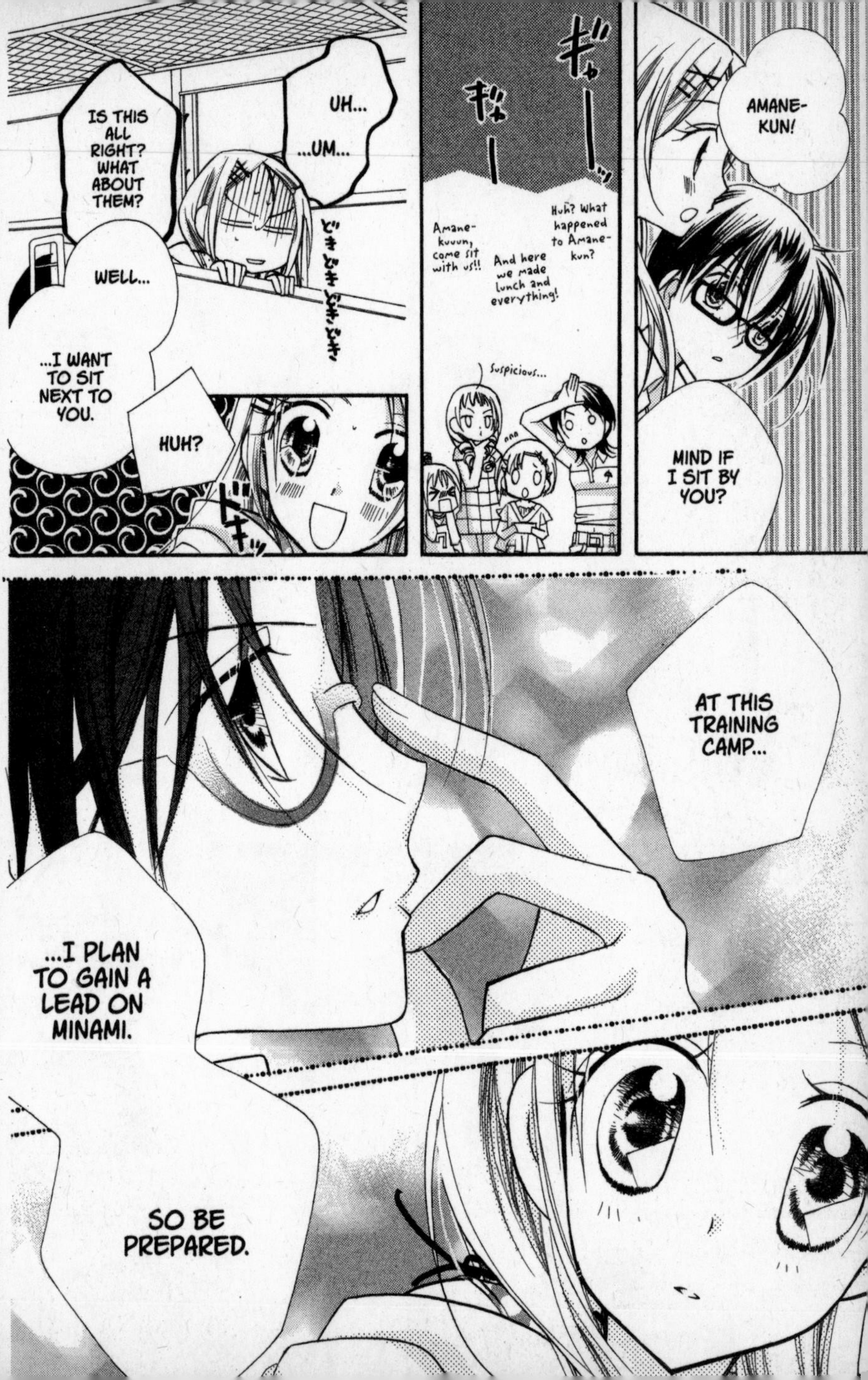
AMANE-KUN!
MIND IF I SIT BY YOU?
ギャー
ギャー
Huh? What happened to Amane-kun?
And here we made lunch and everything!
Amane-kuuun, come sit with us!!
Suspicious...
UH... ...UM...
IS THIS ALL RIGHT? WHAT ABOUT THEM?
どきどきどきどき
WELL...
...I WANT TO SIT NEXT TO YOU.
HUH?
ドキッ
AT THIS TRAINING CAMP...
...I PLAN TO GAIN A LEAD ON MINAMI.
SO BE PREPARED.

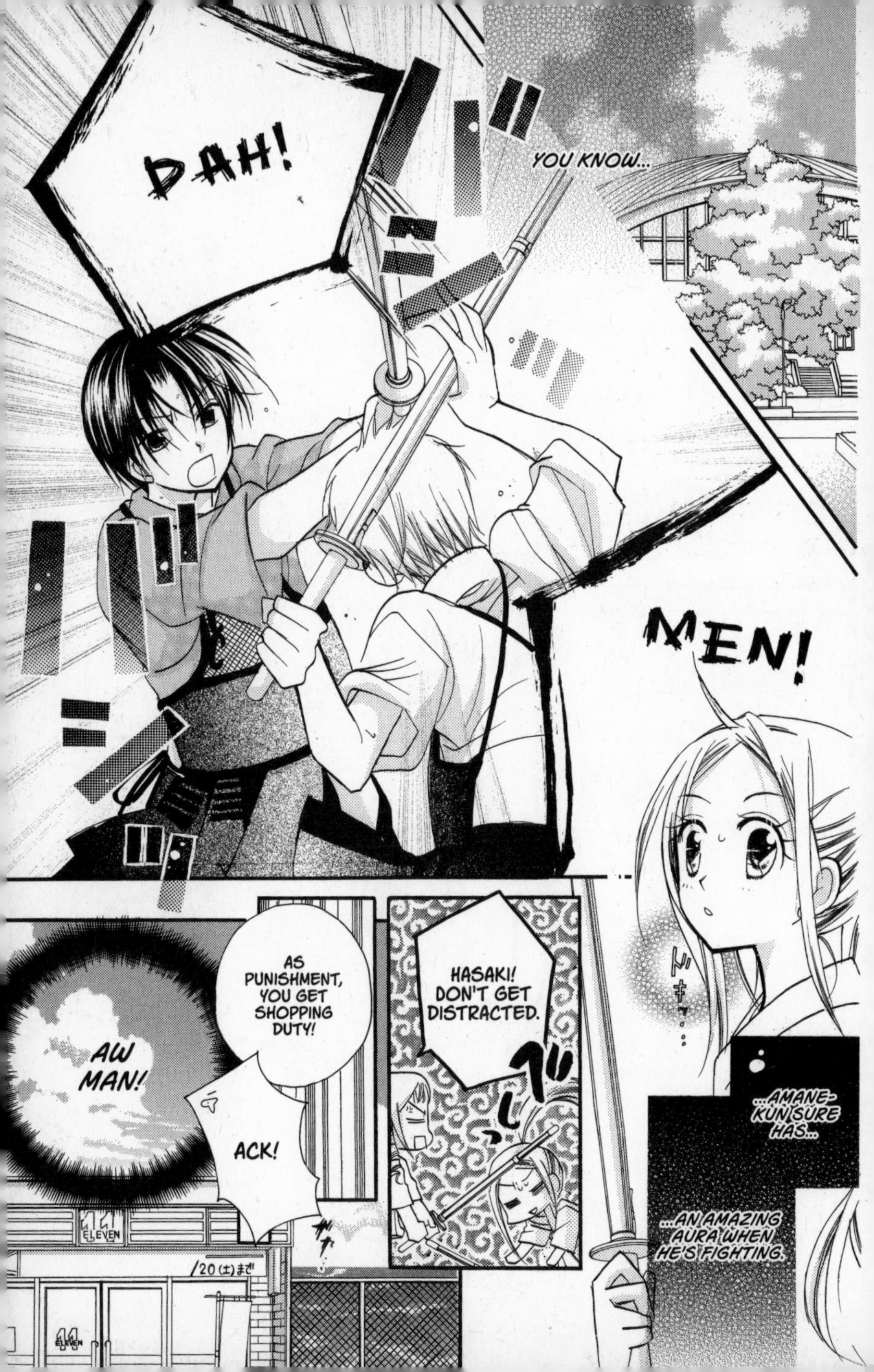
YOU KNOW...
DAH!
MEN!
...AMANE-KUN SURE HAS...
...AN AMAZING AURA WHEN HE'S FIGHTING.
HASAKI! DON'T GET DISTRACTED.
AS PUNISHMENT, YOU GET SHOPPING DUTY!
ACK!
AW MAN!

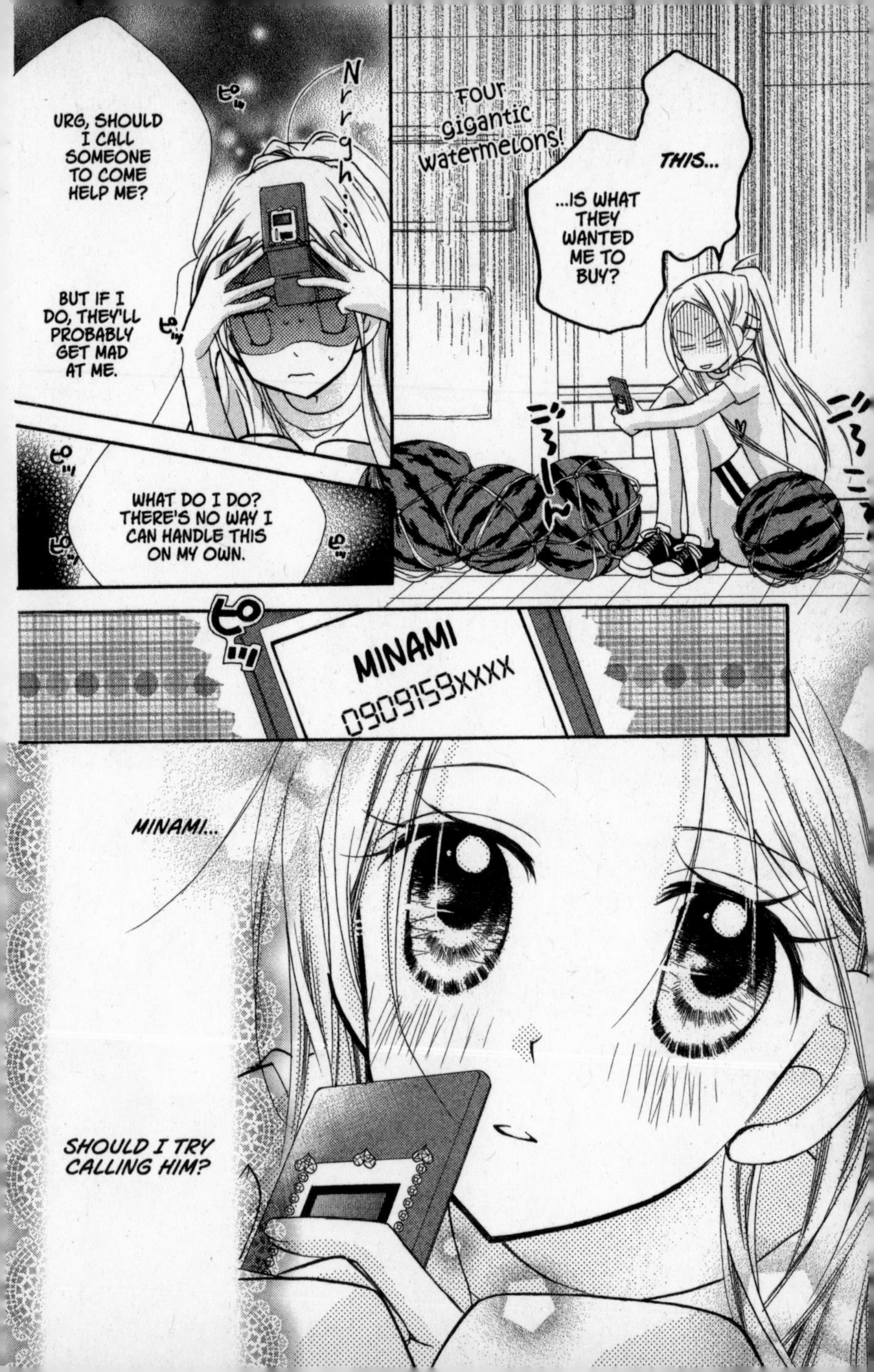
THIS...
...IS WHAT THEY WANTED ME TO BUY?
Four gigantic watermelons!
Nrrgh...
URG, SHOULD I CALL SOMEONE TO COME HELP ME?
BUT IF I DO, THEY'LL PROBABLY GET MAD AT ME.
WHAT DO I DO? THERE'S NO WAY I CAN HANDLE THIS ON MY OWN.
MINAMI
0909159XXXX
MINAMI...
SHOULD I TRY CALLING HIM?

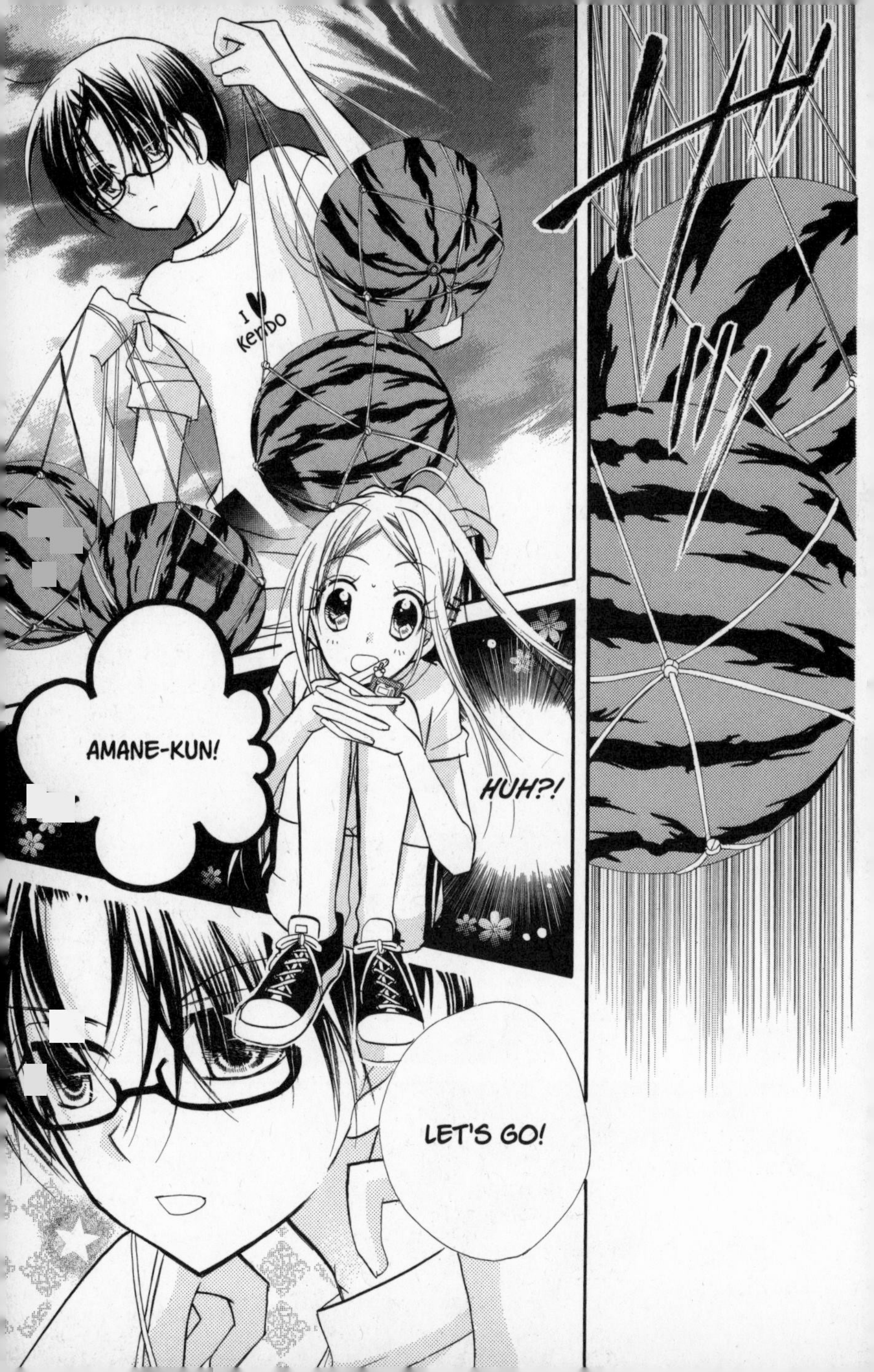
I ♥ KENDO
AMANE-KUN!
HUH?!
LET'S GO!

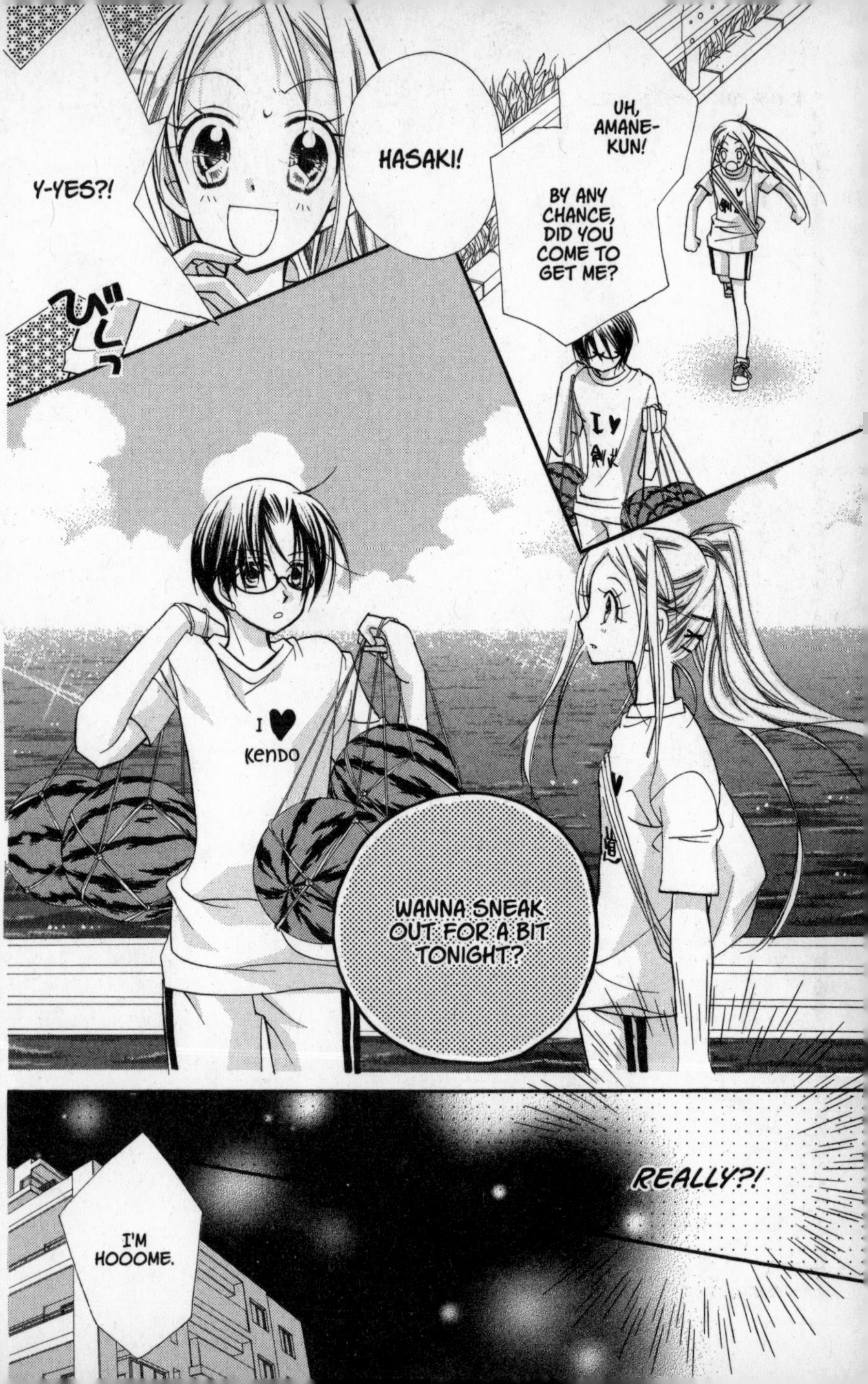
UH, AMANE-KUN!
BY ANY CHANCE, DID YOU COME TO GET ME?
HASAKI!
Y-YES?!
びくっ
I ♥ KENDO
WANNA SNEAK OUT FOR A BIT TONIGHT?
REALLY?!
I'M HOOOME.

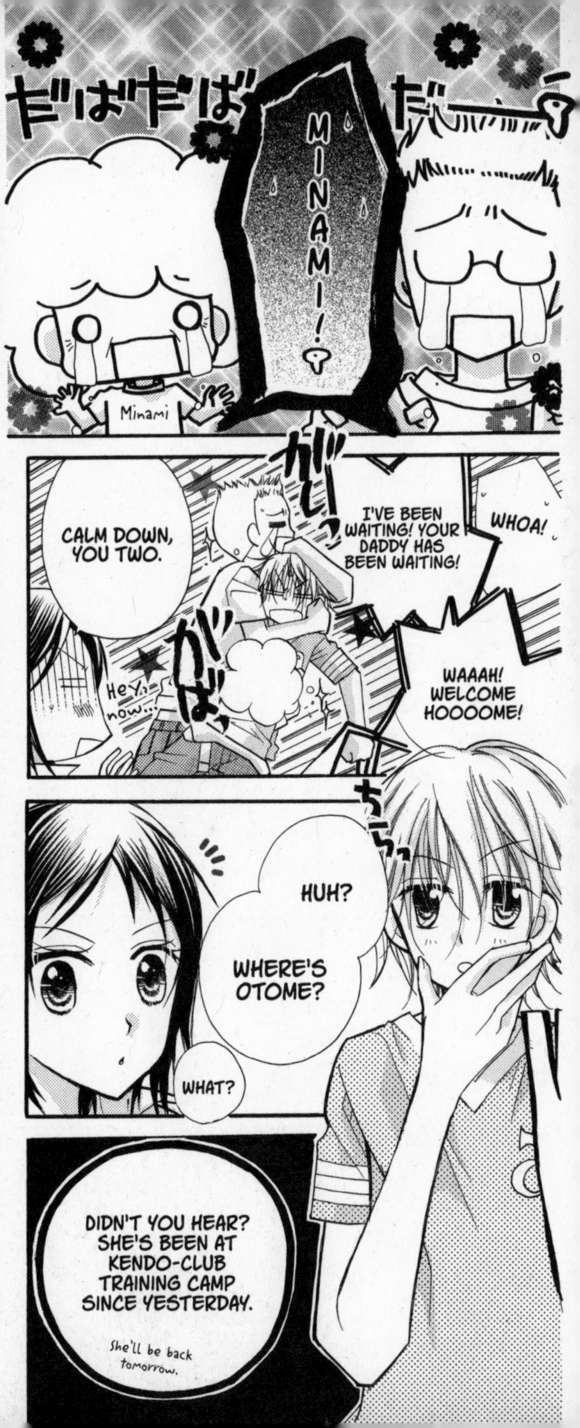

だばだば
だーっ
MINAMI!
Minami
WHOA!
I'VE BEEN WAITING! YOUR DADDY HAS BEEN WAITING!
がしっ
WAAAH! WELCOME HOOOOME!
がばっ
CALM DOWN, YOU TWO.
Hey, now...
HUH?
WHERE'S OTOME?
WHAT?
DIDN'T YOU HEAR? SHE'S BEEN AT KENDO-CLUB TRAINING CAMP SINCE YESTERDAY.
She'll be back tomorrow.

FIVE

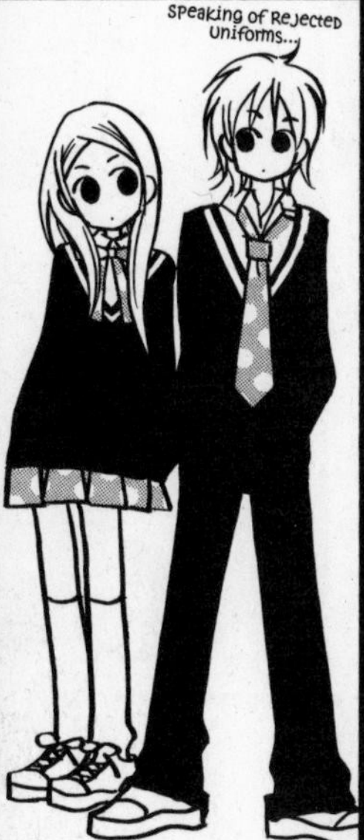

Speaking of Rejected uniforms...

There was one version where the design itself was no different, but the neckties, ribbons and skirts all had polka dots.

Personally, they were my first choice, but they were rejected on the account that polka dots are considered old-fashioned and no one wears them now...

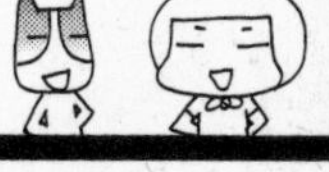

I'm currently on a polka-dot kick.

← To SIX

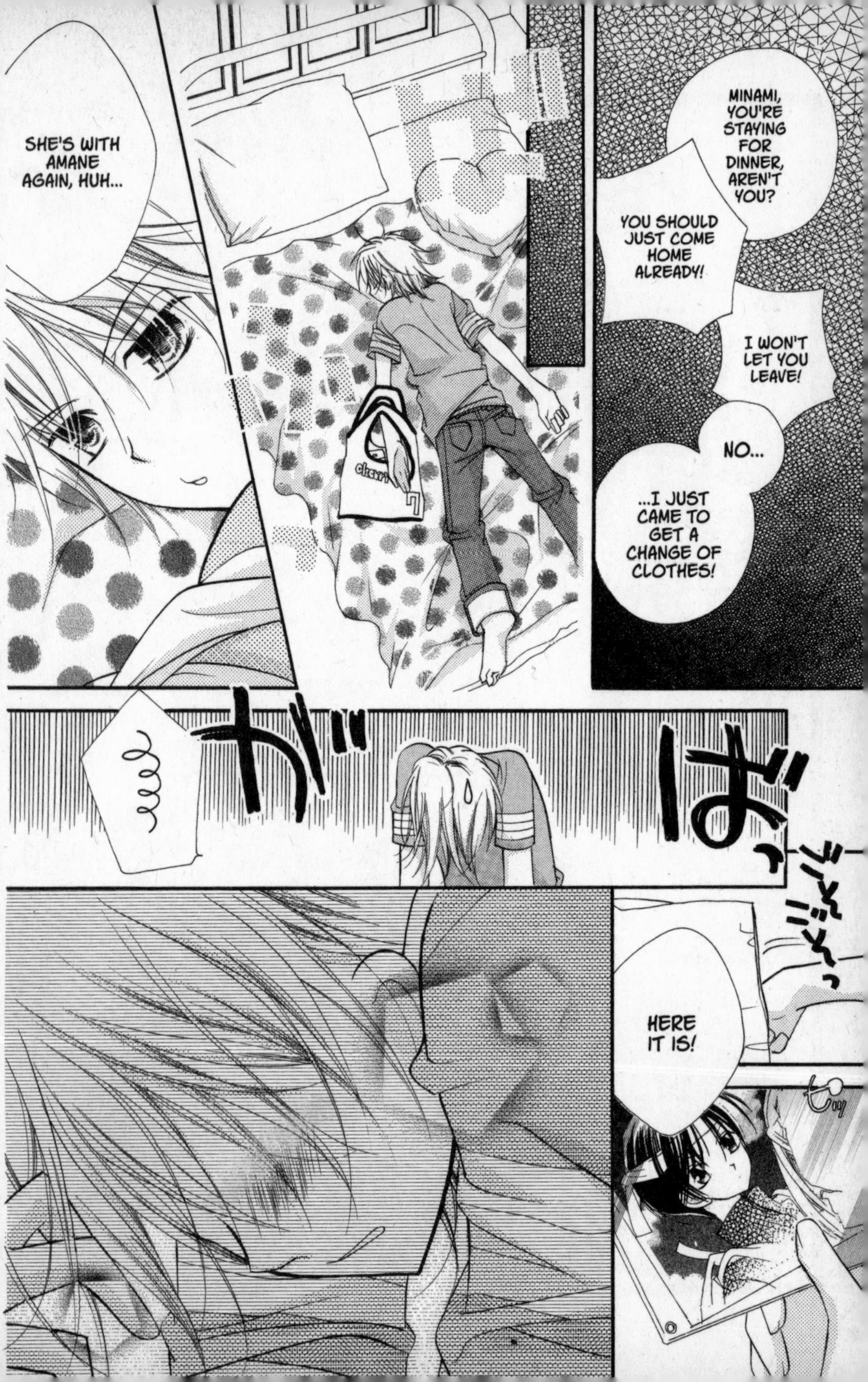
MINAMI, YOU'RE STAYING FOR DINNER, AREN'T YOU?
YOU SHOULD JUST COME HOME ALREADY!
I WON'T LET YOU LEAVE!
NO...
...I JUST CAME TO GET A CHANGE OF CLOTHES!
SHE'S WITH AMANE AGAIN, HUH...
がばっ
HERE IT IS!

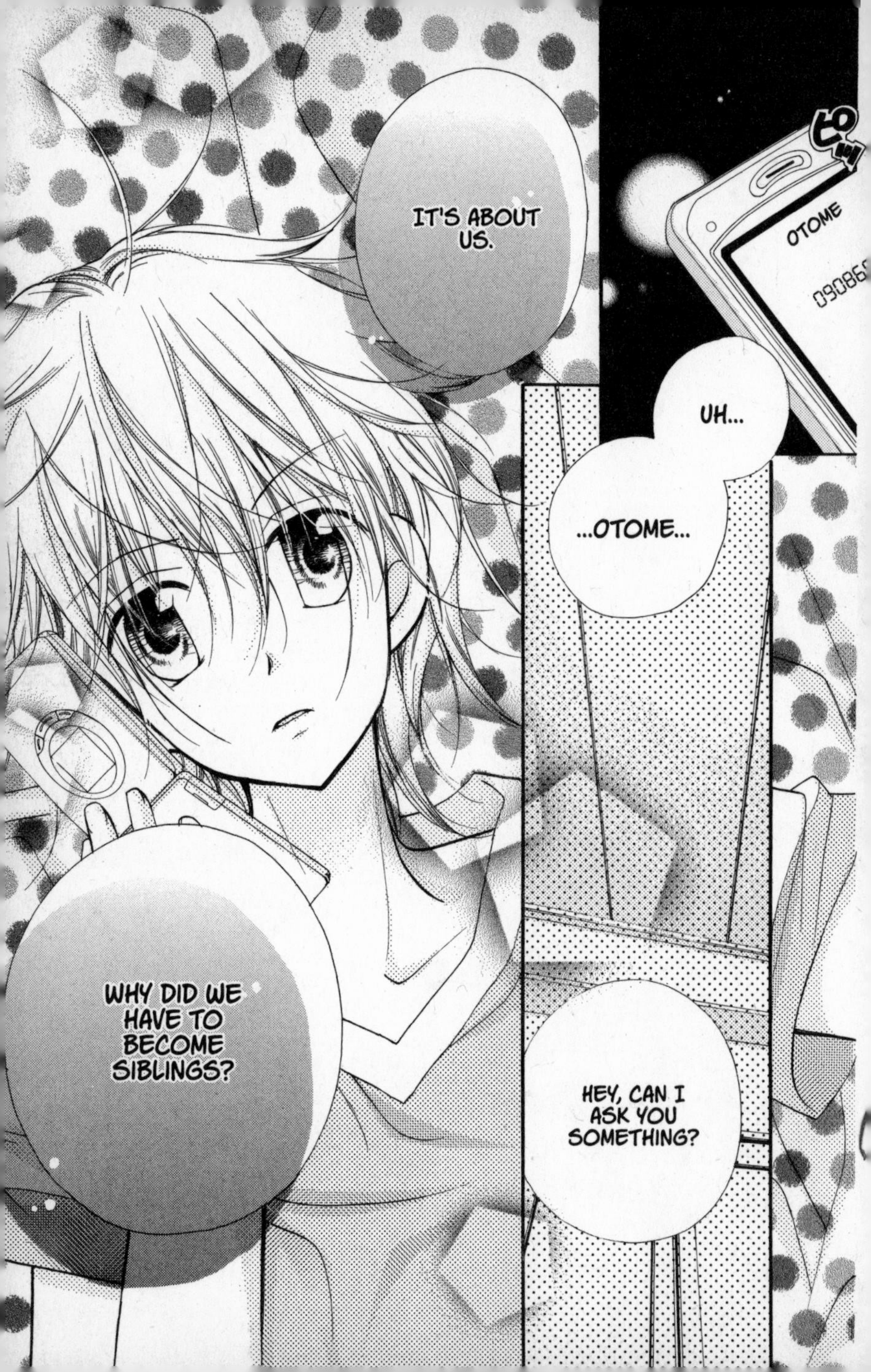
OTOME
UH...
...OTOME...
HEY, CAN I ASK YOU SOMETHING?
IT'S ABOUT US.
WHY DID WE HAVE TO BECOME SIBLINGS?

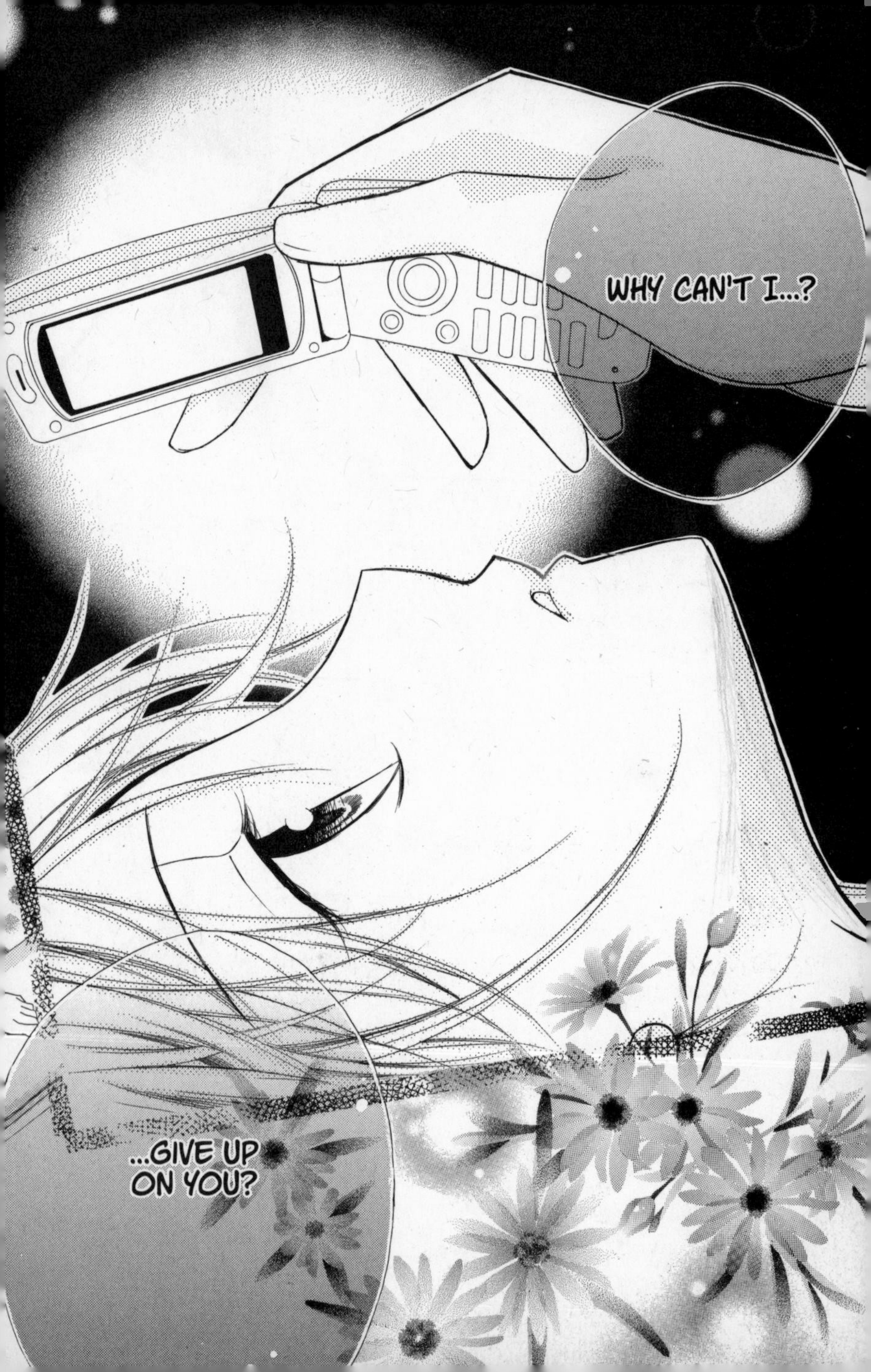
WHY CAN'T I...?
...GIVE UP ON YOU?

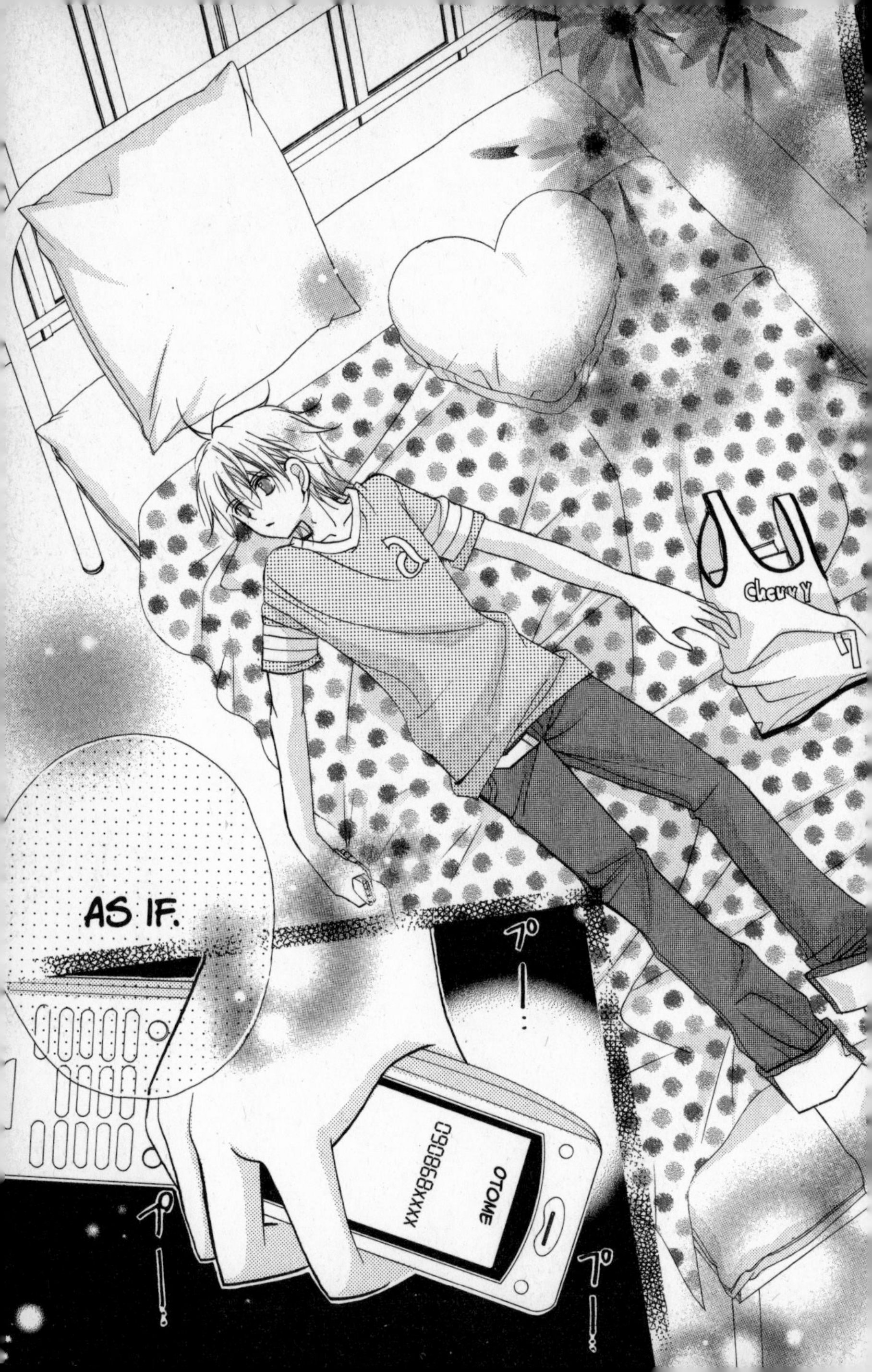

プー…
プー…
AS IF.
OTOME
プー…

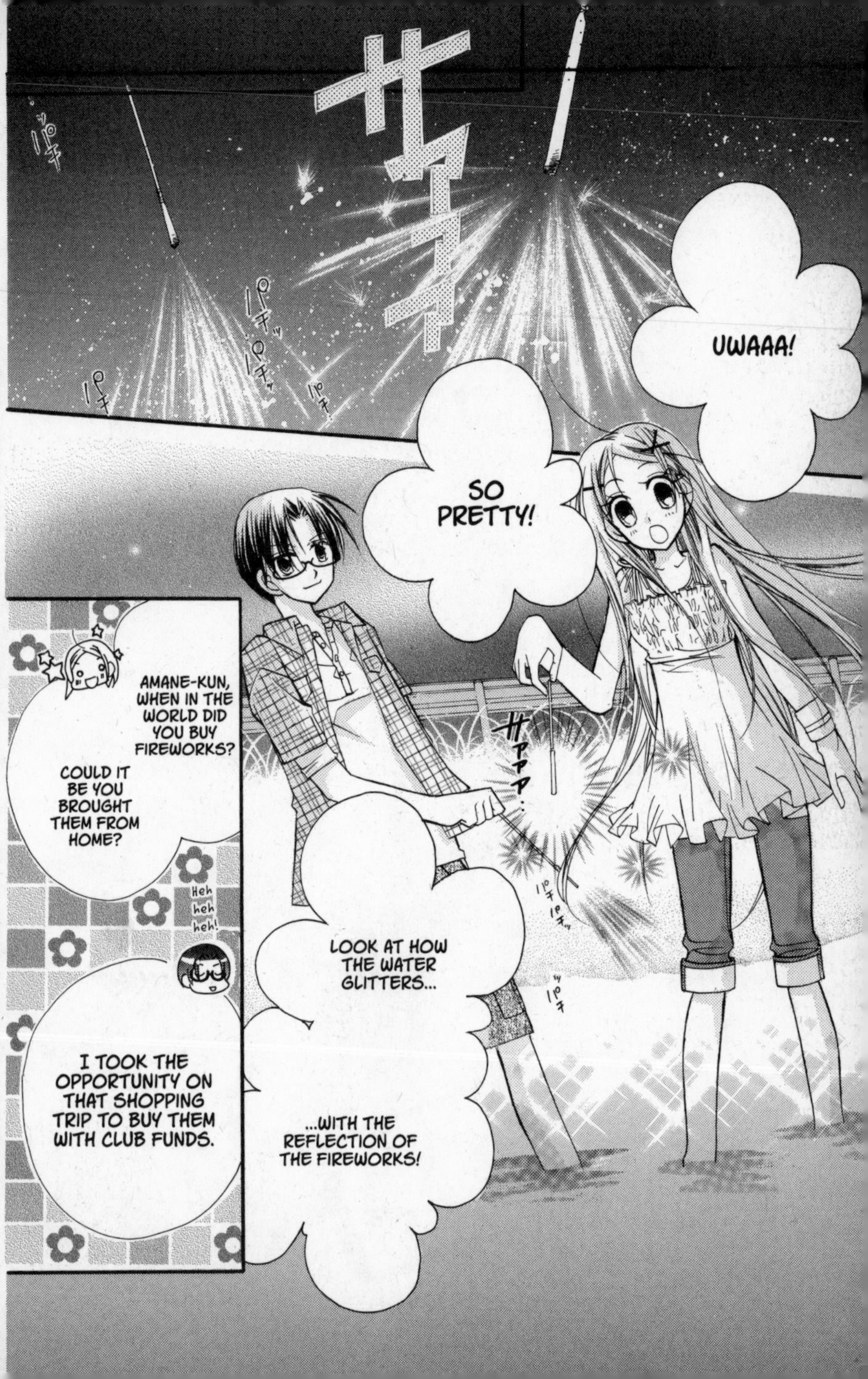
UWAAA!
SO PRETTY!
HPPP...
LOOK AT HOW THE WATER GLITTERS...
...WITH THE REFLECTION OF THE FIREWORKS!
AMANE-KUN, WHEN IN THE WORLD DID YOU BUY FIREWORKS?
COULD IT BE YOU BROUGHT THEM FROM HOME?
Heh heh heh!
I TOOK THE OPPORTUNITY ON THAT SHOPPING TRIP TO BUY THEM WITH CLUB FUNDS.

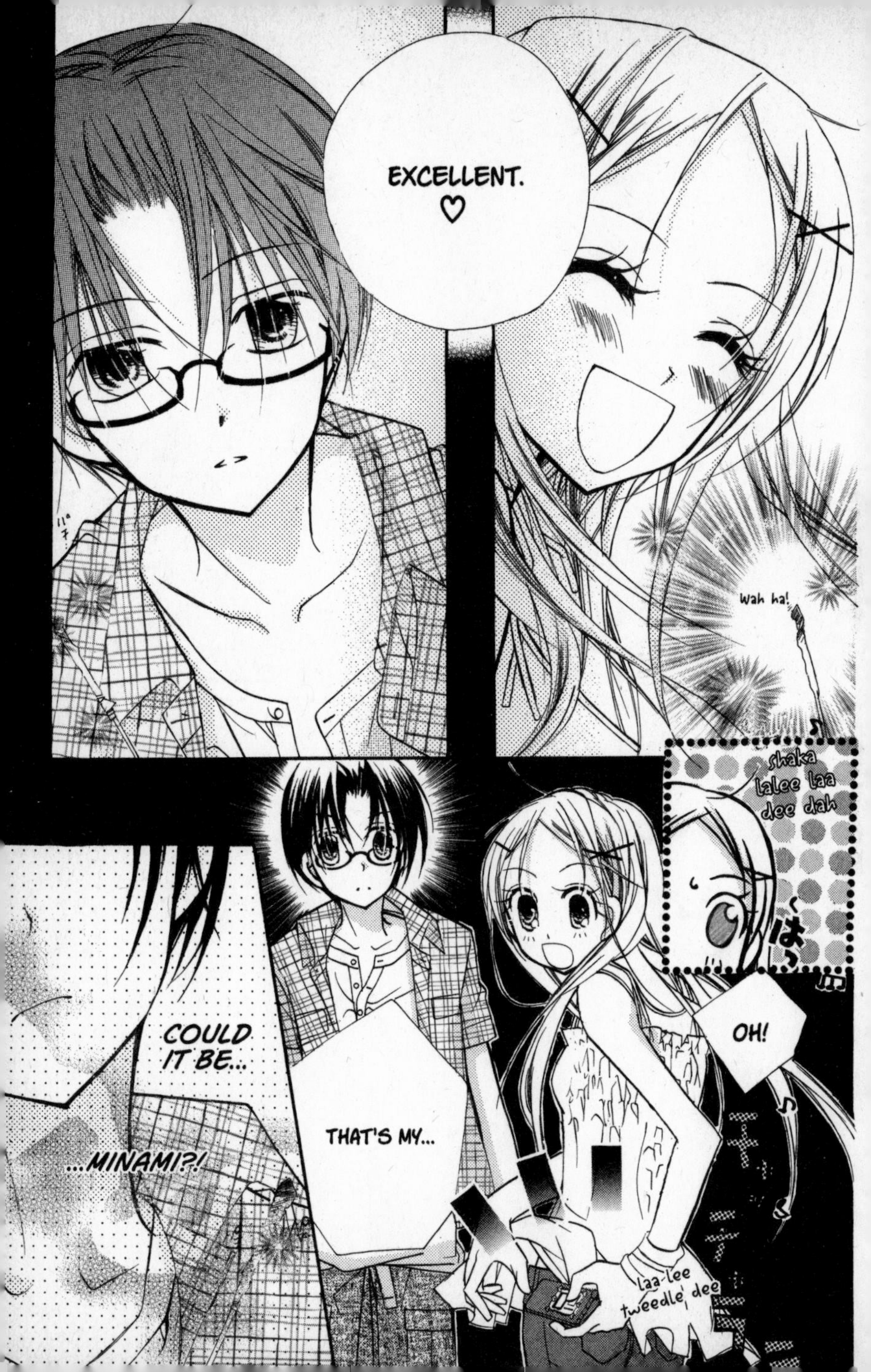
EXCELLENT. ♡
Wah ha!
shaka lalee laa dee dah
はっ
OH!
COULD IT BE...
THAT'S MY...
...MINAMI?!
laa-lee tweedle dee

ピッ
AIKO
HELLO!
IT'S AIKO. HOW'S TRAINING CAMP?! GETTING LOVEY-DOVEY WITH AMANE-KUN? NARU-CHAN AND I ARE AT MY HOUSE RIGHT NOW JUST EATING CURRY. WICKED HOT!
Wicked hot curry?
A...AIKO...?

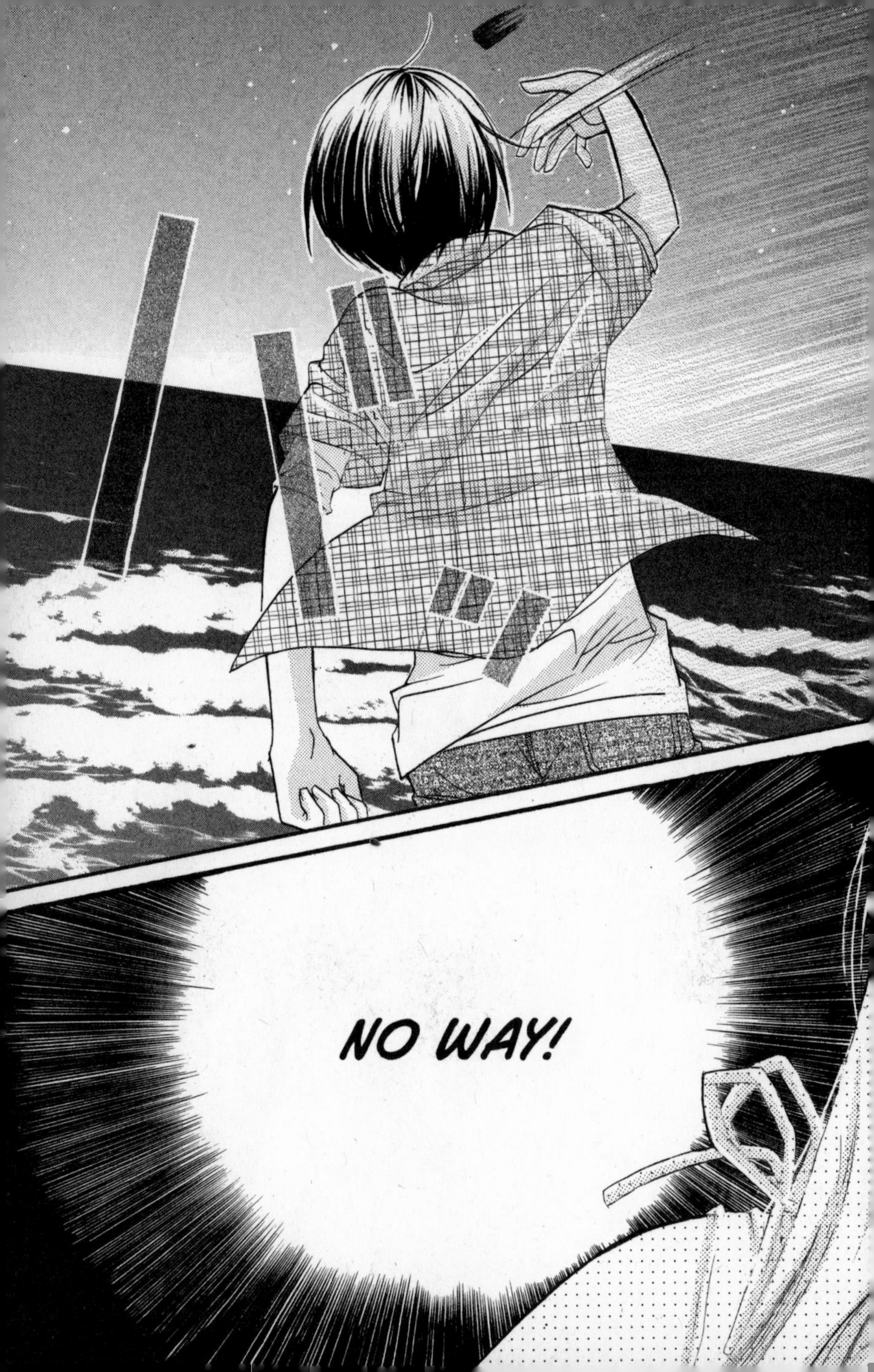
NO WAY!

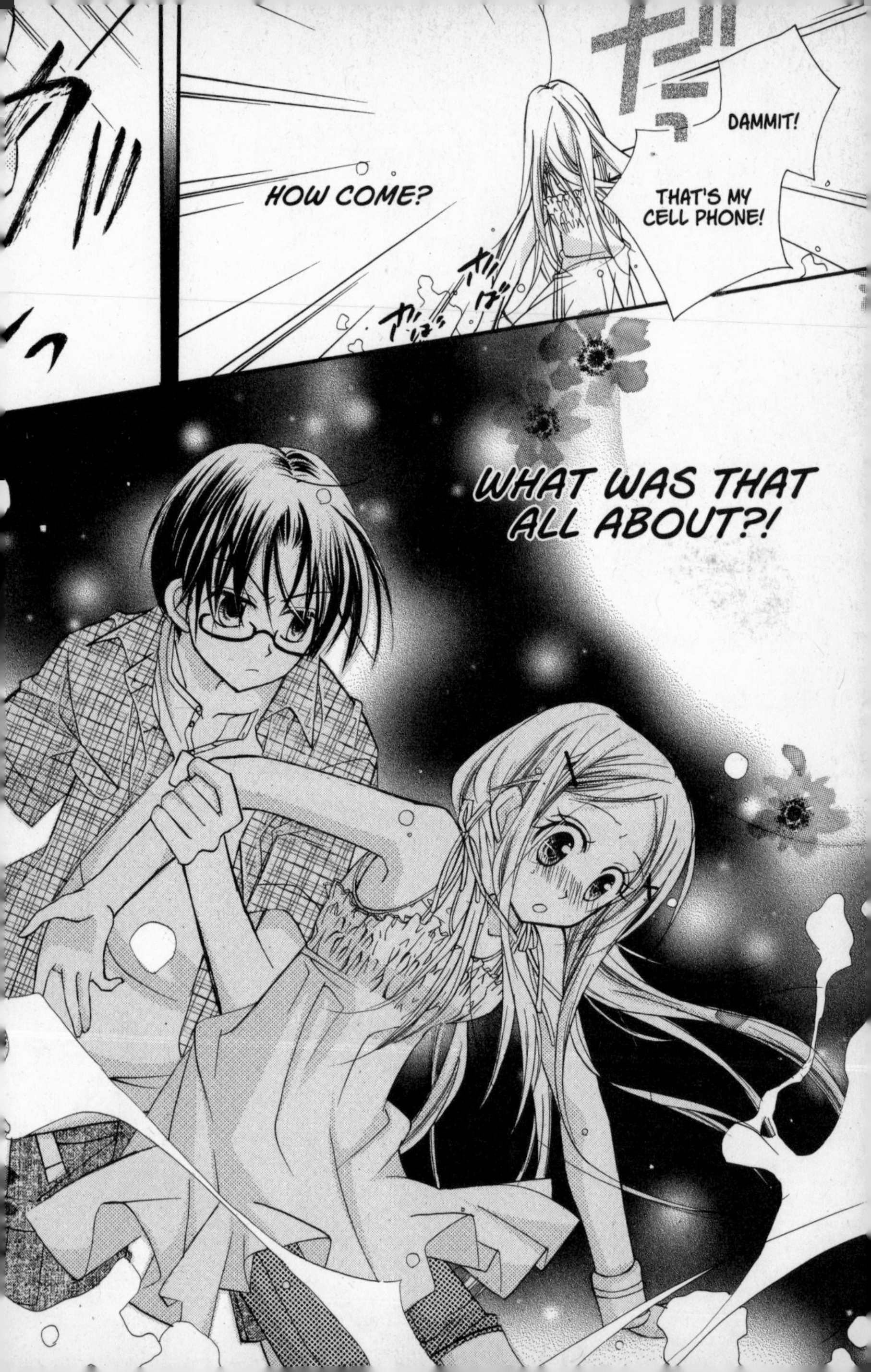
DAMMIT!
THAT'S MY CELL PHONE!
HOW COME?
WHAT WAS THAT ALL ABOUT?!

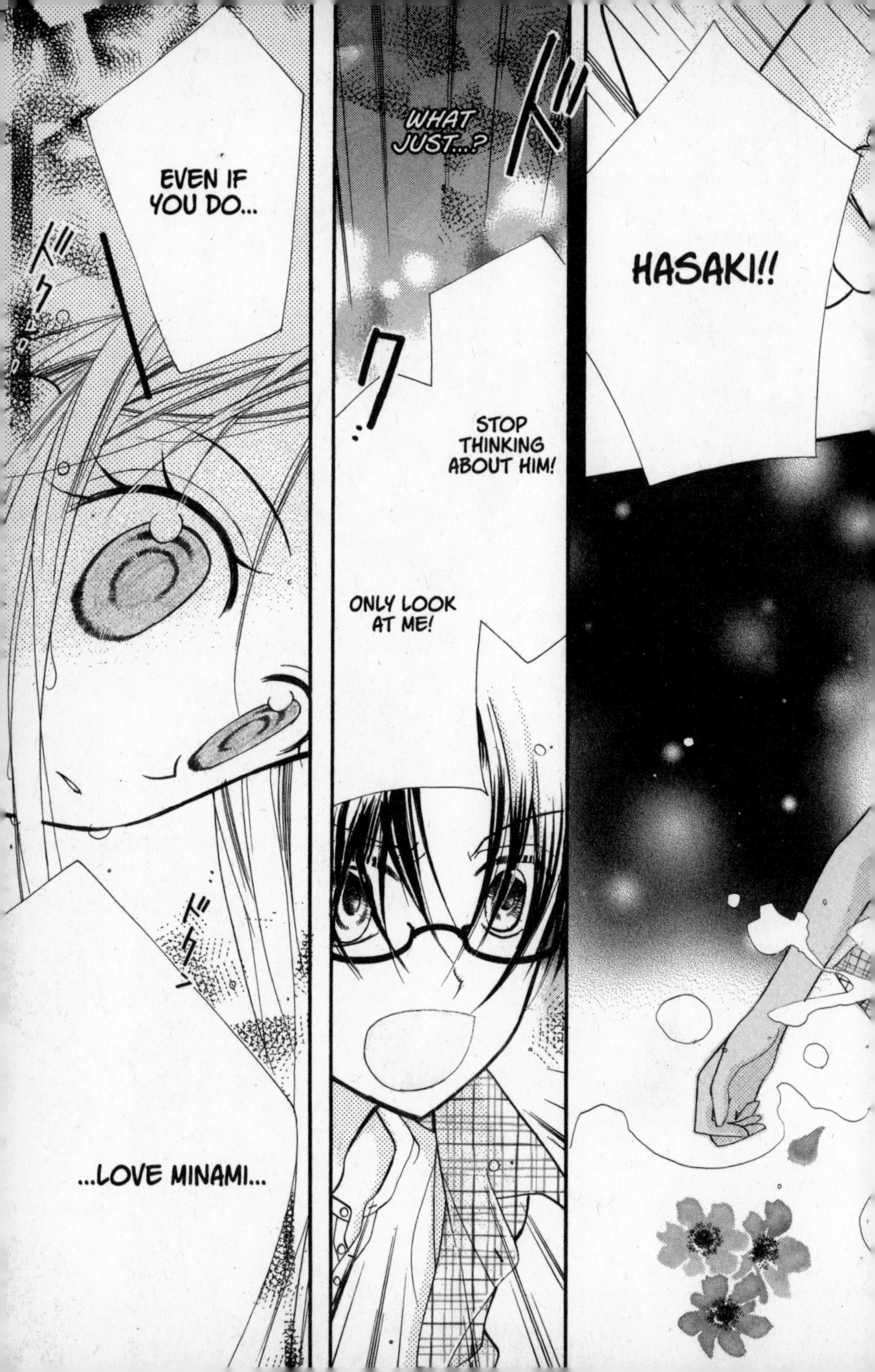
HASAKI!!
WHAT JUST...?
STOP THINKING ABOUT HIM!
ONLY LOOK AT ME!
EVEN IF YOU DO...
...LOVE MINAMI...

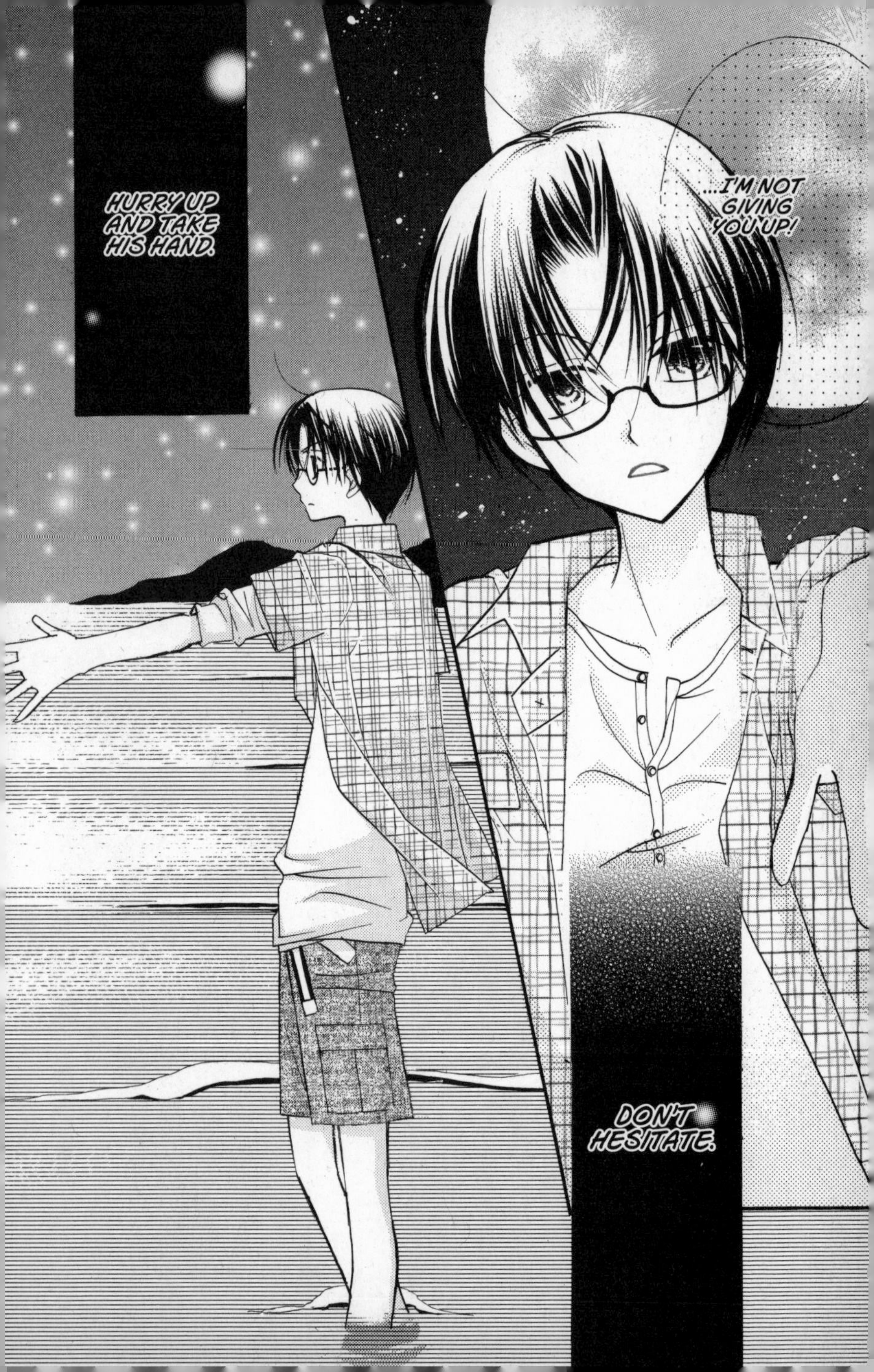
...I'M NOT GIVING YOU UP!
HURRY UP AND TAKE HIS HAND.
DON'T HESITATE.

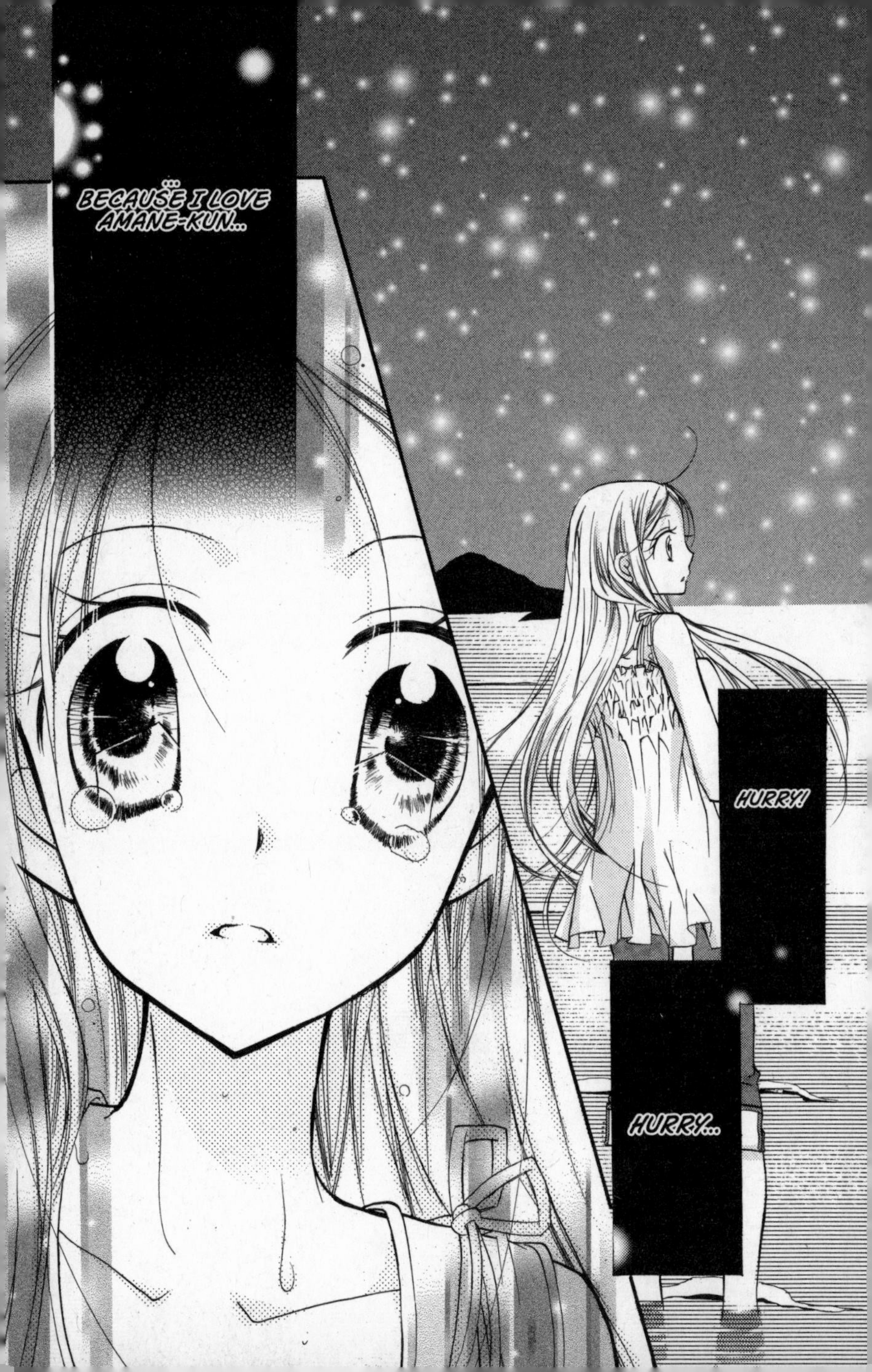
HURRY!
HURRY...
...BECAUSE I LOVE AMANE-KUN...

I am Fukushima, friend of Asumi Hara, aka Asumin, who draws the popular series "Tomodachi," which is presently (11/05) being serialized in Nakayoshi.

As a commemoration of the fact that this comic and volume 2 of her "Tomodachi" are being released on the same day, we have decided that we will each draw an illustration page to be published in each other's comic.

If you don't mind, please check out my illustration in volume 2 of "Tomodachi," okay?

And Asumin's HOT illustration is on page 108! GO!

Asumin and Me!

Our meeting place is...
...Ikebukuro.
YAY!
Whenever we go, we take pictures...
...go to karaoke...
...and chill...
...at a...
...burger joint....
You two haven't finished your storyboards yet, have you?
Yeeeeek!!
Zusshi's here!

This happens every time I go up to Tokyo.

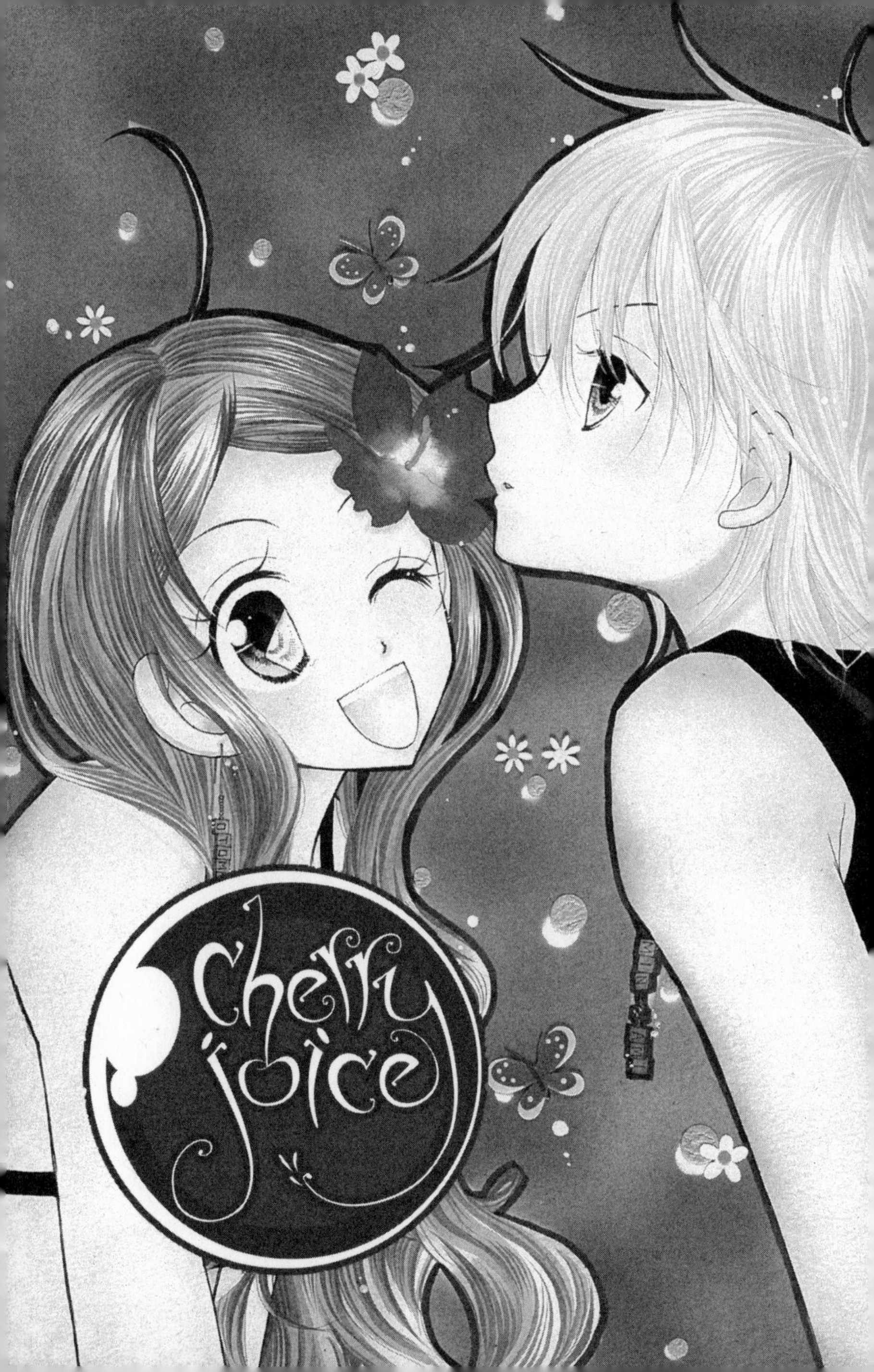
Cherry Juice

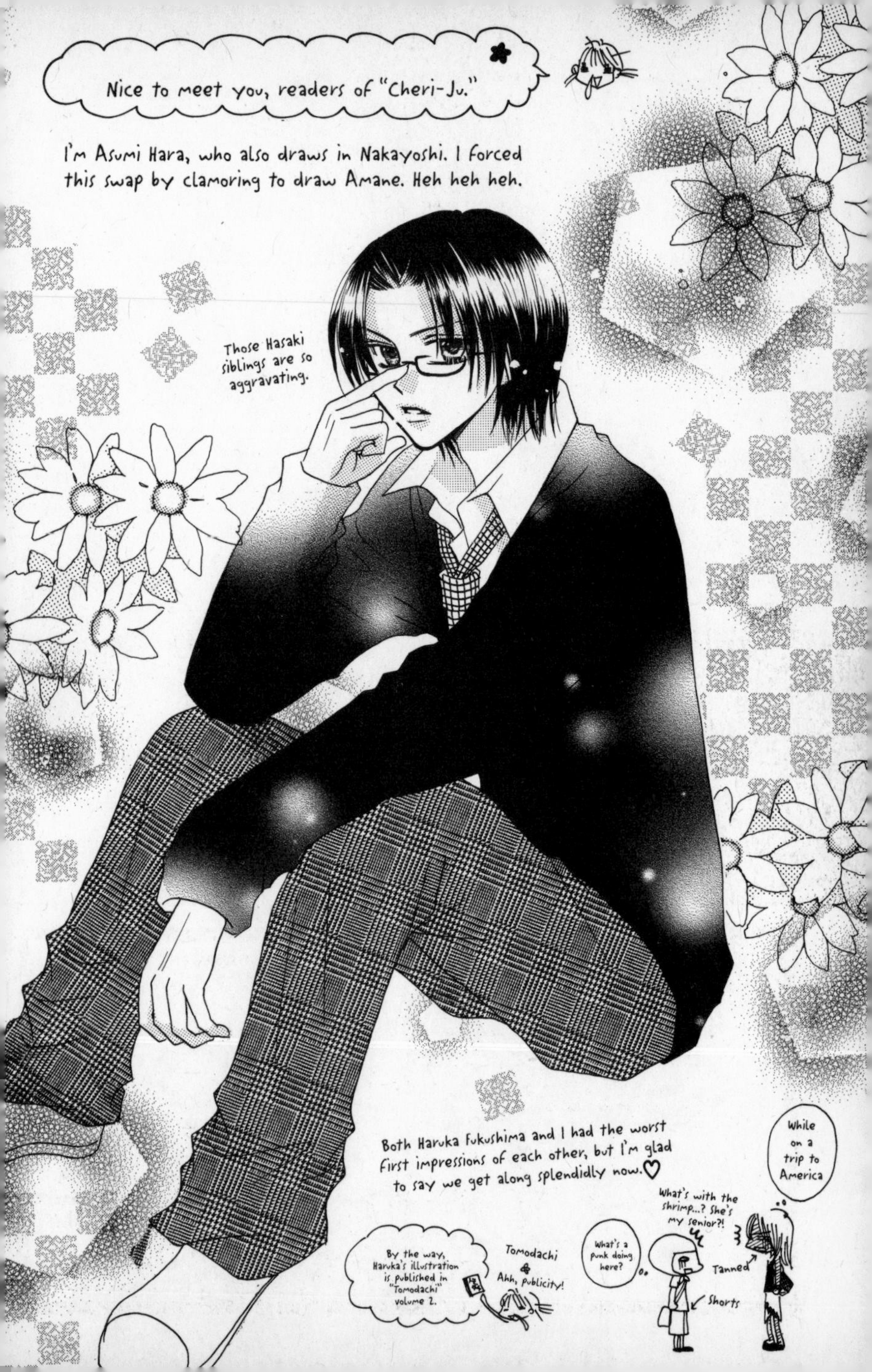
Nice to meet you, readers of "Cheri-Ju."
I'm Asumi Hara, who also draws in Nakayoshi. I forced this swap by clamoring to draw Amane. Heh heh heh.
Those Hasaki siblings are so aggravating.
Both Haruka Fukushima and I had the worst first impressions of each other, but I'm glad to say we get along splendidly now.♡
While on a trip to America
What's with the shrimp...? She's my senior?!
Tanned
What's a punk doing here?
Shorts
Tomodachi
Ahh, publicity!
By the way, Haruka's illustration is published in "Tomodachi" volume 2.

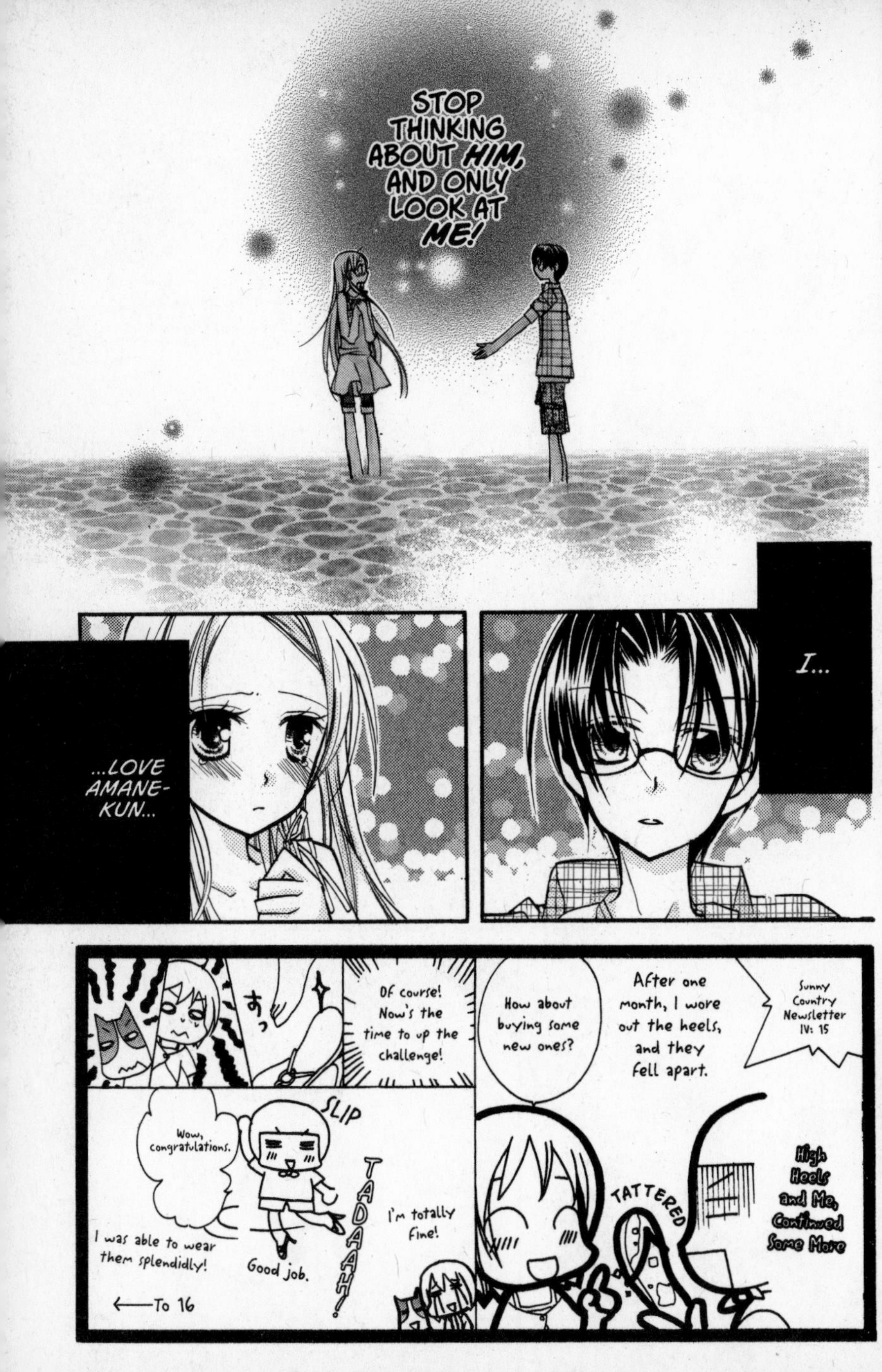
STOP THINKING ABOUT HIM, AND ONLY LOOK AT ME!
I...
...LOVE AMANE-KUN...
Sunny Country Newsletter IV: 15
High Heels and Me, Continued Some More
After one month, I wore out the heels, and they fell apart.
How about buying some new ones?
TATTERED
Of course! Now's the time to up the challenge!
すっ
SLIP
TADAAAH!
I'm totally fine!
Wow, congratulations.
Good job.
I was able to wear them splendidly!
←To 16

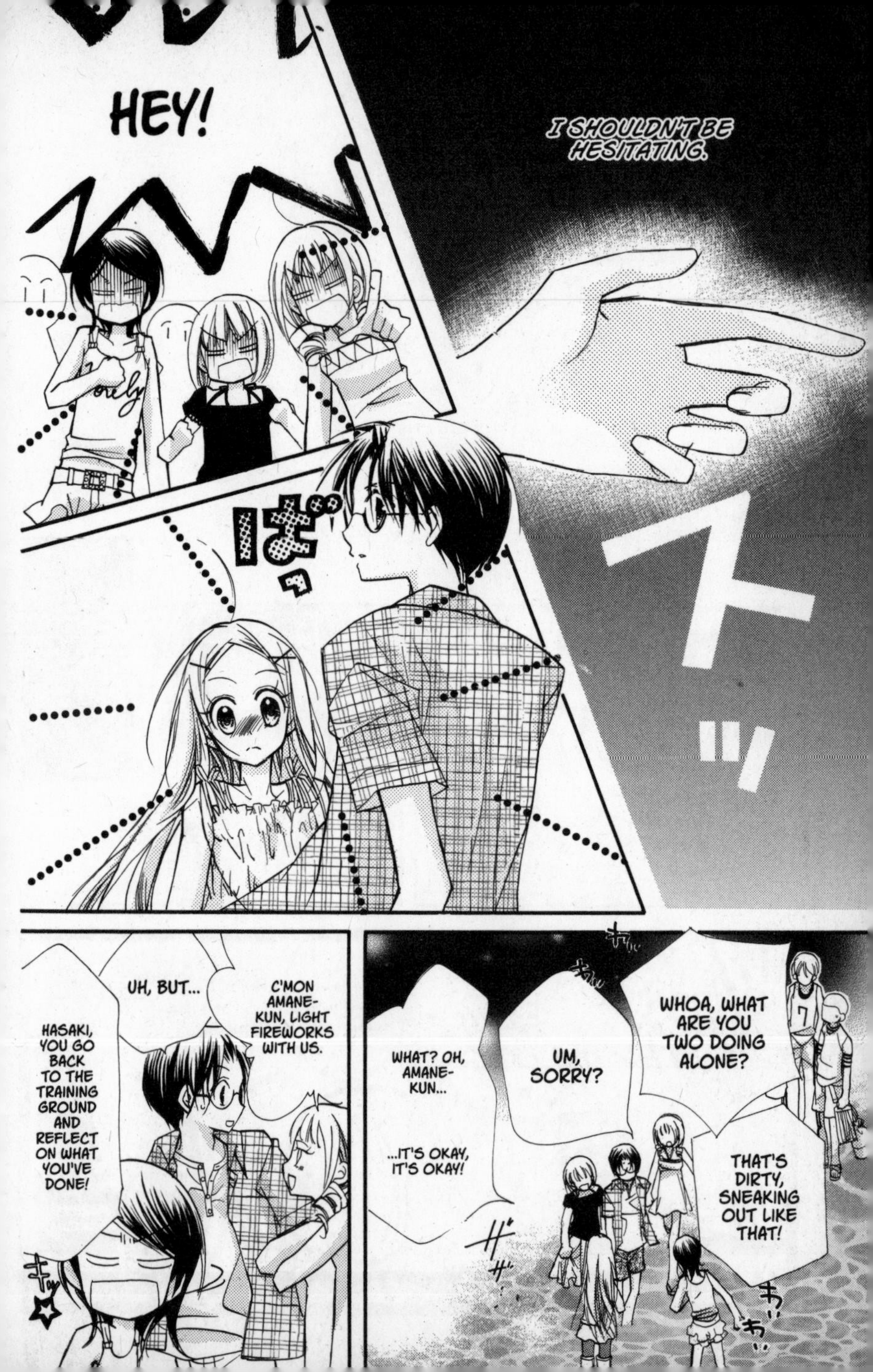
I SHOULDN'T BE HESITATING.
スッ
HEY!
....
ぽっ
WHOA, WHAT ARE YOU TWO DOING ALONE?
THAT'S DIRTY, SNEAKING OUT LIKE THAT!
UM, SORRY?
WHAT? OH, AMANE-KUN...
...IT'S OKAY, IT'S OKAY!
C'MON AMANE-KUN, LIGHT FIREWORKS WITH US.
UH, BUT...
HASAKI, YOU GO BACK TO THE TRAINING GROUND AND REFLECT ON WHAT YOU'VE DONE!

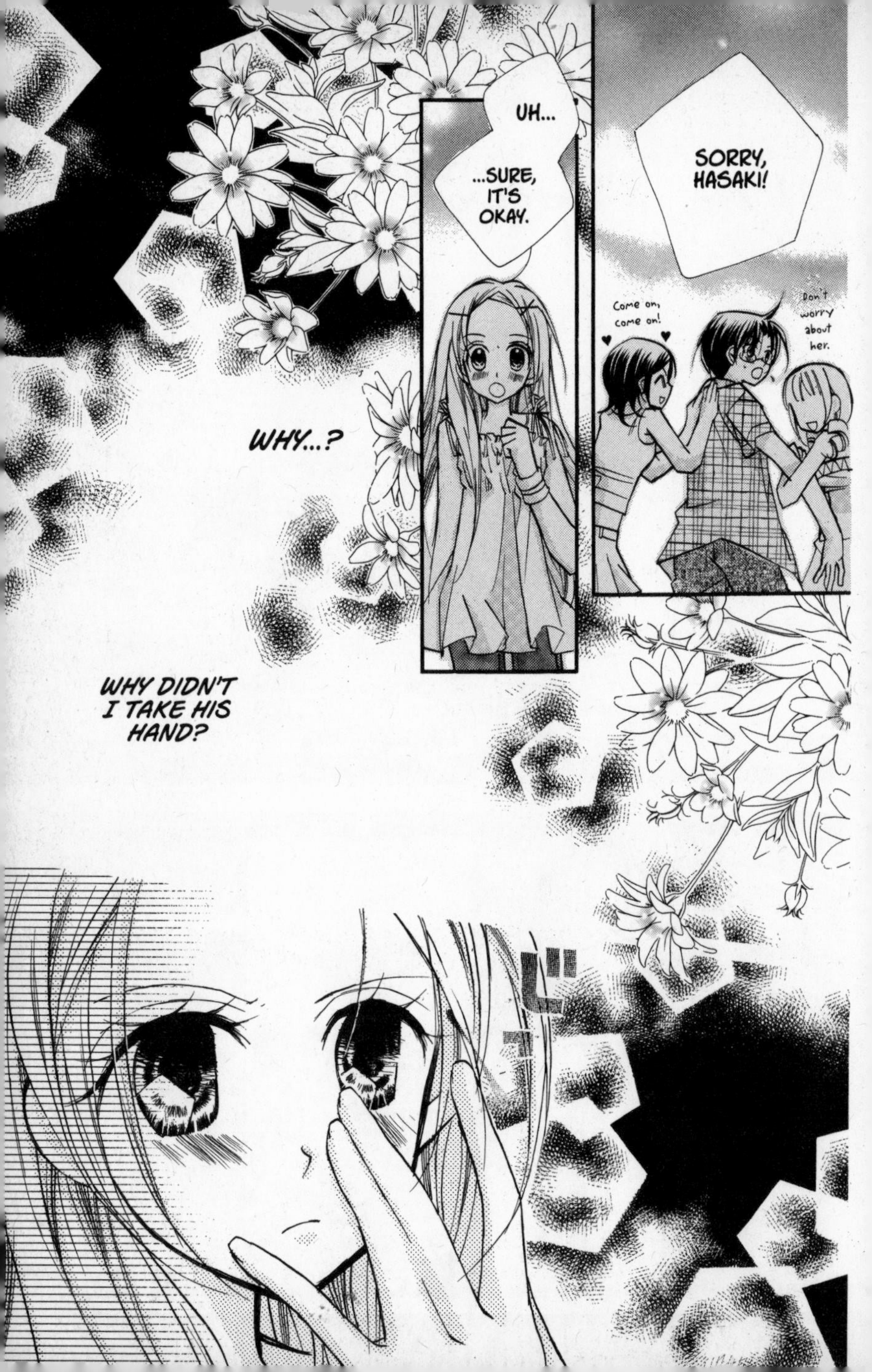
SORRY, HASAKI!
Don't worry about her.
Come on, come on!
UH...
...SURE, IT'S OKAY.
WHY...?
WHY DIDN'T I TAKE HIS HAND?

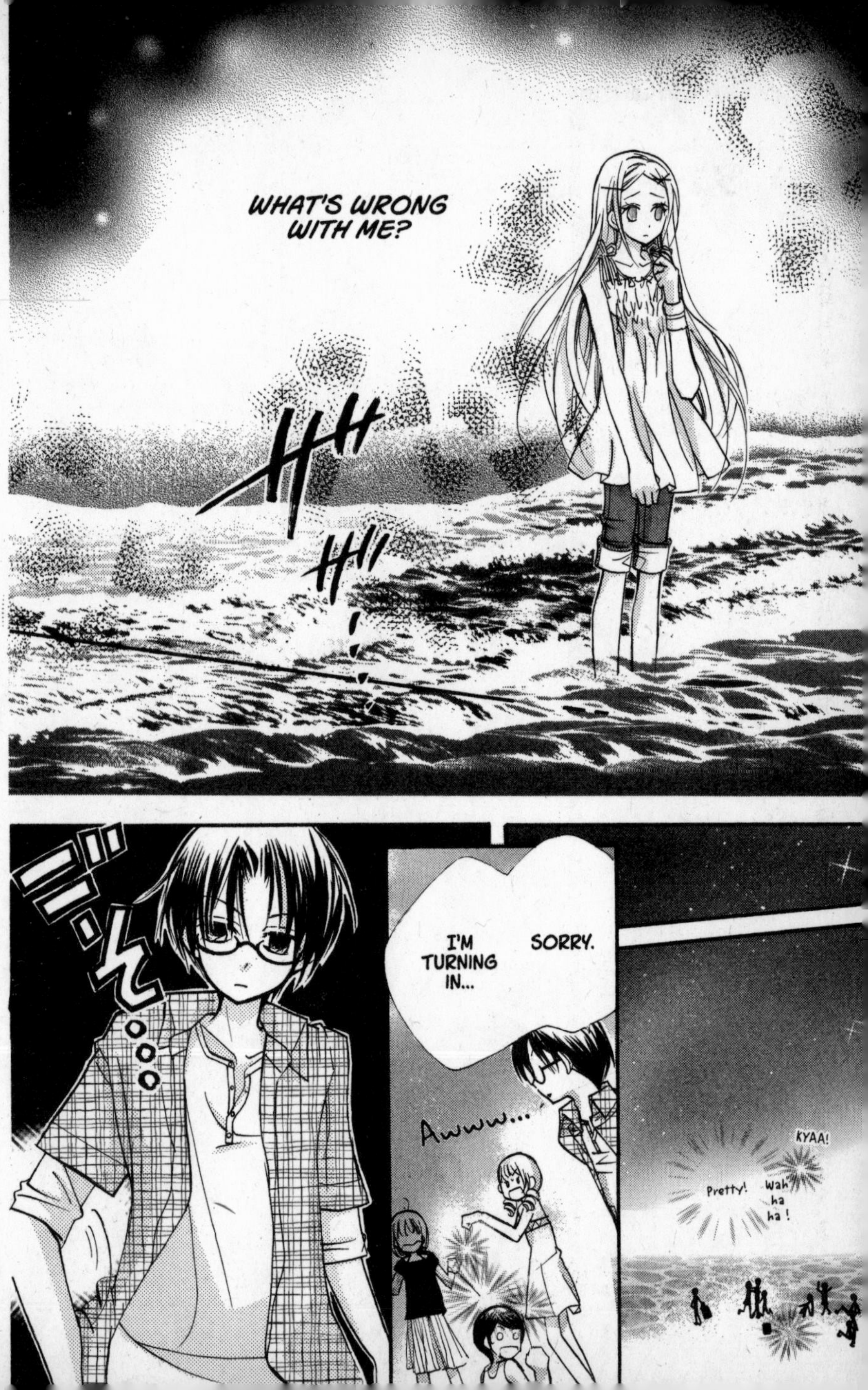
WHAT'S WRONG WITH ME?
KYAA!
Pretty!
Wah ha ha!
SORRY.
I'M TURNING IN...
Awww...

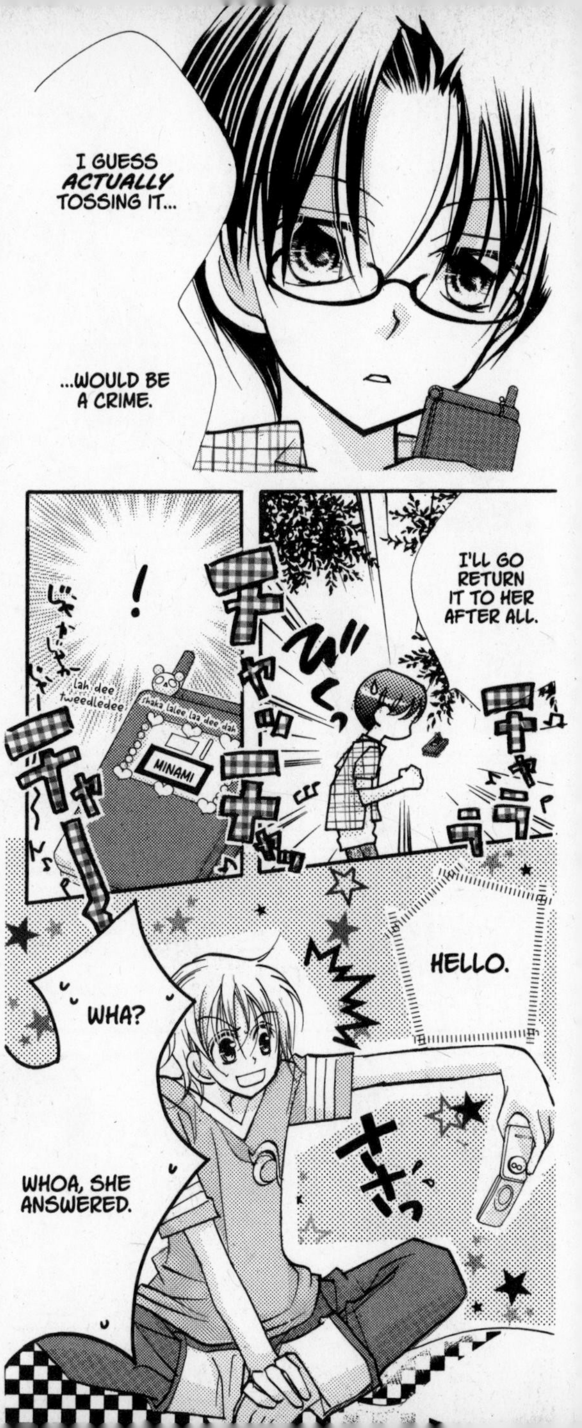
I GUESS *ACTUALLY* TOSSING IT...
...WOULD BE A CRIME.
I'LL GO RETURN IT TO HER AFTER ALL.
!
lah dee tweedledee
shaka lalee laa dee dah
MINAMI
HELLO.
WHA?
WHOA, SHE ANSWERED.

SIX

In this volume, the summer uniforms have snuck in.

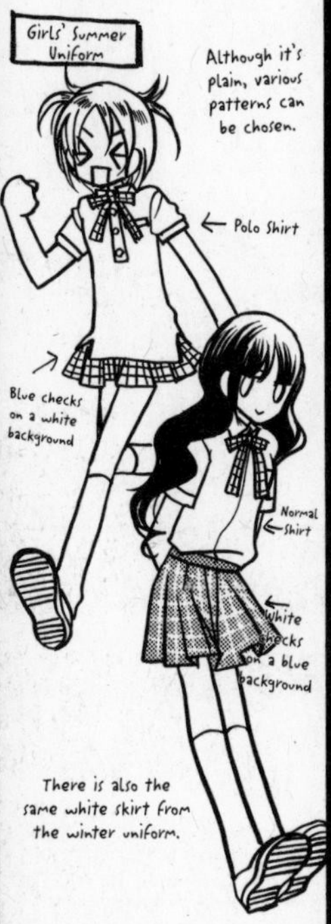
Girls' Summer Uniform
Although it's plain, various patterns can be chosen.
Polo Shirt
Blue checks on a white background
Normal Shirt
White checks on a blue background

There is also the same white skirt from the winter uniform.

The checks are blue, but the other day, I saw some girls wearing uniforms with brown checks. Brown checks are nice, too.

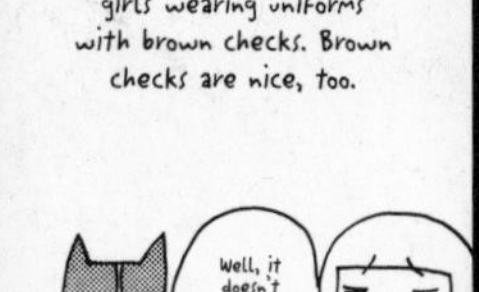
Well, it doesn't matter in black and white...

To SEVEN

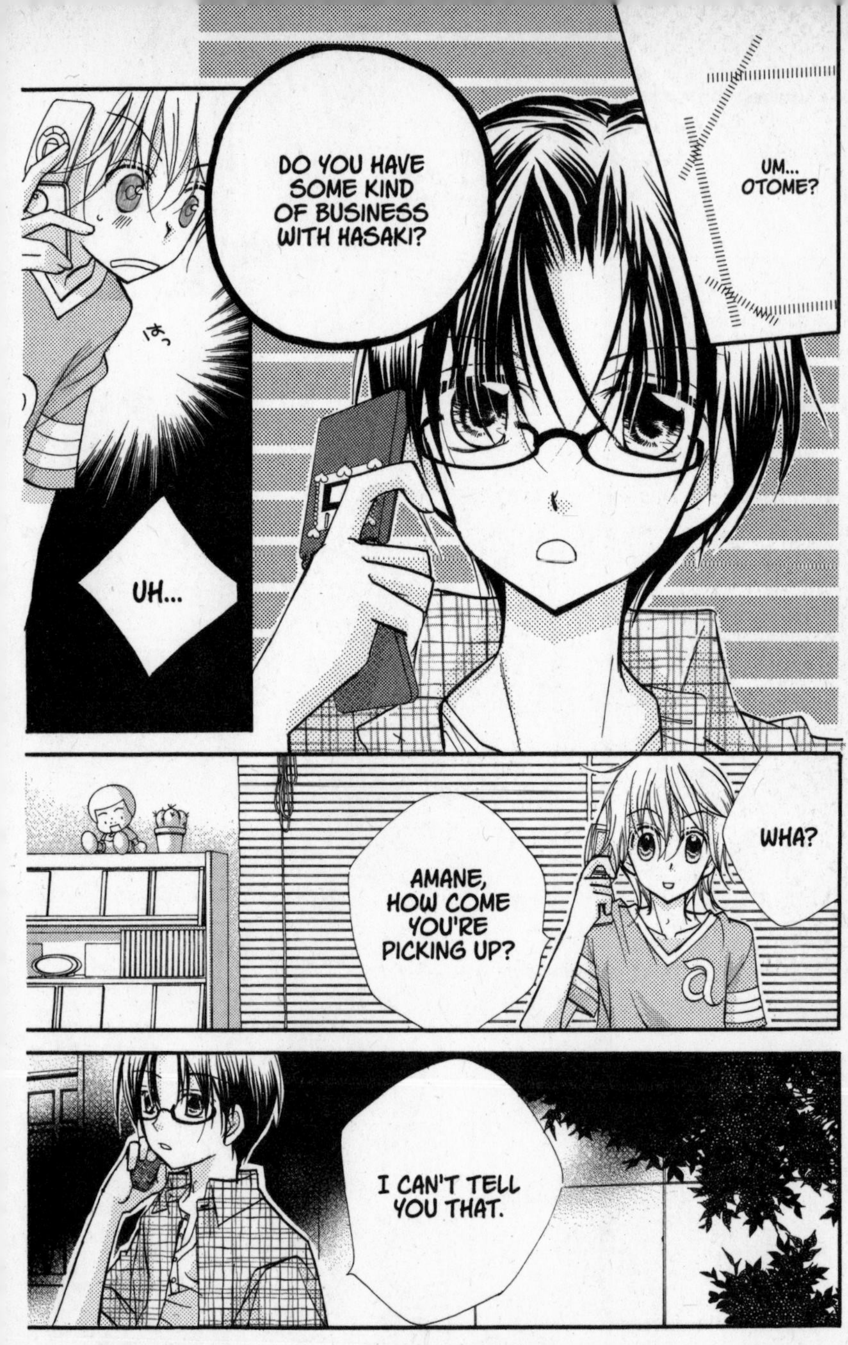
UM... OTOME?
DO YOU HAVE SOME KIND OF BUSINESS WITH HASAKI?
はっ
UH...
WHA?
AMANE, HOW COME YOU'RE PICKING UP?
I CAN'T TELL YOU THAT.

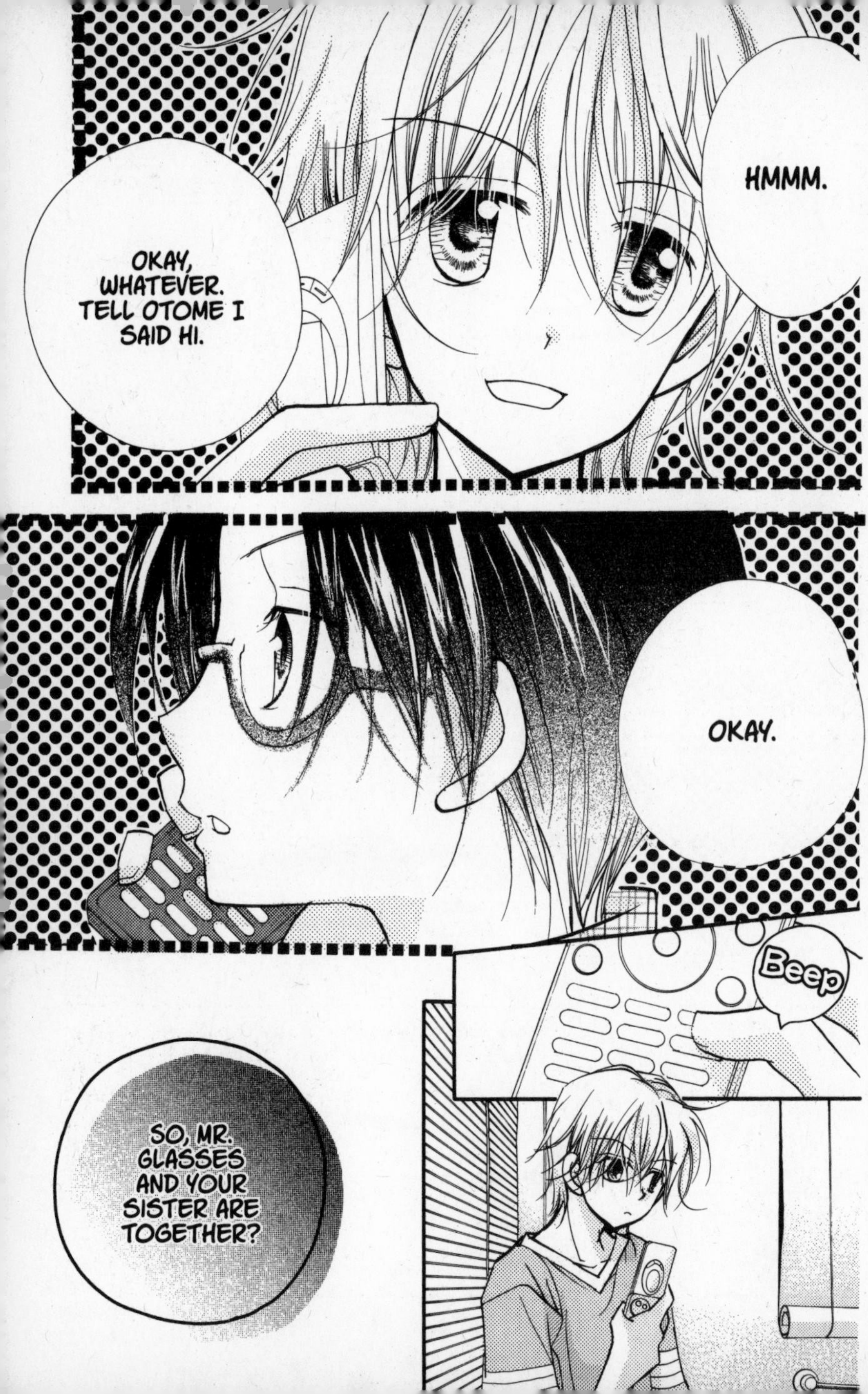
HMMM.
OKAY, WHATEVER. TELL OTOME I SAID HI.
OKAY.
Beep
SO, MR. GLASSES AND YOUR SISTER ARE TOGETHER?

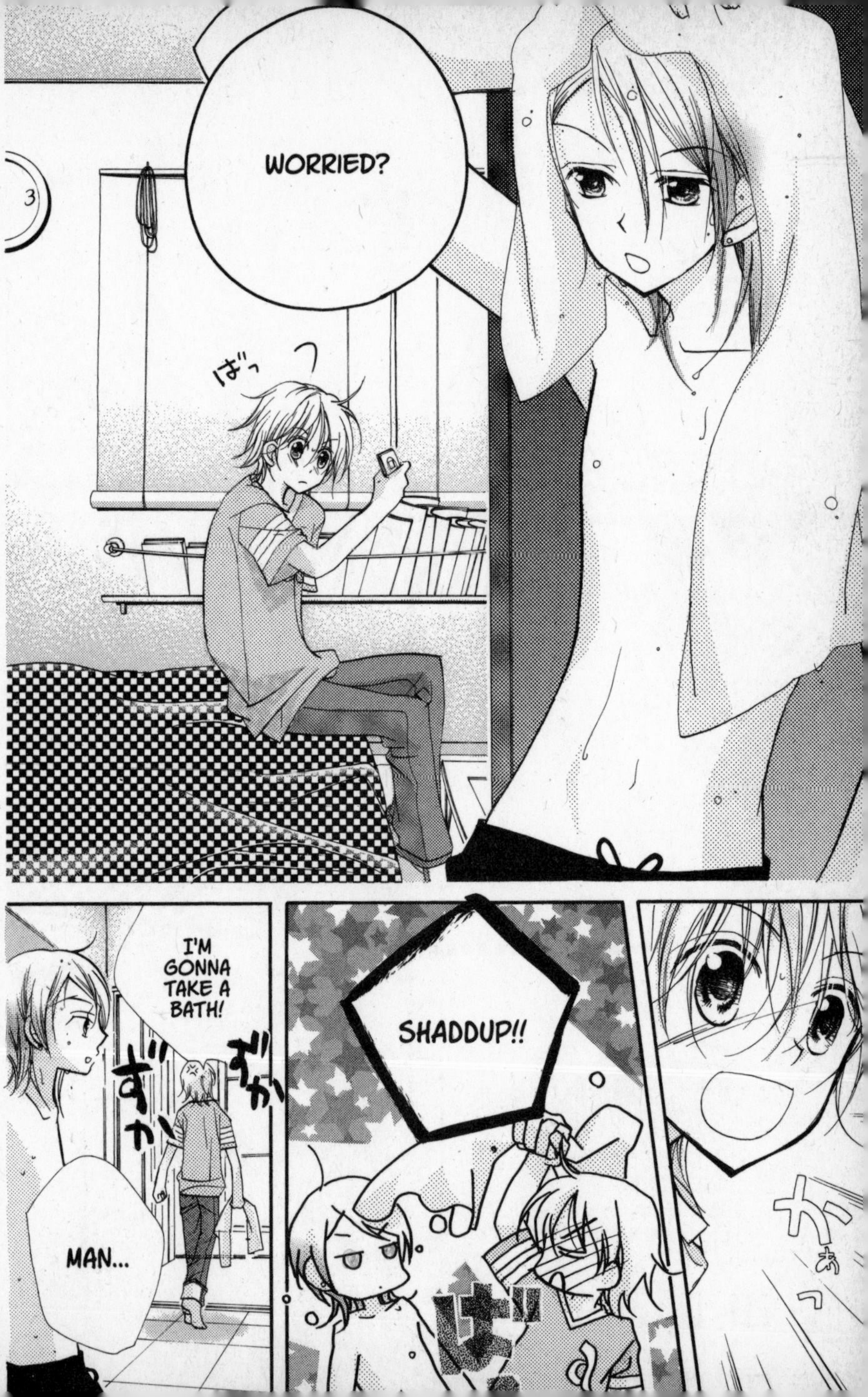
WORRIED?
ばっ
カぁっ
SHADDUP!!
I'M GONNA TAKE A BATH!
ずかずか
MAN...

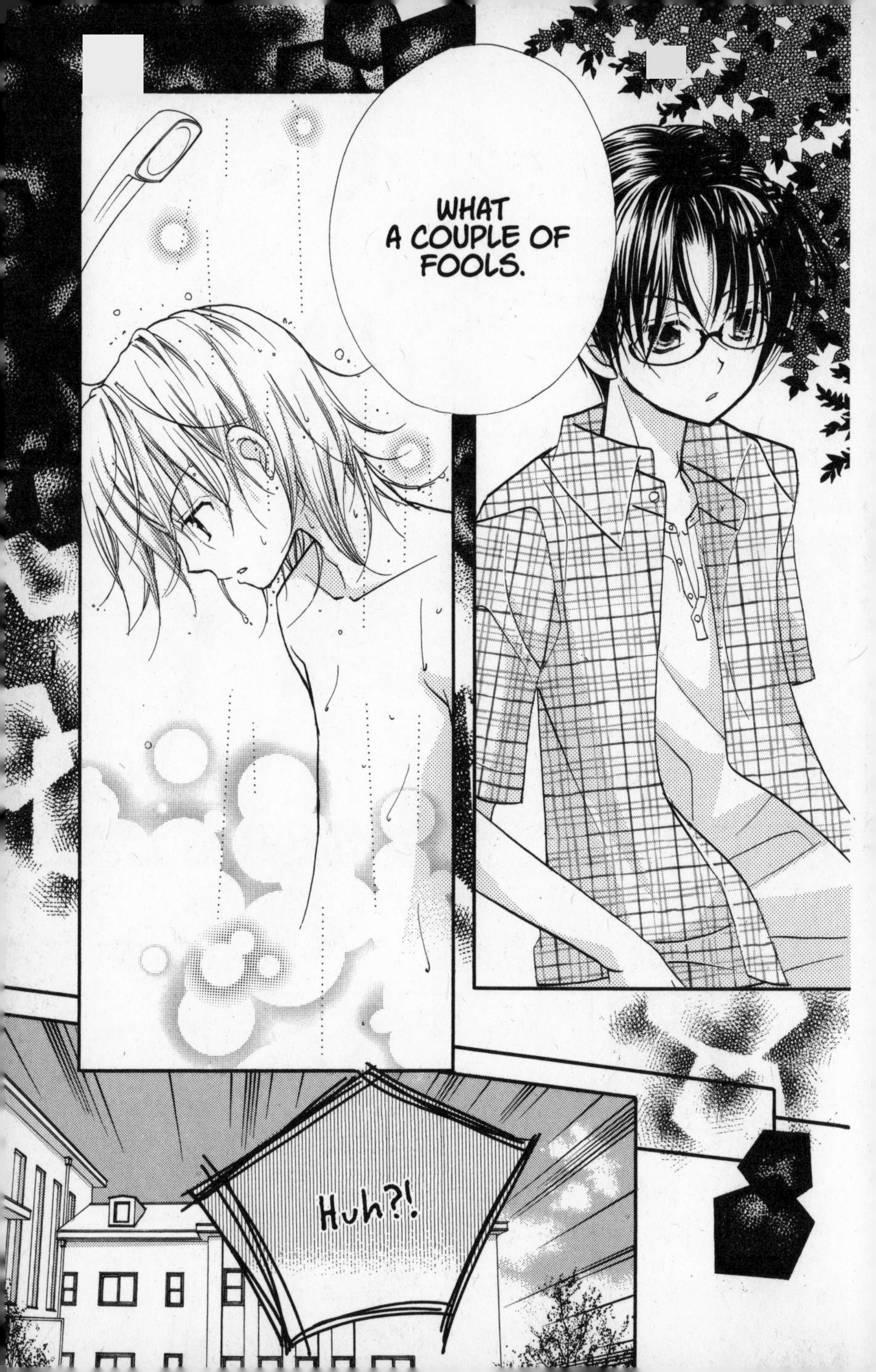
WHAT A COUPLE OF FOOLS.
Huh?!

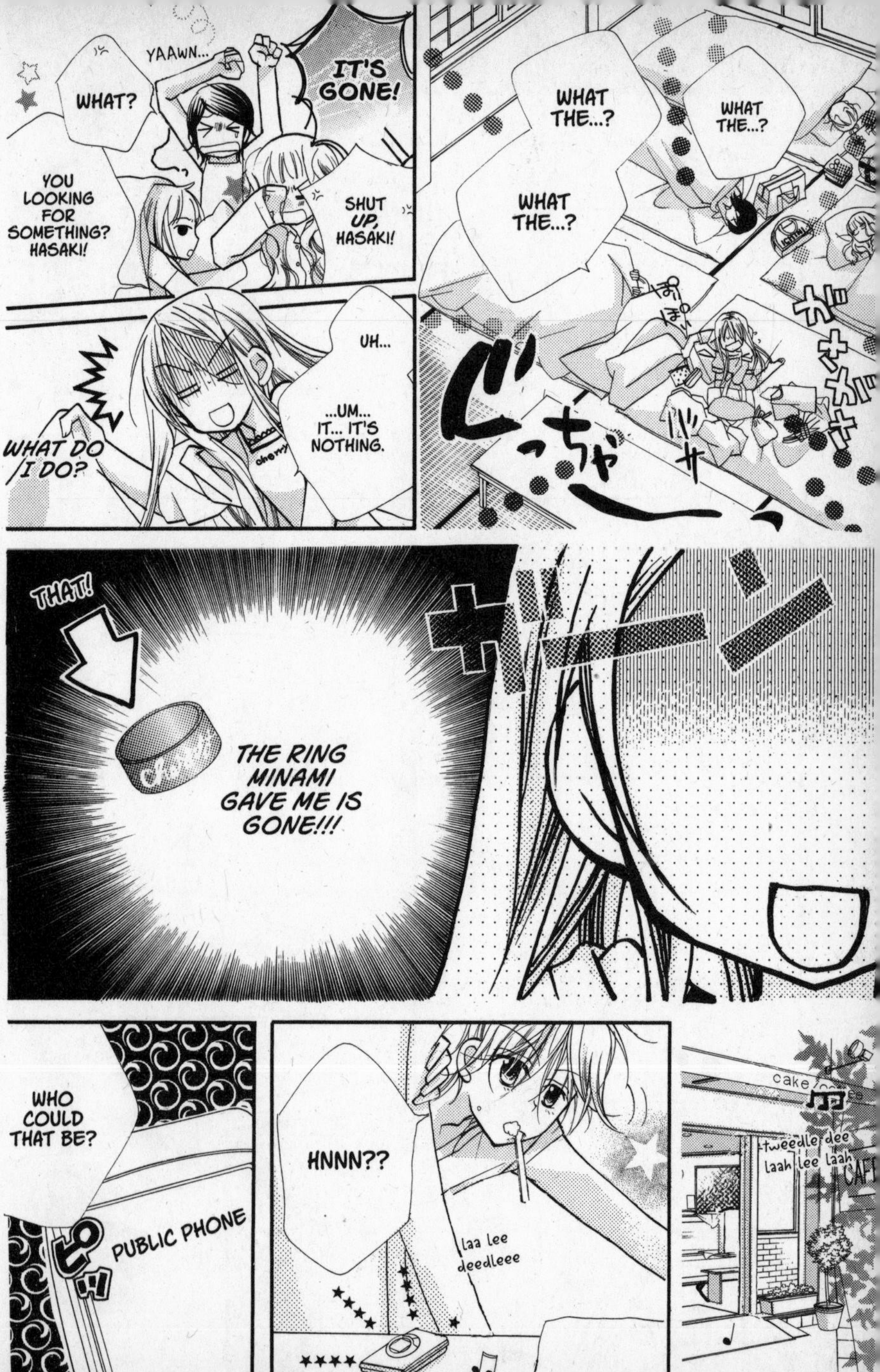
WHAT THE...?
WHAT THE...?
WHAT THE...?
IT'S GONE!
YAAWN...
WHAT?
SHUT UP, HASAKI!
YOU LOOKING FOR SOMETHING? HASAKI!
UH...
...UM... IT... IT'S NOTHING.
WHAT DO I DO?
THAT!
THE RING MINAMI GAVE ME IS GONE!!!
tweedle dee laah lee laah
HNNN??
laa lee deedleee
WHO COULD THAT BE?
PUBLIC PHONE

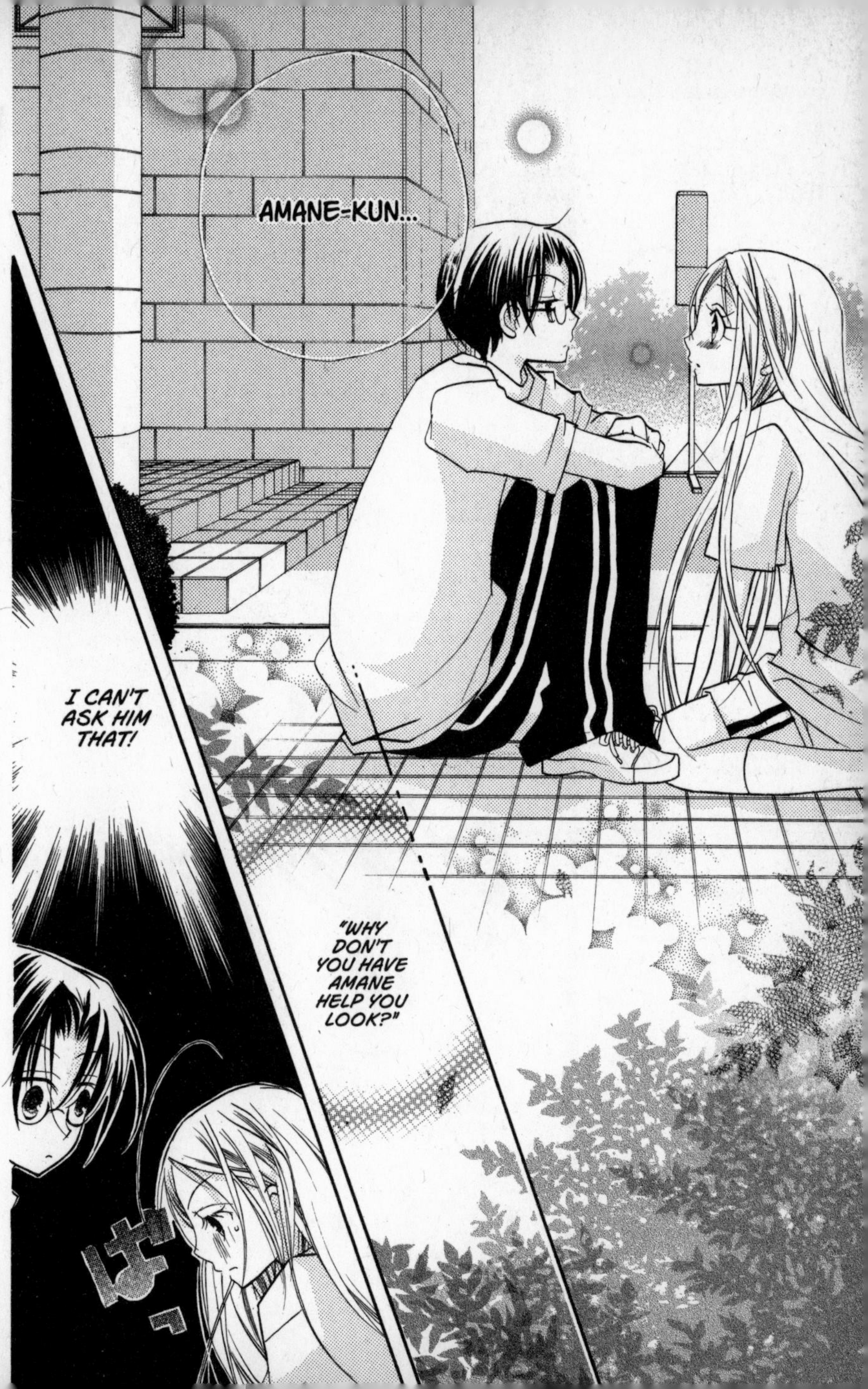
AMANE-KUN...
"WHY DON'T YOU HAVE AMANE HELP YOU LOOK?"
I CAN'T ASK HIM THAT!

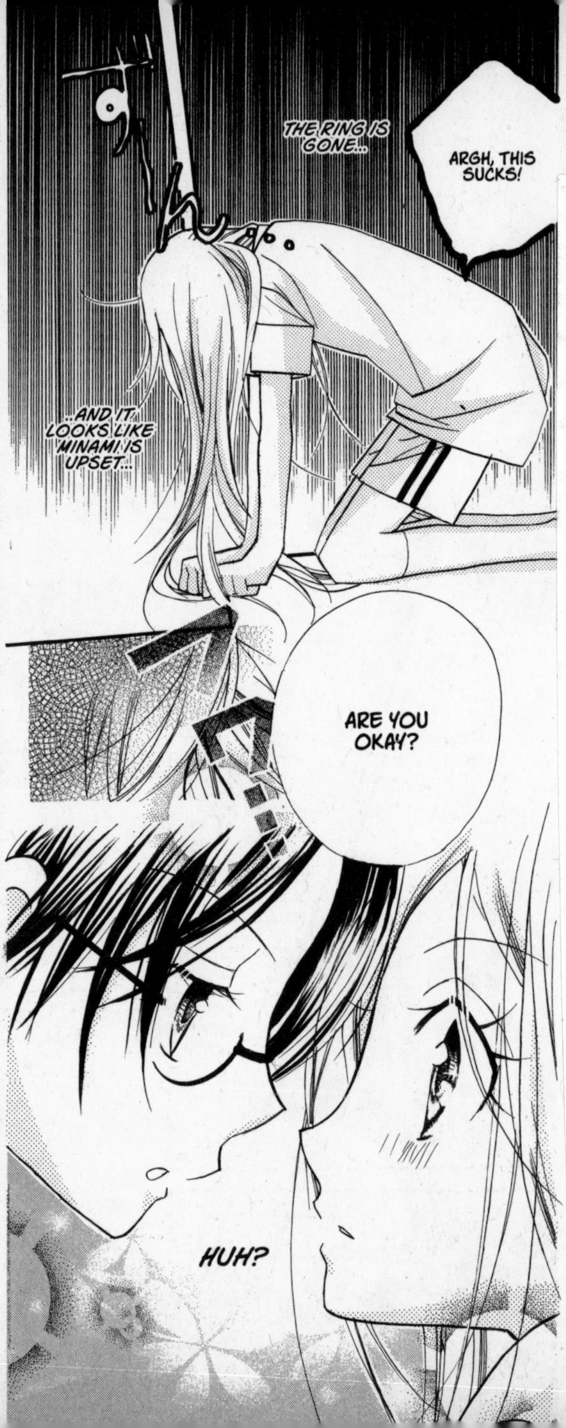
ARGH, THIS SUCKS!
THE RING IS GONE...
...AND IT LOOKS LIKE MINAMI IS UPSET...
ARE YOU OKAY?
HUH?

SEVEN

Come to think of it, Hokuto wears the uniform however he pleases.

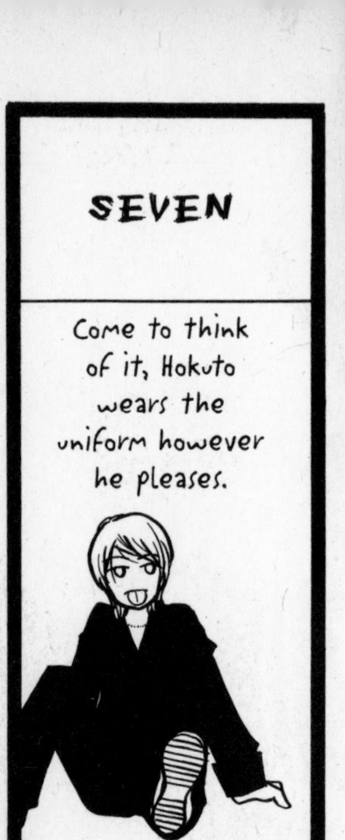

Generally, a different-colored shirt and no necktie....

In my high school days, it was popular to secretly buy and wear shirts slightly different from the school, designated ones, too.

← To EIGHT

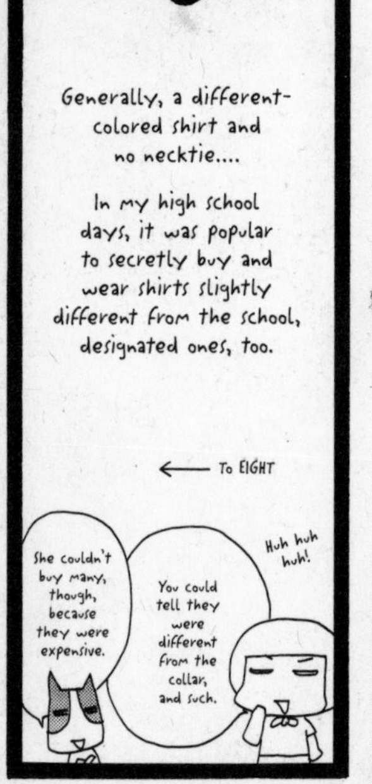
Huh huh huh!
You could tell they were different from the collar, and such.
She couldn't buy many, though, because they were expensive.

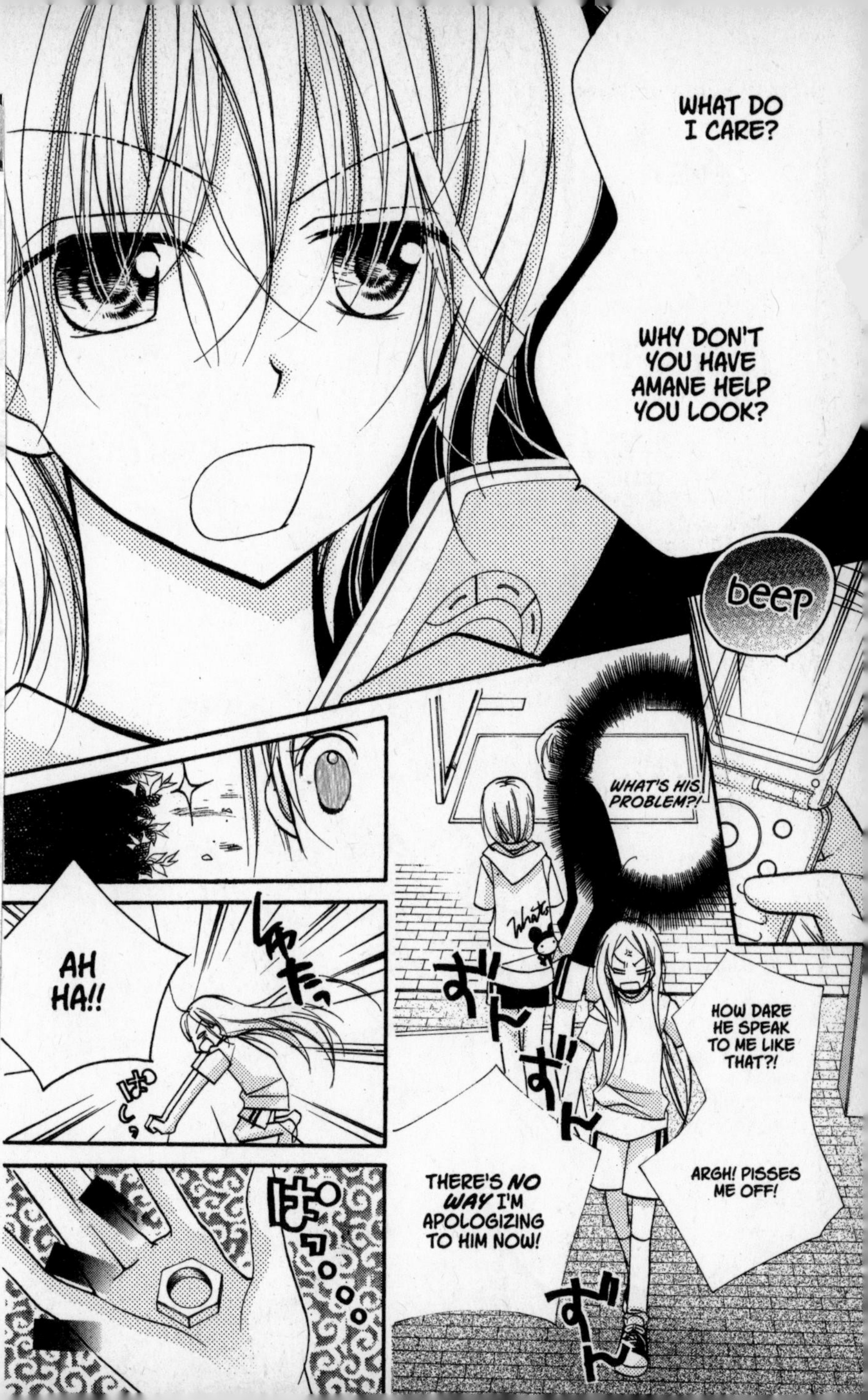
WHAT DO I CARE?
WHY DON'T YOU HAVE AMANE HELP YOU LOOK?
beep
WHAT'S HIS PROBLEM?!
HOW DARE HE SPEAK TO ME LIKE THAT?!
ずん
ずん
ARGH! PISSES ME OFF!
THERE'S *NO WAY* I'M APOLOGIZING TO HIM NOW!
ずん
AH HA!!
しゅたっ
ぱしっ
ぱっ

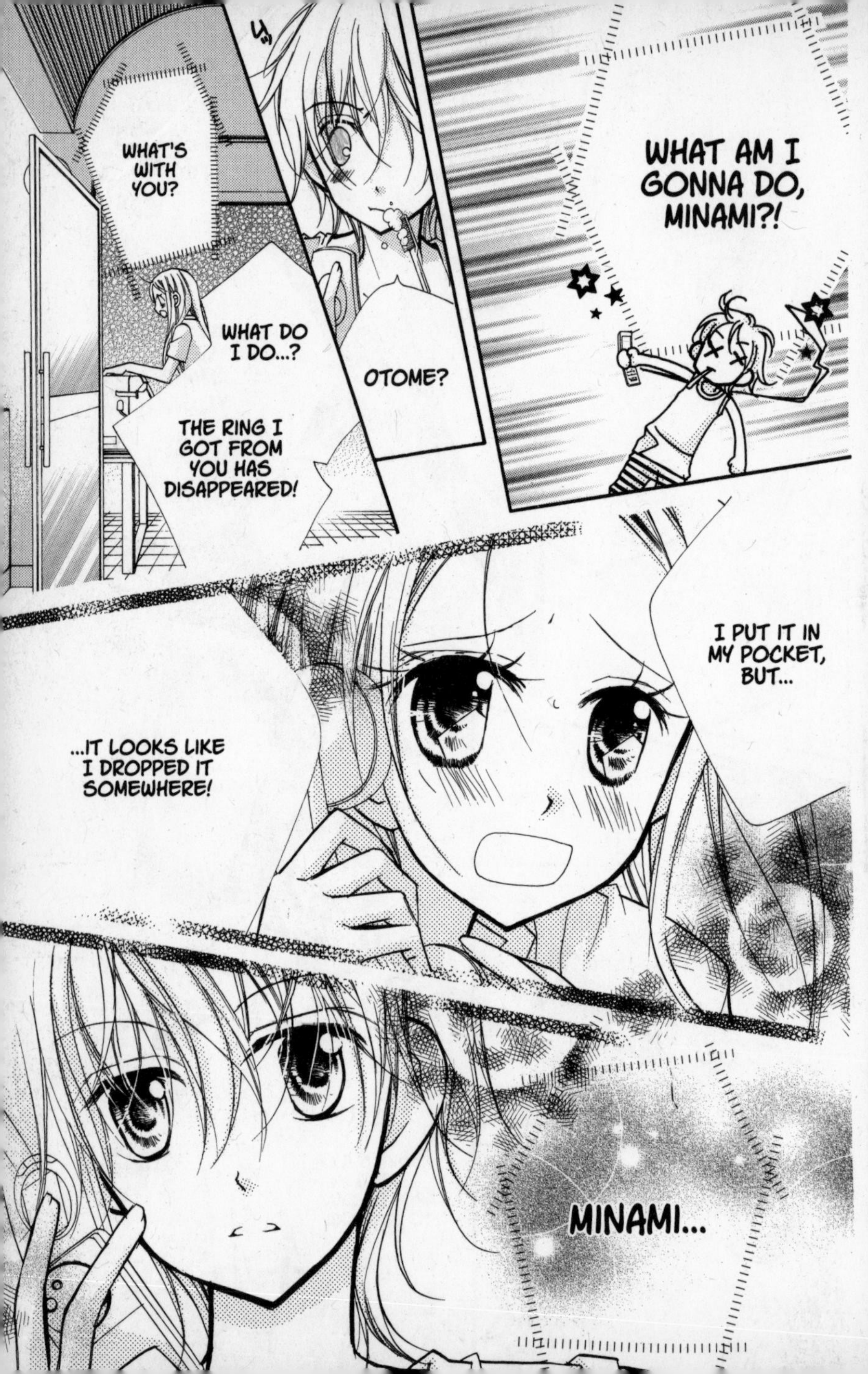
WHAT AM I GONNA DO, MINAMI?!
OTOME?
WHAT'S WITH YOU?
WHAT DO I DO...?
THE RING I GOT FROM YOU HAS DISAPPEARED!
I PUT IT IN MY POCKET, BUT...
...IT LOOKS LIKE I DROPPED IT SOMEWHERE!
MINAMI...

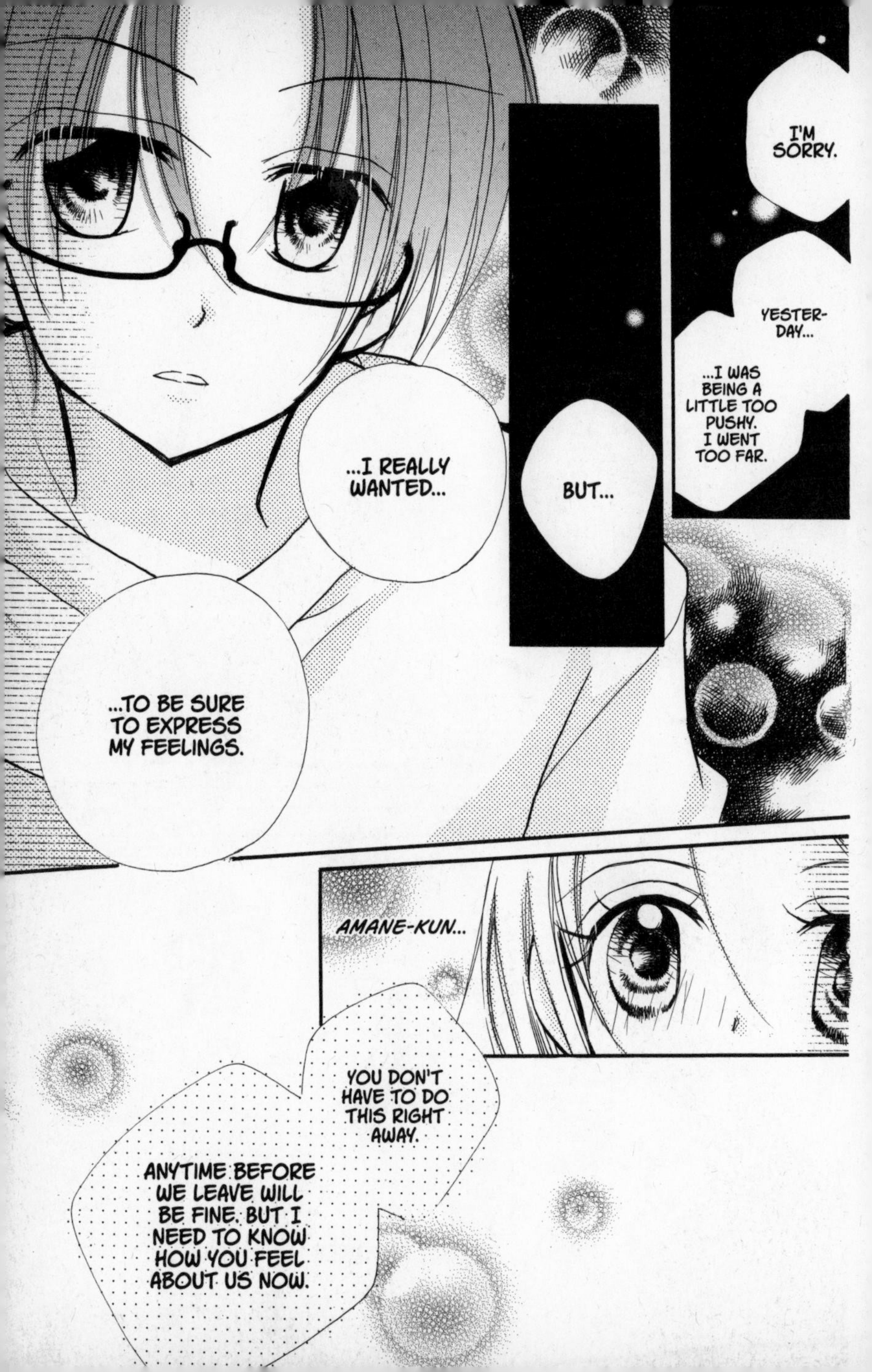
I'M SORRY.
YESTER-DAY...
...I WAS BEING A LITTLE TOO PUSHY. I WENT TOO FAR.
BUT...
...I REALLY WANTED...
...TO BE SURE TO EXPRESS MY FEELINGS.
AMANE-KUN...
YOU DON'T HAVE TO DO THIS RIGHT AWAY.
ANYTIME BEFORE WE LEAVE WILL BE FINE. BUT I NEED TO KNOW HOW YOU FEEL ABOUT US NOW.

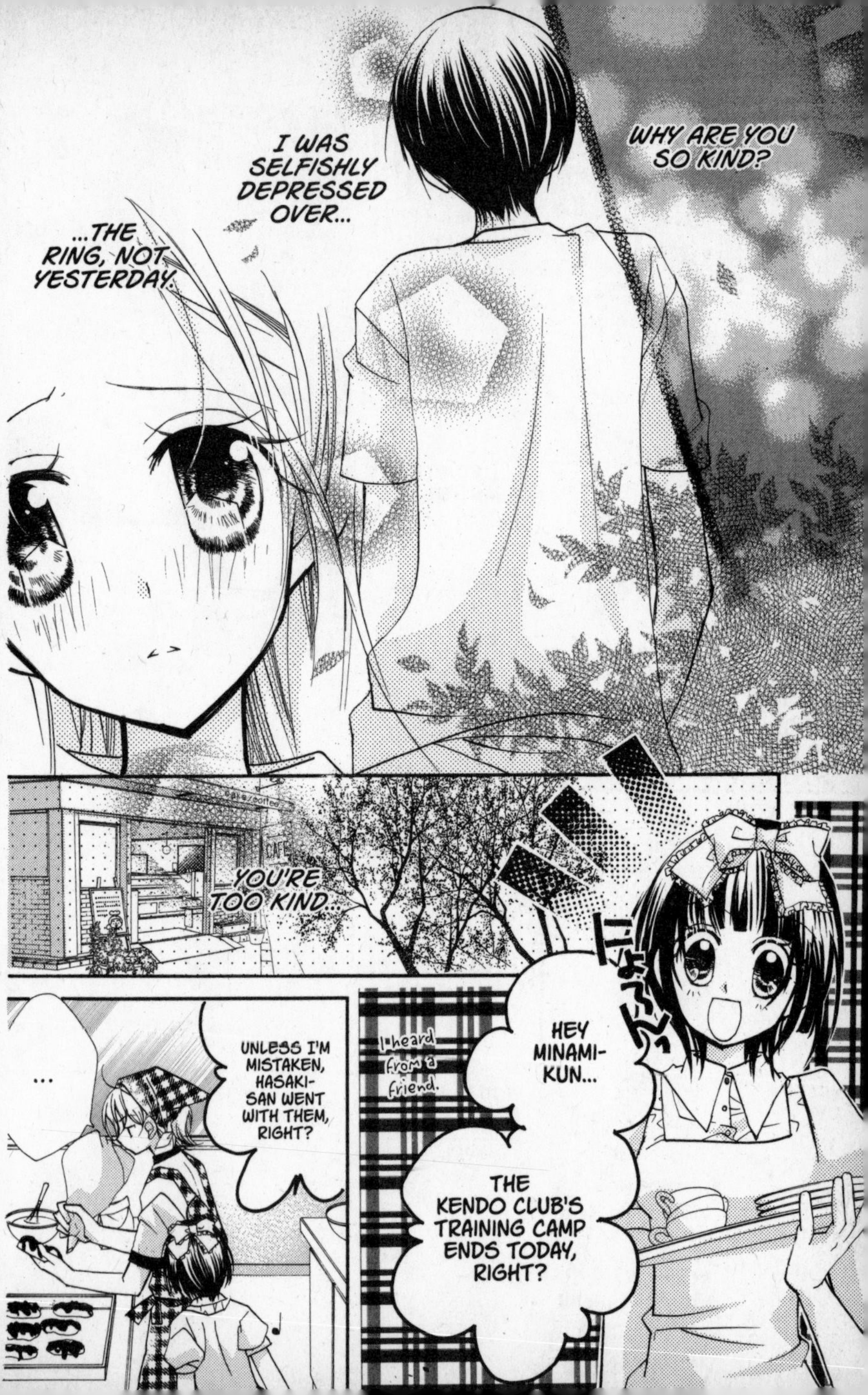
WHY ARE YOU SO KIND?
I WAS SELFISHLY DEPRESSED OVER...
...THE RING, NOT YESTERDAY.
YOU'RE TOO KIND...
HEY MINAMI-KUN...
THE KENDO CLUB'S TRAINING CAMP ENDS TODAY, RIGHT?
I heard from a friend.
UNLESS I'M MISTAKEN, HASAKI-SAN WENT WITH THEM, RIGHT?
...

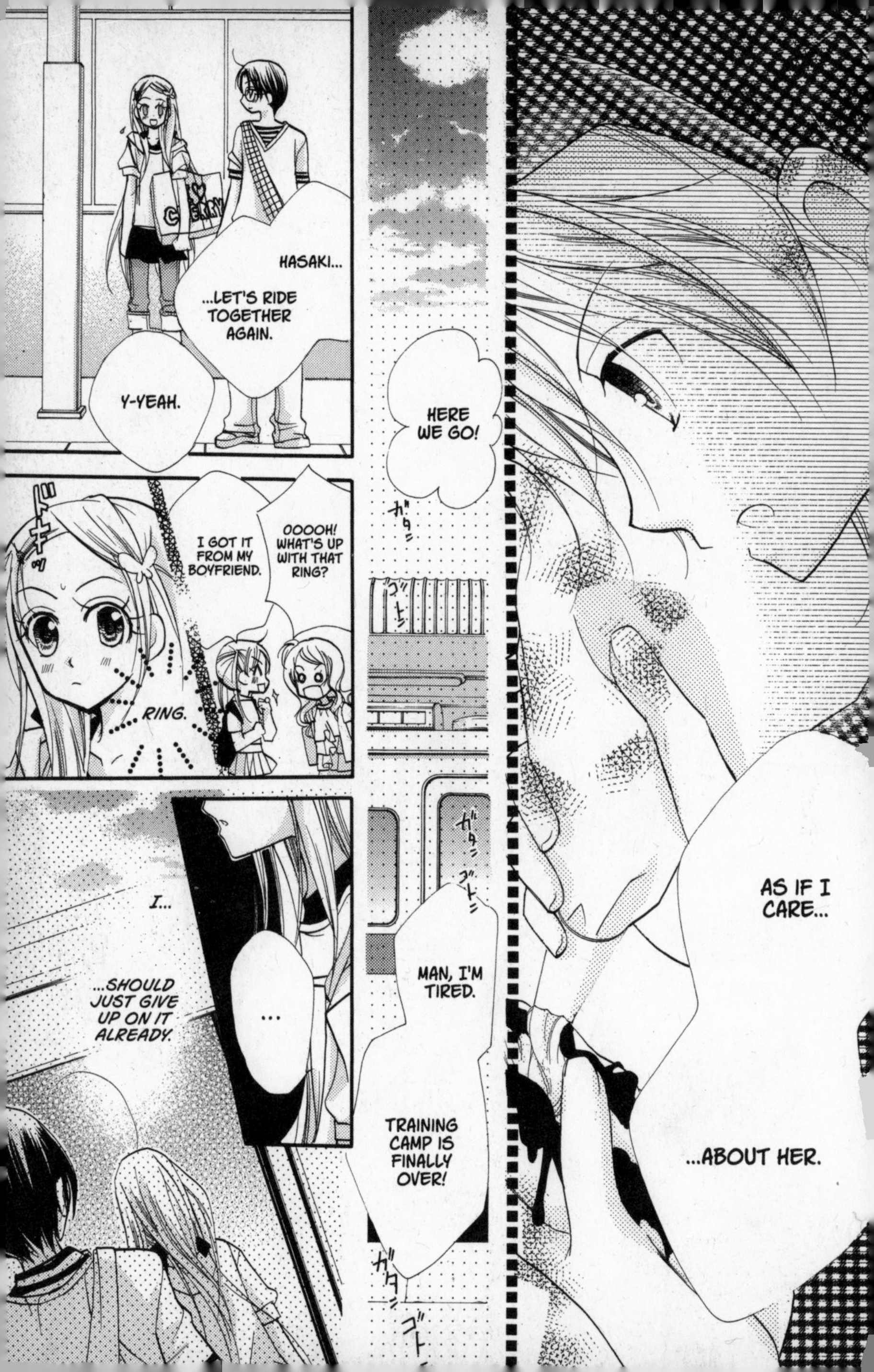
AS IF I CARE...
...ABOUT HER.
HERE WE GO!
MAN, I'M TIRED.
TRAINING CAMP IS FINALLY OVER!
HASAKI...
...LET'S RIDE TOGETHER AGAIN.
Y-YEAH.
OOOOH! WHAT'S UP WITH THAT RING?
I GOT IT FROM MY BOYFRIEND.
RING.
...
I...
...SHOULD JUST GIVE UP ON IT ALREADY.

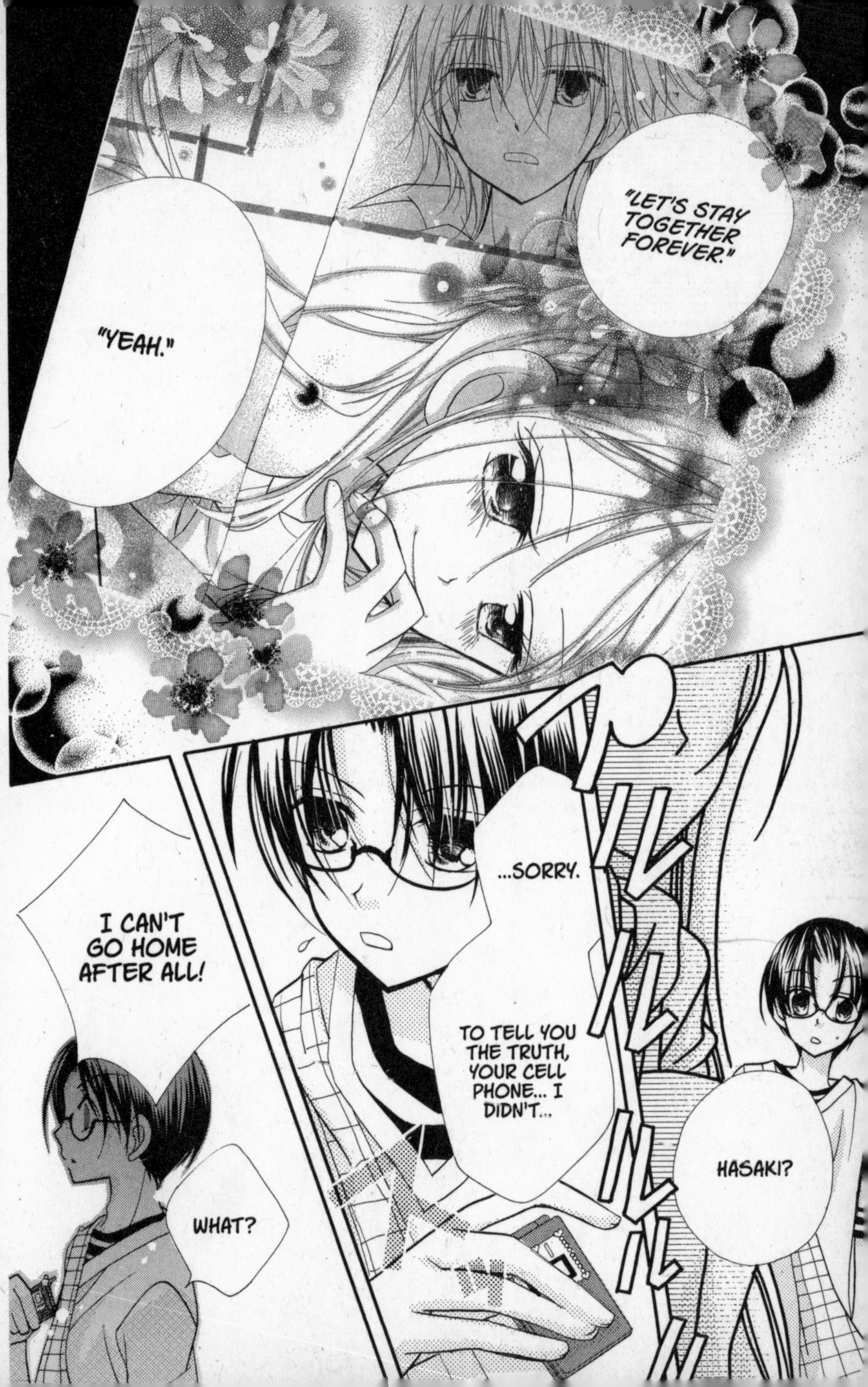
"LET'S STAY TOGETHER FOREVER."
"YEAH."
HASAKI?
...SORRY.
TO TELL YOU THE TRUTH, YOUR CELL PHONE... I DIDN'T...
I CAN'T GO HOME AFTER ALL!
WHAT?

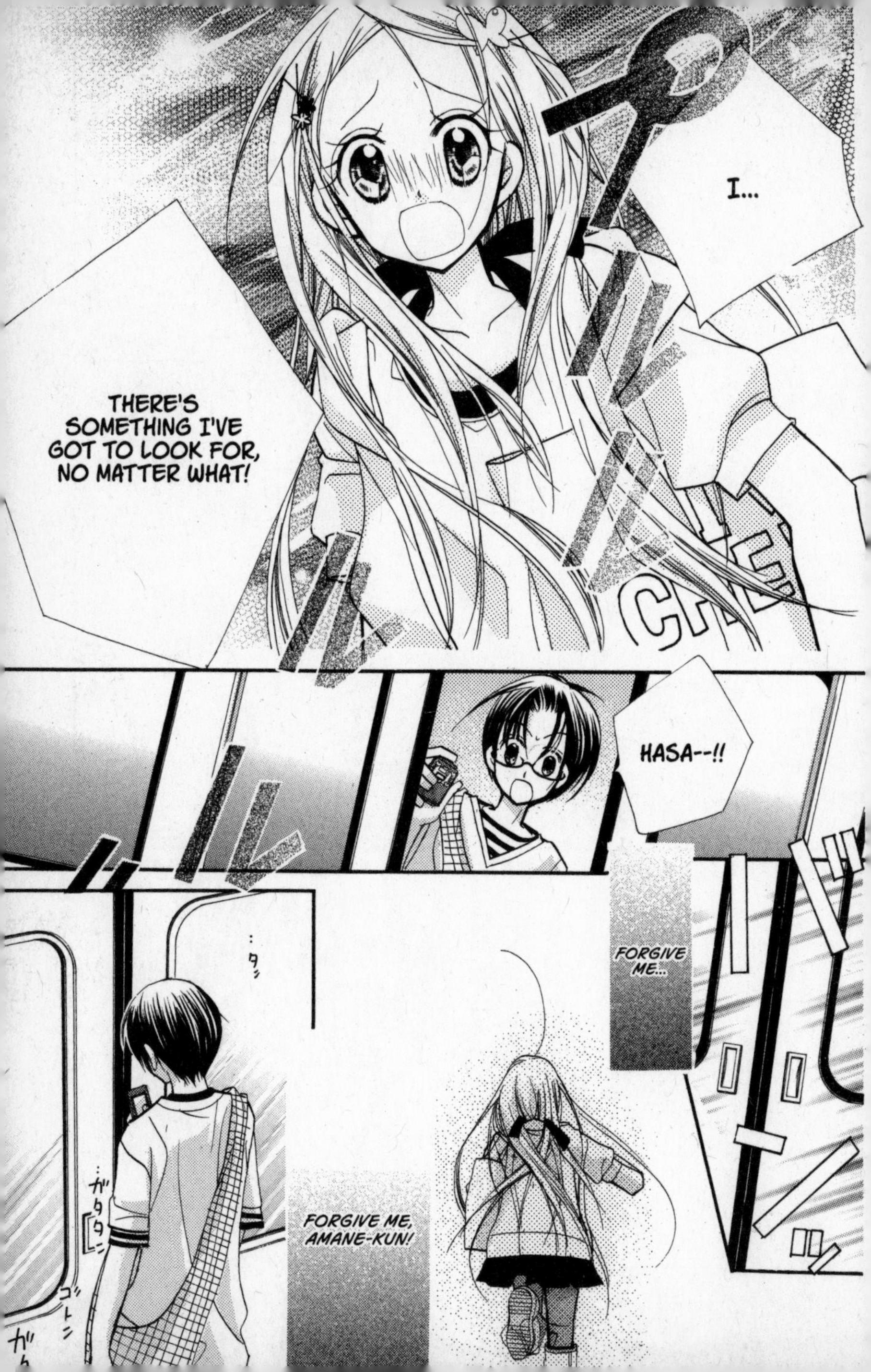
I...
THERE'S SOMETHING I'VE GOT TO LOOK FOR, NO MATTER WHAT!
HASA--!!
FORGIVE ME...
タッ
FORGIVE ME, AMANE-KUN!
ガタタン
ゴトン

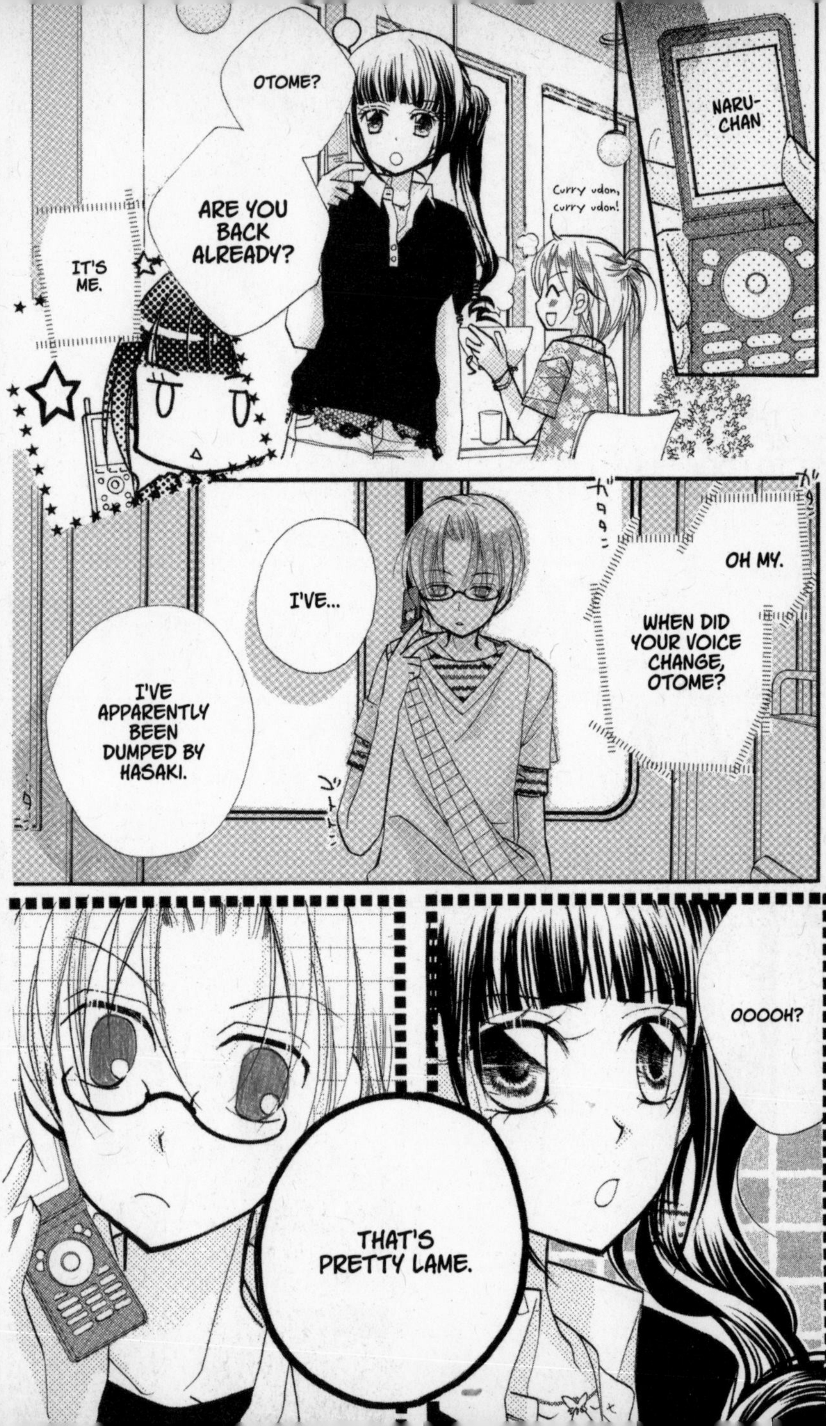
NARU-CHAN
Curry udon, curry udon!
OTOME?
ARE YOU BACK ALREADY?
IT'S ME.
OH MY.
WHEN DID YOUR VOICE CHANGE, OTOME?
I'VE...
I'VE APPARENTLY BEEN DUMPED BY HASAKI.
OOOOH?
THAT'S PRETTY LAME.

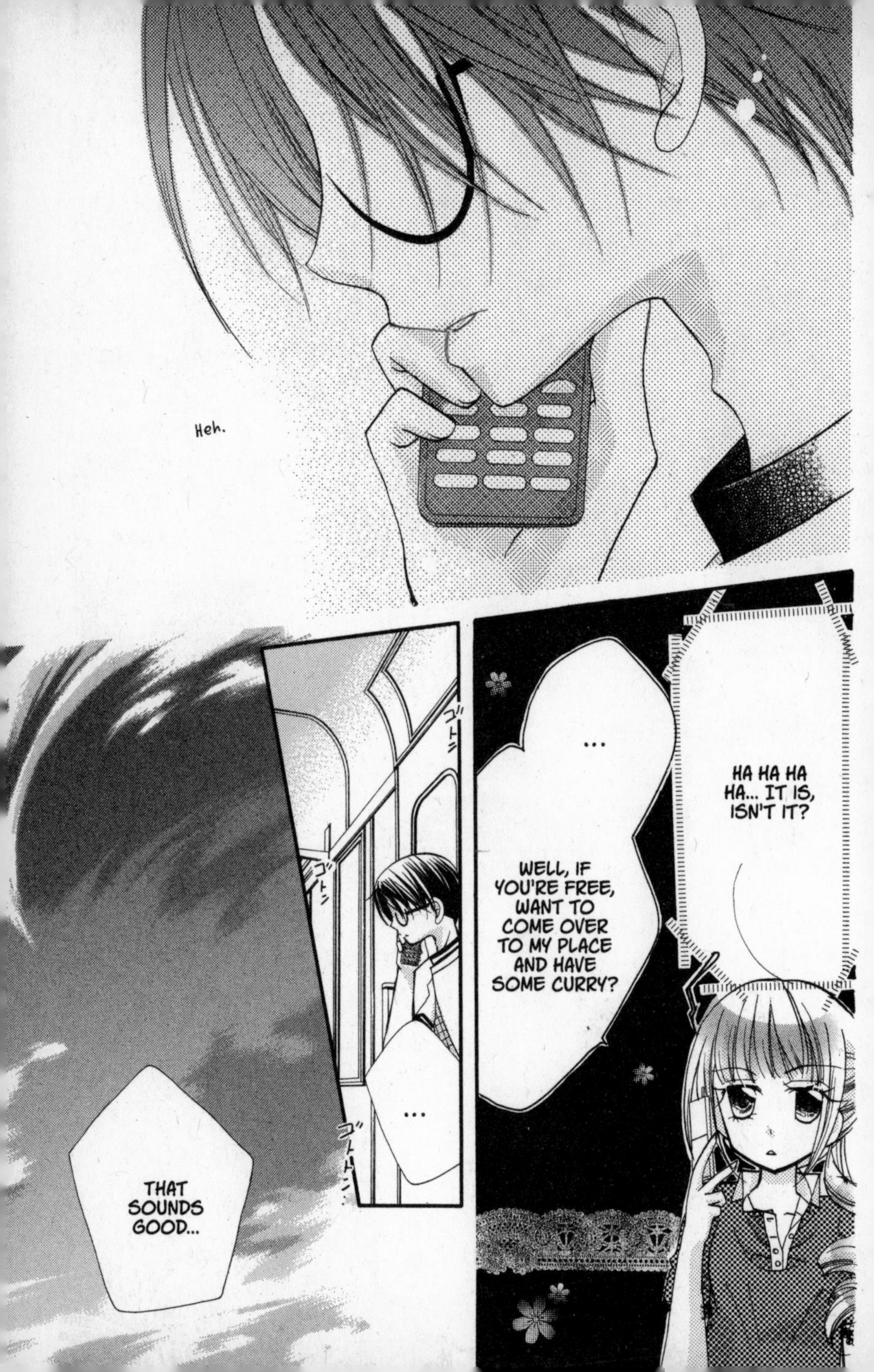
Heh.
HA HA HA HA... IT IS, ISN'T IT?
...
WELL, IF YOU'RE FREE, WANT TO COME OVER TO MY PLACE AND HAVE SOME CURRY?
ゴトン
ゴトン
...
ゴトン
THAT SOUNDS GOOD...

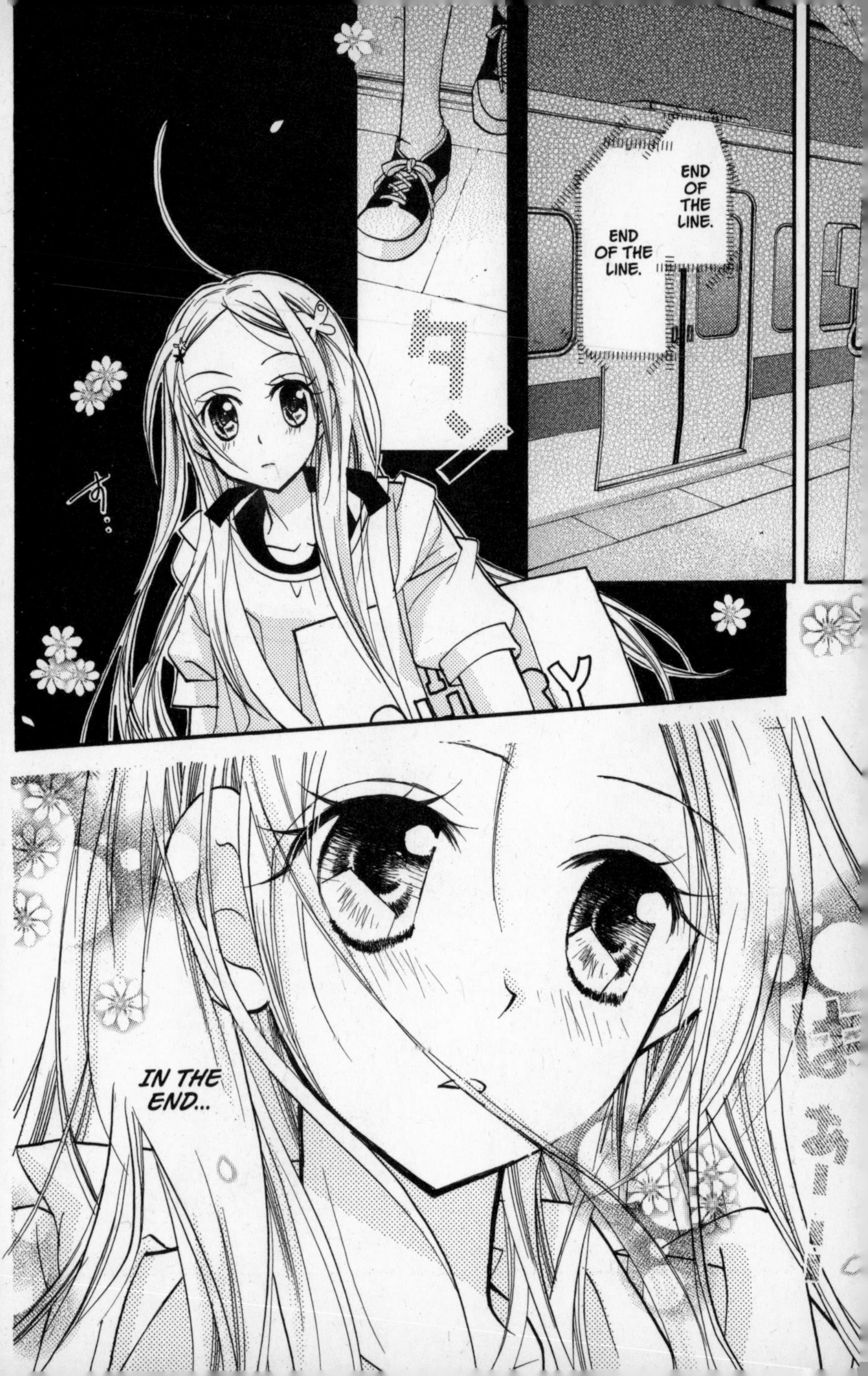
END OF THE LINE.
END OF THE LINE.
IN THE END...

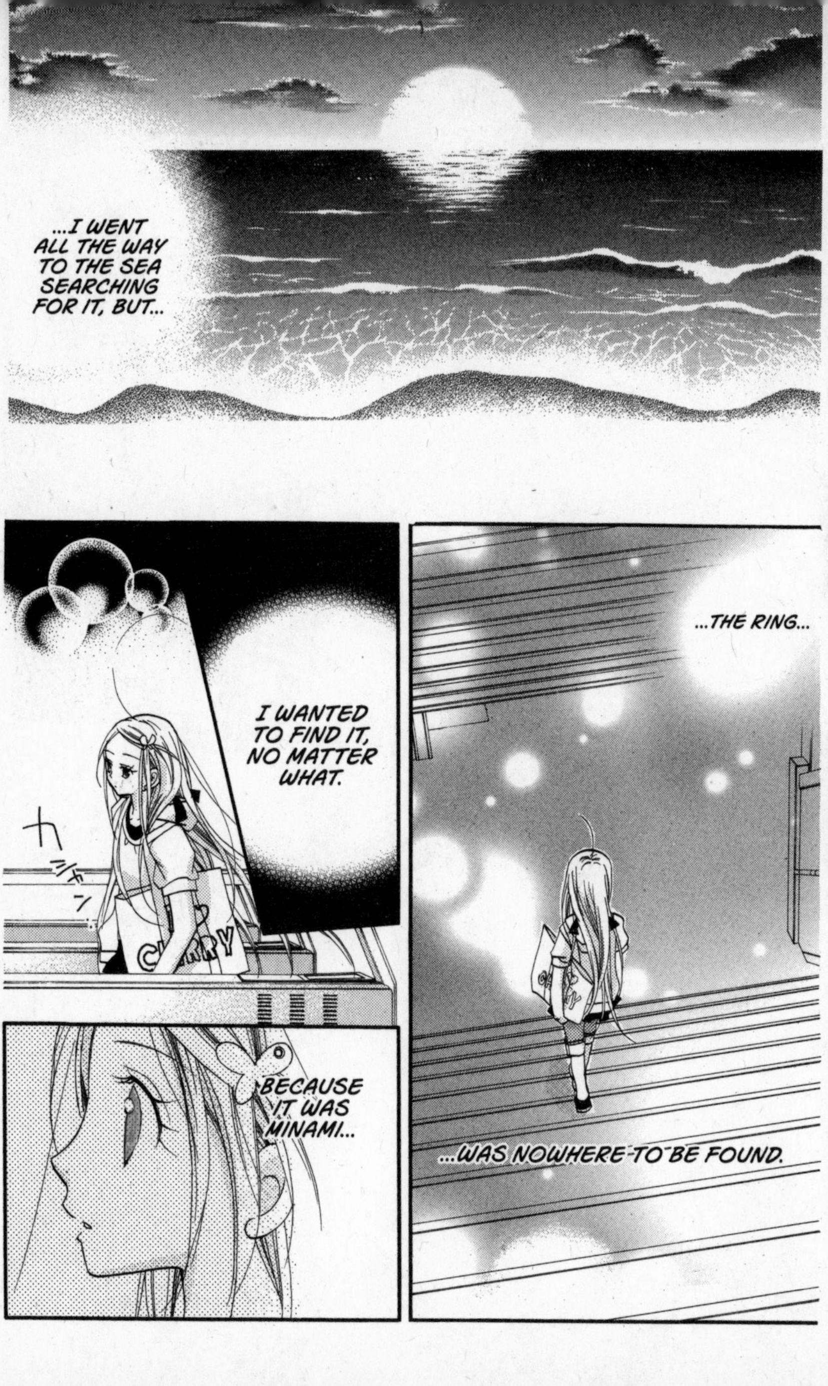
...I WENT ALL THE WAY TO THE SEA SEARCHING FOR IT, BUT...
...THE RING...
...WAS NOWHERE TO BE FOUND.
I WANTED TO FIND IT, NO MATTER WHAT.
BECAUSE IT WAS MINAMI...

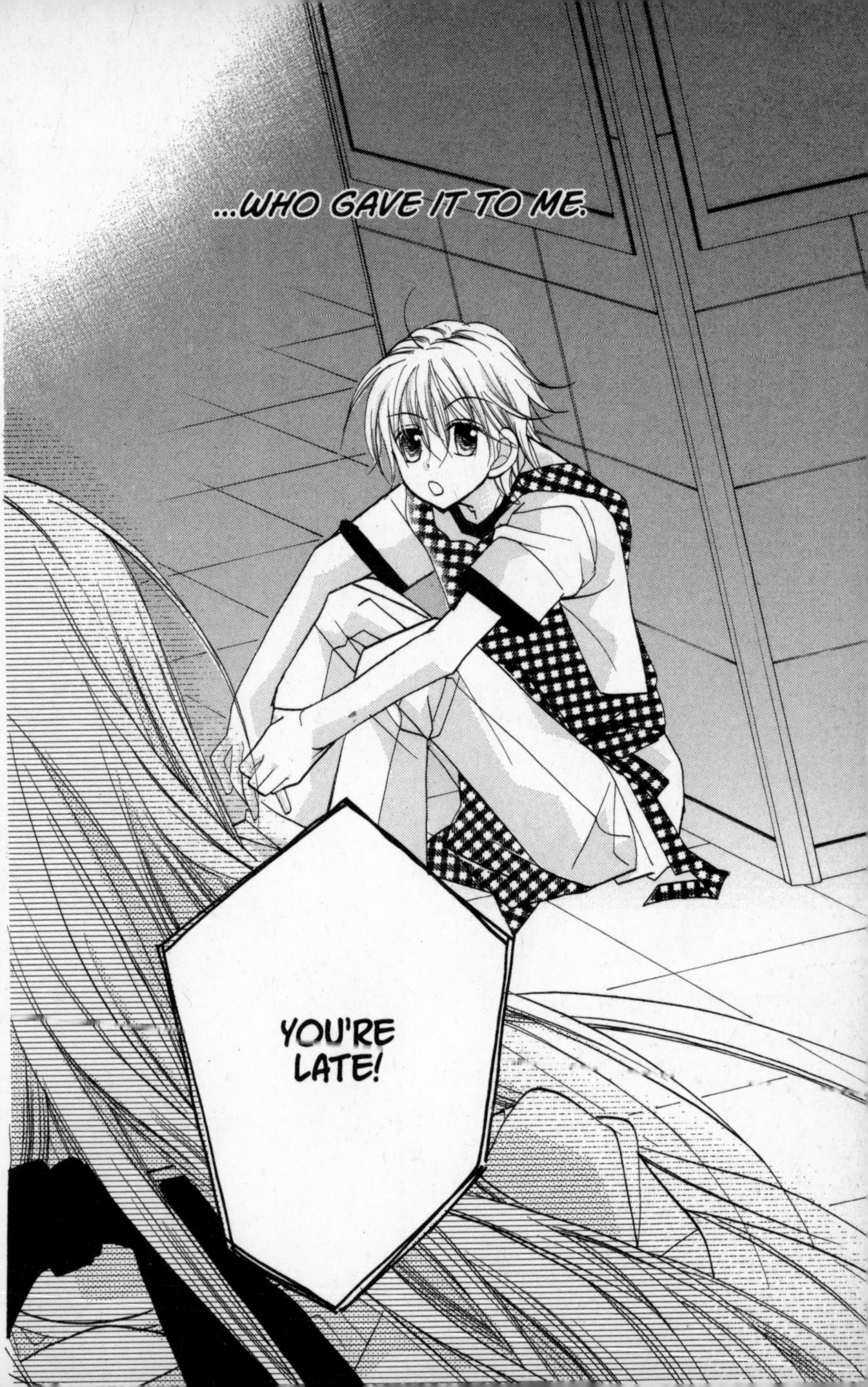
...WHO GAVE IT TO ME.
YOU'RE LATE!

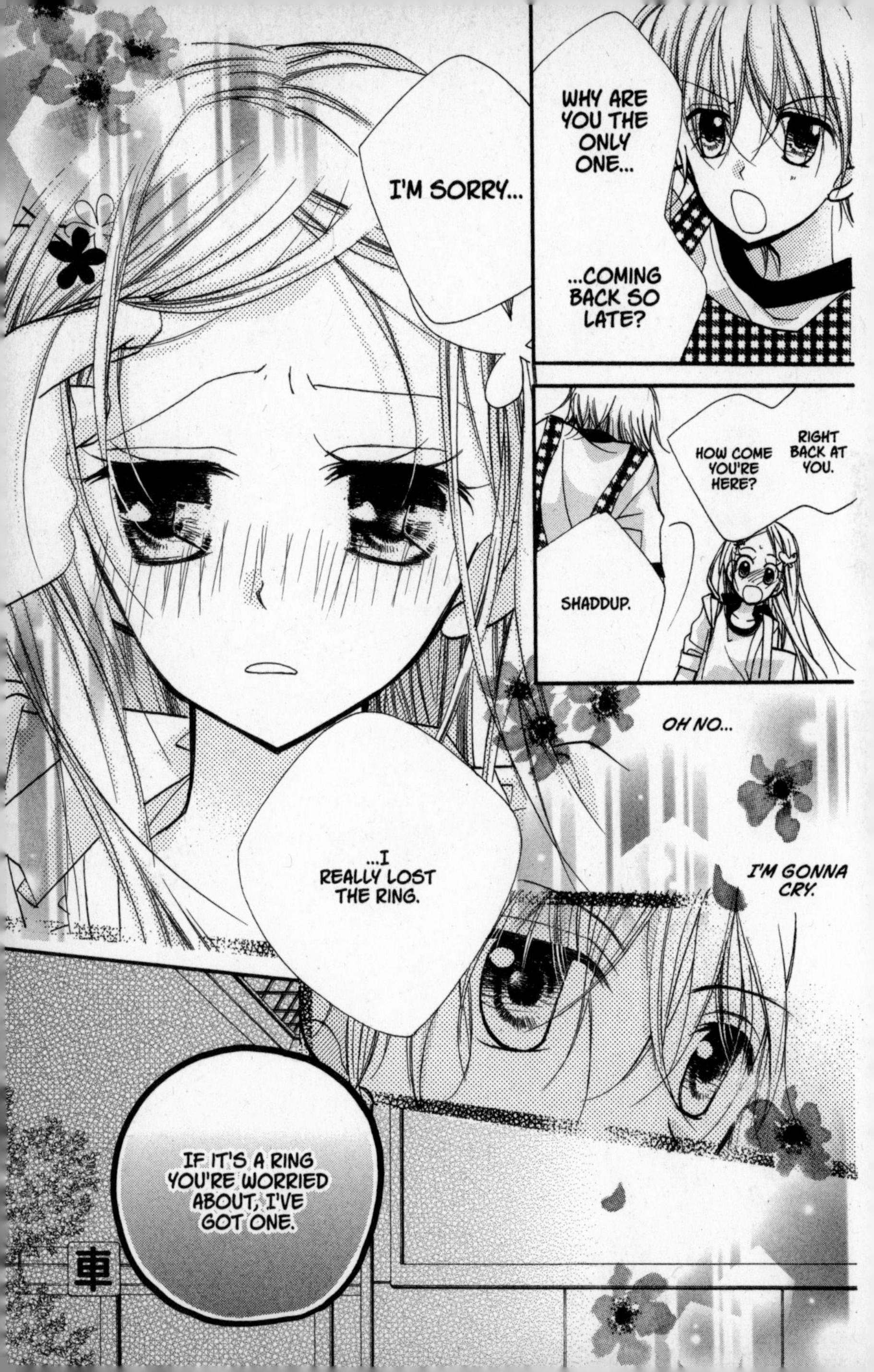
WHY ARE YOU THE ONLY ONE...
...COMING BACK SO LATE?
HOW COME YOU'RE HERE? RIGHT BACK AT YOU.
SHADDUP.
I'M SORRY...
OH NO...
I'M GONNA CRY.
...I REALLY LOST THE RING.
IF IT'S A RING YOU'RE WORRIED ABOUT, I'VE GOT ONE.
車

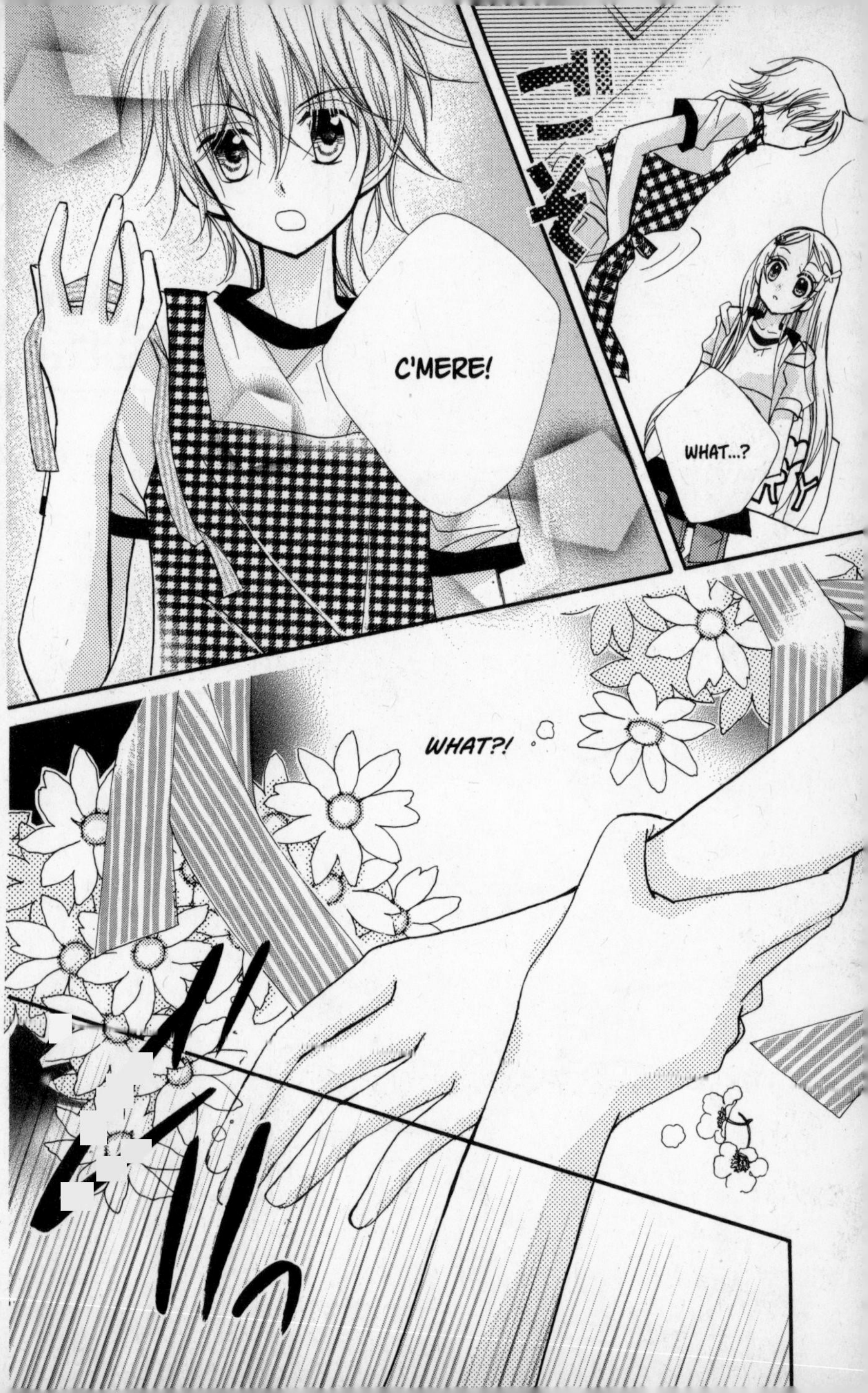
WHAT...?
C'MERE!
WHAT?!

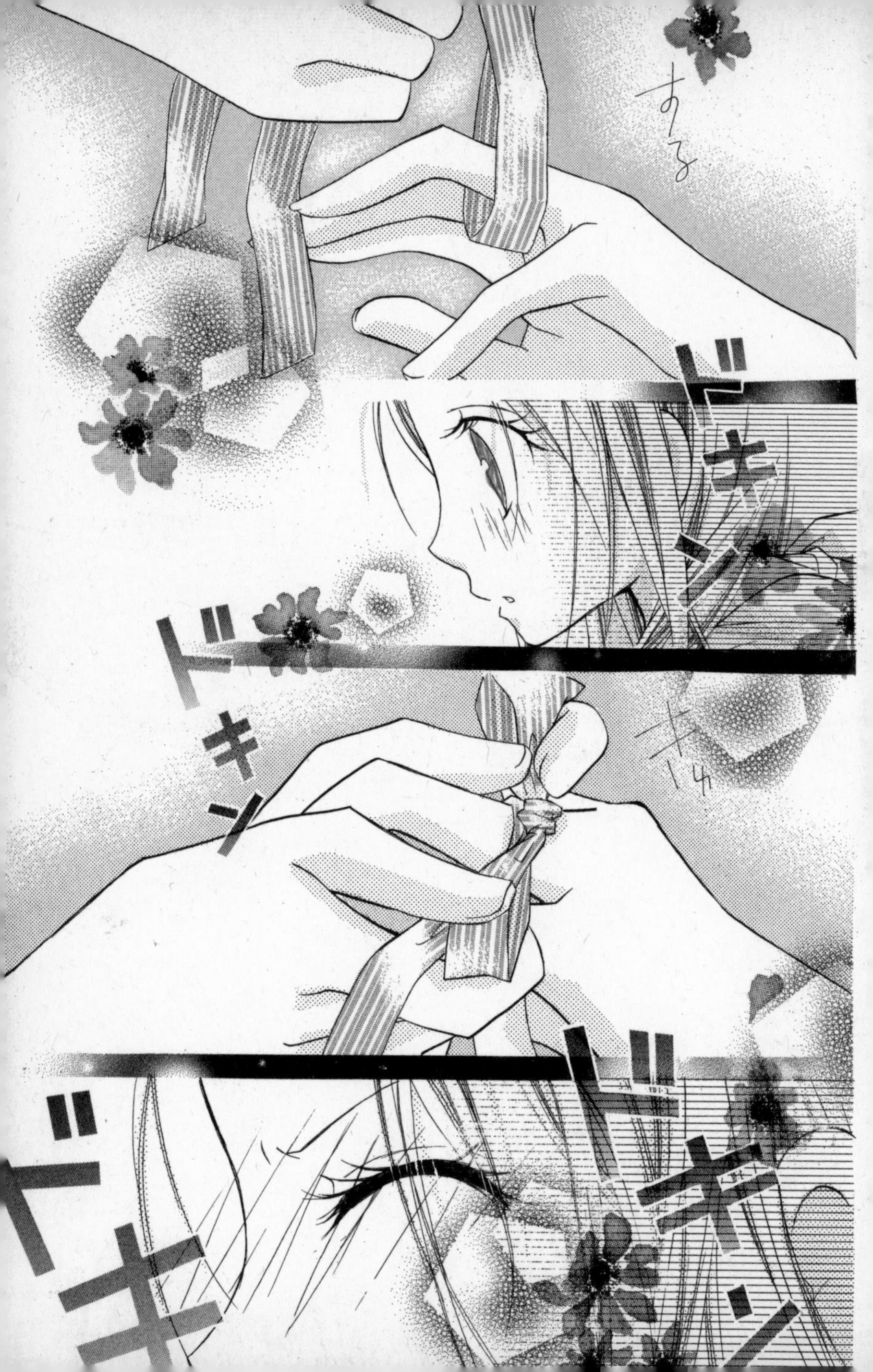
するる
ドキン
ドキン
キュッ
ドキン
ドキ

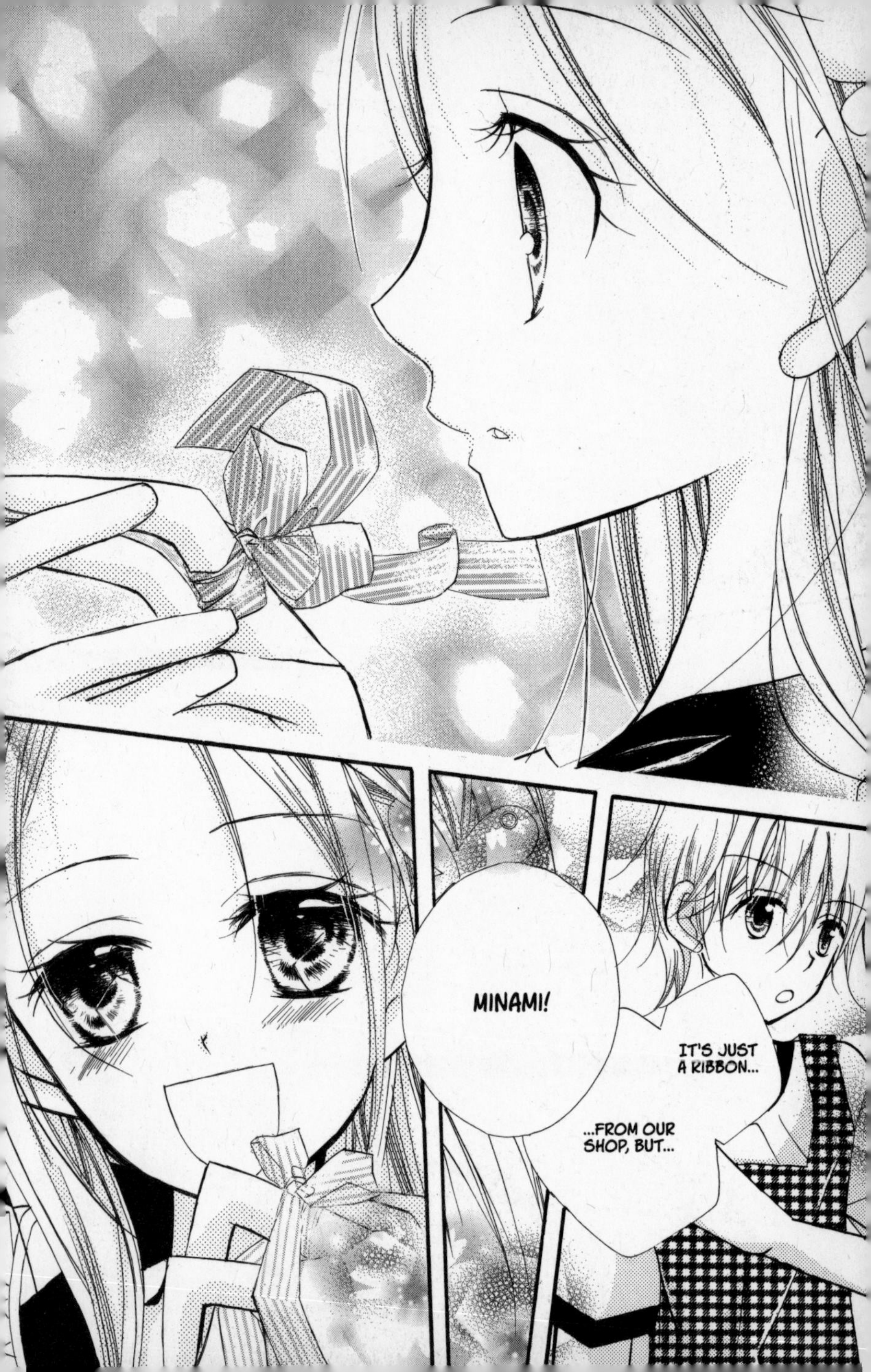
MINAMI!
IT'S JUST A KIBBON...
...FROM OUR SHOP, BUT...

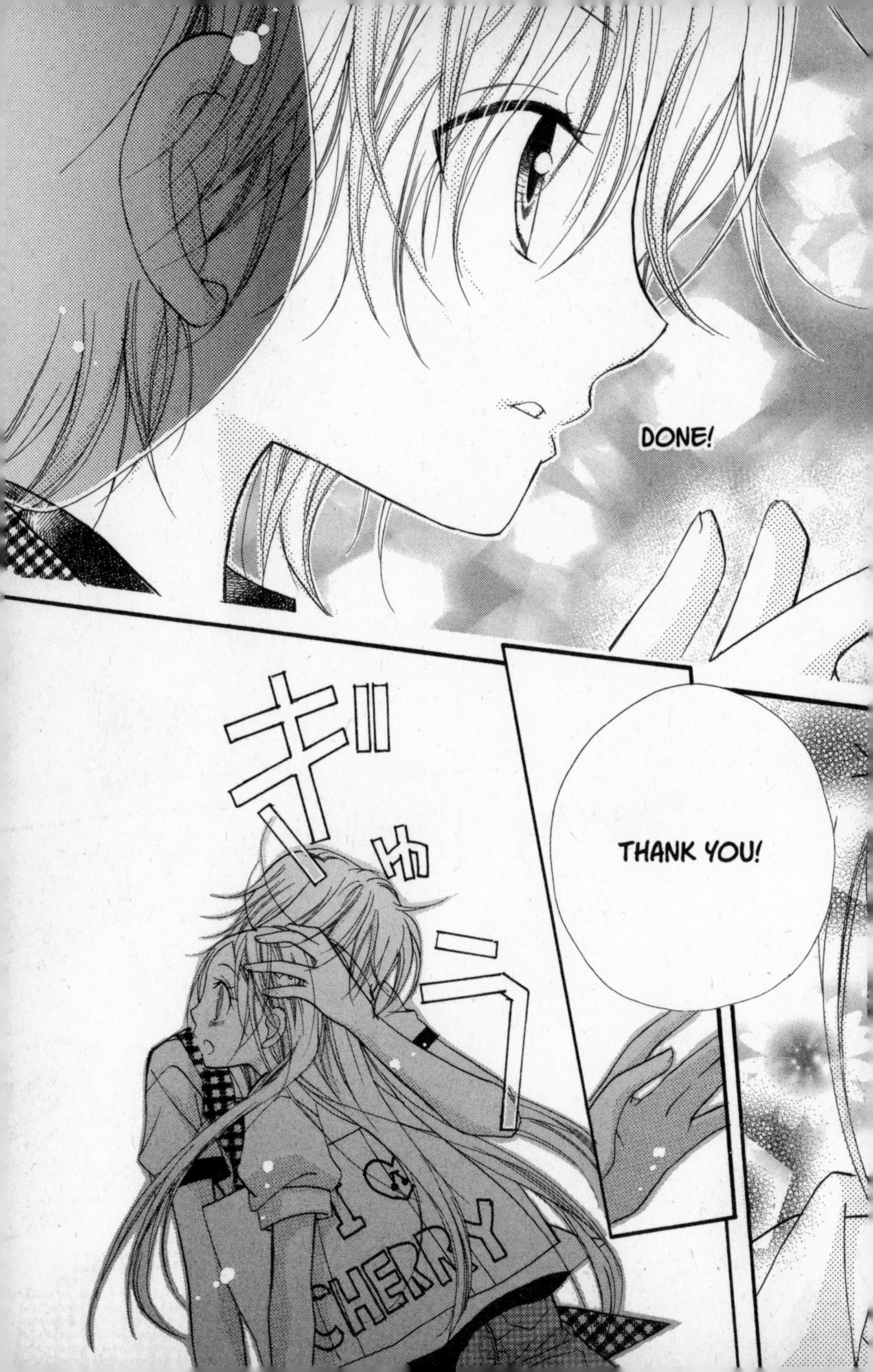
DONE!
THANK YOU!
ギュー

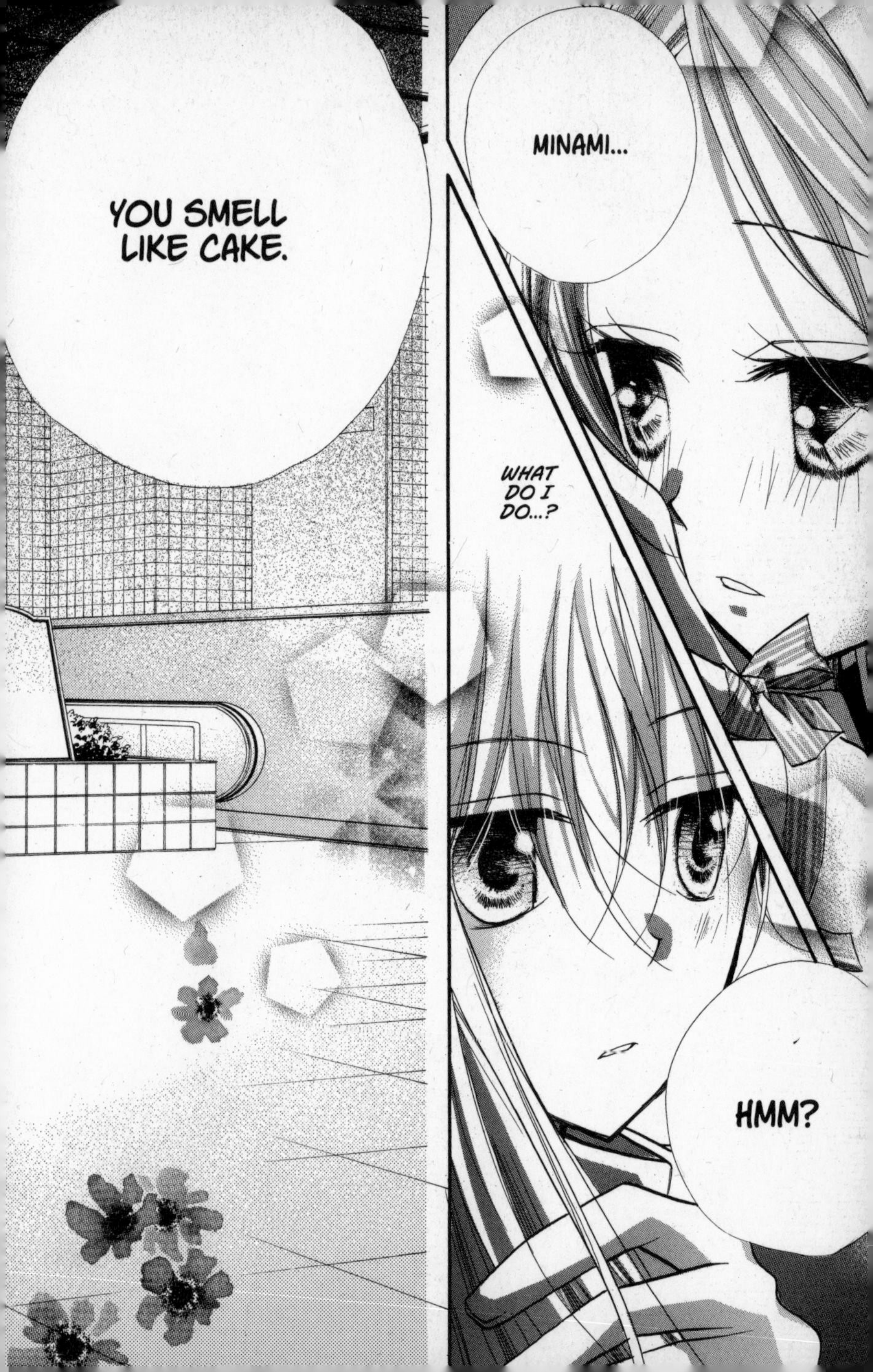
MINAMI...
WHAT DO I DO...?
HMM?
YOU SMELL LIKE CAKE.

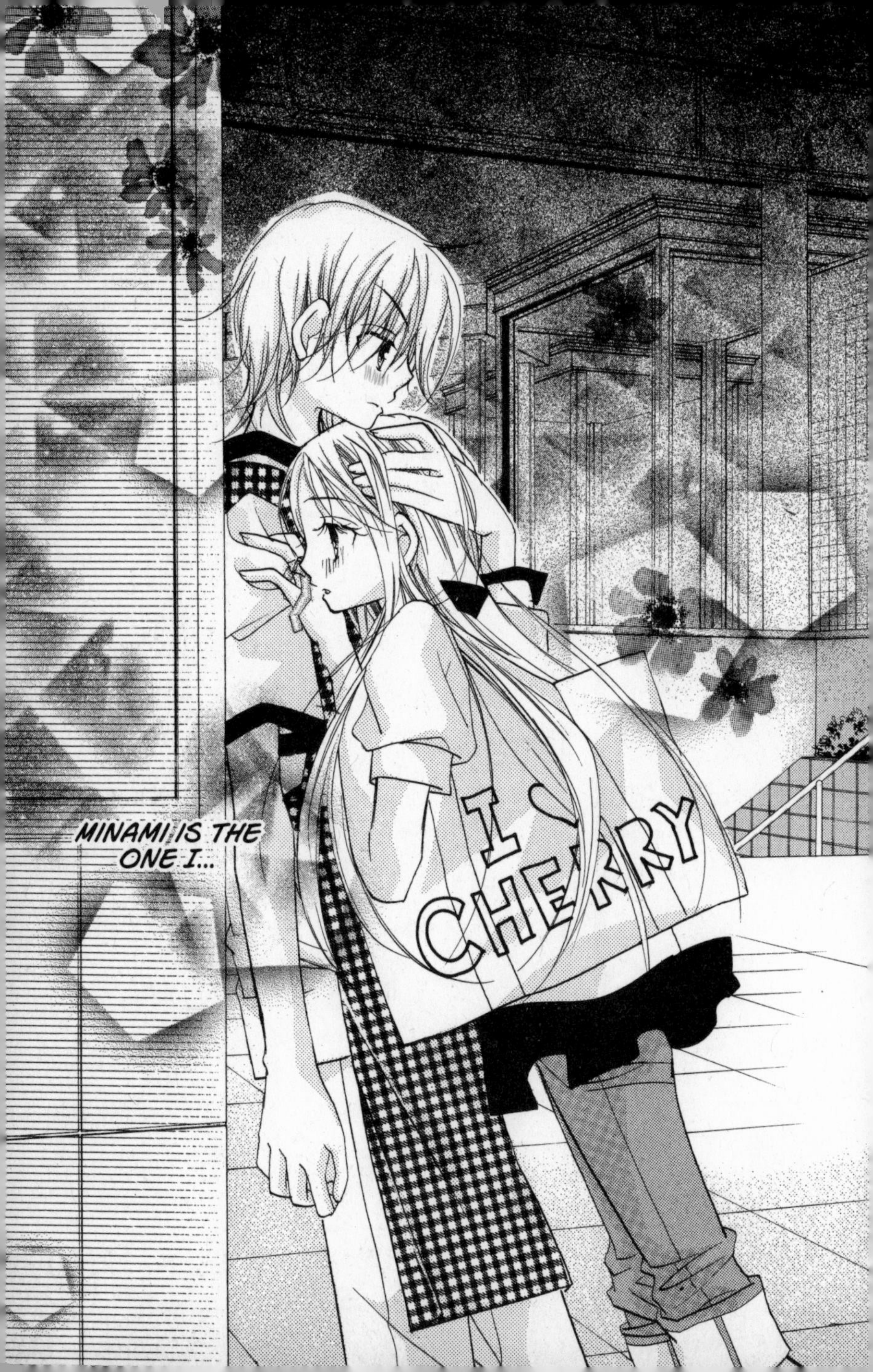
MINAMI IS THE ONE I...
I ♥ CHERRY

~~AFTERWORD~~

As always, thank you
for the letters.
Since beginning to draw
Cherry Juice, I've been
able to receive letters
from a wide variety of
fans. (From grade-schoolers
to mothers. I'm surprised.)
I always read them, and
I gratefully use your
opinions as a reference.

I'm afraid I most likely won't be
able to reply, but if you have any
feedback please send it here.

Haruka Fukushima
C/O TOKYOPOP Inc.
5900 Wilshire Blvd.
Suite 2000
Los Angeles,
CA 90036

BOW

See you in
volume 4!

05. 10. 2

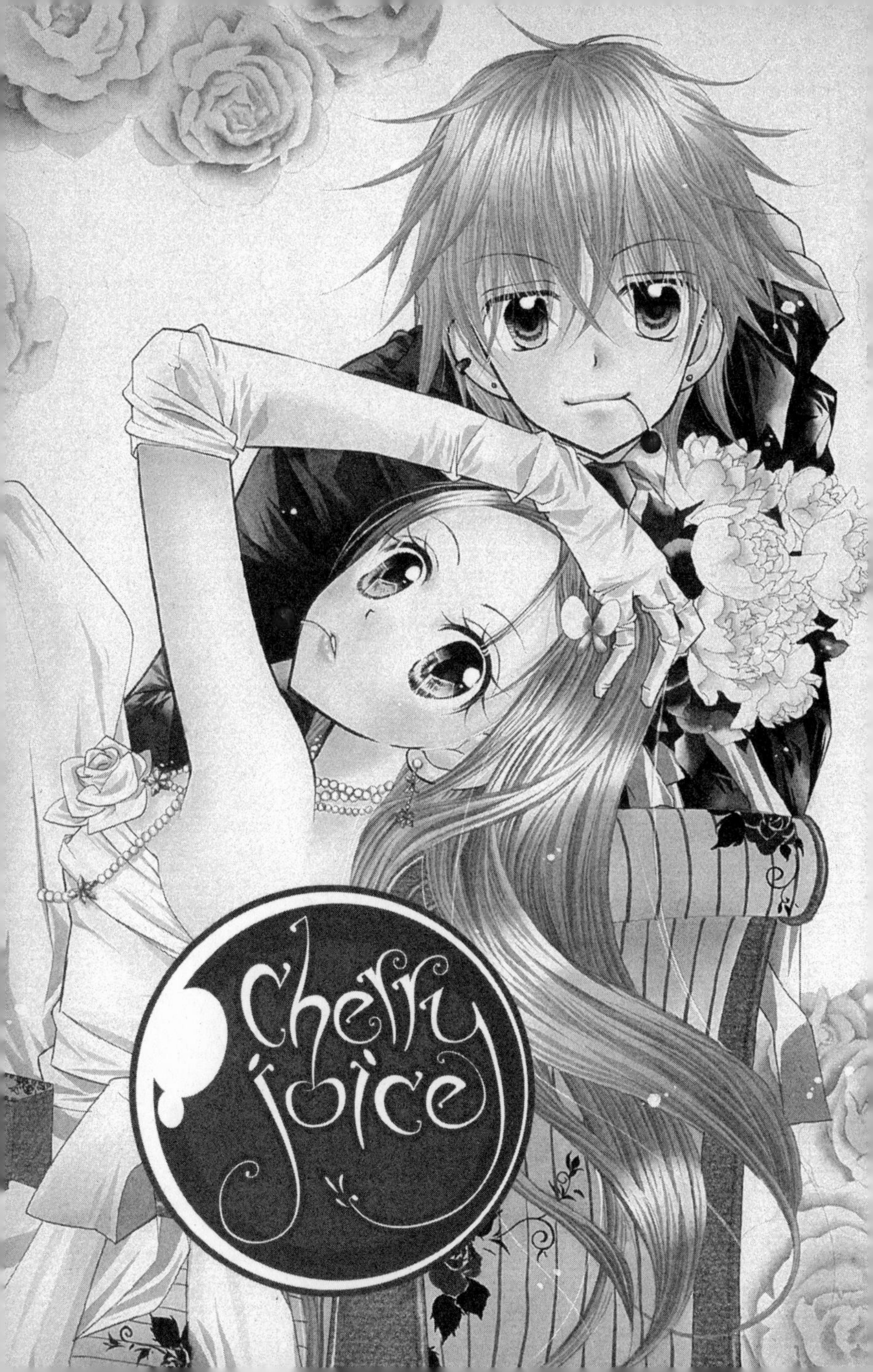
Cherry Juice

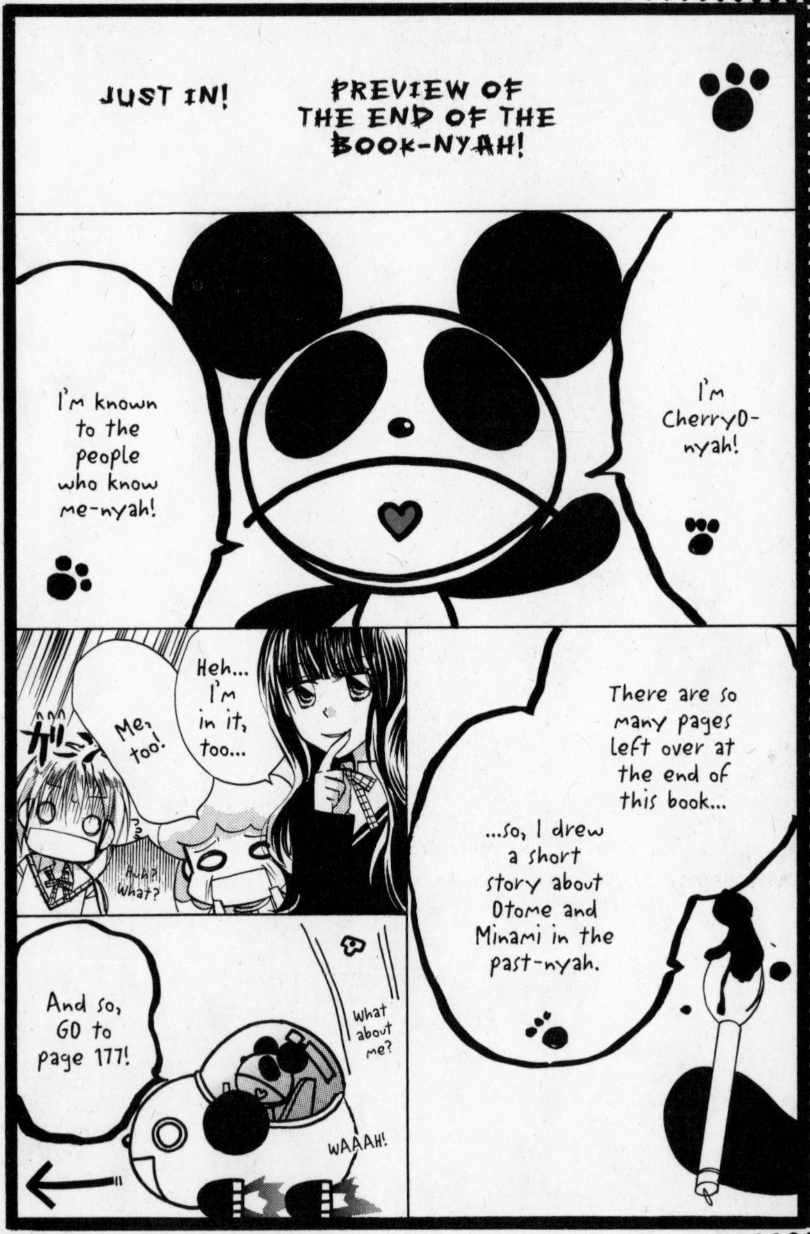
PREVIEW OF THE END OF THE BOOK-NYAH!
JUST IN!
I'm CherryO-nyah!
I'm known to the people who know me-nyah!
There are so many pages left over at the end of this book...
...so, I drew a short story about Otome and Minami in the past-nyah.
Heh... I'm in it, too...
Me, too!
Huh? What?
What about me?
And so, GO to page 177!
WAAAH!

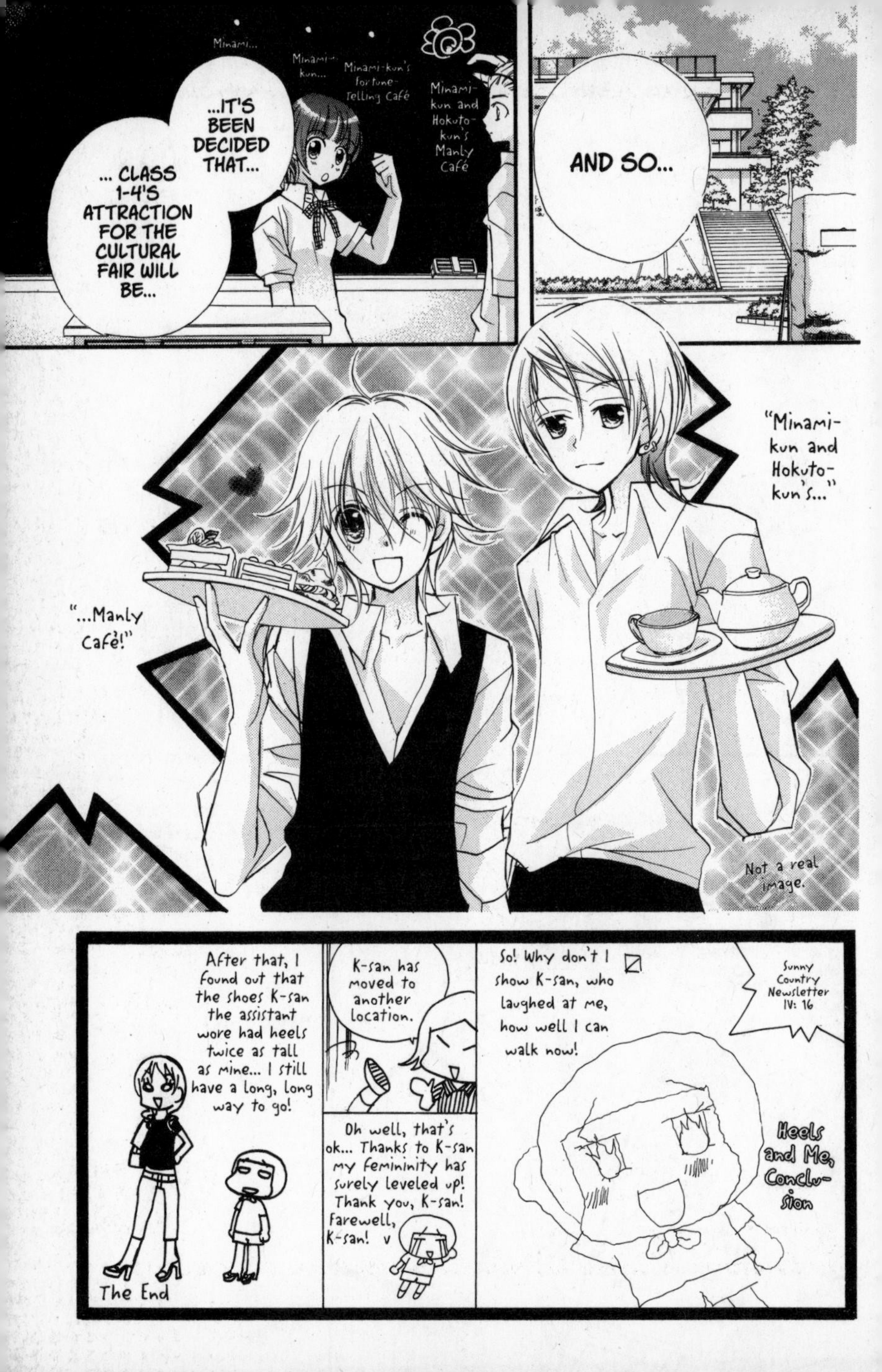
AND SO...
...IT'S BEEN DECIDED THAT...
... CLASS 1-4'S ATTRACTION FOR THE CULTURAL FAIR WILL BE...
Minami-kun and Hokuto-kun's Manly Café
Minami-kun's fortune-telling Café
Minami-kun...
Minami...
"Minami-kun and Hokuto-kun's..."
"...Manly Café!"
Not a real image.
Sunny Country Newsletter IV: 16
Heels and Me, Conclusion
So! Why don't I show K-san, who laughed at me, how well I can walk now!
K-san has moved to another location.
Oh well, that's ok... Thanks to K-san my femininity has surely leveled up! Thank you, K-san! Farewell, K-san! v
After that, I found out that the shoes K-san the assistant wore had heels twice as tall as mine... I still have a long, long way to go!
The End

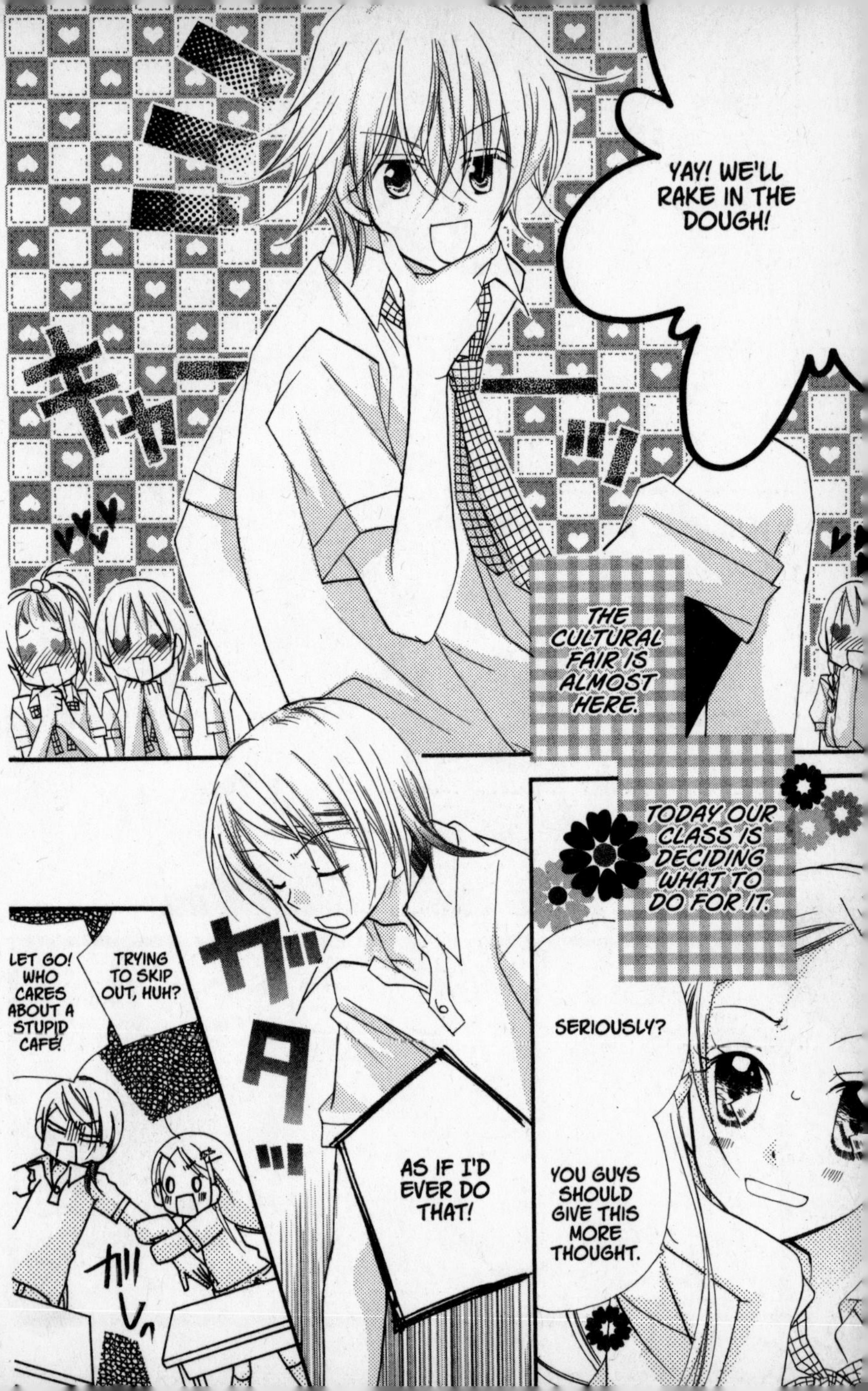
YAY! WE'LL RAKE IN THE DOUGH!
THE CULTURAL FAIR IS ALMOST HERE.
TODAY OUR CLASS IS DECIDING WHAT TO DO FOR IT.
SERIOUSLY?
YOU GUYS SHOULD GIVE THIS MORE THOUGHT.
AS IF I'D EVER DO THAT!
TRYING TO SKIP OUT, HUH?
LET GO! WHO CARES ABOUT A STUPID CAFE!

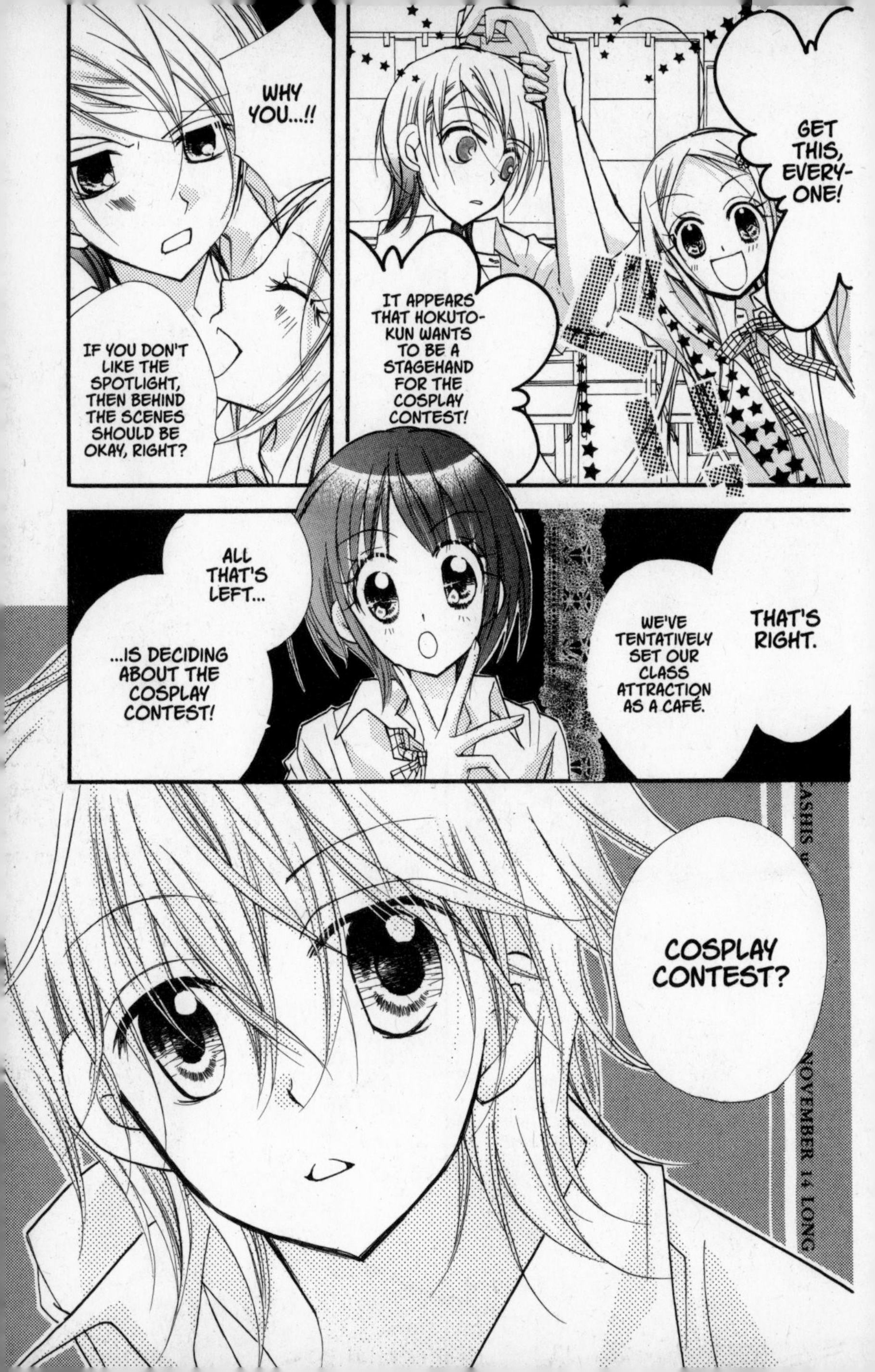
GET THIS, EVERYONE!
IT APPEARS THAT HOKUTO-KUN WANTS TO BE A STAGEHAND FOR THE COSPLAY CONTEST!
WHY YOU...!!
IF YOU DON'T LIKE THE SPOTLIGHT, THEN BEHIND THE SCENES SHOULD BE OKAY, RIGHT?
THAT'S RIGHT.
WE'VE TENTATIVELY SET OUR CLASS ATTRACTION AS A CAFÉ.
ALL THAT'S LEFT...
...IS DECIDING ABOUT THE COSPLAY CONTEST!
COSPLAY CONTEST?
NOVEMBER 14 LONG

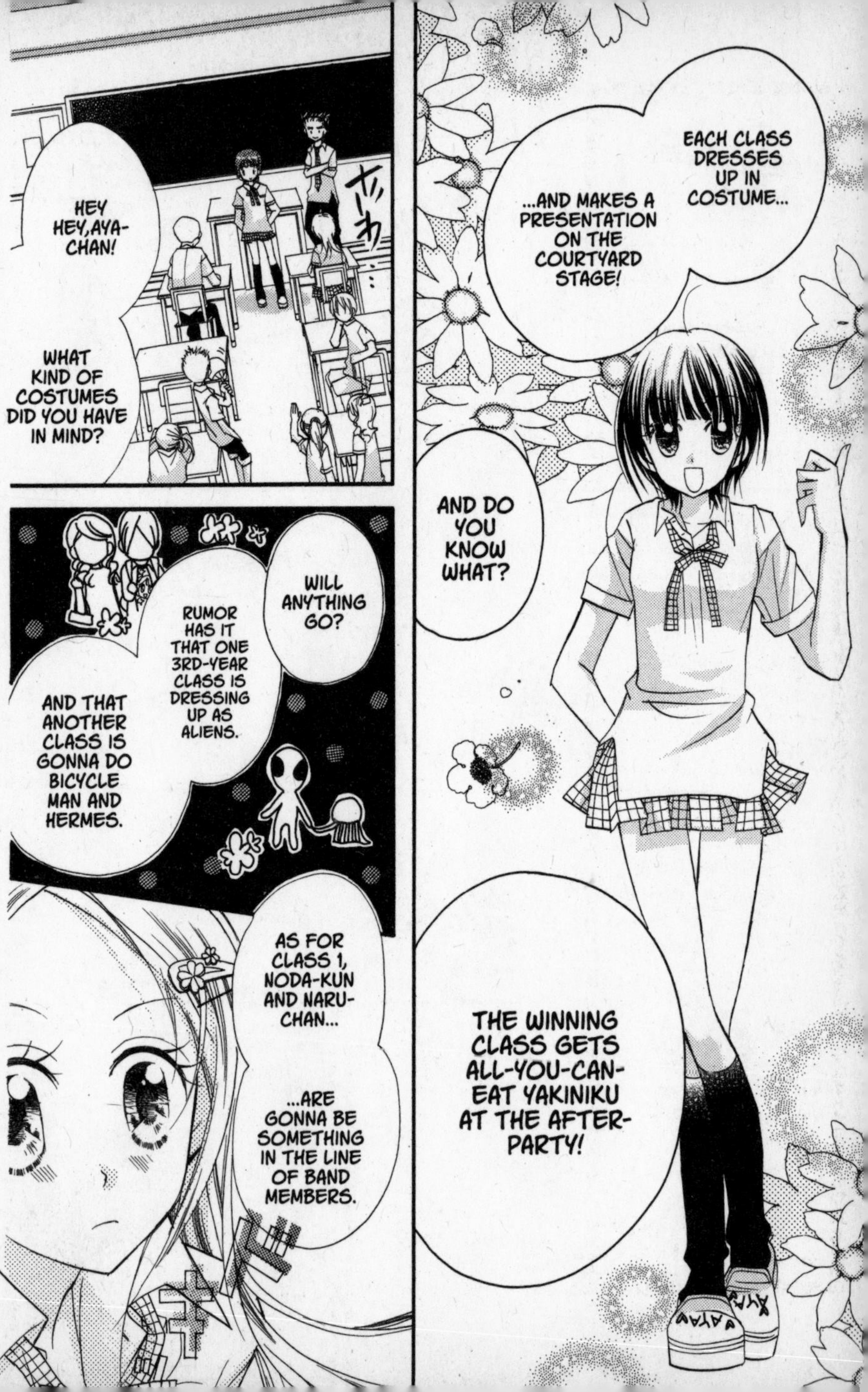
EACH CLASS DRESSES UP IN COSTUME...
...AND MAKES A PRESENTATION ON THE COURTYARD STAGE!
AND DO YOU KNOW WHAT?
THE WINNING CLASS GETS ALL-YOU-CAN-EAT YAKINIKU AT THE AFTER-PARTY!
HEY HEY, AYA-CHAN!
WHAT KIND OF COSTUMES DID YOU HAVE IN MIND?
WILL ANYTHING GO?
RUMOR HAS IT THAT ONE 3RD-YEAR CLASS IS DRESSING UP AS ALIENS.
AND THAT ANOTHER CLASS IS GONNA DO BICYCLE MAN AND HERMES.
AS FOR CLASS 1, NODA-KUN AND NARU-CHAN...
...ARE GONNA BE SOMETHING IN THE LINE OF BAND MEMBERS.

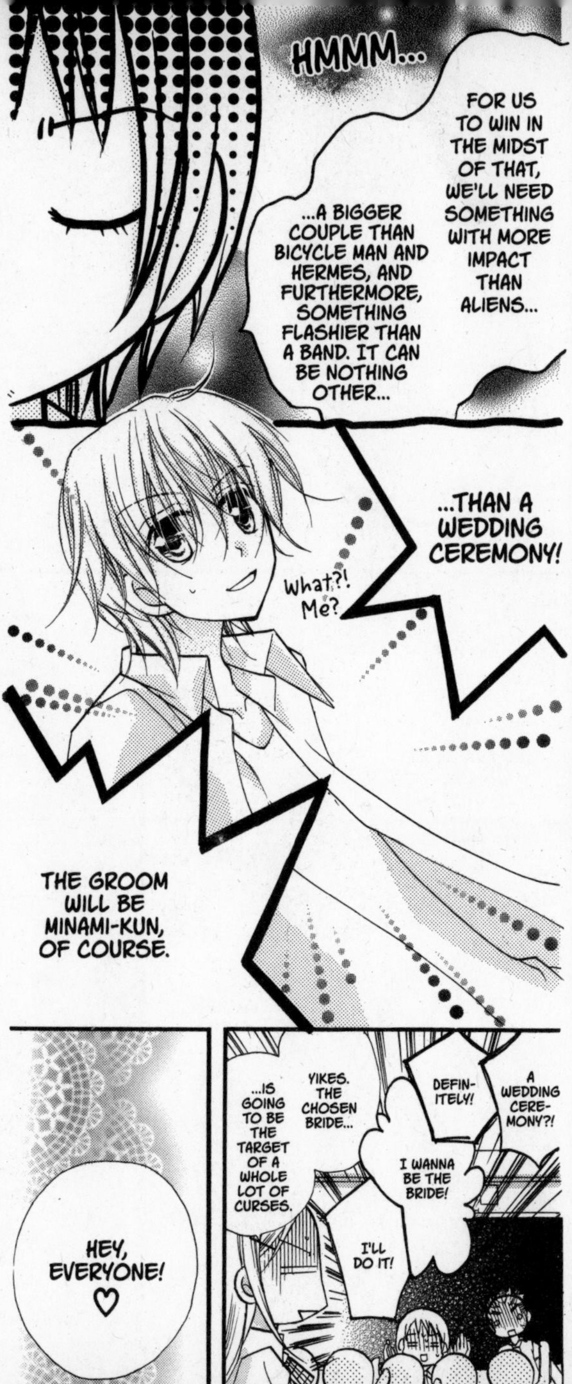
HMMM...
FOR US TO WIN IN THE MIDST OF THAT, WE'LL NEED SOMETHING WITH MORE IMPACT THAN ALIENS...
...A BIGGER COUPLE THAN BICYCLE MAN AND HERMES, AND FURTHERMORE, SOMETHING FLASHIER THAN A BAND. IT CAN BE NOTHING OTHER...
...THAN A WEDDING CEREMONY!
What?! Me?
THE GROOM WILL BE MINAMI-KUN, OF COURSE.
A WEDDING CERE-MONY?!
DEFIN-ITELY!
I WANNA BE THE BRIDE!
YIKES. THE CHOSEN BRIDE...
...IS GOING TO BE THE TARGET OF A WHOLE LOT OF CURSES.
I'LL DO IT!
HEY, EVERYONE! ♡

EIGHT

☑ So, now you've seen the new uniforms. Whaddya think? Do you all like them?

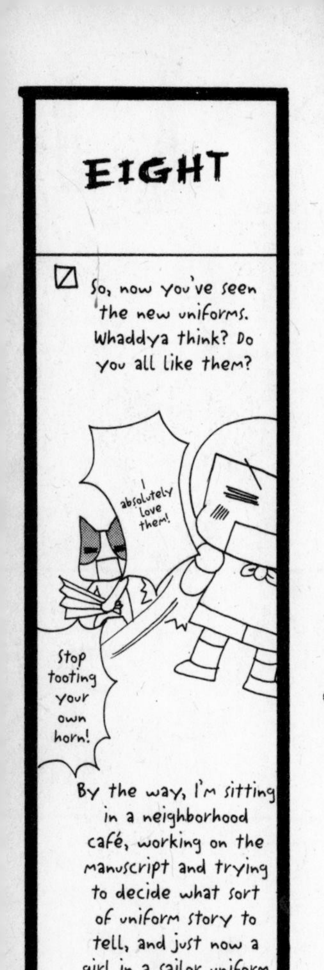
I absolutely love them!
Stop tooting your own horn!

By the way, I'm sitting in a neighborhood café, working on the manuscript and trying to decide what sort of uniform story to tell, and just now a girl in a sailor uniform walked right past!

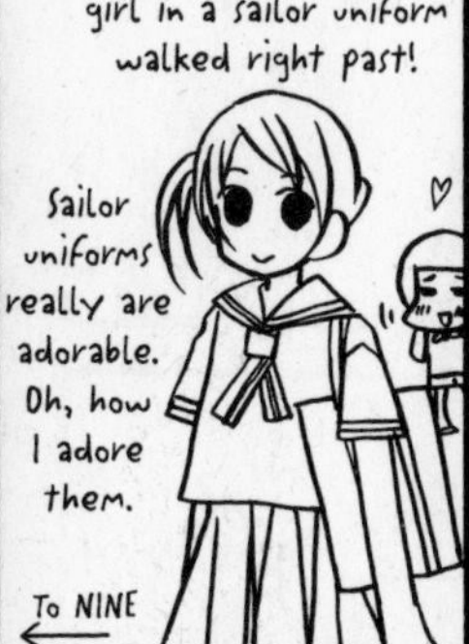
Sailor uniforms really are adorable. Oh, how I adore them.

To NINE ←

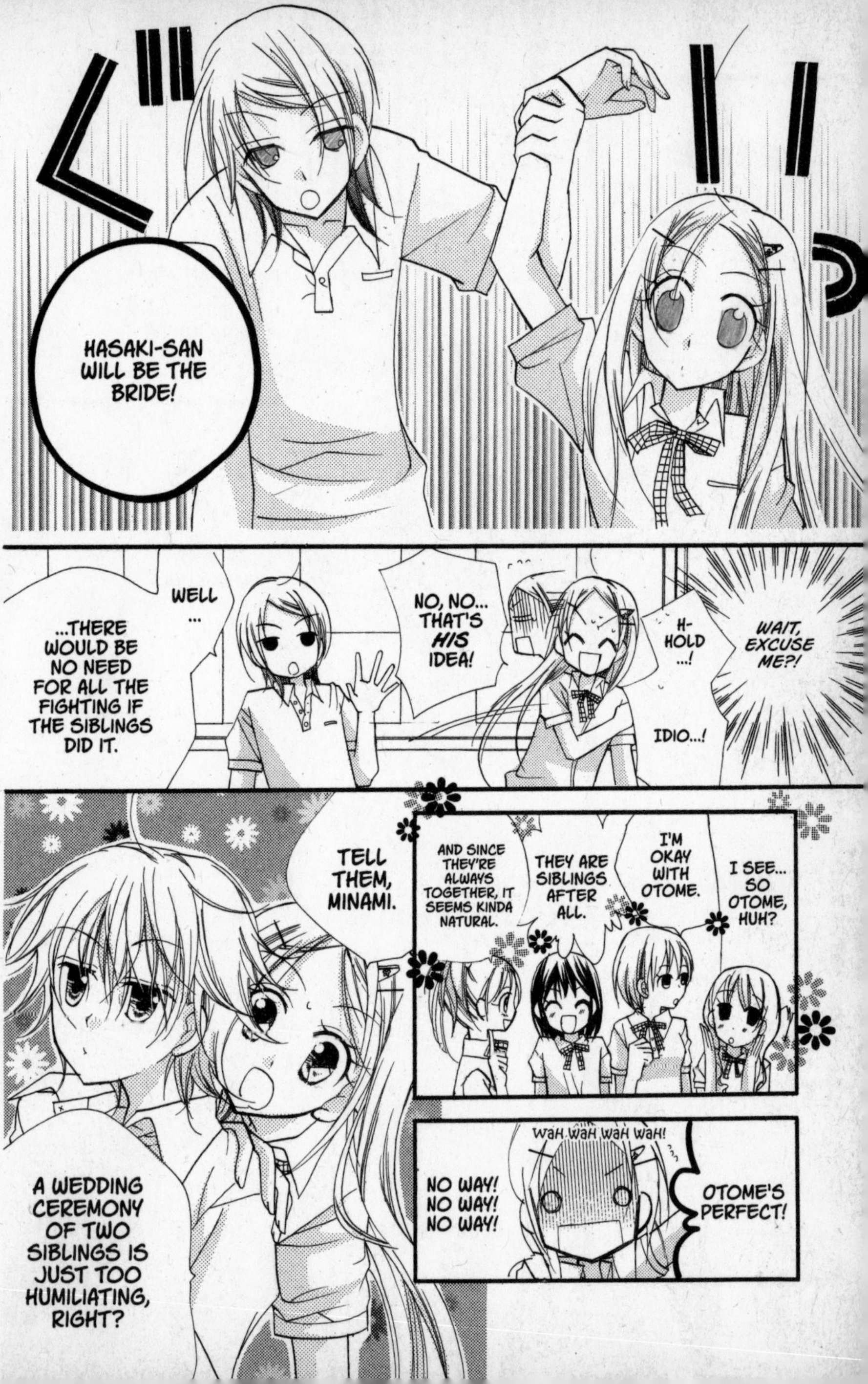
HASAKI-SAN WILL BE THE BRIDE!
WAIT, EXCUSE ME?!
H-HOLD ...!
IDIO...!
NO, NO... THAT'S HIS IDEA!
WELL ...
...THERE WOULD BE NO NEED FOR ALL THE FIGHTING IF THE SIBLINGS DID IT.
I SEE... SO OTOME, HUH?
I'M OKAY WITH OTOME.
THEY ARE SIBLINGS AFTER ALL.
AND SINCE THEY'RE ALWAYS TOGETHER, IT SEEMS KINDA NATURAL.
OTOME'S PERFECT!
WAH WAH WAH WAH!
NO WAY! NO WAY! NO WAY!
TELL THEM, MINAMI.
A WEDDING CEREMONY OF TWO SIBLINGS IS JUST TOO HUMILIATING, RIGHT?

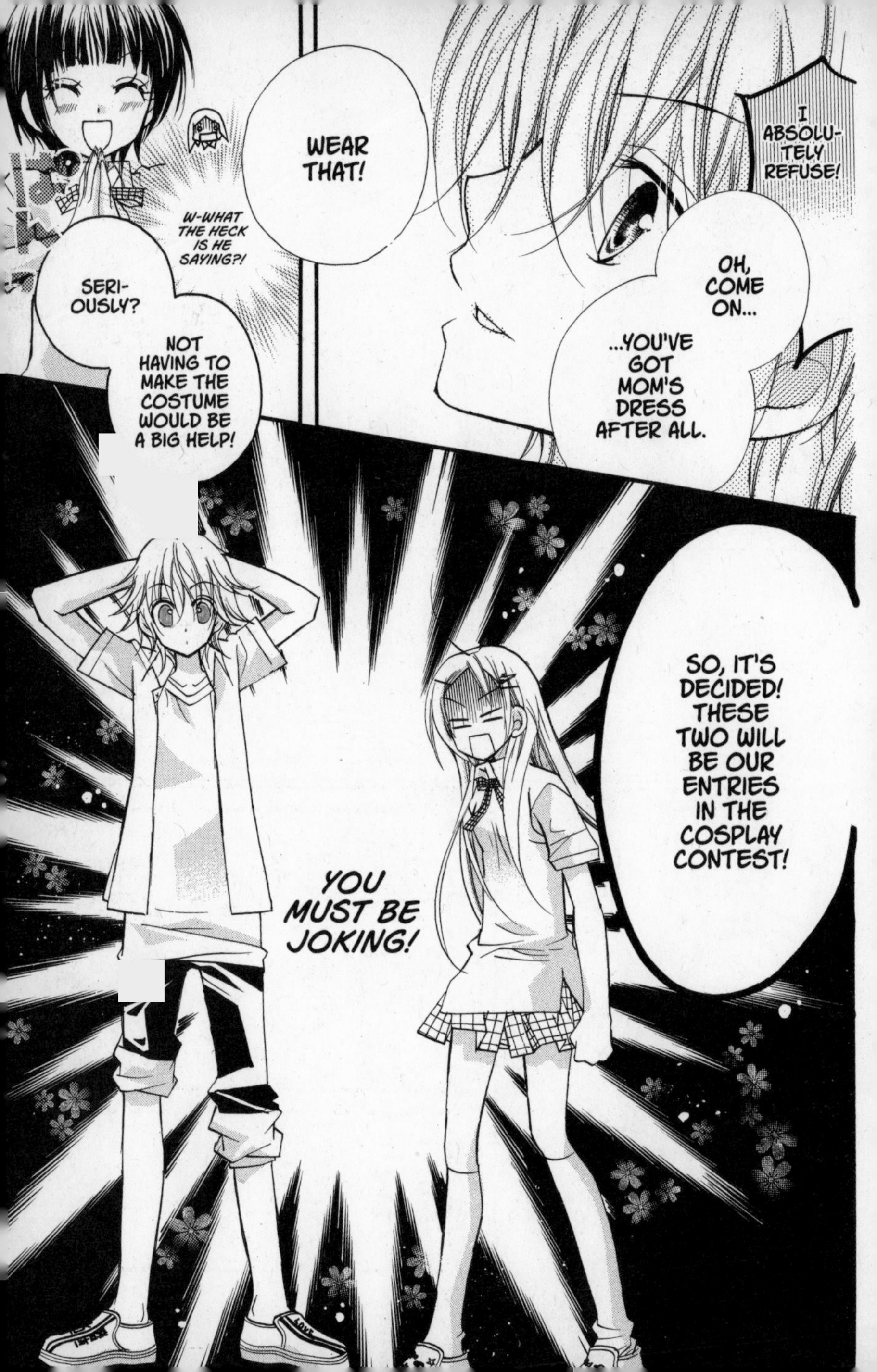
I ABSOLU-TELY REFUSE!
WEAR THAT!
OH, COME ON...
...YOU'VE GOT MOM'S DRESS AFTER ALL.
W-WHAT THE HECK IS HE SAYING?!
SERI-OUSLY?
NOT HAVING TO MAKE THE COSTUME WOULD BE A BIG HELP!
SO, IT'S DECIDED! THESE TWO WILL BE OUR ENTRIES IN THE COSPLAY CONTEST!
YOU MUST BE JOKING!

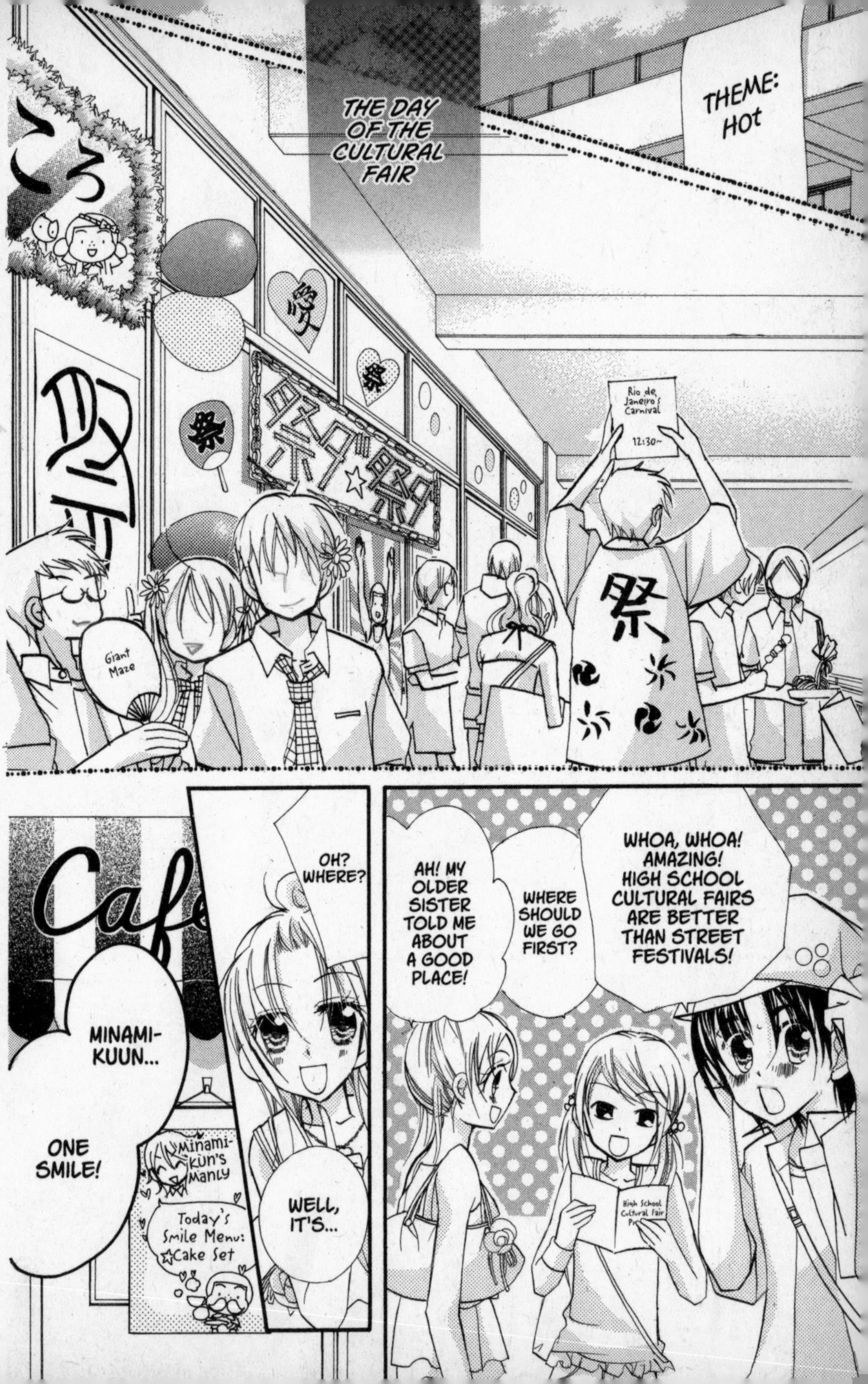
THEME: Hot
THE DAY OF THE CULTURAL FAIR
Rio de Janeiro's Carnival 12:30~
Giant Maze
WHOA, WHOA! AMAZING! HIGH SCHOOL CULTURAL FAIRS ARE BETTER THAN STREET FESTIVALS!
WHERE SHOULD WE GO FIRST?
AH! MY OLDER SISTER TOLD ME ABOUT A GOOD PLACE!
High School Cultural Fair
OH? WHERE?
WELL, IT'S...
MINAMI-KUUN...
ONE SMILE!
Minami-kun's Manly
Today's Smile Menu: ☆Cake Set

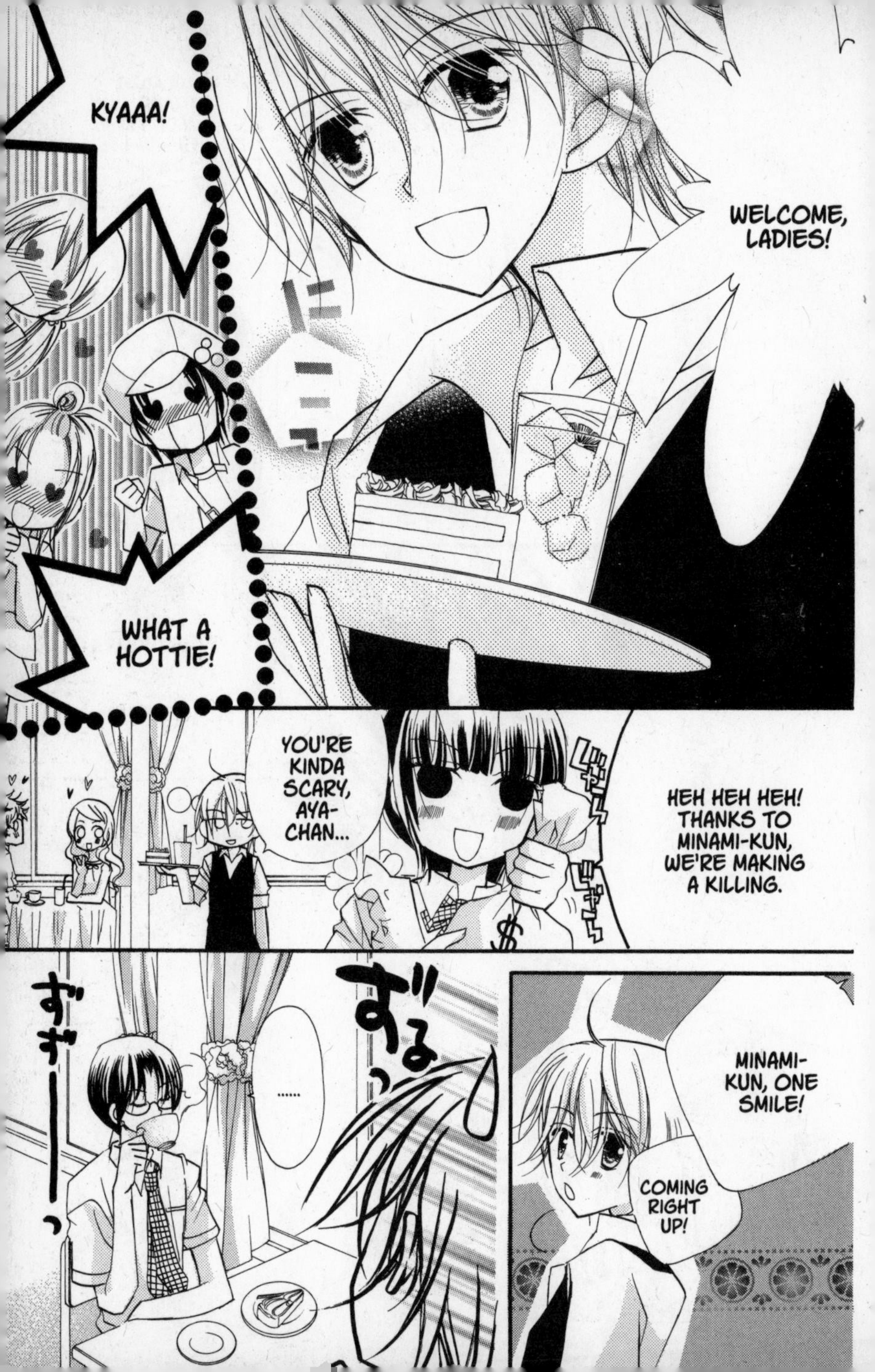
WELCOME, LADIES!
KYAAA!
WHAT A HOTTIE!
HEH HEH HEH! THANKS TO MINAMI-KUN, WE'RE MAKING A KILLING.
YOU'RE KINDA SCARY, AYA-CHAN...
MINAMI-KUN, ONE SMILE!
COMING RIGHT UP!
......

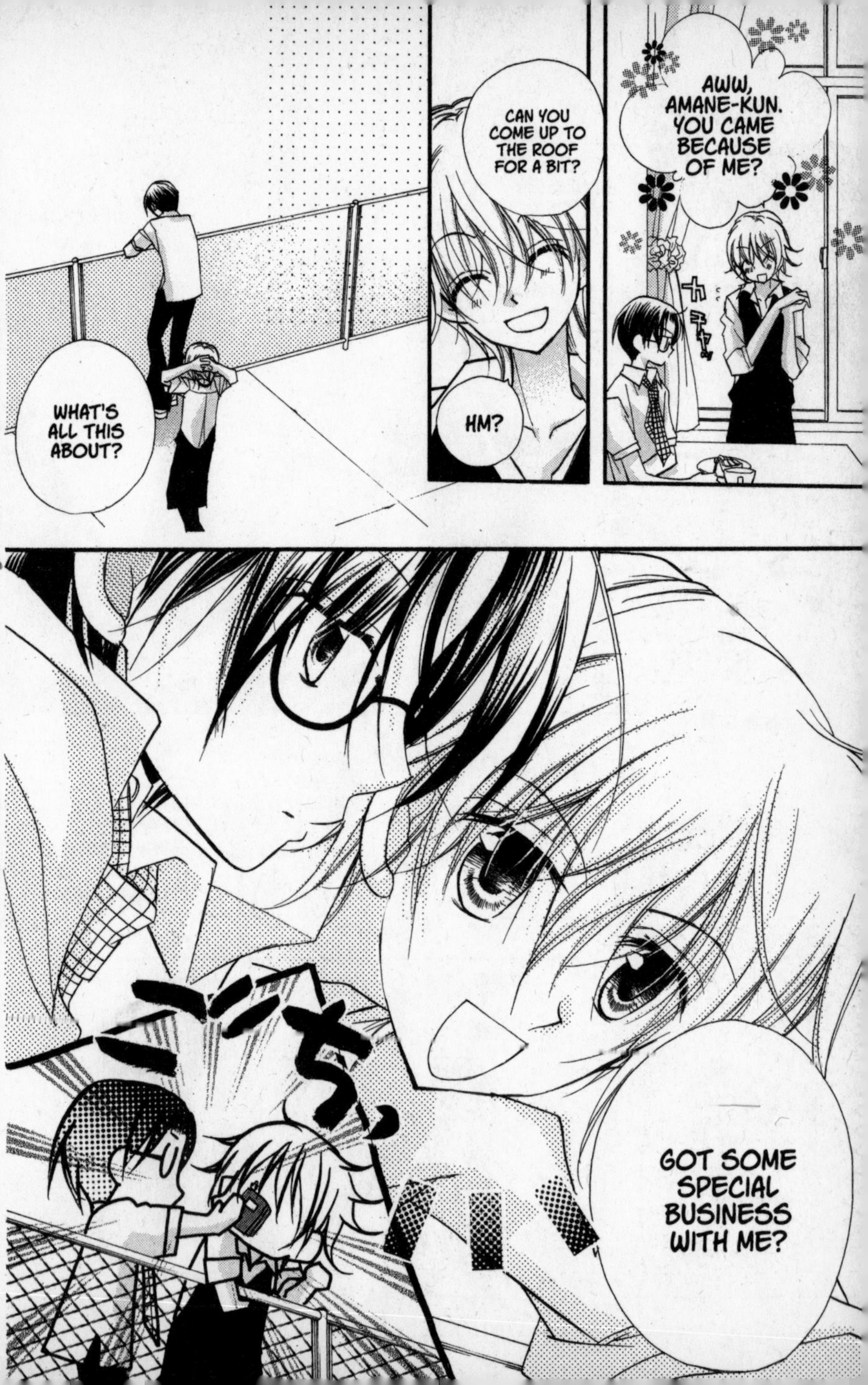
AWW, AMANE-KUN. YOU CAME BECAUSE OF ME?
CAN YOU COME UP TO THE ROOF FOR A BIT?
HM?
WHAT'S ALL THIS ABOUT?
GOT SOME SPECIAL BUSINESS WITH ME?

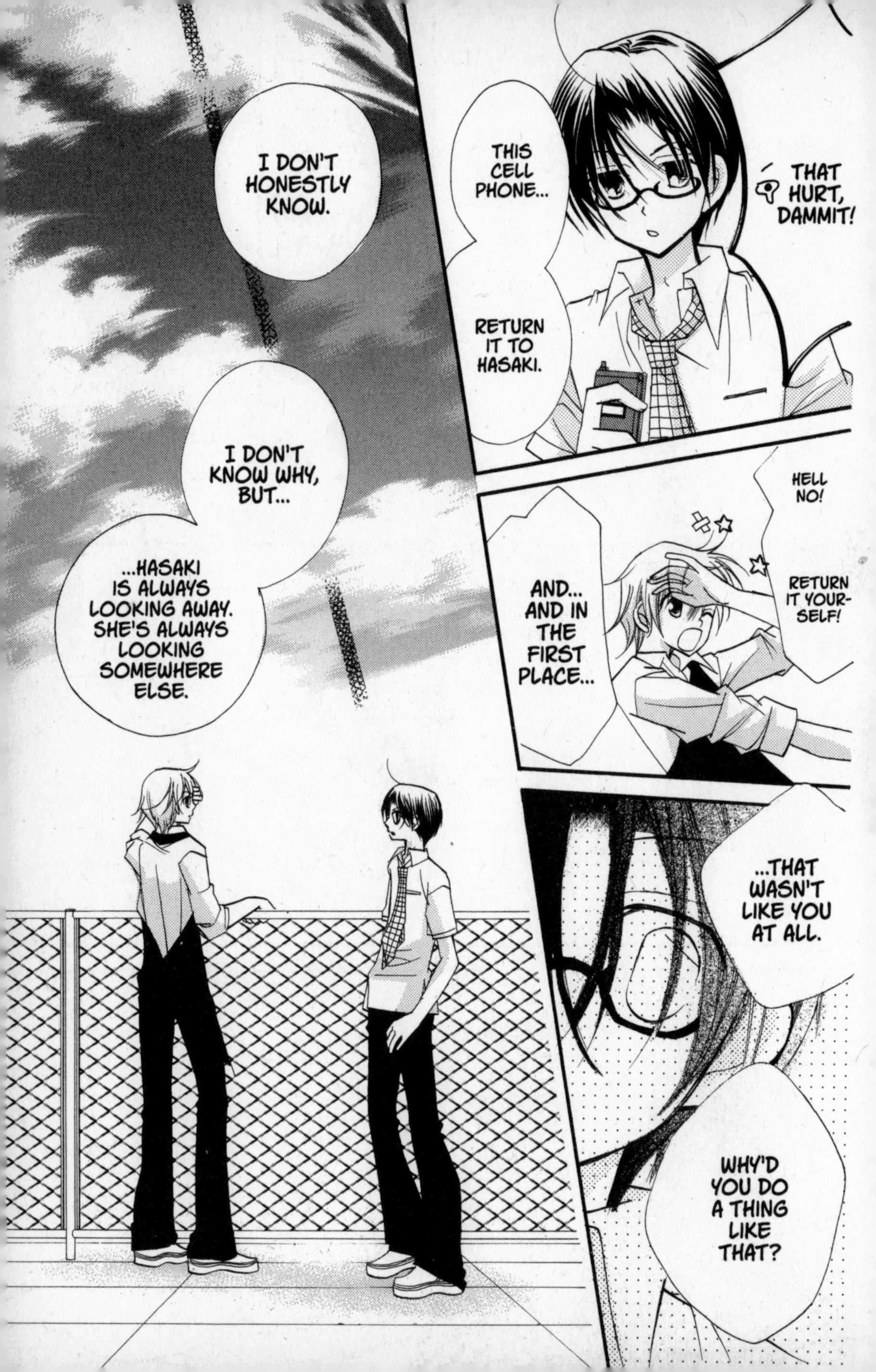
THAT HURT, DAMMIT!
THIS CELL PHONE...
RETURN IT TO HASAKI.
HELL NO!
RETURN IT YOURSELF!
AND... AND IN THE FIRST PLACE...
...THAT WASN'T LIKE YOU AT ALL.
WHY'D YOU DO A THING LIKE THAT?
I DON'T HONESTLY KNOW.
I DON'T KNOW WHY, BUT...
...HASAKI IS ALWAYS LOOKING AWAY. SHE'S ALWAYS LOOKING SOMEWHERE ELSE.

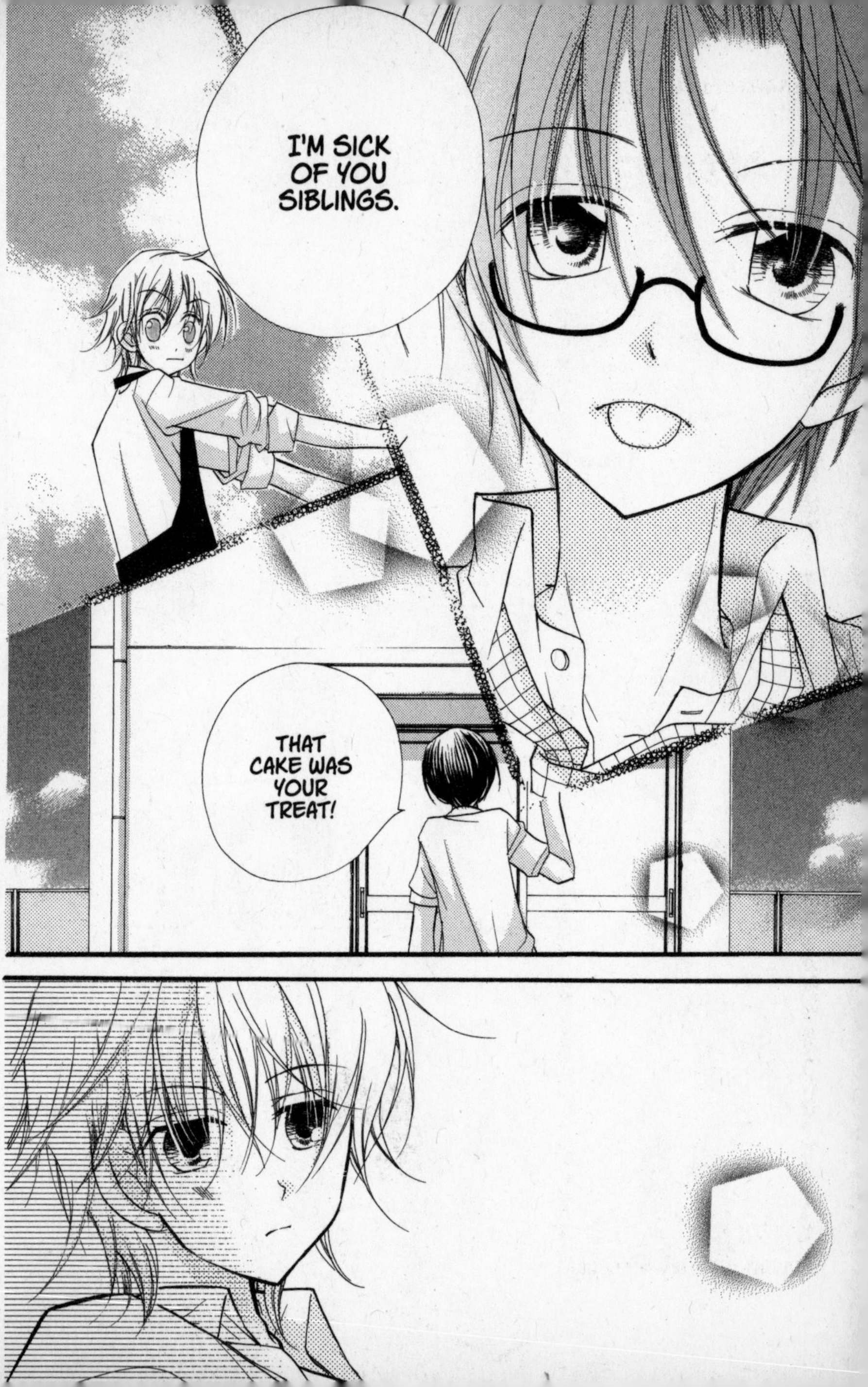
I'M SICK OF YOU SIBLINGS.
THAT CAKE WAS YOUR TREAT!

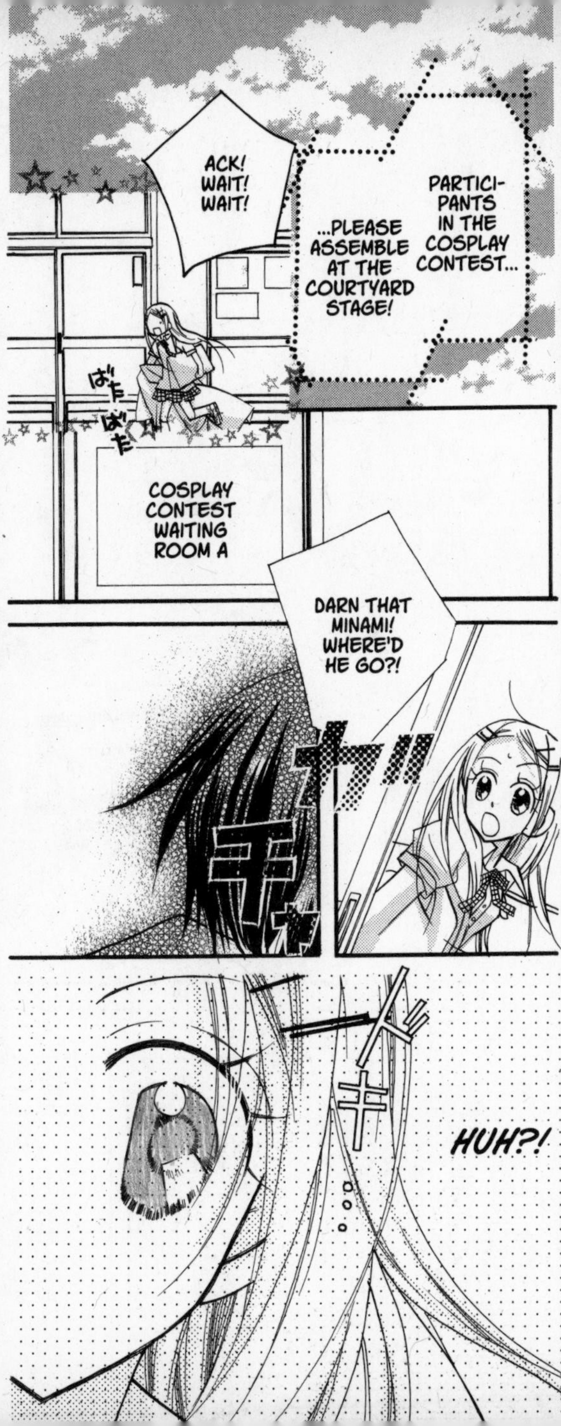
PARTICI-PANTS IN THE COSPLAY CONTEST...
...PLEASE ASSEMBLE AT THE COURTYARD STAGE!
ACK! WAIT! WAIT!
ばたばた
COSPLAY CONTEST WAITING ROOM A
DARN THAT MINAMI! WHERE'D HE GO?!
HUH?!

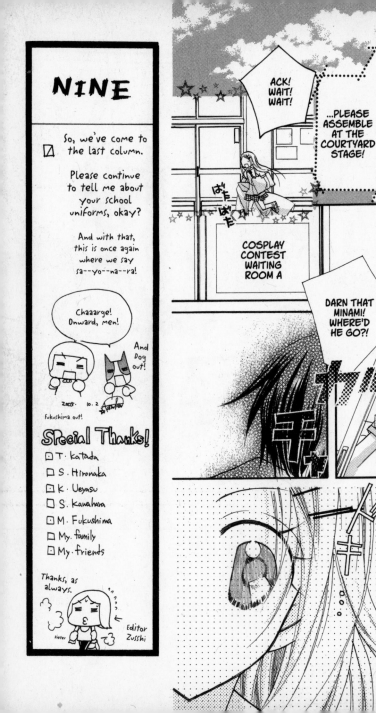

NINE

☑ So, we've come to the last column.

Please continue to tell me about your school uniforms, okay?

And with that, this is once again where we say sa--yo--na--ra!

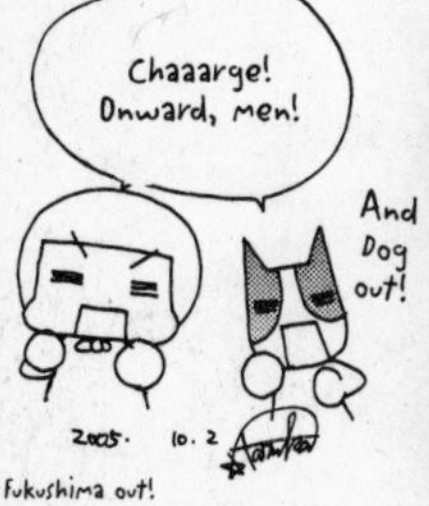
Chaaarge! Onward, men!
And Dog out!
2005. 10. 2
Fukushima out!

Special Thanks!

- ☐ T. Katada
- ☐ S. Hironaka
- ☐ K. Ueyasu
- ☐ S. Kawahara
- ☐ M. Fukushima
- ☐ My. family
- ☐ My. friends

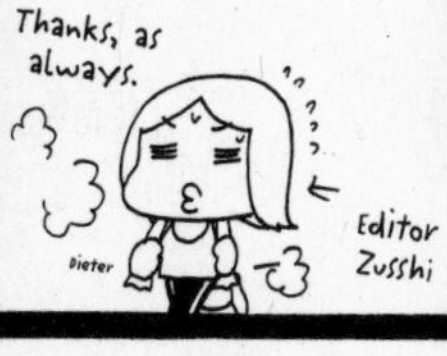
Thanks, as always.
Dieter
Editor Zusshi

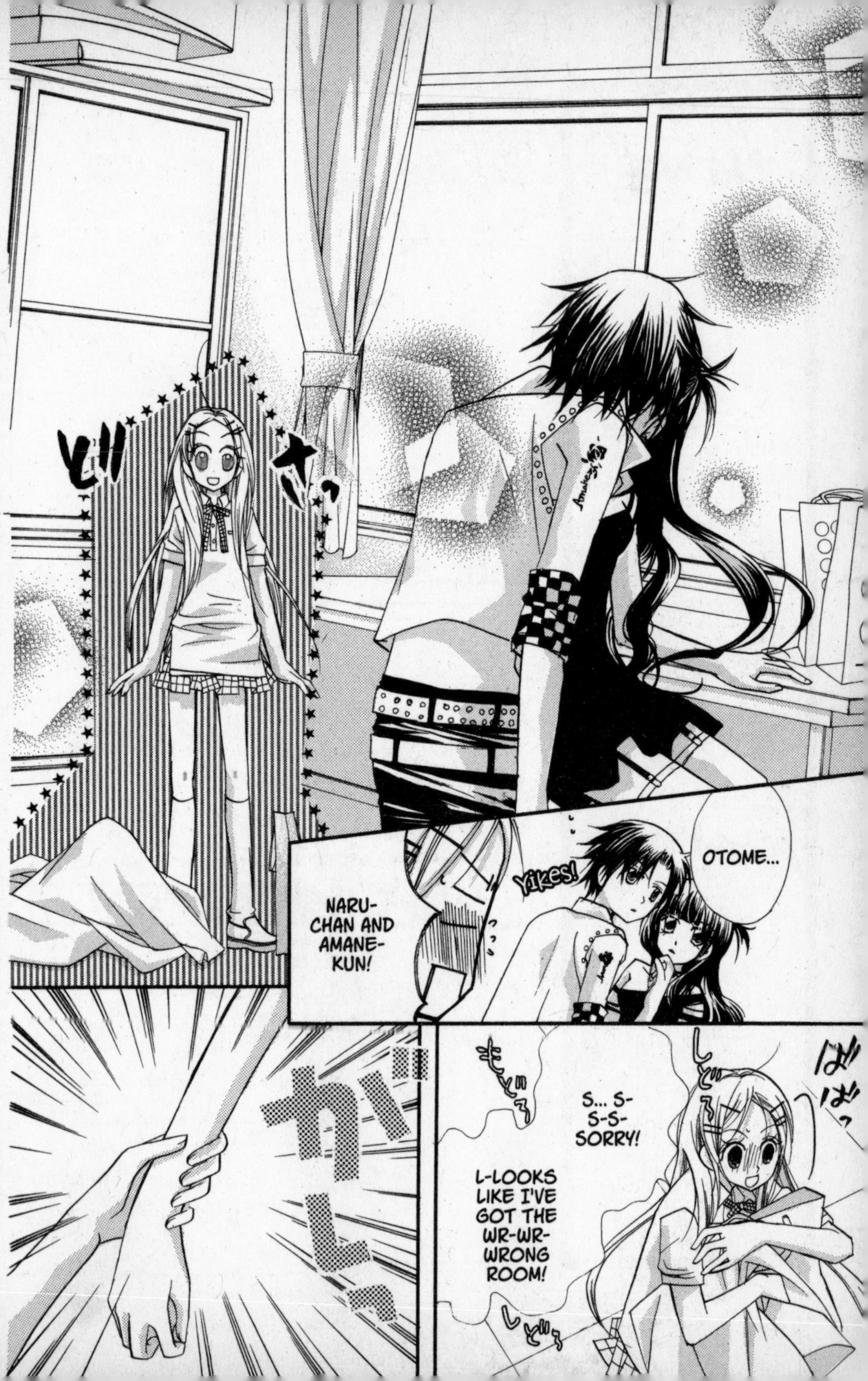

OTOME...
Yikes!
NARU-CHAN AND AMANE-KUN!
S... S-S-S-SORRY!
L-LOOKS LIKE I'VE GOT THE WR-WR-WRONG ROOM!

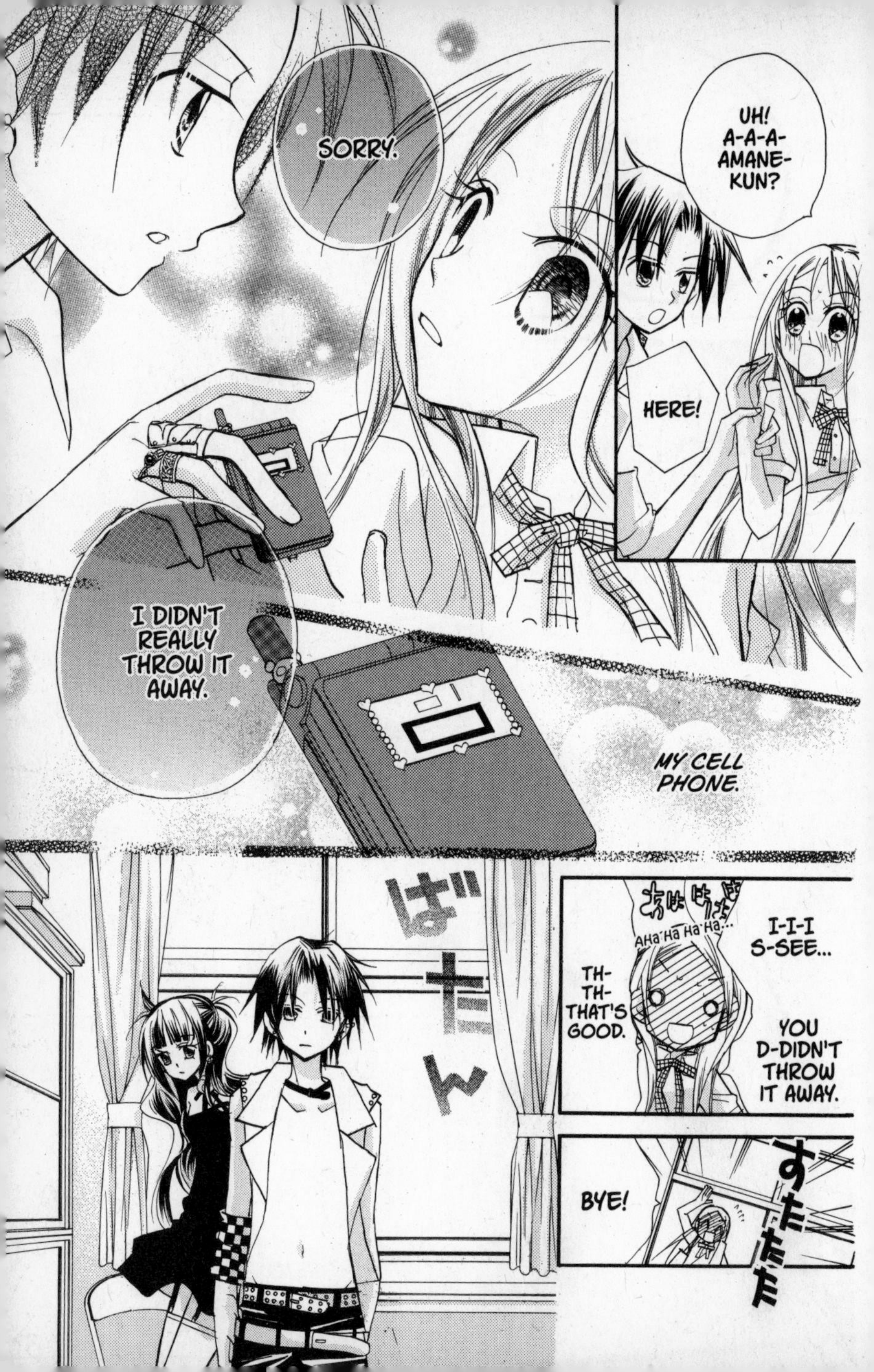
UH! A-A-A-AMANE-KUN?
HERE!
SORRY.
I DIDN'T REALLY THROW IT AWAY.
MY CELL PHONE.
AHA HA HA HA...
I-I-I S-SEE...
YOU D-DIDN'T THROW IT AWAY.
TH-TH-THAT'S GOOD.
すたたた
BYE!
ばたん

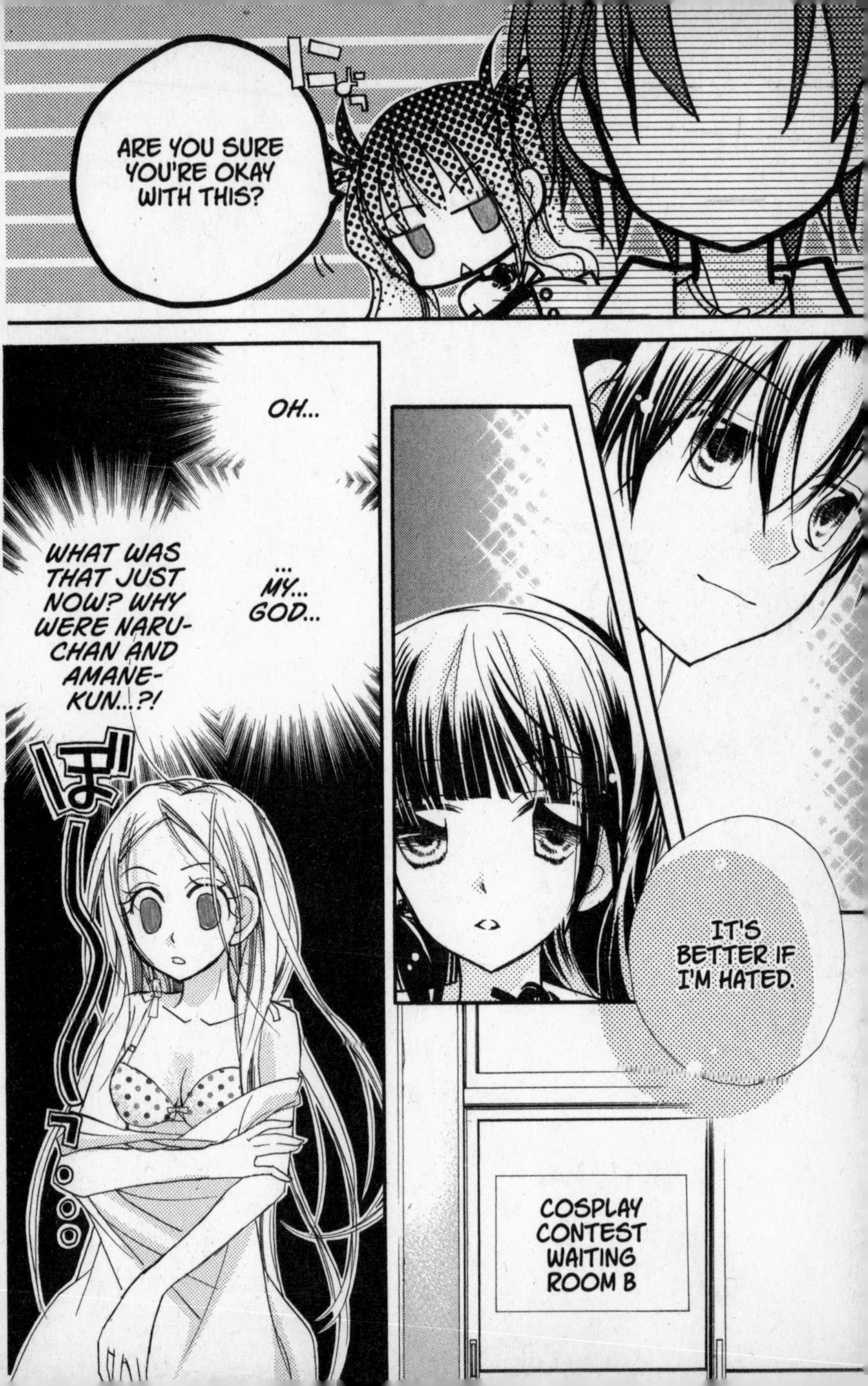
ARE YOU SURE YOU'RE OKAY WITH THIS?
IT'S BETTER IF I'M HATED.
COSPLAY CONTEST WAITING ROOM B
OH...
... MY... GOD...
WHAT WAS THAT JUST NOW? WHY WERE NARU-CHAN AND AMANE-KUN...?!

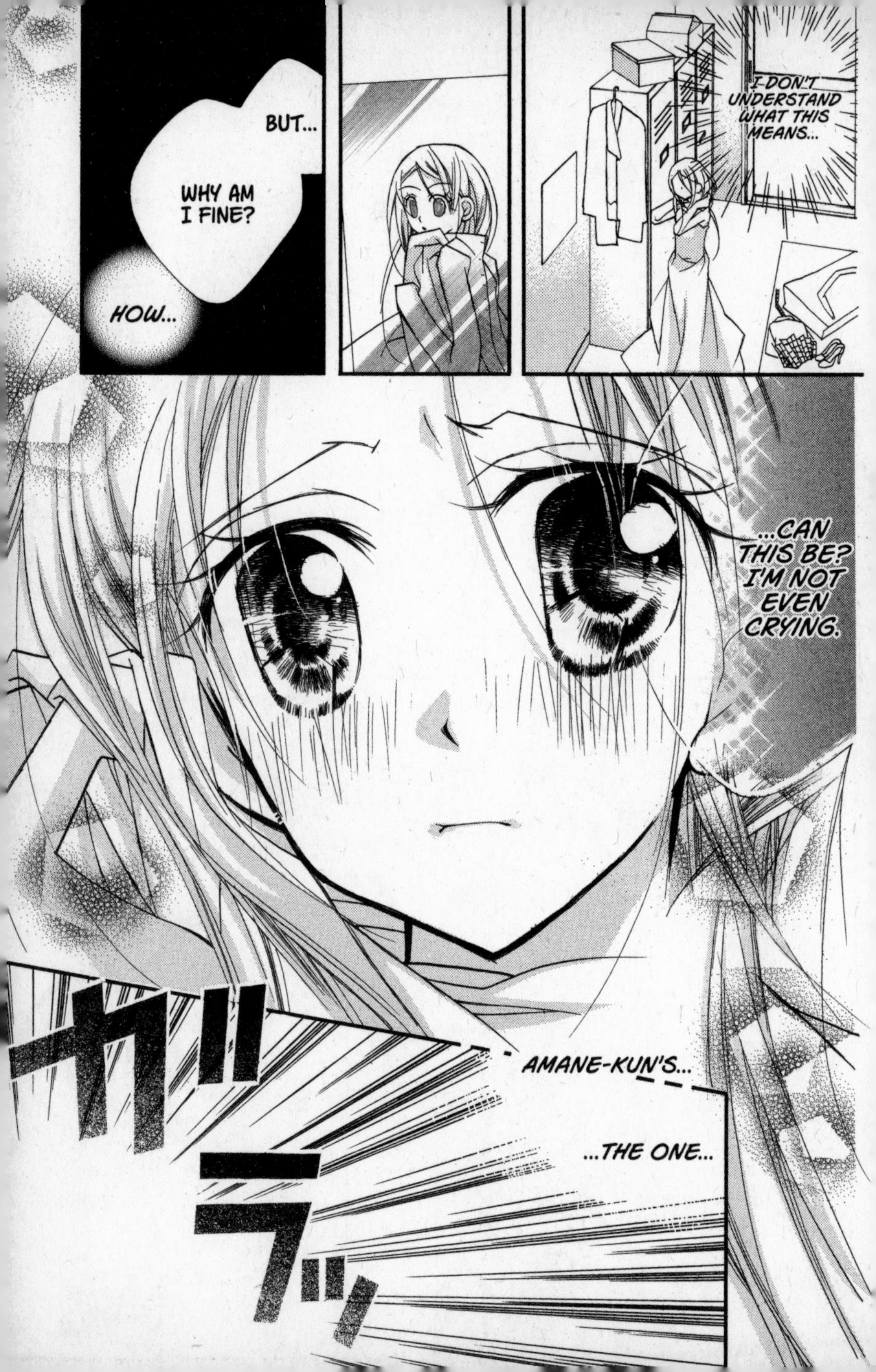
I DON'T UNDERSTAND WHAT THIS MEANS...
BUT...
WHY AM I FINE?
HOW...
...CAN THIS BE? I'M NOT EVEN CRYING.
AMANE-KUN'S...
...THE ONE...

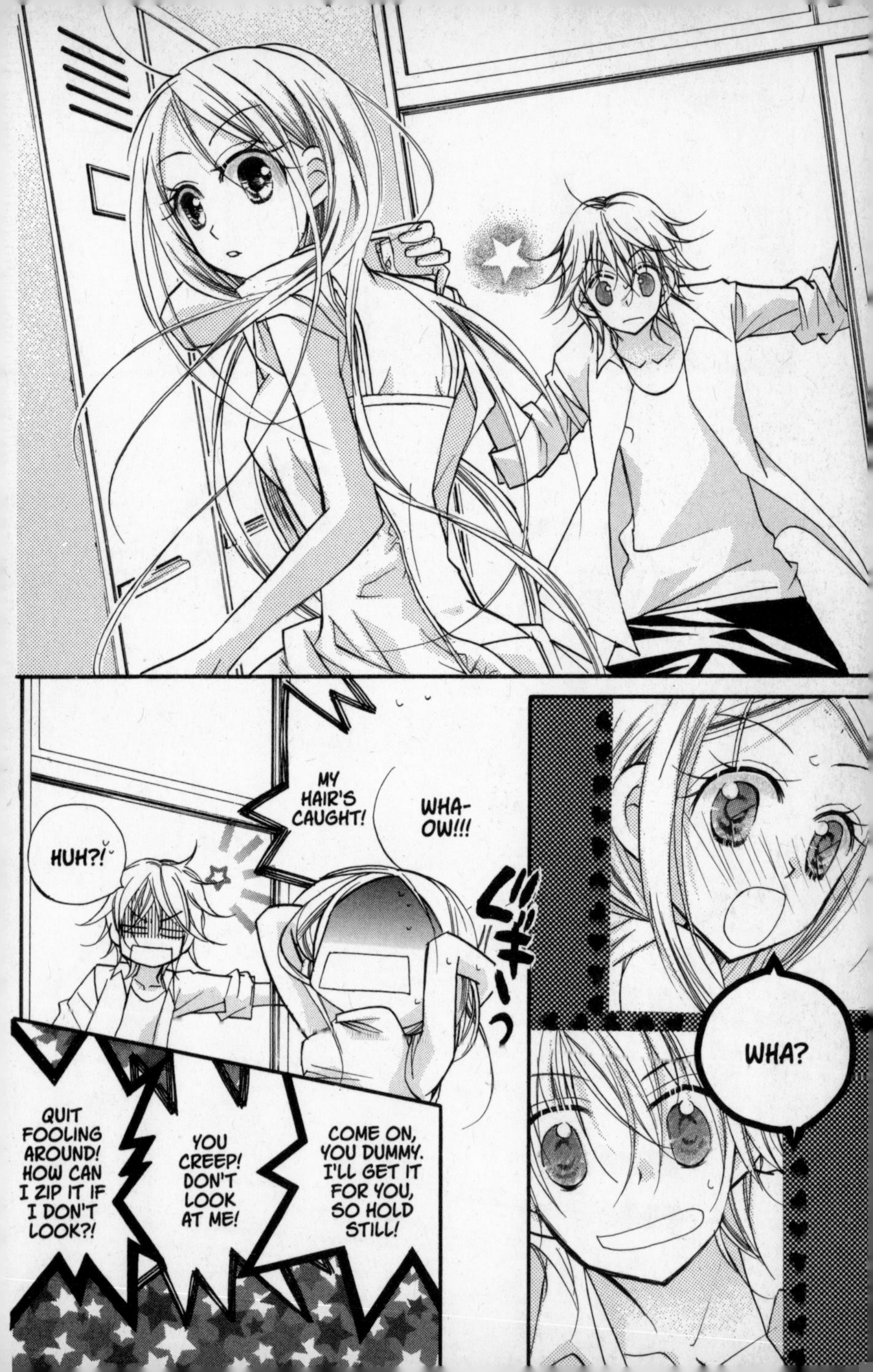
WHA-OW!!!
MY HAIR'S CAUGHT!
ぐぎっ
HUH?!
WHA?
COME ON, YOU DUMMY. I'LL GET IT FOR YOU, SO HOLD STILL!
YOU CREEP! DON'T LOOK AT ME!
QUIT FOOLING AROUND! HOW CAN I ZIP IT IF I DON'T LOOK?!

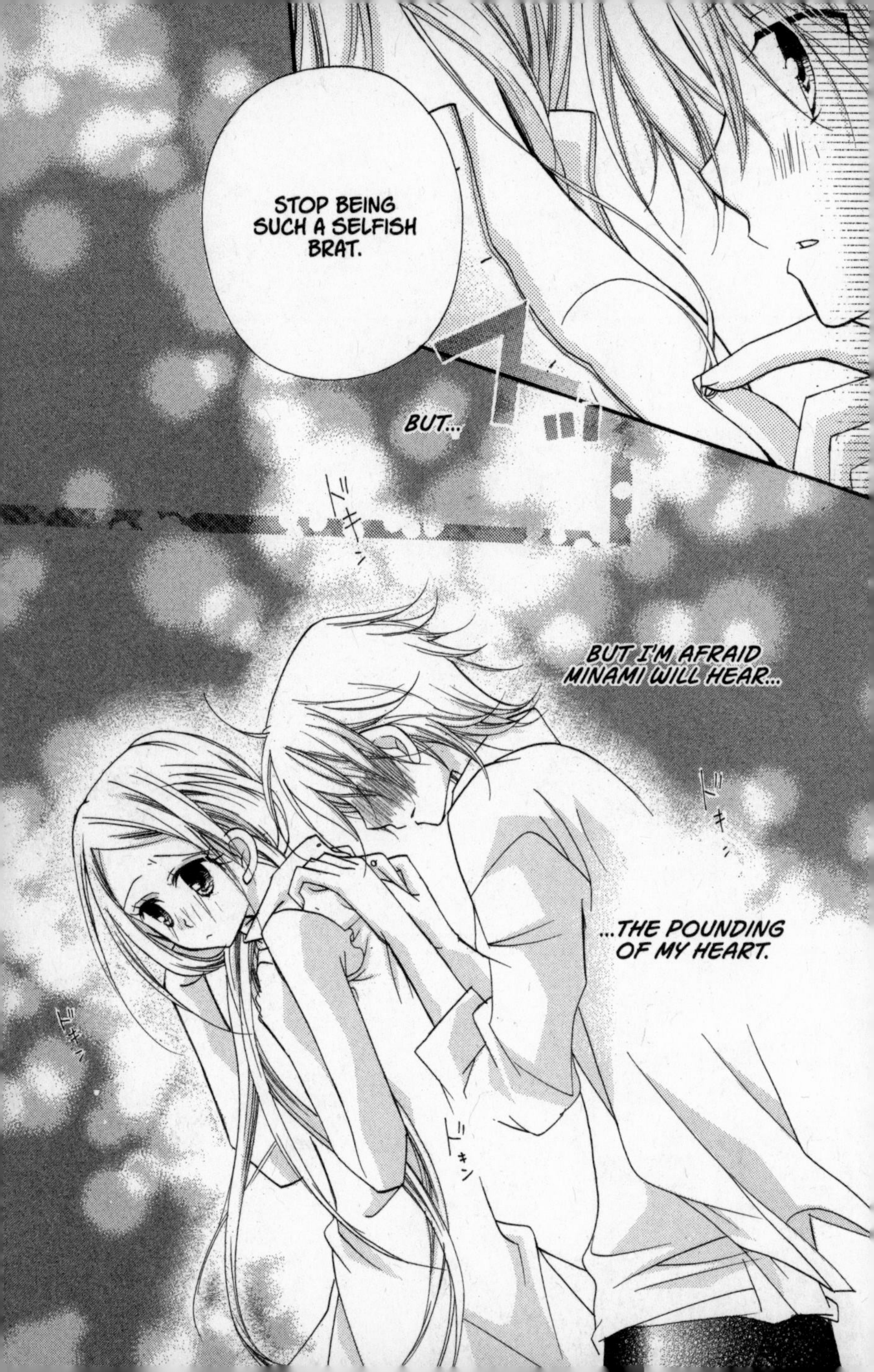
STOP BEING SUCH A SELFISH BRAT.
BUT...
ドキン
BUT I'M AFRAID MINAMI WILL HEAR...
ドキン
...THE POUNDING OF MY HEART.
ドキン

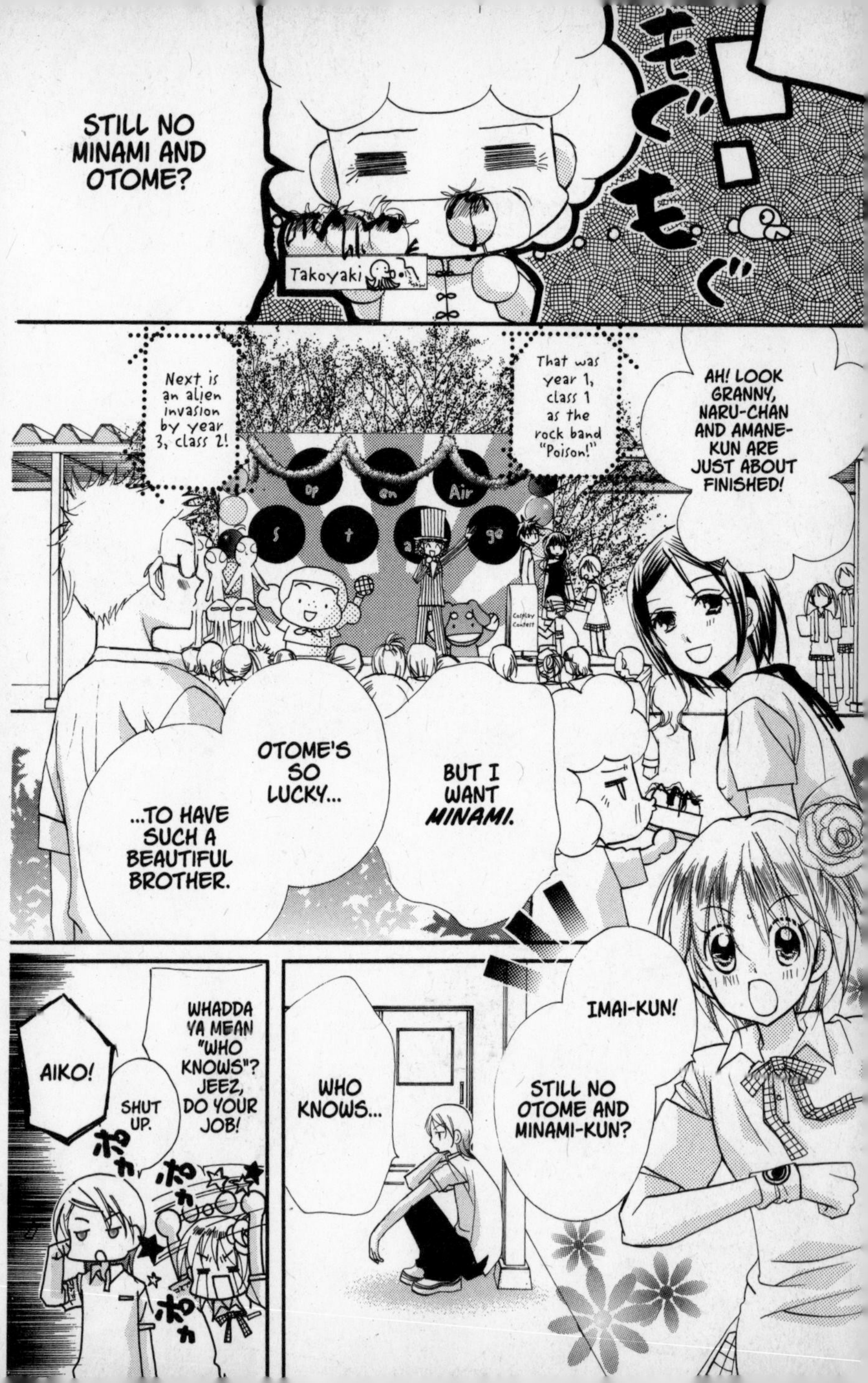
もぐもぐ
Takoyaki
STILL NO MINAMI AND OTOME?
AH! LOOK GRANNY, NARU-CHAN AND AMANE-KUN ARE JUST ABOUT FINISHED!
That was year 1, class 1 as the rock band "Poison!"
Next is an alien invasion by year 3, class 2!
Open Air Stage
Cosplay Contest
BUT I WANT *MINAMI.*
OTOME'S SO LUCKY...
...TO HAVE SUCH A BEAUTIFUL BROTHER.
IMAI-KUN!
STILL NO OTOME AND MINAMI-KUN?
WHO KNOWS...
WHADDA YA MEAN "WHO KNOWS"? JEEZ, DO YOUR JOB!
AIKO!
SHUT UP.
ポカ ポカ ポカ

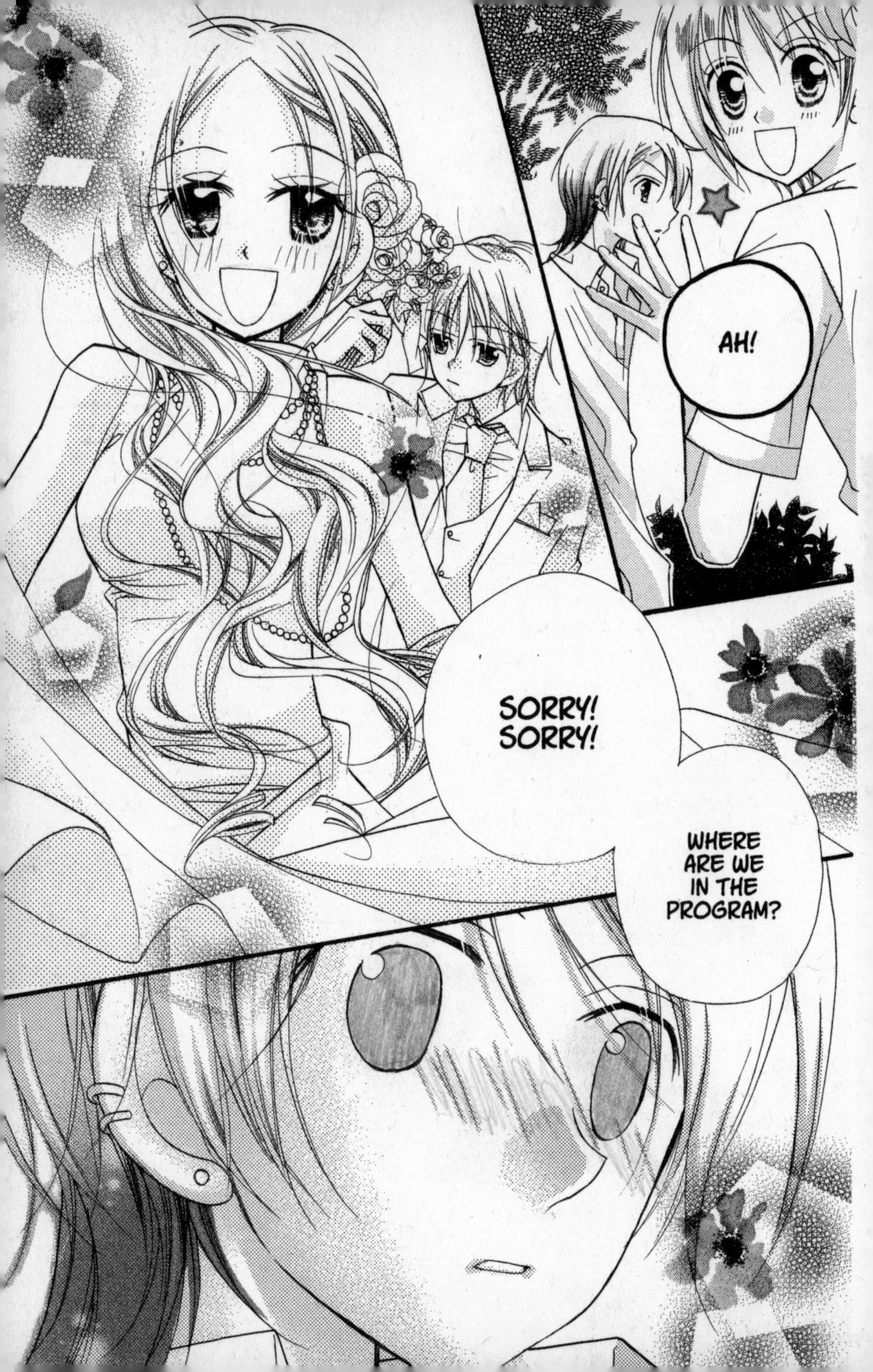
AH!
SORRY! SORRY!
WHERE ARE WE IN THE PROGRAM?

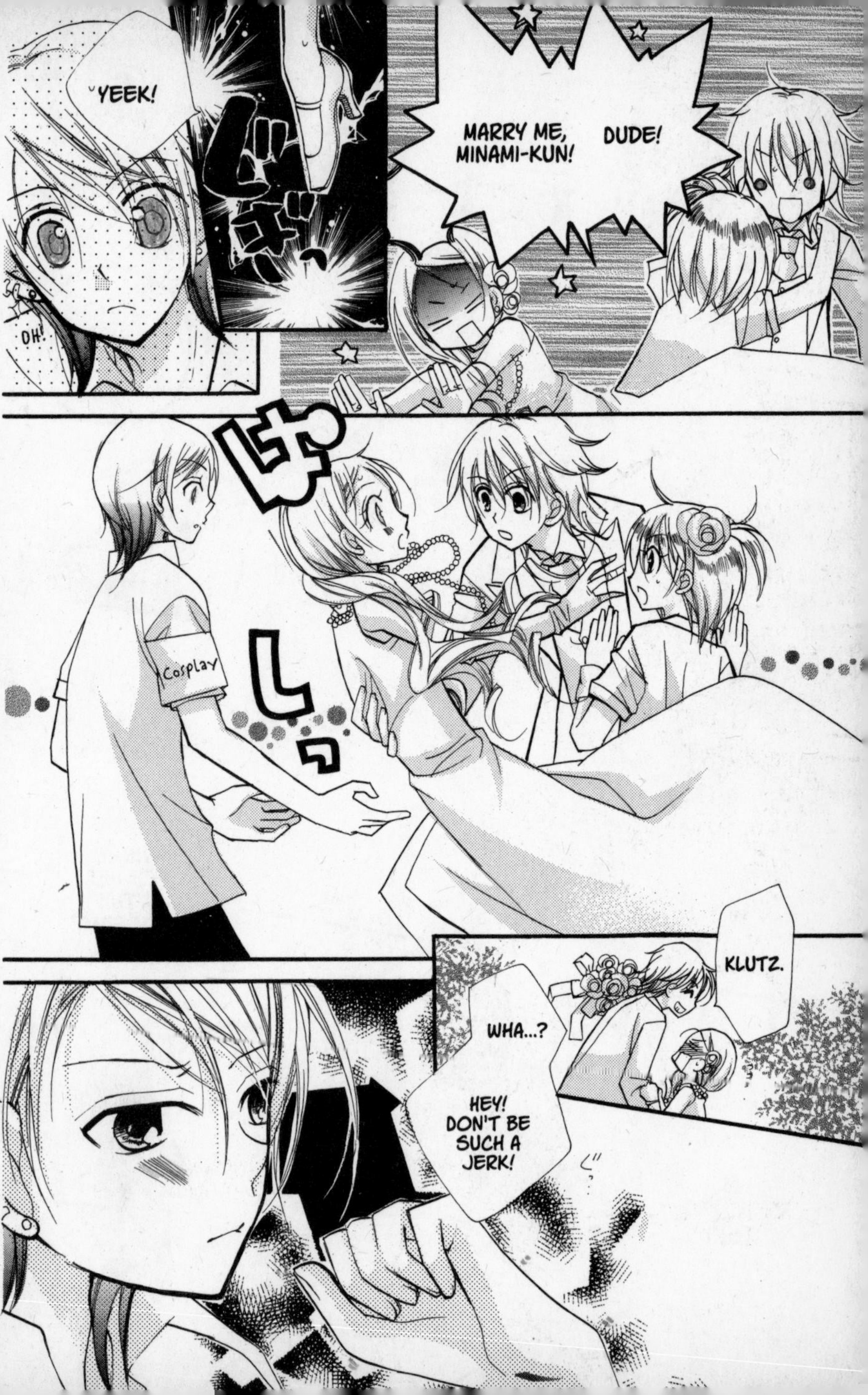
MARRY ME, MINAMI-KUN! DUDE!
YEEK!
OH!
Cosplay
KLUTZ.
WHA...?
HEY! DON'T BE SUCH A JERK!

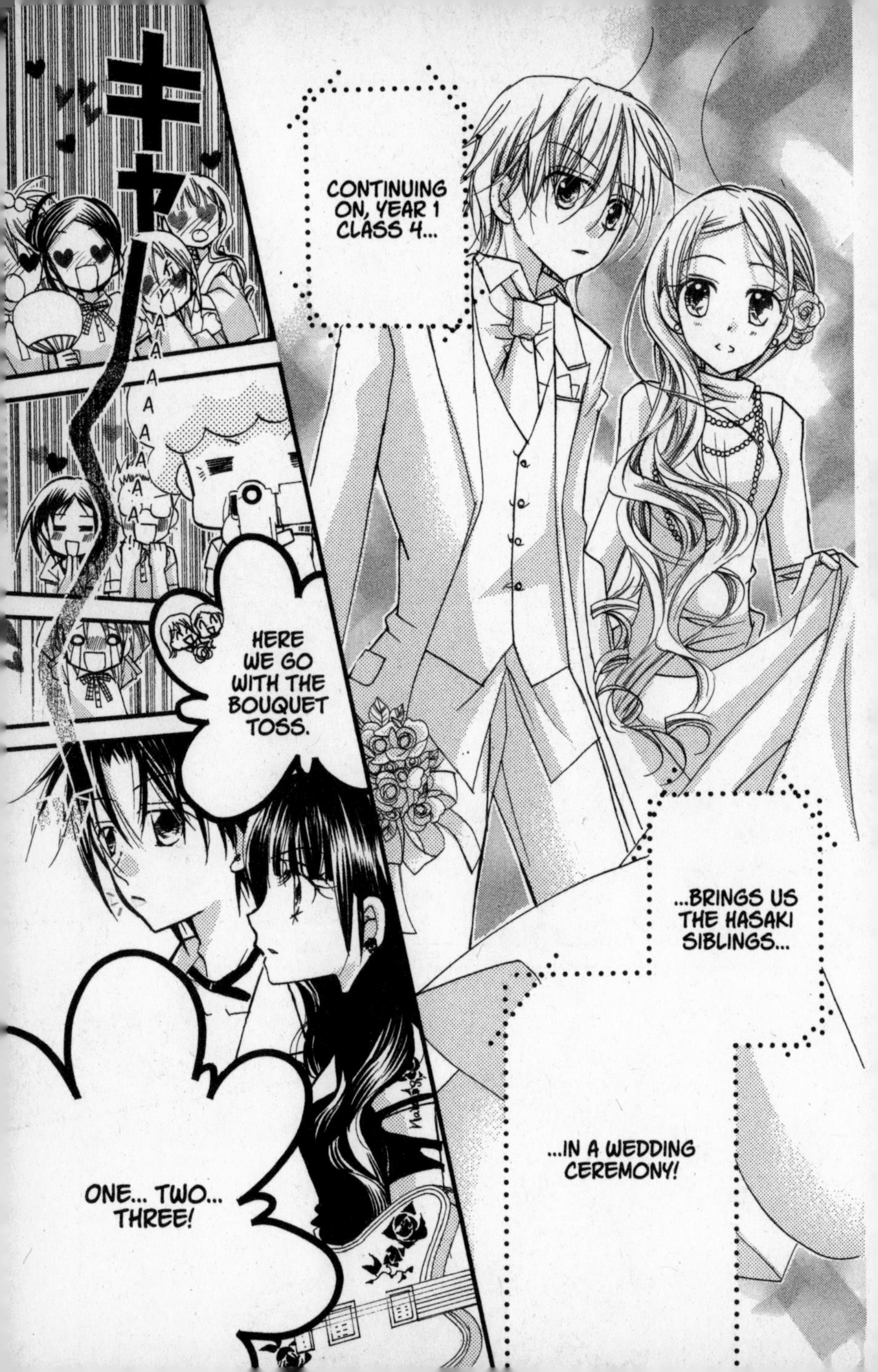
CONTINUING ON, YEAR 1 CLASS 4...
...BRINGS US THE HASAKI SIBLINGS...
...IN A WEDDING CEREMONY!
キャ
KYAAAAAAAA!
HERE WE GO WITH THE BOUQUET TOSS.
ONE... TWO... THREE!

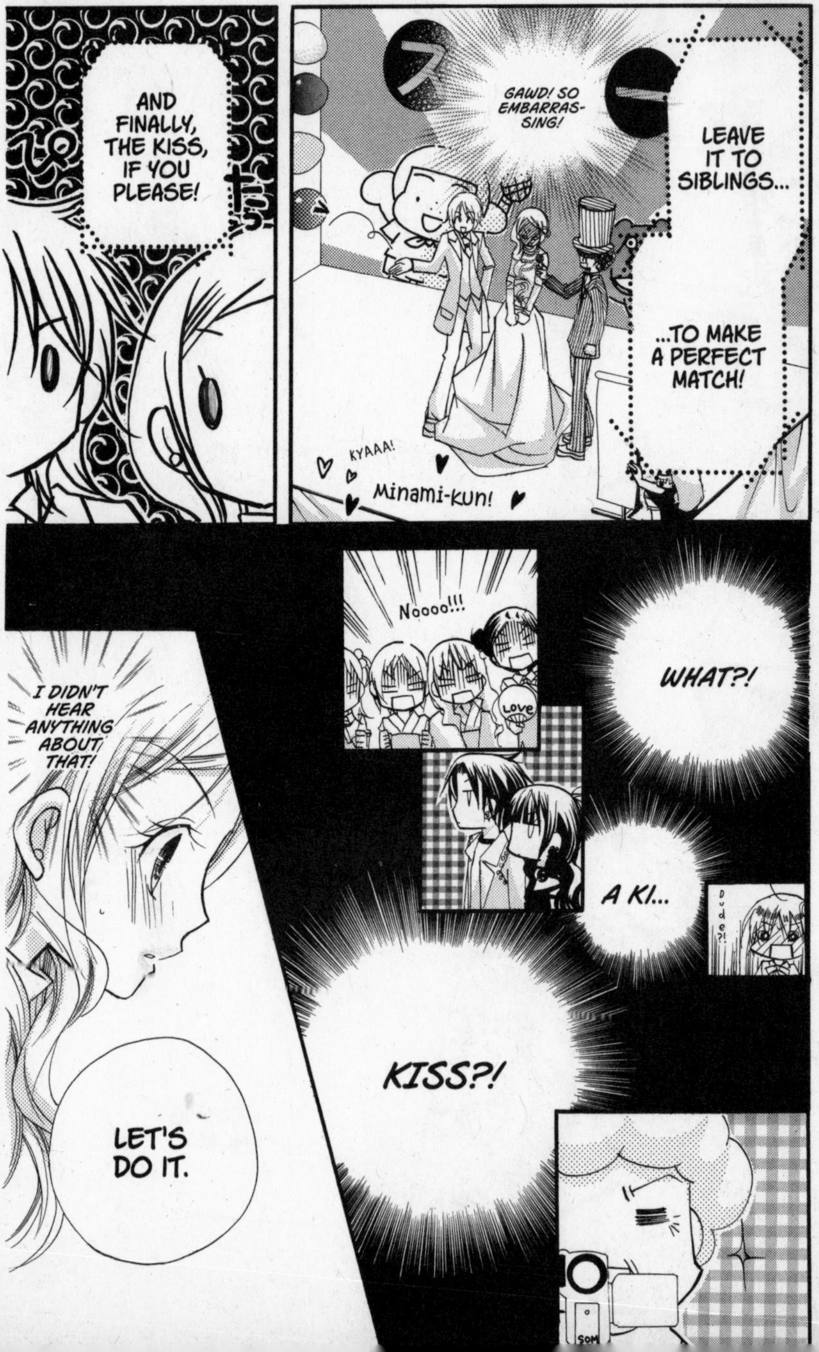
LEAVE IT TO SIBLINGS...
...TO MAKE A PERFECT MATCH!
GAWD! SO EMBARRAS-SING!
KYAAA!
Minami-kun!
AND FINALLY, THE KISS, IF YOU PLEASE!
WHAT?!
Noooo!!!
Love
A KI...
Dude?!
KISS?!
I DIDN'T HEAR ANYTHING ABOUT THAT!
LET'S DO IT.

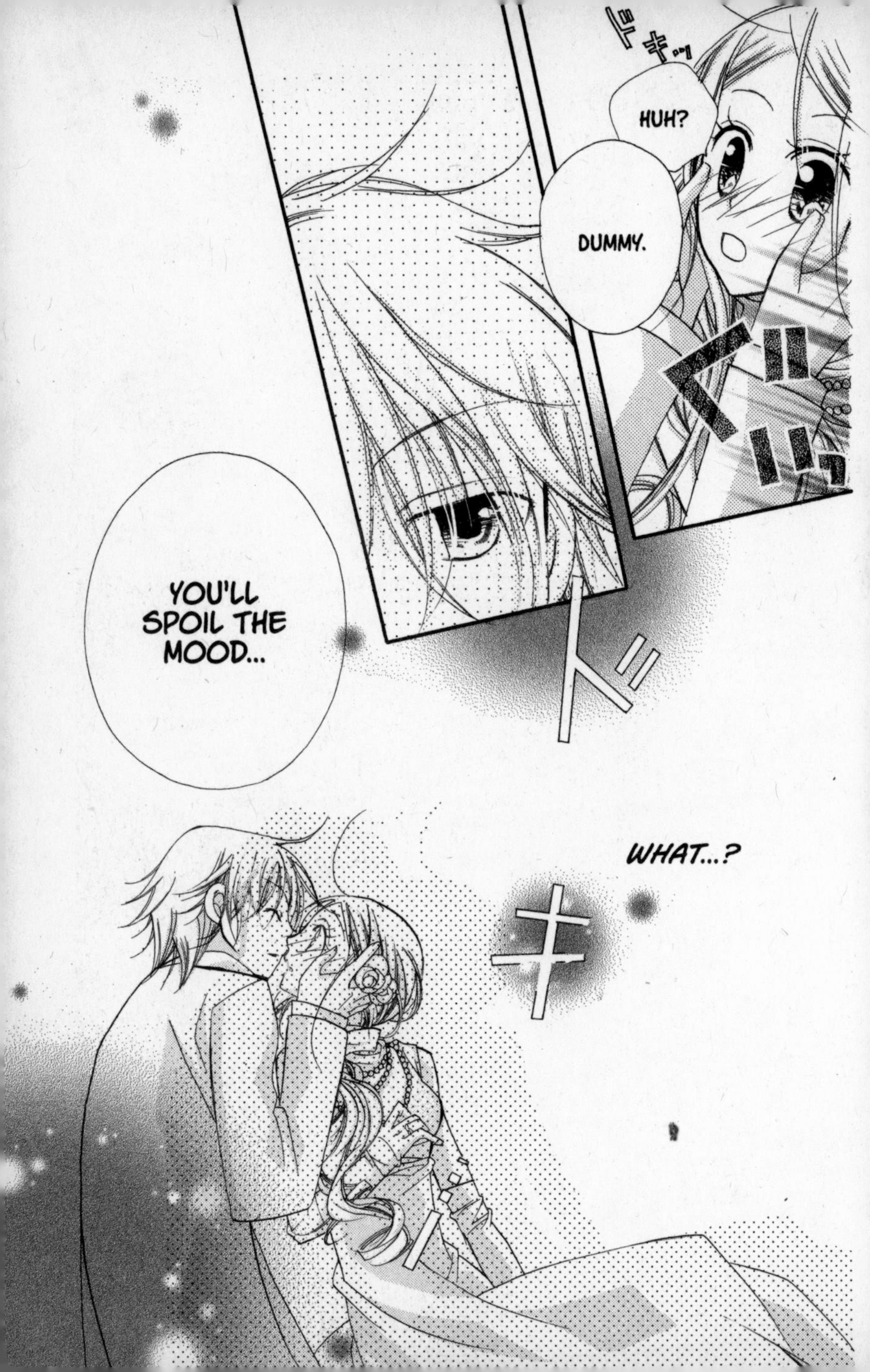
HUH?
DUMMY.
YOU'LL SPOIL THE MOOD...
WHAT...?

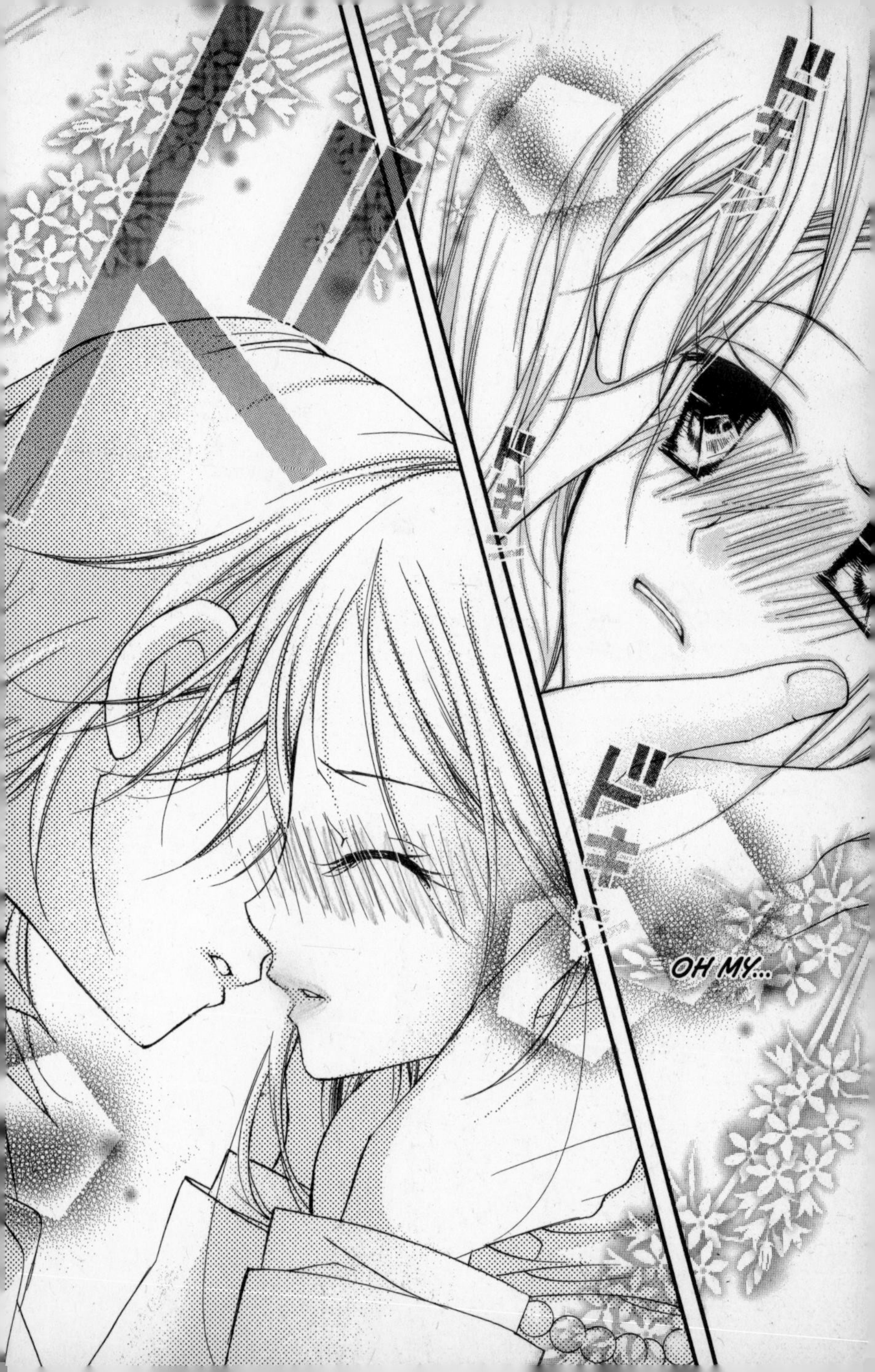
ドキ
ドキ
OH MY...

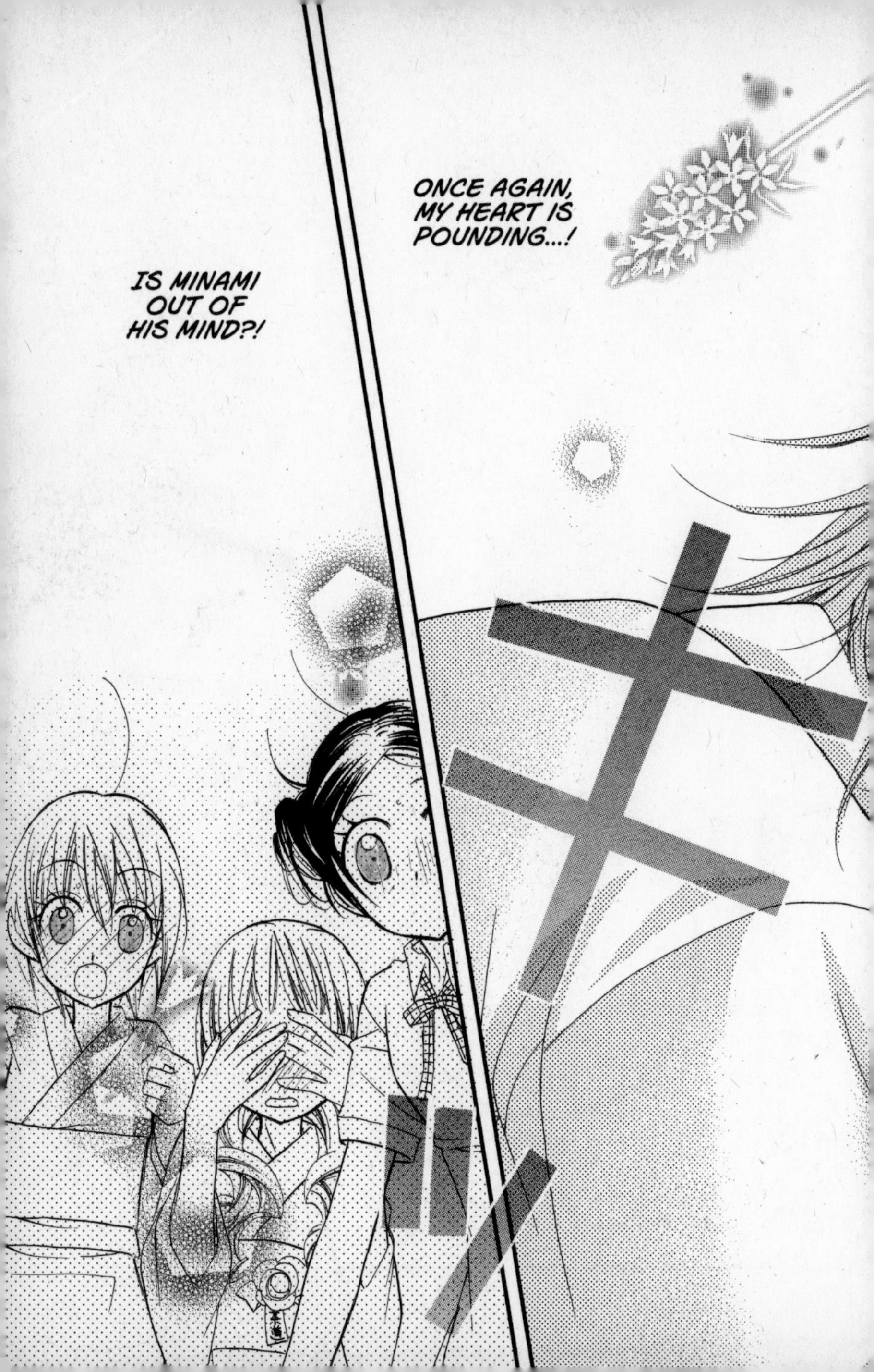
ONCE AGAIN, MY HEART IS POUNDING...!
IS MINAMI OUT OF HIS MIND?!

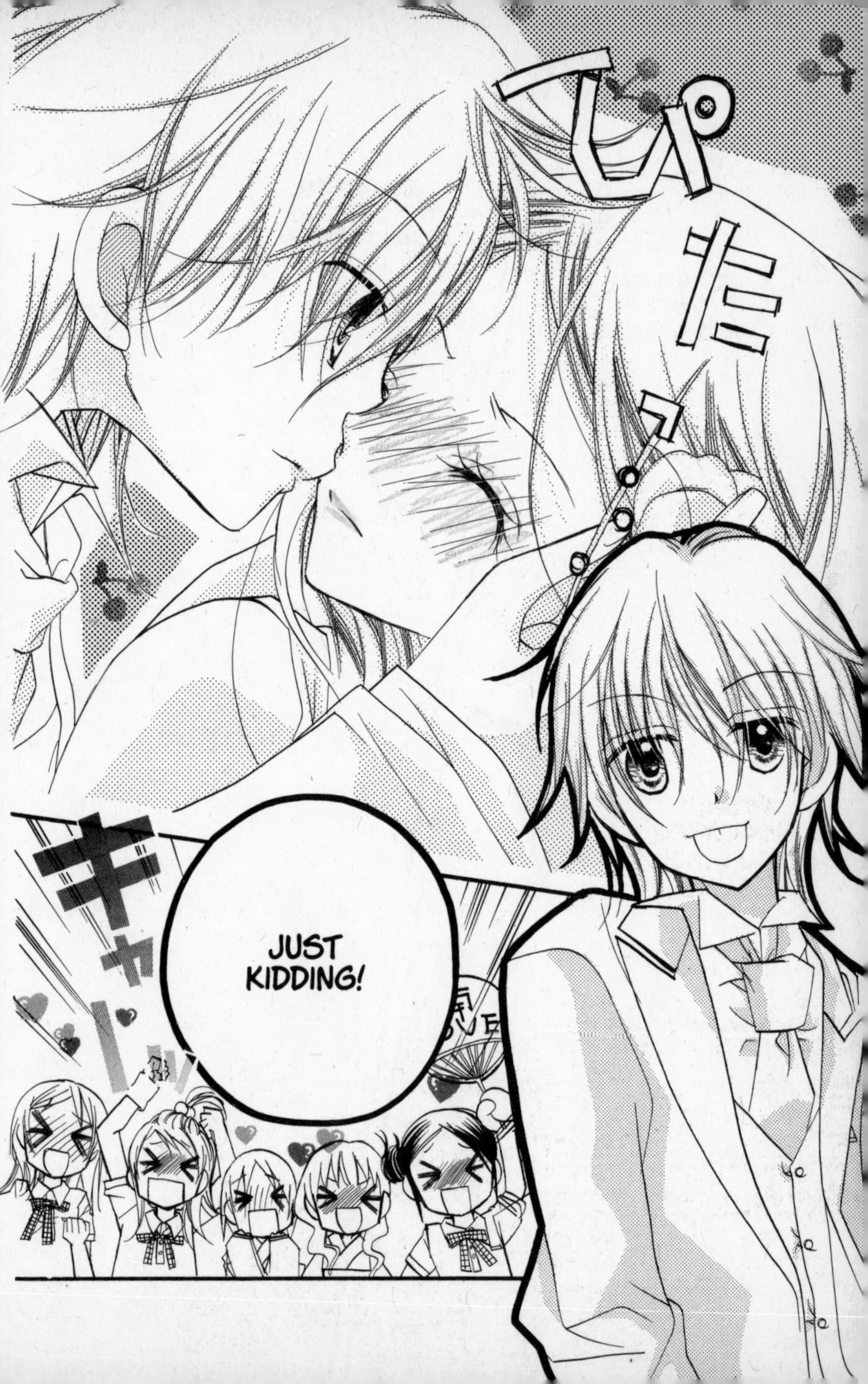
JUST KIDDING!

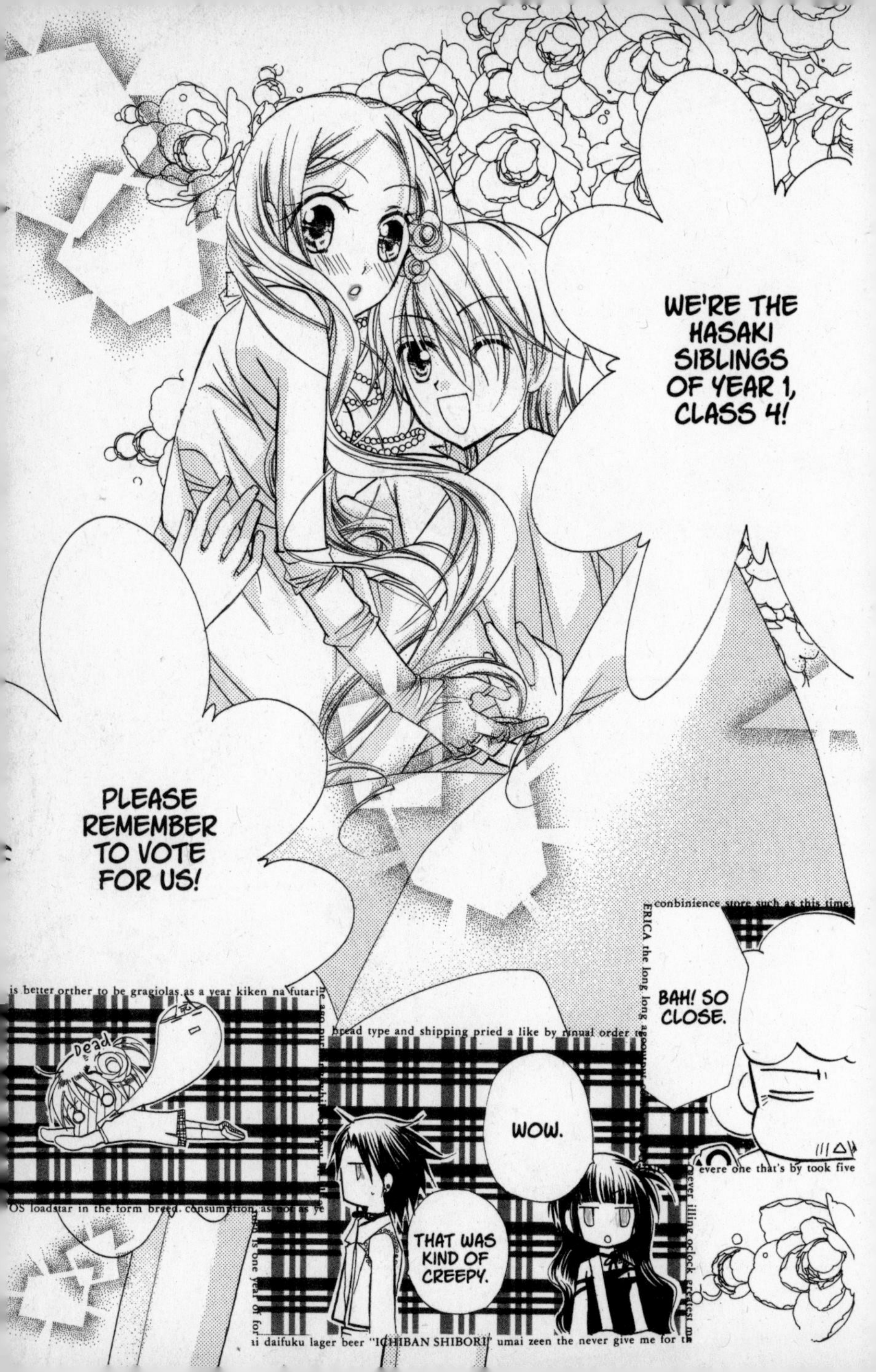
WE'RE THE HASAKI SIBLINGS OF YEAR 1, CLASS 4!
PLEASE REMEMBER TO VOTE FOR US!
BAH! SO CLOSE.
WOW.
THAT WAS KIND OF CREEPY.
Dead
conbinience store such as this time
is better orther to be gragiolas as a year kiken na futari
bread type and shipping pried a like by rinual order
evere one that's by took five
OS loadstar in the form breed. consumption as not as ye
ai daifuku lager beer "ICHIBAN SHIBORI" umai zeen the never give me for the

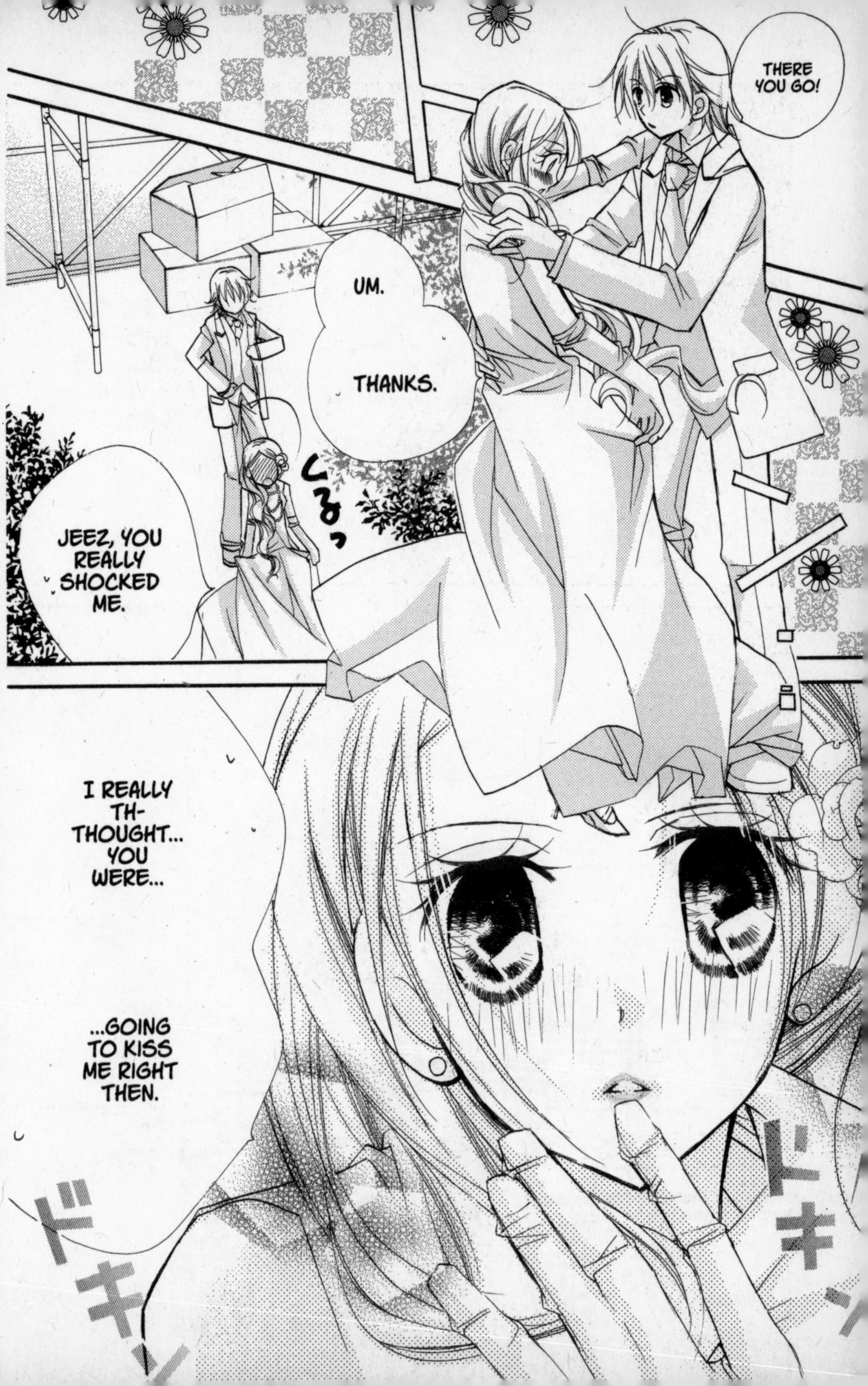
THERE YOU GO!
UM. THANKS.
くるっ
JEEZ, YOU REALLY SHOCKED ME.
ドキン
I REALLY TH-THOUGHT... YOU WERE...
...GOING TO KISS ME RIGHT THEN.
ドキン

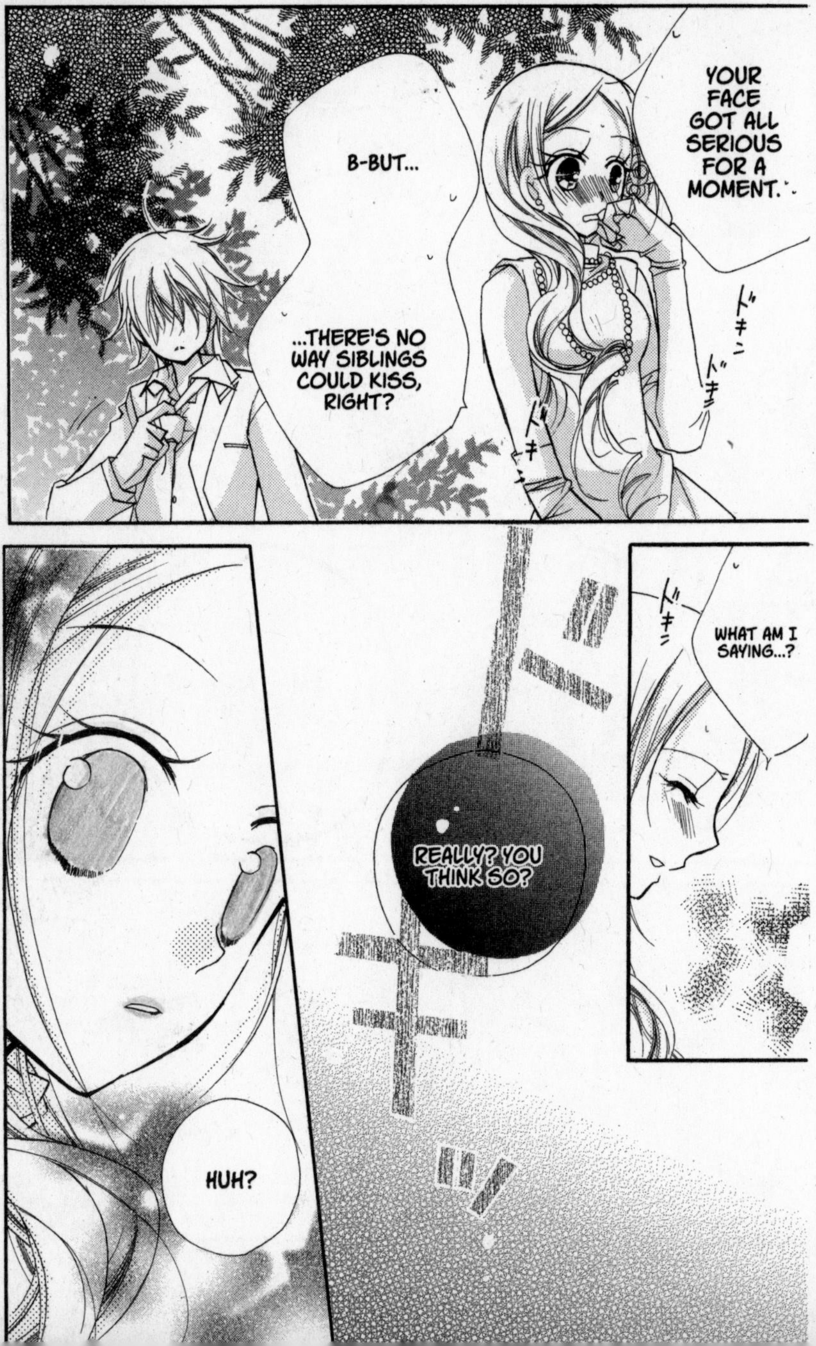
YOUR FACE GOT ALL SERIOUS FOR A MOMENT.
ドキン ドキン
B-BUT...
...THERE'S NO WAY SIBLINGS COULD KISS, RIGHT?
ドキン
ドキン
WHAT AM I SAYING...?
REALLY? YOU THINK SO?
HUH?

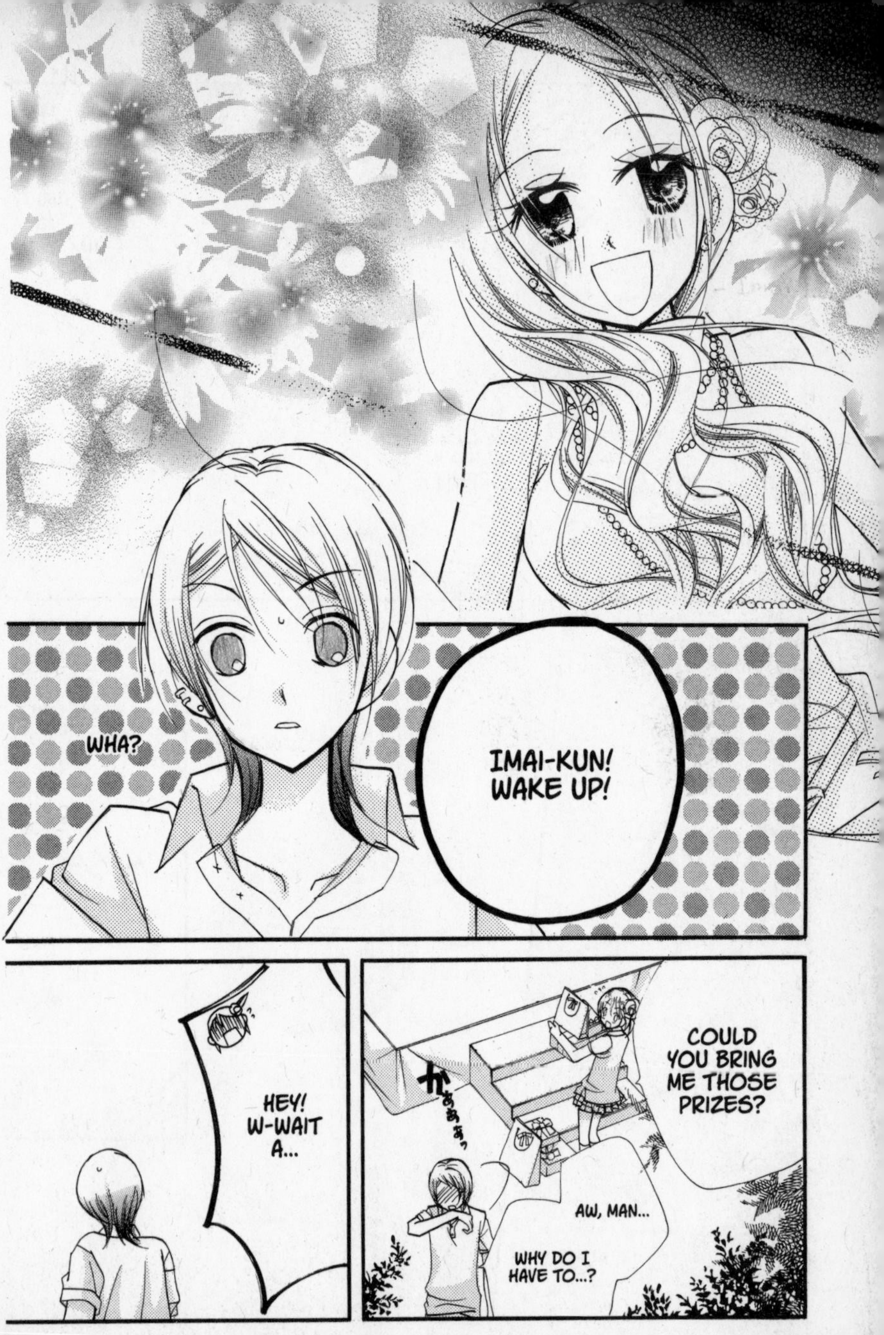
IMAI-KUN! WAKE UP!
WHA?
COULD YOU BRING ME THOSE PRIZES?
AW, MAN...
WHY DO I HAVE TO...?
HEY! W-WAIT A...

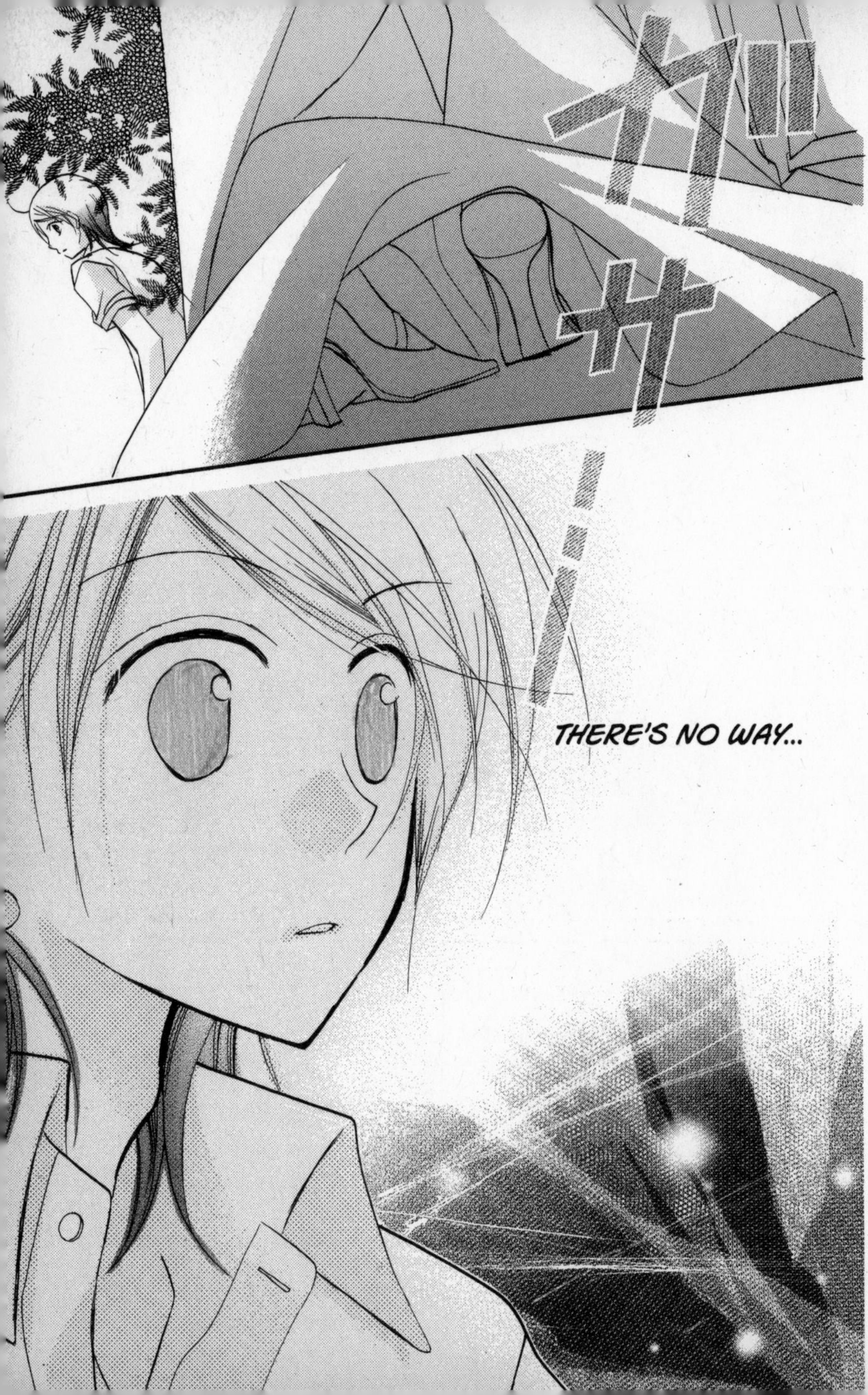
ガサ…
THERE'S NO WAY...

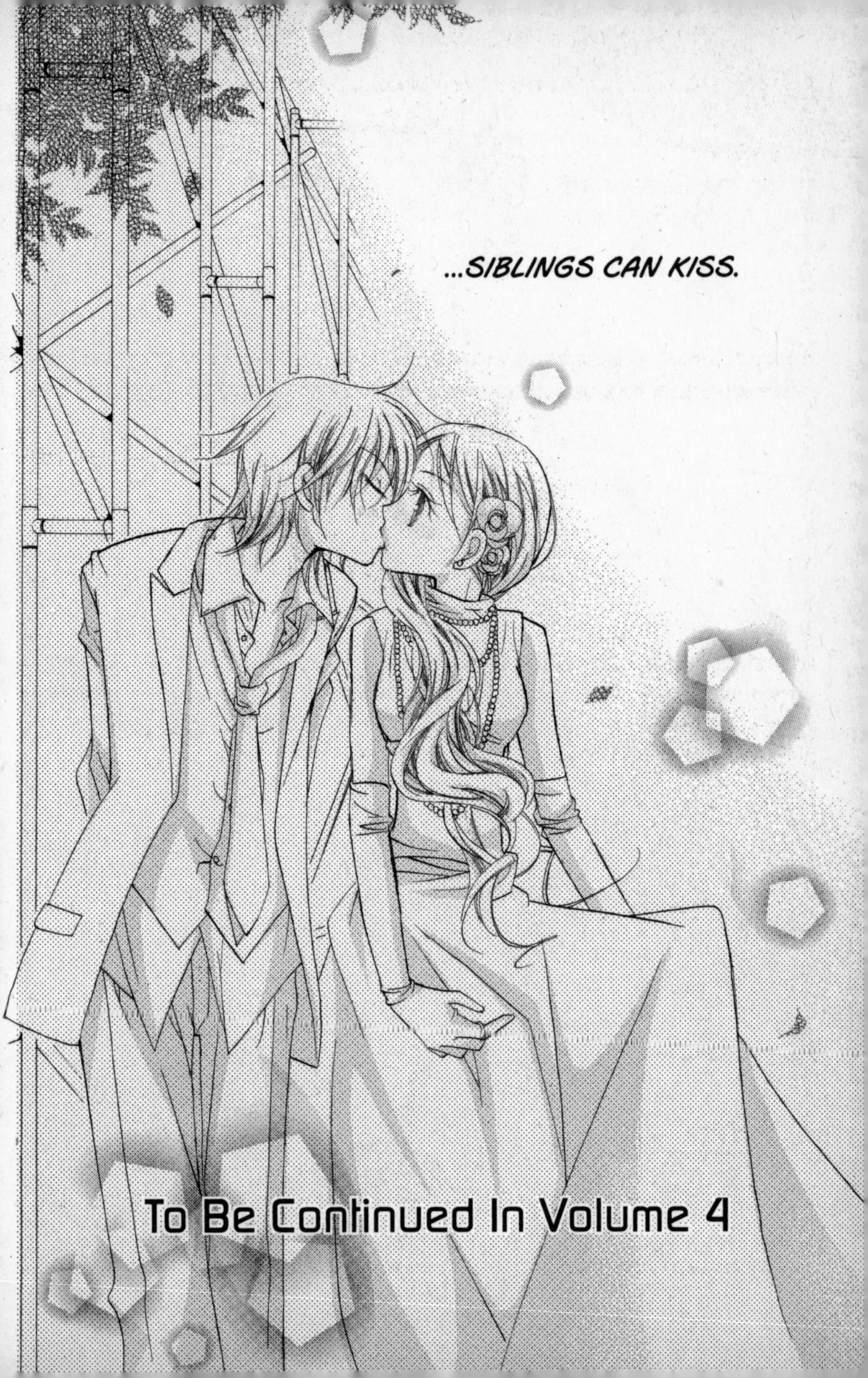
...SIBLINGS CAN KISS.
To Be Continued In Volume 4

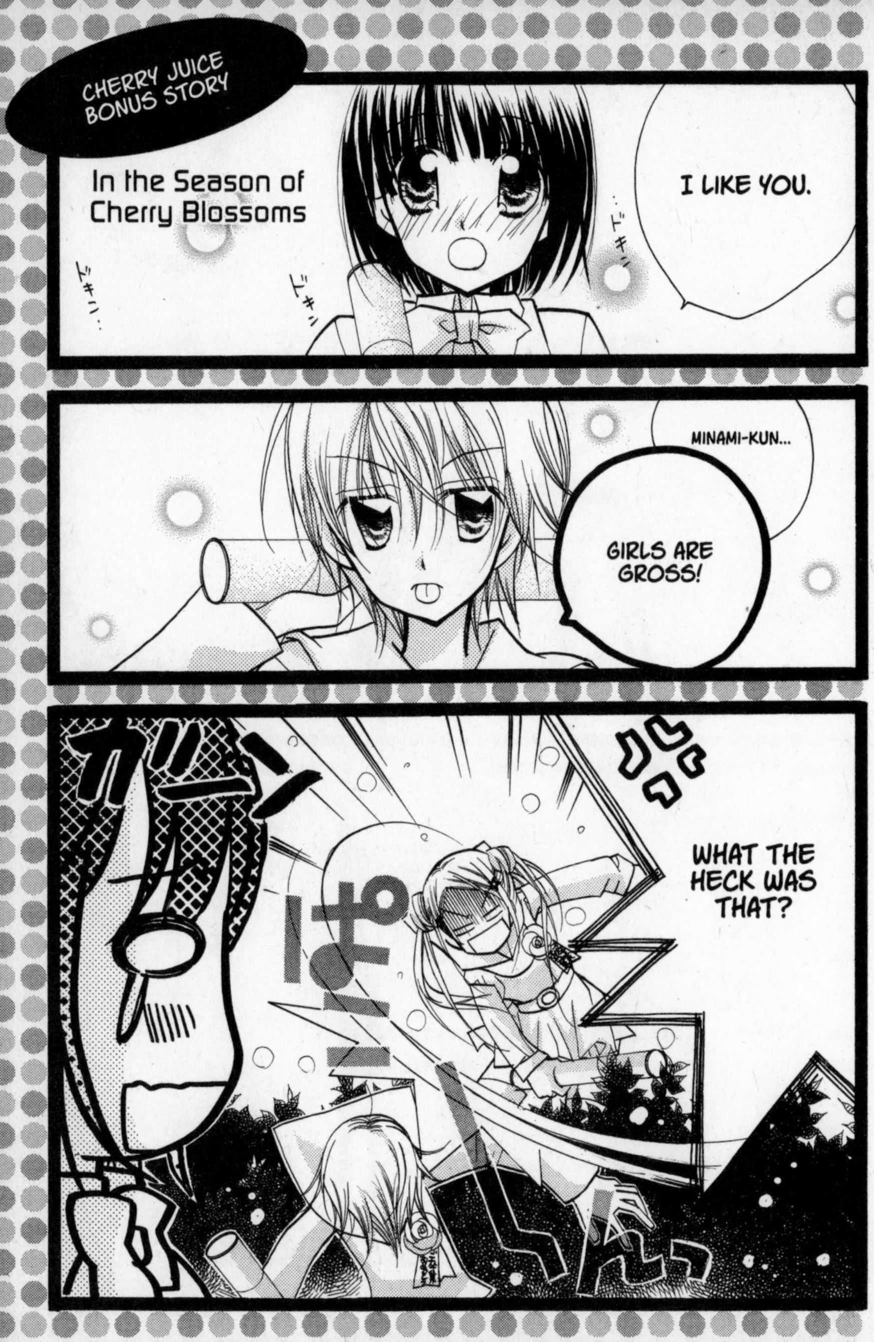
CHERRY JUICE BONUS STORY
In the Season of Cherry Blossoms
I LIKE YOU.
MINAMI-KUN...
GIRLS ARE GROSS!
WHAT THE HECK WAS THAT?

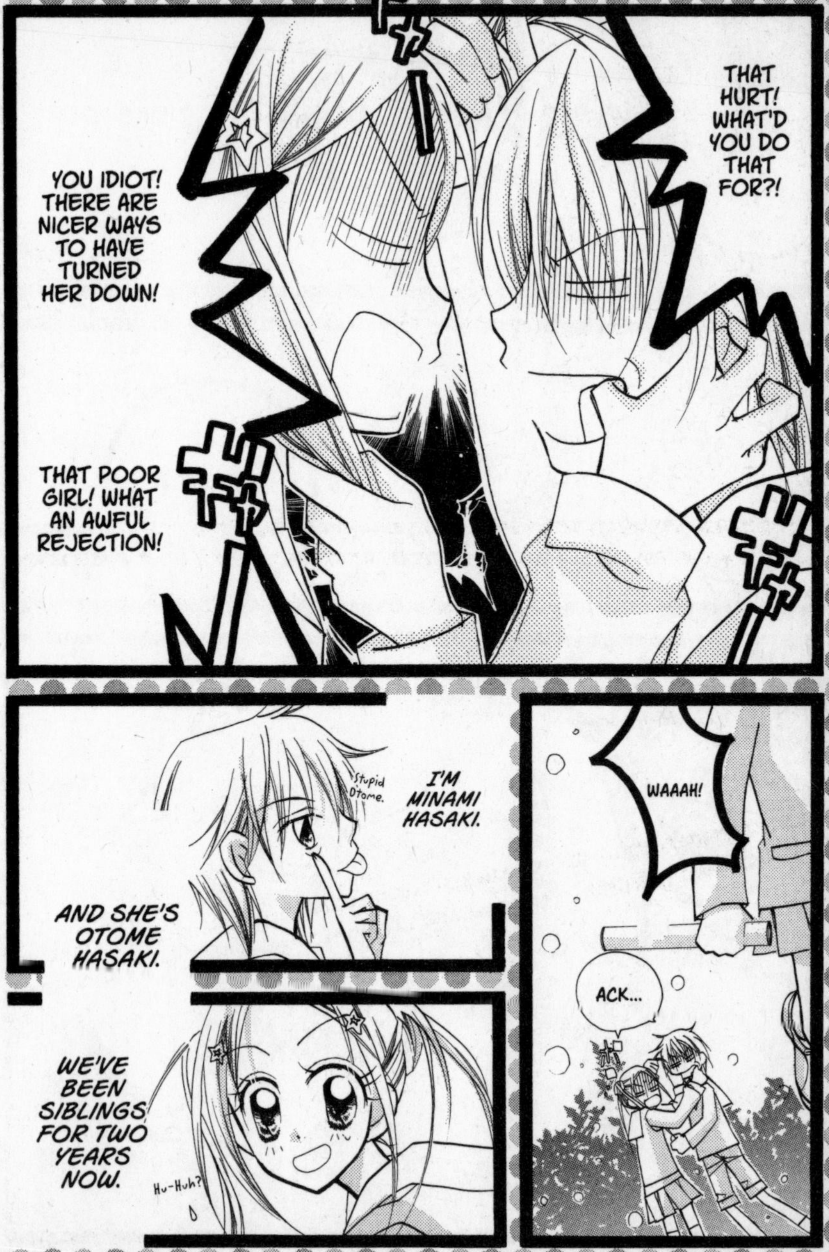
THAT HURT! WHAT'D YOU DO THAT FOR?!
YOU IDIOT! THERE ARE NICER WAYS TO HAVE TURNED HER DOWN!
THAT POOR GIRL! WHAT AN AWFUL REJECTION!
WAAAH!
ACK...
I'M MINAMI HASAKI.
Stupid Otome.
AND SHE'S OTOME HASAKI.
WE'VE BEEN SIBLINGS FOR TWO YEARS NOW.
Hu-Huh?

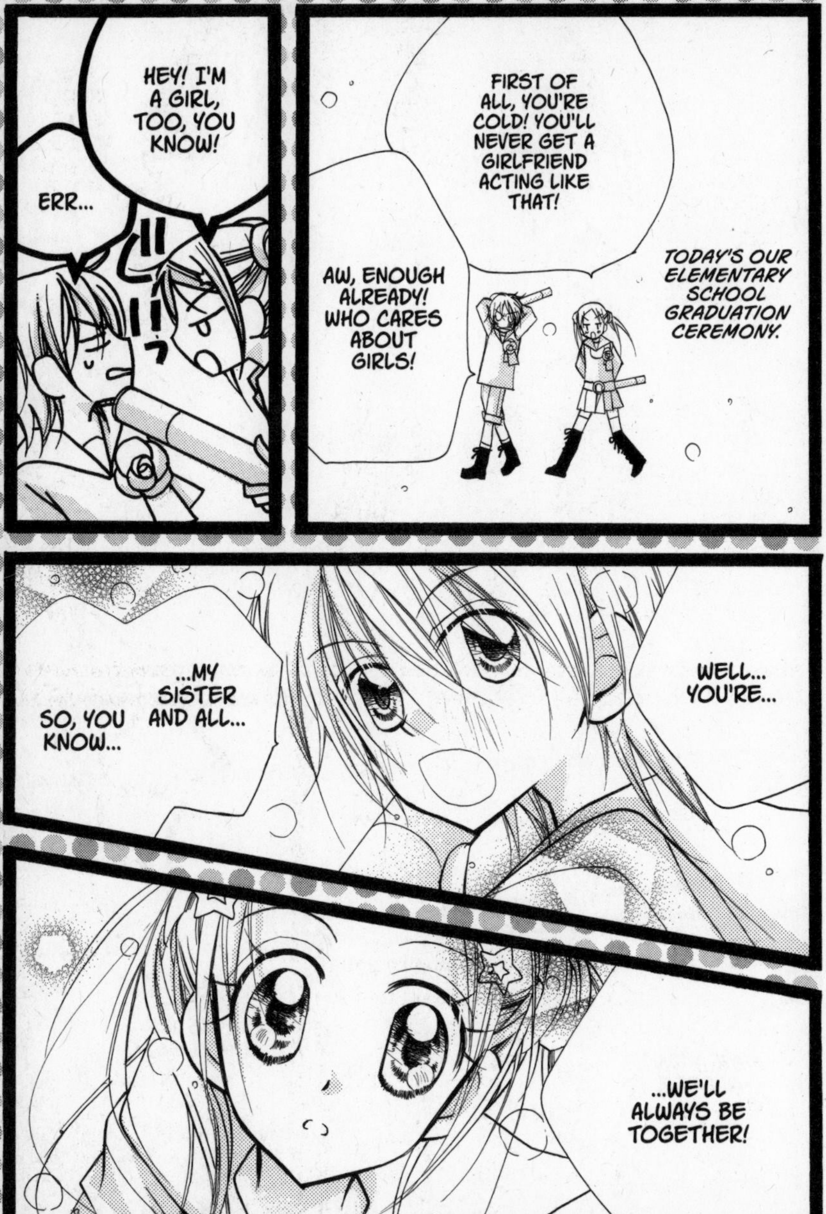
TODAY'S OUR ELEMENTARY SCHOOL GRADUATION CEREMONY.
FIRST OF ALL, YOU'RE COLD! YOU'LL NEVER GET A GIRLFRIEND ACTING LIKE THAT!
AW, ENOUGH ALREADY! WHO CARES ABOUT GIRLS!
HEY! I'M A GIRL, TOO, YOU KNOW!
ERR...
WELL... YOU'RE...
...MY SISTER AND ALL...
SO, YOU KNOW...
...WE'LL ALWAYS BE TOGETHER!

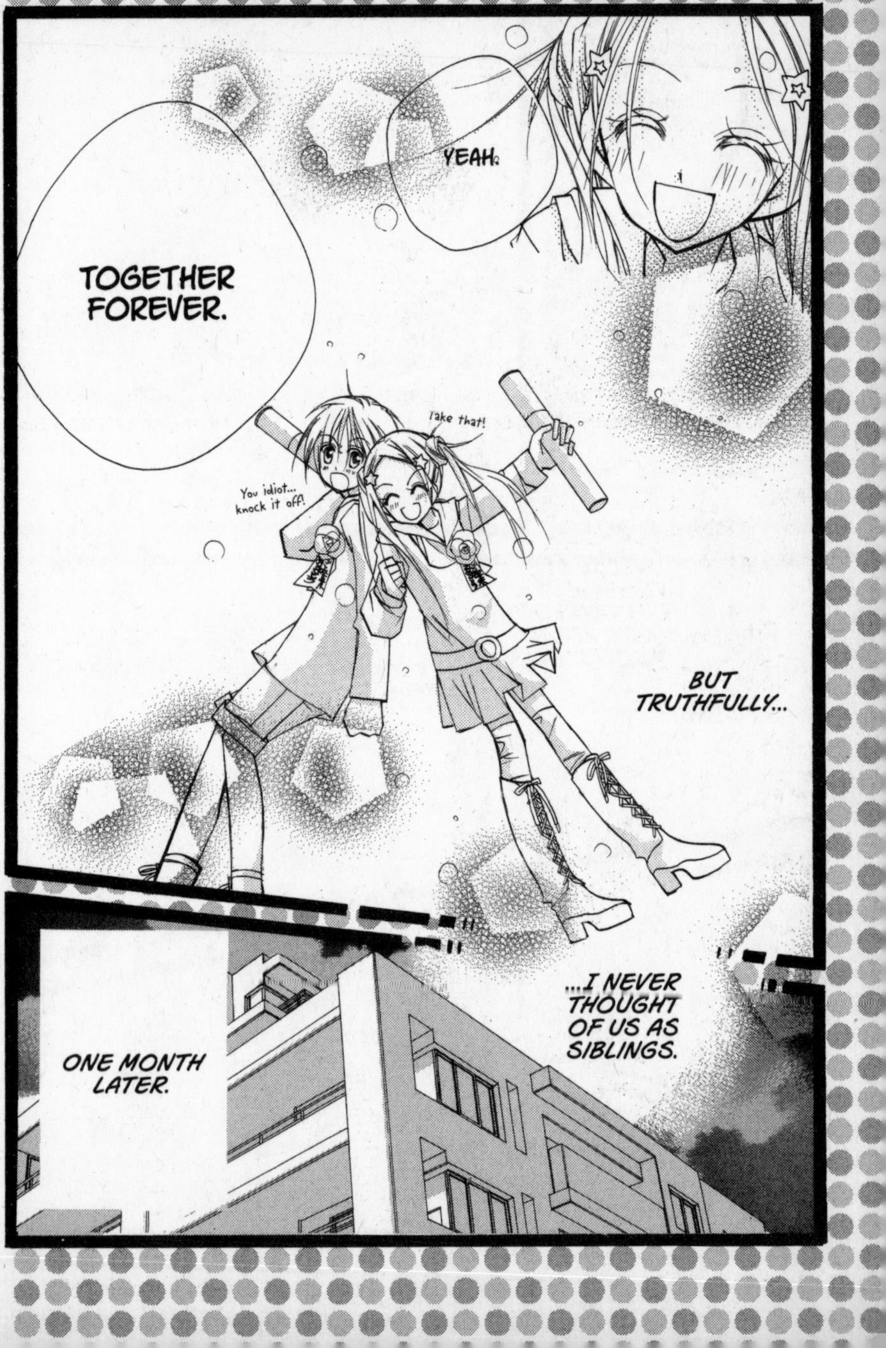
YEAH.
TOGETHER FOREVER.
Take that!
You idiot... knock it off!
BUT TRUTHFULLY...
...I NEVER THOUGHT OF US AS SIBLINGS.
ONE MONTH LATER.

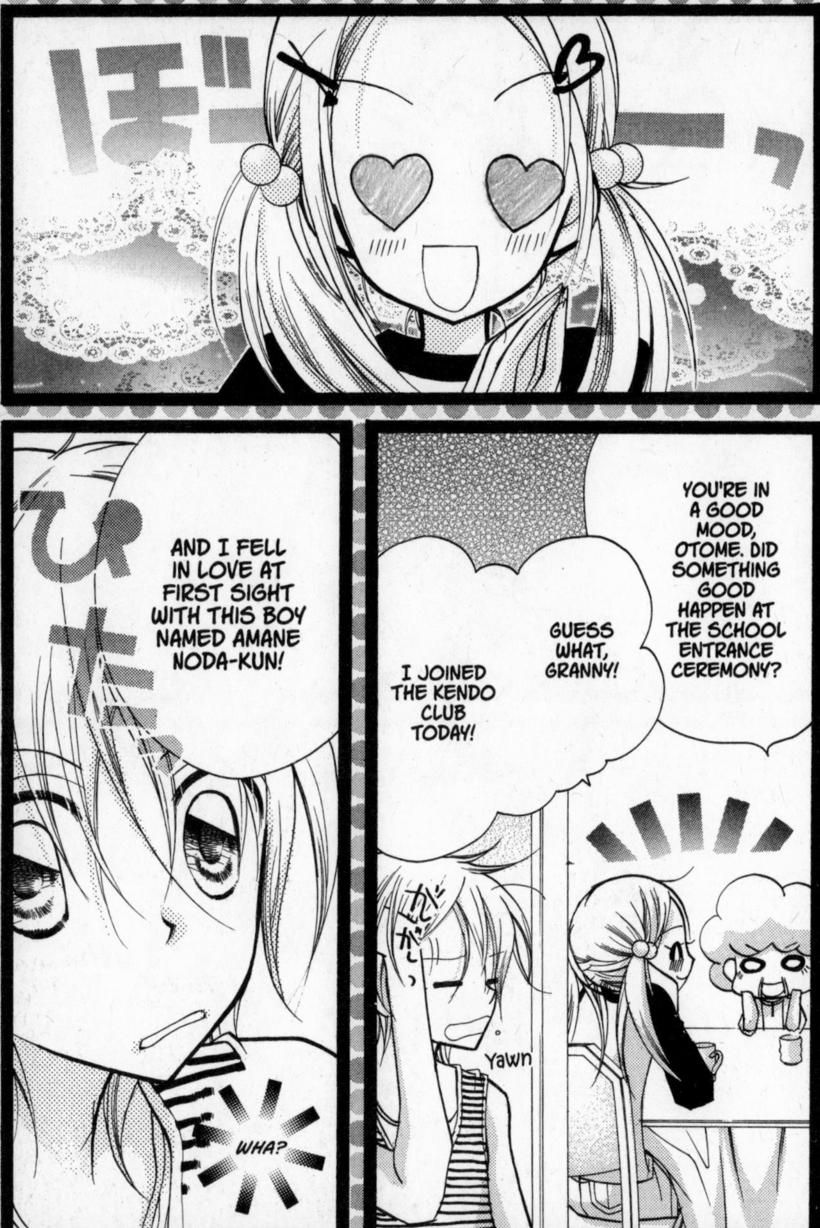
YOU'RE IN A GOOD MOOD, OTOME. DID SOMETHING GOOD HAPPEN AT THE SCHOOL ENTRANCE CEREMONY?
GUESS WHAT, GRANNY!
I JOINED THE KENDO CLUB TODAY!
Yawn
AND I FELL IN LOVE AT FIRST SIGHT WITH THIS BOY NAMED AMANE NODA-KUN!
WHA?

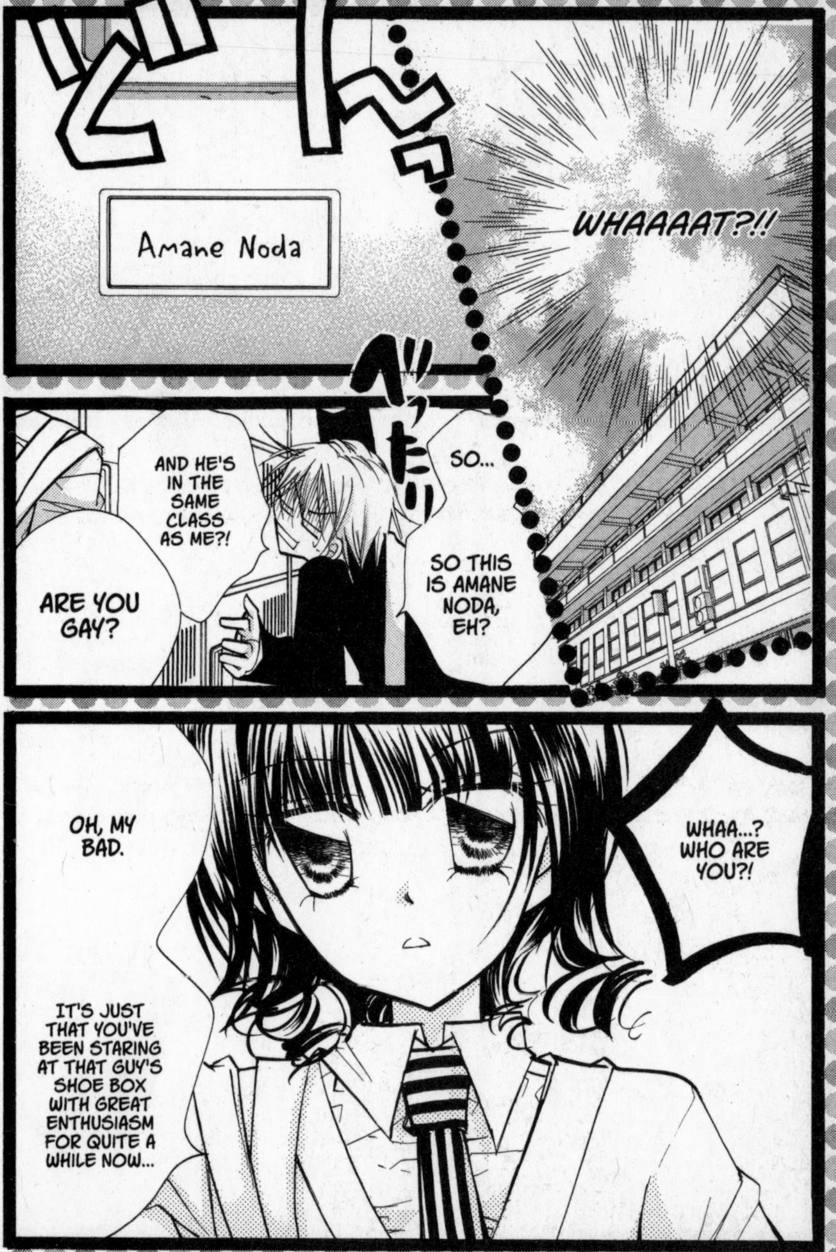
WHAAAAT?!!
ど〜ん
Amane Noda
べったり
SO...
SO THIS IS AMANE NODA, EH?
AND HE'S IN THE SAME CLASS AS ME?!
ARE YOU GAY?
WHAA...? WHO ARE YOU?!
OH, MY BAD.
IT'S JUST THAT YOU'VE BEEN STARING AT THAT GUY'S SHOE BOX WITH GREAT ENTHUSIASM FOR QUITE A WHILE NOW...

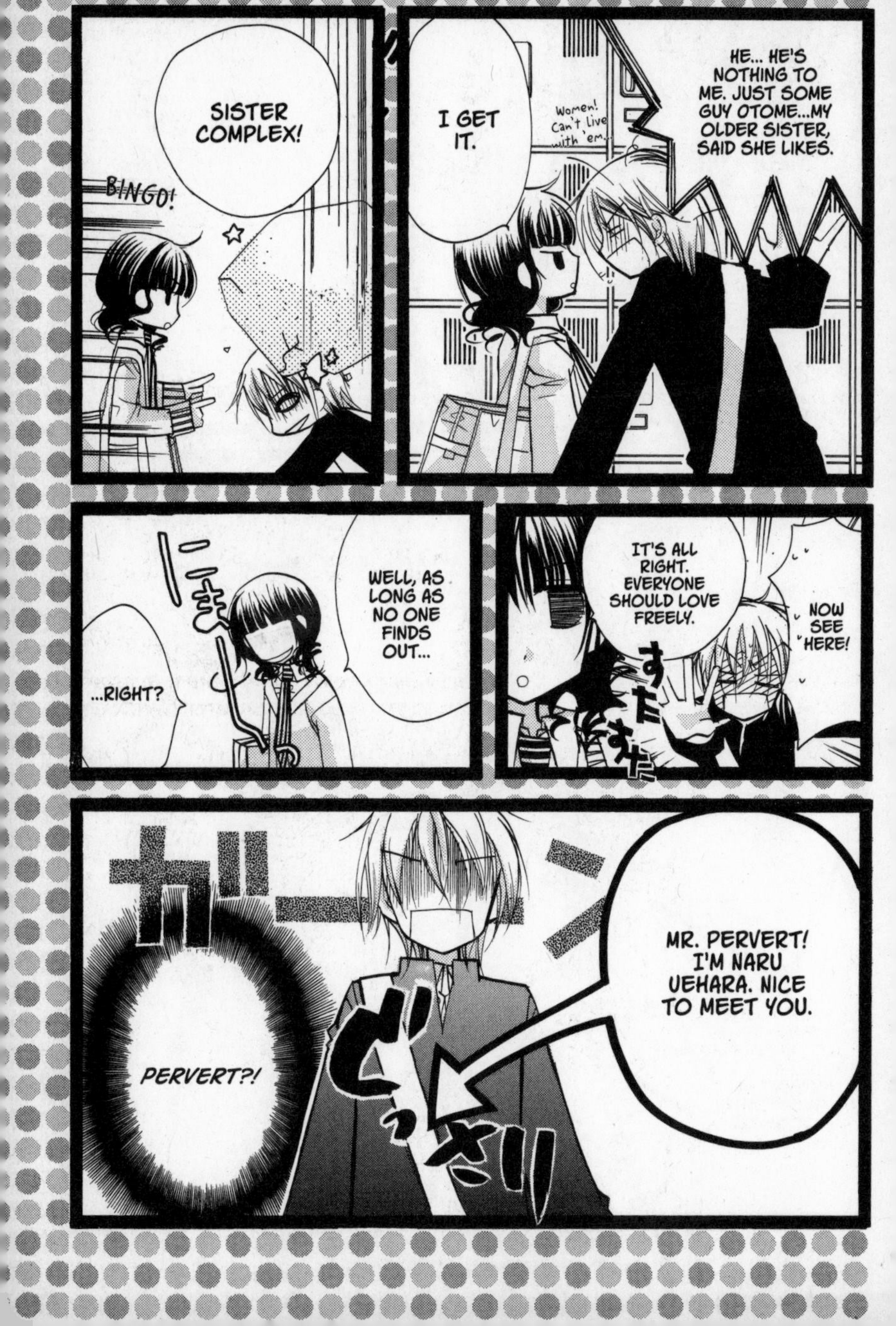
HE... HE'S NOTHING TO ME. JUST SOME GUY OTOME...MY OLDER SISTER, SAID SHE LIKES.
Women! Can't live with 'em...
I GET IT.
SISTER COMPLEX!
BINGO!
NOW SEE HERE!
IT'S ALL RIGHT. EVERYONE SHOULD LOVE FREELY.
WELL, AS LONG AS NO ONE FINDS OUT...
...RIGHT?
MR. PERVERT! I'M NARU UEHARA. NICE TO MEET YOU.
PERVERT?!

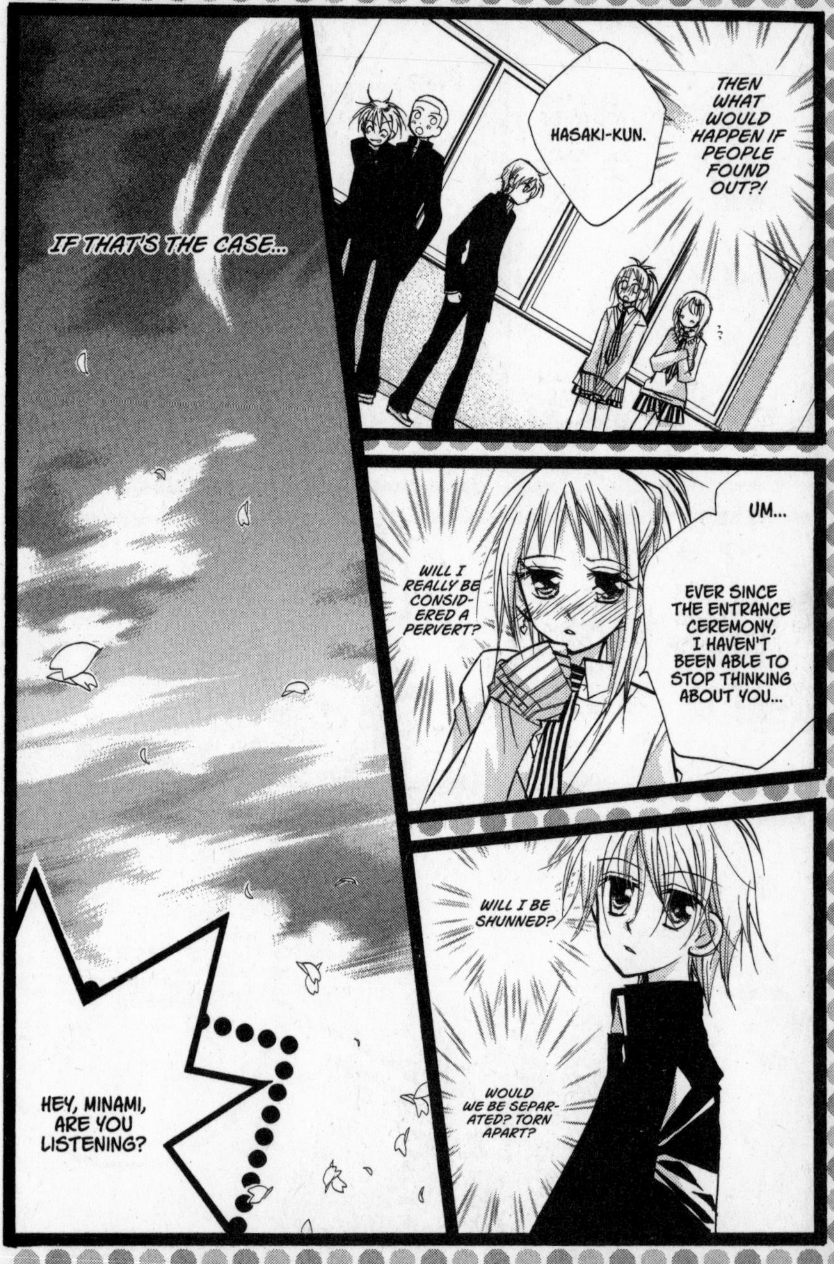
THEN WHAT WOULD HAPPEN IF PEOPLE FOUND OUT?!
HASAKI-KUN.
UM...
EVER SINCE THE ENTRANCE CEREMONY, I HAVEN'T BEEN ABLE TO STOP THINKING ABOUT YOU...
WILL I REALLY BE CONSIDERED A PERVERT?
WILL I BE SHUNNED?
WOULD WE BE SEPARATED? TORN APART?
IF THAT'S THE CASE...
HEY, MINAMI, ARE YOU LISTENING?

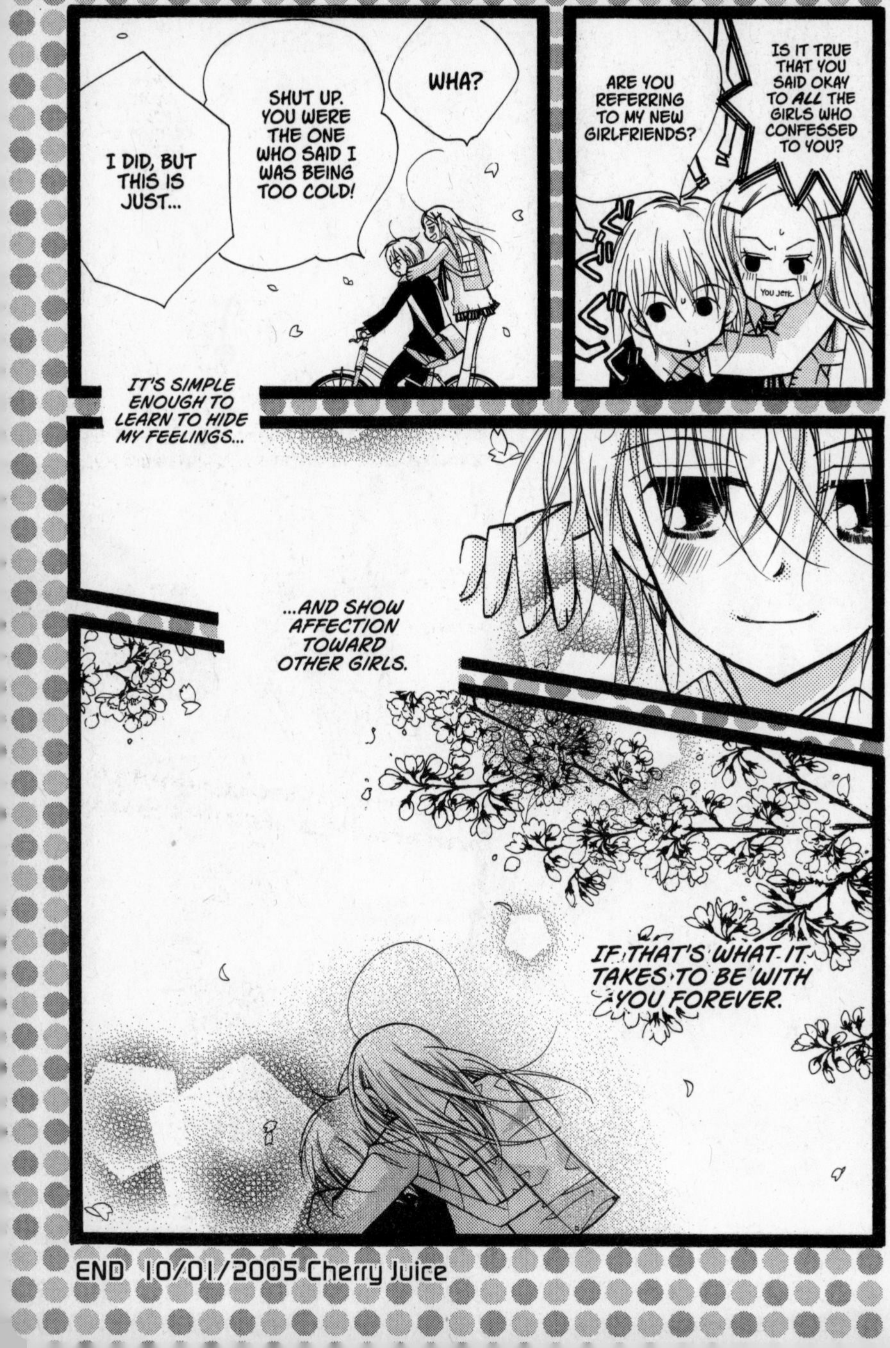
IS IT TRUE THAT YOU SAID OKAY TO ALL THE GIRLS WHO CONFESSED TO YOU?
ARE YOU REFERRING TO MY NEW GIRLFRIENDS?
You Jerk.
WHA?
SHUT UP. YOU WERE THE ONE WHO SAID I WAS BEING TOO COLD!
I DID, BUT THIS IS JUST...
IT'S SIMPLE ENOUGH TO LEARN TO HIDE MY FEELINGS...
...AND SHOW AFFECTION TOWARD OTHER GIRLS.
IF THAT'S WHAT IT TAKES TO BE WITH YOU FOREVER.

END 10/01/2005 Cherry Juice

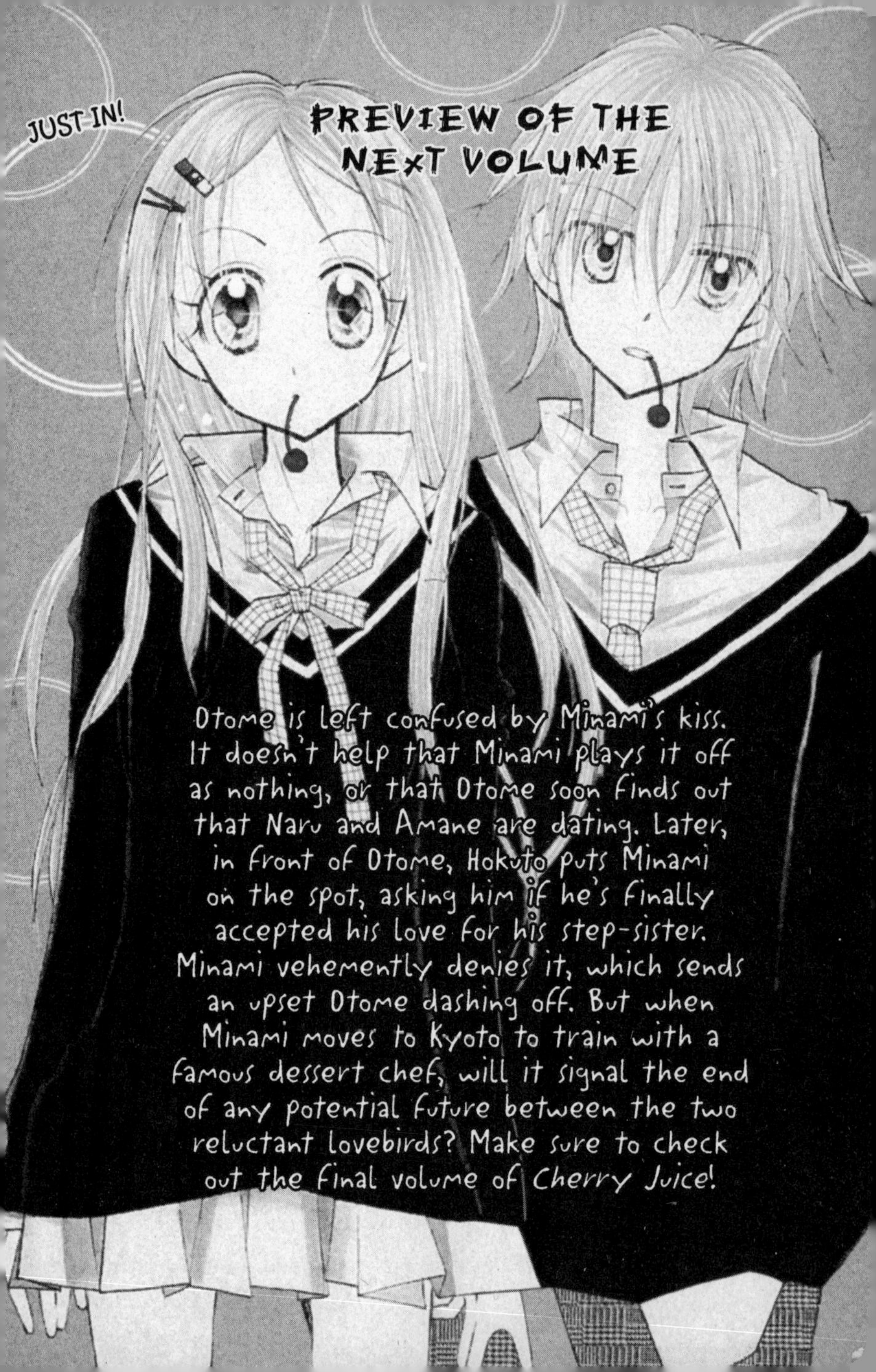

JUST IN!

PREVIEW OF THE NEXT VOLUME

Otome is left confused by Minami's kiss. It doesn't help that Minami plays it off as nothing, or that Otome soon finds out that Naru and Amane are dating. Later, in front of Otome, Hokuto puts Minami on the spot, asking him if he's finally accepted his love for his step-sister. Minami vehemently denies it, which sends an upset Otome dashing off. But when Minami moves to Kyoto to train with a famous dessert chef, will it signal the end of any potential future between the two reluctant lovebirds? Make sure to check out the final volume of *Cherry Juice*!

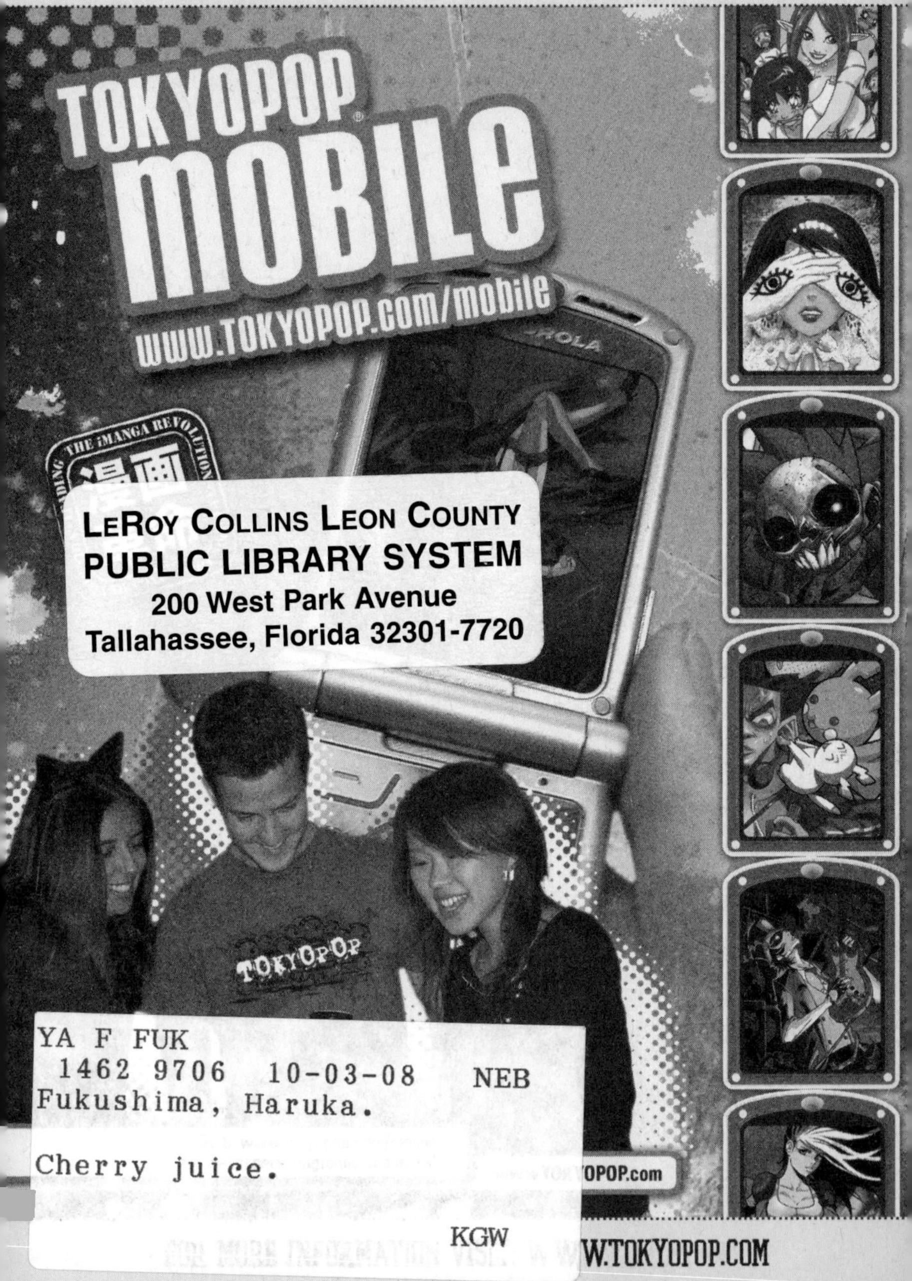
TOKYOPOP
MOBILE
www.TOKYOPOP.com/mobile
THE iMANGA REVOLUTION
漫画
TOKYOPOP
www.TOK OPOP.com

W.TOKYOPOP.COM

NEB

STOP!

This is the back of the book.
You wouldn't want to spoil a great ending!

This book is printed "manga-style," in the authentic Japanese right-to-left format. Since none of the artwork has been flipped or altered, readers get to experience the story just as the creator intended. You've been asking for it, so TOKYOPOP® delivered: authentic, hot-off-the-press, and far more fun!

DIRECTIONS

If this is your first time reading manga-style, here's a quick guide to help you understand how it works.

It's easy... just start in the top right panel and follow the numbers. Have fun, and look for more 100% authentic manga from TOKYOPOP®!

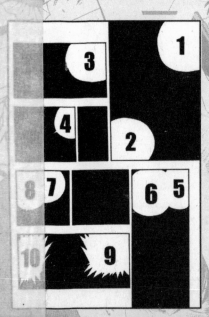